Modernising Charity Law

Recent Developments and Future Directions

Edited by

Myles McGregor-Lowndes and Kerry O'Halloran

Queensland University of Technology, Australia

Edward Elgar

Cheltenham, UK • Northampton, MA, USA

Published by
Edward Elgar Publishing Limited
The Lypiatts
15 Lansdown Road
Cheltenham
Glos GL50 2JA
UK

Edward Elgar Publishing, Inc.
William Pratt House
9 Dewey Court
Northampton
Massachusetts 01060
USA

A catalogue record for this book
is available from the British Library

Library of Congress Control Number: 2010922144

Mixed Sources
Product group from well-managed
forests and other controlled sources
www.fsc.org Cert no. SA-COC-1565
FSC © 1996 Forest Stewardship Council

ISBN 978 1 84980 250 5

Printed and bound by MPG Books Group, UK

Contents

PART III   THE FUTURE OF CIVIL SOCIETY
           ORGANISATIONS

Contributors

Dr Oonagh B. Breen is a Senior Lecturer at University College Dublin School of Law, and currently a visiting Research Fellow at the Hauser Center for Nonprofit Organizations, Harvard University. Dr Breen specialises in the area of comparative charity law regulation and policy.

Lindsay Driscoll has spent over 30 years in the field of charity law and governance in a number of different roles including a term as a Charity Commissioner. She is currently a consultant with the firm of Bates, Wells and Braithwaite, Solicitors, in London.

Dr Jonathan Garton is a Reader in Law in the Charity Law Unit at the University of Liverpool. He is the author of *The Regulation of Organised Civil Society* (Hart, 2009) and the charities volume of *Halsbury's Laws of England* (Lexis, 2010).

Dr Michael Gousmett is an independent researcher in the charity sector in New Zealand. He was formerly General Manager of the Pacific Leprosy Foundation (1989–2007), and adviser to charities on governance, strategic planning, accounting, taxation and legal issues.

Laird Hunter, QC is a partner in the Richards Hunter law firm in Edmonton, Alberta, Canada. Since 1975, his practice has concentrated on matters for nonprofits and charities. He was intervenor counsel at the Canadian Supreme Court in *Vancouver Society of Immigrant and Visible Minority Women v Minister of National Revenue* (1998) and the *Amateur Youth Soccer Association* case (2007). Mr Hunter has had a long-standing involvement in public policy matters related to charities of various sorts. He is recognised for his skill in charity and nonprofit law by Lexpert and The Best Lawyers in Canada.

Fr Brian Lucas is a graduate in law from the University of Sydney. Ordained a Catholic priest in 1980, he is General Secretary of the Australian Catholic Bishops Conference. He is a co-author of the *Church Administration Handbook*.

Professor Myles McGregor-Lowndes is Director of the Australian Centre for Philanthropy and Nonprofit Studies and has an ongoing interest in regulatory reform in the Third Sector. He is an advisory member to the Australian Board of Taxation, member of the Australian Taxation Office Charities Consultative Committee and Chair of the Australian Council for International Development Code of Conduct Committee.

Debra Morris is Reader in Charity Law and Policy at the University of Liverpool, UK. She is also Director of the Charity Law Unit, University of Liverpool, where she leads research on various projects concerned with aspects of charity law.

Professor Kerry O'Halloran is an academic lawyer who has written several charity law books and is currently Adjunct Professor at the Australian Centre for Philanthropy and Nonprofit Studies, Queensland University of Technology, Brisbane.

Anne Robinson is the founder and principal of Prolegis Lawyers, which specialises in providing legal services to charitable organisations and other nonprofits. She has been involved in governance of nonprofit organisations for 25 years, including being on the boards of two independent schools and chairing the boards of trustees of two hospital and religious institutions. She has been a Director of World Vision Australia for the past ten years, and the Board Chairman since 2005, and is also a director of World Vision International.

Professor Karla W. Simon is Professor of Law and Director of Faculty Development at the Columbus School of Law, Catholic University of America. She is a scholar of the nonprofit sector world-wide, and her most recent published work concerns civil society in China and Japan.

Dr Matthew Turnour is the Managing Partner of Neumann & Turnour Lawyers and a lecturer at the Australian Centre for Philanthropy and Nonprofit Studies, Queensland University of Technology, Brisbane. He was awarded his doctorate in 2009 for a dissertation entitled 'Beyond Charity: Outlines of a Jurisprudence for Civil Society' in which he expounded an alternative approach to jurisprudence for civil society organisations.

Bob Wyatt has been executive director of The Muttart Foundation since 1989. He has been involved in issues of charitable regulation for much of that time, including serving as co-chair of the Joint Regulatory Table, part of Canada's Voluntary Sector Initiative. He was Executive-in-Residence at the Australian Centre for Philanthropy and Nonprofit Studies in 2005–06.

Foreword

The energy, scholarship and working knowledge evident in the presentations and exchange of ideas at the international Modernising Charity Law conference held in Brisbane in April 2009 has been maintained in the production of this collection of papers that originated at the conference. The conference was held at a critical time for reflection on significant reforms affecting charities and charity law in some jurisdictions and consideration of the possibility of greater reform in other jurisdictions, against the impact of the global financial crisis. As with any good conference, general themes emerged during the presentation of the papers and panel discussions that did not necessarily reflect the anticipated structure of the conference. This has been accommodated by the ordering of the chapters in this volume to cover these themes in a methodical way (rather than the order in which papers were presented), as is explained in the introduction to the volume.

The work of charities was important to English society when the Statute of Elizabeth was enacted in 1601. Charities remain important to the functioning of society in each jurisdiction, but their role and the regulation and nature of charities have changed significantly since 1601 and will continue to change to meet the challenges of a dynamic society that demands transparency and accountability where any use of public funds or benefit arising from charitable status is involved.

This volume is an excellent resource for those who wish to make a comparative study of recent developments in charity law in a number of jurisdictions, or wish to gain a better understanding of the current issues in the area of charity law and the regulation of charities, or simply wish to ponder on the possibilities for future reforms. I congratulate the Australian Centre for Philanthropy and Nonprofit Studies at the Queensland University of Technology for its foresight in organising the Modernising Charity Law conference and the authors of this volume, not only for their scholarship, but for cooperating to produce this cohesive work to enable the benefits of the engagement at that conference to be available to a much wider audience.

Justice Debra Mullins
Supreme Court of Queensland, Brisbane

Acknowledgements

The Modernising Charity Law Conference and the subsequent published proceedings were funded by a Founding Chairman grant from The Atlantic Philanthropies and a contribution by the Queensland University of Technology Faculty of Business. We also acknowledge the generous support and encouragement of Professor Harvey Dale, Founding President of The Atlantic Philanthropies, Professor of Philanthropy and the Law at the New York University School of Law, and Director of the National Center on Philanthropy and the Law.

Table of cases

Table of statutes

Subordinate legislation

UNITED STATES

Introduction

Myles McGregor-Lowndes

This volume about modernising charity law results from a conference held at the Australian Centre for Philanthropy and Nonprofit Studies at the Queensland University of Technology in April 2009. It came at a pivotal moment in Australian charity law reform, as the first term federal Labor government began a number of overlapping inquiries touching upon charity reform. Many hoped that this government would eventually lay down a blueprint for charity law reform in Australia and perhaps even Third Sector reform, which had generated only glimmers of interest under the previous 13 years of conservative administration.

A previous conference was held at the Centre in 2001 – the impetus being the recommendations of the Charity Definition Inquiry,[1] which held much promise – and it resulted in a collection of papers being published in a special issue of *Third Sector Review*.[2] That conference brought together scholars and regulators from across the globe, including United Kingdom and Canadian policy makers who were at that time tasked with providing options to reform charity law and regulation in their respective countries. The Australian legislative outcome of the Charity Definition Inquiry was meagre when compared with reform in the UK, New Zealand and Singapore: a very short Act applying only to the federal jurisdiction and addressing just three issues.[3] The draft bill was much more ambitious, but attracted significant opposition from the sector and legal practitioners as it departed from the carefully crafted inquiry recommendations.

The 2009 conference again brought together scholars and regulators from around the globe, but also included Australian politicians, their advisors, research staff involved in the various inquiries touching on charity law issues, the leadership of sector bodies and legal practitioners. The first two days of the conference focused on the jurisdictional charity reform process that had developed since 2001 and an assessment of how those reforms were now faring. What were the drivers for public policy choices during the process? What were the lessons to be learnt from other jurisdictions? Will the changes to the public benefit test actually work in the field? The third day was given over to examining the strategies to increase philanthropic behaviour by reviewing recent initiatives in a number of jurisdictions. Is there a magic gold bullet to fire at the hearts of increasing numbers of high net worth individuals and mega-corporations? Or is it a case of silver buckshot?

Although the conference presentations are available as streamed video from the Centre's web site, it was believed worthwhile to publish a more scholarly record of parts of the conference.[4] The conference papers and this publication stand as a record across the charity law jurisdictions of the series of reforms that rival the Statute of Elizabeth in their breadth and effect. Whether Australia follows such a course remains to be seen.

OVERVIEW

Chapter 1 conflates a number of conference papers into a broad overview of the legislative and judicial activity in relation to charities since 2001 in the UK, Canada, New Zealand, Singapore and Australia. It provides a necessary background to the rest of the chapters, which deal with specific issues of modernising charity law. Clearly the UK jurisdictions have led the way with a series of reforms which, on any measure, are significant and bold. While there are differences in the detail between the UK jurisdictions there is enough commonality to discern broad areas of agreement such as: additional charitable purpose heads; review of the public benefit test; greater disclosure; new hybrid legal structures; an appeals tribunal and a streamlined regulatory framework with an independent charities regulator at its centre.

Singapore is a fascinating example of a small nation with big ambitions and the political will to encourage charity to play a more significant role in its developing civil society. New Zealand has had less ambitious vision, but still made some significant progress in reforming the regulatory framework for charities with the establishment of a commission and register. At the other end of the scale are Canada and Australia.

The Canadian Voluntary Sector Initiative delivered a report with 75 recommendations, of which 69 were adopted. However, most of these reforms do not go anywhere near the more adventurous policy agenda of the UK jurisdictions. A change in federal government and the federal structure have dulled any appetite for further reform at present, apart from hybrid social enterprise legal forms. Australia, another federation, has moved little since 2001. There have been the minor reforms introduced in the federal jurisdiction by the Extension of Charitable Purpose Act 2004, the introduction of a new form of tax effective private foundation, and some other minor tax incentives. The major driver has been taxation regulator activism which has seen an ongoing review of the register of charities and tax deductible entities; publishing of formal rulings on a range of charity tax issues, including its definition; and after a drought of over three decades, several High Court decisions arising from charity taxation disputes.

In some jurisdictions, such as the UK, the reform outcomes are now starting to bite and regret may surface. For others the journey is just beginning and some even have the luxury of learning from the experience of others.

PEMSEL PLUS

Chapter 2 by Lindsay Driscoll and Chapter 3 by Oonagh Breen examine in detail the modernising reforms in England and Ireland respectively. Lindsay Driscoll, who has been a constant player in UK charity law reform, in the role of sector representative, charity commissioner or legal practitioner, gives a measured account of the critical issues. Her view of the streamlined administration framework of the Charity Commission and Tribunal is instructive and represents what is probably the current model in comparison to some other charity law jurisdictions. While the statutory definition and the new heads of charity appear radical to an external observer, she makes the argument that the guidances of the Charity Commission in recent years had all but paved the way for such formal recognition of the new heads. However, as she notes, the new charity law tribunal and courts are yet to have the final word on whether this statutory formalisation of incremental policy development might allow some adventuresome judicial decision making. It is here that there may be some future regrets.

In Chapter 3, Oonagh Breen examines the reforms in Ireland, which, although not as advanced in implementation as in England and Wales, represent a significant stride in charity law and regulation modernisation. While it has many similarities to English reforms, the emerging charity law framework in Ireland has a number of interesting features such as: the separation of the previous strong tax exemption–charitable status nexus; exclusion of amateur sport, human rights and peace related organisations; retention of the public benefit presumption solely for religious purposes; and a mandatory five-year review of the statute.

PUBLIC BENEFIT

Chapters 4 and 5 address the issue of public benefit in the formulation of the definition of charity from two different perspectives. Debra Morris

examines the reformulation issues in England and Karla Simon examines
developments in Japan and China. It is one of the most controversial
issues on the modernising charity law agenda. At common law there was
a long-held presumption that purposes within the first three heads of
charity were for the public benefit. The effect of the presumption was that,
when the charitable status of an organisation established for the relief of
poverty, the advancement of education, or the advancement of religion
was being considered, the organisation's purpose was presumed to be for
the public benefit, unless there was evidence that it was not. By contrast,
organisations established for all other purposes, which did not benefit
from that presumption, were required, at the time that their status was
being considered, to provide evidence that their purpose was for the public
benefit. Tampering with this state of affairs by reversing the presumption
is a significant reform, with implications for many long-established charitable entities (for example, fee-paying schools).

The general inclination to an audit society where all are called upon
to justify their existence and actions when public funds, concessions or
privileges are involved does not auger well for charities. There is little
public support for relieving organisations claiming to be for the public
benefit from having to show good evidence to support their claim. Clearly
we have a major deficit in tools to measure such claims, many of which
involve intangible notions and go to the heart of our difficulties in understanding what is public and private, what is a benefit, how direct a benefit
must be and how much of the public must benefit. The first three heads
of charitable purposes all have organisations on the margins which, if
called upon, are going to have measurement and evidence difficulties in
demonstrating their public benefit. Religion probably represents the most
contentious area.

Debra Morris details the background, statutory provisions and regulatory implementation of the reformed public benefit test in the English
jurisdiction. This could perhaps be the single most probable cause for
migrane among charity lawyers, regulators and trustees in England. The
Charity Commission has expended considerable resources trying to chart
a practical course through waters full of sharp rocks, whirlpools of public
prejudice, the sharks of the popular press and unspoken political compromises. Her well-argued but surprising conclusion that the journey may
return from whence it began can only give those who are about to start the
journey reason to pause and reflect.

In Chapter 5, Karla Simon provides an update on the progress made
in two significant Asian jurisdictions. Japan and China are two civil law
countries that are seeking to develop nonprofit organisations that pursue
Anglo-American public benefit purposes. Japan has made significant

strides since the Kobe earthquake and China is following its own winding path on controlling and facilitating public benefit organisations.

BUSINESS

The boundary between charity and business has been relatively clear with the bright line of the non-distribution constraint combined with a core purposes test. In the past, contentions have revolved around the amount of unrelated trading income, application of tax neutrality principles between sectors and risk to donor funds from charity business ventures. However, new areas of contention are being hotly debated across most jurisdictions. They come in the form of social enterprises, social entrepreneurs and venture philanthropy which use the MBA toolkit to bludgeon wicked problems such as unemployment, poverty, homelessness, and global environmental abuse out of existence. Preoccupied with outcomes and the impacts of market activity, they are unrestrained by pure charitable purposes and non-profit restraints.

Various practitioner-concocted hybrids and boutique statutory vehicles have appeared in the US and UK jurisdictions. There are also legally adventurous partnerships between business and nonprofit organisations, seeking to maximize access either to market capital or to government–donor funds denied to an orthodox business or nonprofit vehicle. The community interest companies (CICs) and low-profit, limited liability companies (L3Cs) are experimental structures between market and State that challenge many of the central tenets of charity law.

Such schemes in Australia have been aided by the judiciary. The Australian High Court decision in *Word Investments*[5] (much to the revenue authority's dismay) entrenched the 'destination of income' test into charity tax law. This test simply means that once it is shown that earned income is for charitable purposes, the manner in which the income is raised does not detract from the otherwise charitable objects. This goes against the trend of other comparable jurisdictions and opens the gate for some adventurous boundary blurring.

Oonagh Breen, an Irish legal academic, recently spent time at Harvard University considering all these boundary issues in different jurisdictions. As a consequence, Chapter 6 tracks both the traditional issues of separation of business and charity, alleged unfair competition and the emergence of hybrid forms between market, state and nonprofit. The detailed examination of the laws and regulations in each jurisdiction exposes the challenges for all participants seeking to shift formerly well-accepted bright lines.

GOVERNMENT

Governments have an interest in the performance of charities providing public goods to the community, which it might otherwise have to provide or reap the consequences of a dissatisfied community. When governments believe that they should provide all public goods, then charity is often left to its own devices or in some instances actively suppressed. One can loosely draw parallels between the state as it was at the time of the 1601 Preamble and the modern UK state. The fear of general revolution in the days of the Preamble driving state intervention has been replaced by the loss of political power for public goods not delivered at the right cost to taxpayers. The changing shape of modern government has impacted on the boundaries of charity. The Preamble's list of schools, universities, hospitals, roads, bridges, jetties and prisons once provided by charity are now regularly provided by consortia in which big business and international financiers play a leading role; and charity plays little, if any, in many jurisdictions. This is particularly the case in the UK, where government experimentation with public–private finance initiatives has brought the finances, skills, competitiveness and profit motive of the business world to bear on areas of utility and service provision that were once the heartland of charity.

This trend has not meant that charity has a lesser overall relationship with government, as the new public management strategy for the rollback of the welfare state has driven the use of the nonprofit sector as a delivery mechanism for community and welfare services. Recently, the growth of the non-profit sector in many jurisdictions has been due to contractual arrangements for specific programs and services, rather than general grants to aid the purposes of organisations. The position of government as the largest financier in such semi-markets allows considerable coercive power over those in such a market space, leading to one-sided contracts, shifting of risk to others who are not the most able to finance it, and underfunding.

Is the modernisation of charity law about a state agenda seeking to harness the resources of charity for the 'cheaper, better and faster' delivery of community services, or lofty notions of partnership and facilitation of a vibrant independent sector for democratic enhancement?

In Chapter 7, Kerry O'Halloran traces the developments in this area from the initial charity–government boundary in the Preamble to the more recent legal developments in the various UK jurisdictions. The '*Pemsel* plus' formulation and the new regulatory mechanisms indicate where the new boundaries are to be found and how they are shaping the relationship between the state, charities and the community.

RELIGION

There is no part of the law of charities more replete with paradox than the third head, the advancement of religion. It was missing in the Preamble, apart from 'the repair of churches', but within a few years had been recognised by the judiciary as extending to an exceptionally wide array of purposes. The initial omission is more confounding, considering that religion formed the core of the misty beginnings of pious uses and the legal notion of an equitable trust. To cause complete confusion much of this was developed in the ecclesiastical courts! The paradox does not stop there as religion has been present consistently in the base motivation of the creation and sustaining of significant charitable activities across all the heads and the ages. Evidence is now overwhelming that adherence to a faith and more importantly worship attendance is the best predictor of high and regular giving and volunteering to any cause, not just to those which are religious.[6] Yet this force for public good is riven with infamous examples of religion motivating, justifying or being associated with human genocide, unspeakable inhumanity across nations, races and families often lasting for generations. How can something which has produced so much public benefit also produce so much public harm?

One could continue identifying the paradoxes, puzzles and inconsistencies in this head of charity, but just one more will probably reduce readers (other than hardened charity lawyers) to despair, when a prominent English charity law text claims, 'The rationale for treating the advancement of religion as charitable has not been discussed in the English cases'.[7] Clearly the unique position of the formal church in western history – from once being a state unto itself to being a state-established institution, and more latterly finding itself in a more level legal playing field of multiple faiths – combined with fluctuating but mostly declining membership, resources, political and moral influence, is part of the explanation of what we see now as paradoxes.

The Australian inquiries into charity or nonprofit regulation have all had submissions from those who, with a fervour and dogmatism worthy of a religious fanatic, rail against the concessions given to religious organisations.[8] The rising glare of sunlight driven by an increasing public appetite for transparency and accountability and tabloid stories about fallen saints has cast a deep shadow over all things religious. The sexual abuse of children in religious institutions across continents and ages, the worldly excesses of some high-profile religious leaders and various sectarian-associated mass violence have taken their toll and as a consequence religion's assumed position as a public good, an anchor sustaining law and social behaviour, and worthy of concessional treatment is open for discussion and justification.

In Chapter 8, Anne Robinson, a practising lawyer retained by many religious bodies, and Father Brian Lucas, lawyer and General Secretary of the Australian Catholic Bishops Conference, examine the issue of religion as a head of charity. As the old assumptions of religious public benefit have already been largely stripped away in the court of tabloid opinion, what are the new rationales which will suffice to persuade politicians and the public that all things religious should remain charitable and worthy of state concessions?

THE FUTURE

Two lawyers from opposite sides of the globe, but with similar concerns about the future shape of the law and regulation of charities, were invited to challenge the incremental model of charity law reform. They have both recently completed doctoral theses proposing radical reform agendas involving not just charities but all civil society organisations. The result is two different but equally challenging examinations of the future of charity law.

In Chapter 9, Jonathan Garton, a UK legal academic, identifies the justification for the state expanding its attention from its preoccupation with charity to the wider view of organised civil society. He applies five justifications for state regulation of all civil society organisations, rather than just charities. In doing so, he identifies what issues are important for the regulation of civil society organisations in comparison with for-profit enterprise, which indicates the shape and extent of such regulation.

In Chapter 10, Matthew Turnour, a charity lawyer, sketches a different architecture for charity law which could be a jurisprudence for all civil society organisations. He proposes a new framework for the common law, rather than incremental statutory intervention. From a reconceptualisation of the heart of charitable purpose, he builds to a multi-dimensional model of the space for civil society organisations which allows for flexible boundaries.

What sets these two contributions apart is that they challenge our legal notions of charity by exploring the rapid advances of other disciplines in understanding charities as nonprofit organisations and then as civil society organisations. A robust challenge is in the making of a legally conceived framework based on the essence of charity, as economics, sociology, administration, psychology and other disciplines make significant strides towards constructing a coherent framework about altruism, philanthropy and volunteerism in modern society.

NOTES

1. Australia, Inquiry into the Definition of Charities and Related Organisations (2001), *Report of the Inquiry into the Definition of Charities and Related Organisations*, Canberra: Treasury.
2. 'Charity Law in the Pacific Rim' (2002), *Third Sector Review*, 8(1) (special issue).
3. Extension of Charitable Purpose Act 2004 (Cth).
4. Available at http://www.bus.qut.edu.au/research/cpns/seminarevent/ ModernisingCharityLawConference.jsp
5. *Commissioner of Taxation of the Commonwealth of Australia v Word Investments Ltd* (2008) 236 CLR 204.
6. For an overview see Bekkers, R. and P. Wiepking (2009), *Generosity and Philanthropy: A Literature Review*, SSRN Working Paper Series No. 1015507, available at http://papers. ssrn.com/sol3/papers.cfm?abstract_id=1015507 (accessed 24 December 2009).
7. Picarda, H. (1999), *The Law and Practice Relating to Charities*, 3rd edn, London: Butterworths, 84.
8. Refer to Chapter 8.

PART I

The charity reform journey since 2001

1. Charity law reforms: overview of progress since 2001

Kerry O'Halloran, Bob Wyatt, Laird Hunter, Michael Gousmett and Myles McGregor-Lowndes

INTRODUCTION

In the UK, Singapore, Canada, New Zealand and Australia, as in many other jurisdictions, charity law is rooted in the common law and anchored on the Statute of Charitable Uses 1601.[1] The *Pemsel*[2] classification of charitable purposes was uniformly accepted, and together with a shared and growing pool of judicial precedents, aided by the 'spirit and intendment' rule,[3] has subsequently allowed the law to develop along much the same lines. In recent years, all the above jurisdictions have embarked on law reform processes designed to strengthen regulatory processes and to statutorily define and encode common law concepts. The reform outcomes are now to be found in a batch of national charity statutes which reflect interesting differences in the extent to which their respective governments have been prepared to balance the modernising of charitable purposes and other common law concepts alongside the customary concern to tighten the regulatory framework.

THE UNITED KINGDOM

The Charities Act 1960, introduced by Westminster and largely replicated in the other jurisdictions of the UK, laid a roughly common baseline for law and practice in the latter part of the 20th century. In England and Wales, the Charity Commissioners (established under the Charitable Trusts Act 1853) had their powers extended by the Charities Act 1960 and further by the Charities Acts of 1992 and 1993. In Scotland, the specific regulation of charities is of more recent origin.[4] The first statute regulating 'Scottish charities' as such was implemented in 1992, when Part I of the Law Reform (Miscellaneous Provisions) (Scotland) Act 1990 came into force. In Northern Ireland, charities have long been regulated by the Charities Act (Northern Ireland) 1964 and the Charities Order (Northern Ireland) 1987. In both Scotland and Northern Ireland, the lead regulatory body has always been the tax-collecting agency.

Following the lead given by England and Wales, certain key outcomes were achieved by the law reform process in each of the jurisdictions, as evidenced in their respective new charity statutes, which re-set a common baseline for charity law in the post-2001 period throughout the UK. These key components consisted of: statutory statements of core common law concepts and a new extended list of charitable purposes; changes to the regulatory framework including a new independent lead regulatory body, a Charity Appeals Tribunal, a Register of Charities and adjustments to the traditional roles of court and Attorney General; and an updating of the law relating to other matters such as trustees, fundraising, cy-près and legal structures.

Reform Outcomes: Core Concepts

It has long been established that to be a charity an entity must be confined exclusively to charitable purposes, be for the public benefit, and be independent, non-profit-distributing and non-political. The outcome of charity law reviews in England and Wales,[5] Scotland[6] and Northern Ireland[7] concluded with statutory statements of these common law concepts.

'Charity'

In England and Wales, 'charity', as defined in section 1 of the 2006 Act, means an 'institution which: (a) is established for charitable purposes only, and (b) falls to be subject to the control of the High Court in the exercise of its jurisdiction with respect to charities'. This definition is replicated in the legislation for Northern Ireland[8] and in Scotland is simply confined to charitable purpose and to public benefit in Scotland or elsewhere.[9] The traditional common law definition therefore remains in place as the standard building block for charity law.

Exclusively charitable

It is well established in the common law jurisdictions that for a trust to be charitable it must be confined exclusively to charitable purposes. In all UK jurisdictions, this rule has been statutorily stated as a continuing component in the legal definition of 'charity'.[10]

The public benefit test

Of the definitional matters that have long constituted the distinguishing characteristics of charity law in a common law context, none is more important than the requirement that to acquire charitable status, and consequent tax exemption privileges, an entity must first satisfy the public benefit test: there must be a real verifiable benefit, and this must accrue to the public or to a significant section of it. This critical component of the gatekeeper role, aided by the 'spirit and intendment' rule, has also provided the only means whereby new interpretations of charitable purposes could be introduced to address contemporary and local manifestations of social need.

A statutory test   The public benefit test now has an unequivocal mandatory application in respect of all charitable purposes in England and Wales,[11] Scotland[12] and Northern Ireland.[13] All jurisdictions have modified this common law test by introducing statutory rules to guide interpretation and provide powers for further guidance to be supplied by the regulator. In both Scotland and Northern Ireland there is now a statutory requirement that in applying the test regard must also be had to any possible negative side effects.[14]

Effect of test on classes of 'poor relations/employees' and on admission fees   One important effect of the statutory public benefit test is the removal of the anomalous exceptions in respect of donor-imposed limitations on the class entitled to benefit. This has been strongly associated with a donor's poor relations or employees, private schools with expensive admission fees, and private hospitals and other health and social care facilities. The removal of any such exemption from the public benefit test is an implied effect of provisions in the English and Scottish statutes, but is more specifically addressed in the Northern Irish legislation.[15]

Test no longer to be applied by the Inland Revenue   The issue as to which agency in the regulatory framework bears responsibility for applying the public benefit test is of crucial importance to charities and for the development of the charitable sector. Where, in keeping with the traditional policing role, that responsibility rested with the tax-collecting agency then, to some degree, the test had to operate in an exclusionary manner as that agency's *raison d'être* required it to protect and maximise the nation's tax revenue base. In all jurisdictions, the legislature has now both vested the new regulatory body with High Court powers and given it lead responsibility relative to the tax-collecting agency, thereby enabling it to use the public benefit test as a potentially powerful means of supporting charities and developing the sector.

Independent

Traditionally, under common law, a charity was required to be a free-standing, independent entity founded by and bound to fulfil the terms of the donor's gift. The charity law reform processes in the UK jurisdictions concluded without any legislative provisions addressing the need to ensure protection for the independence of charities – except for the express stipulation in section 7(4)(b) of the Scottish statute that a body will be held not to satisfy the 'charity test', and thus be debarred from registering as a charity, if 'its constitution expressly permits the Scottish Ministers or a Minister of the Crown to direct or otherwise control its activities'.

Non-profit-distributing

In general, the common law rule is that charities may make profits (or gains) or accumulate surpluses, provided these are not used for the profit or gain of its individual members or for distribution to its owners or members, or to any other person, either while operating or on winding up. In England and Wales the Charities Act 2006 makes no reference to charities and trading,[16] and the other jurisdictions have taken a similar approach. This leaves the common law rule in place.

Non-political

The common law rule draws a distinction between a body with political purposes and one that engages in political activities: the former is not charitable; the latter will be charitable if the activities are ancillary but subordinate to and in furtherance of its non-political purposes. There are references which continue this rule in the Charities Act 2006, the Charities and Trustee Investment (Scotland) Act 2005 and the Charities Act (Northern Ireland) 2008.

The 'spirit and intendment' rule

Traditionally, this rule provided the only means whereby new interpretations of charitable purposes could be introduced to address contemporary and local manifestations of social need. The recent legislation of the UK jurisdictions[17] continues this rule and with it the possibility of allowing further purposes to be added to those already listed as charitable.

Reform Outcomes: Charitable Purposes

The UK jurisdictions have all retained as charitable the set of purposes first identified and listed in the 1601 Statute and as classified in *Pemsel*. The bedrock of charity law in the future will therefore remain firmly based on the *Pemsel* classification and on the accompanying vast body of case law principles and precedents.

Changes to *Pemsel*

An important outcome of the law reform processes in these jurisdictions has been the nature and extent of certain legislative changes made to the *Pemsel* purposes. These include the fact that in all jurisdictions, the task of determining charitable status no longer rests with the tax-collecting agency, which will facilitate a more positive interpretation of *Pemsel* purposes in the future.

Prevention The traditional emphasis on dealing exclusively with effects rather than also with the causes has always been apparent in the case law which stresses the 'relief' of need. An important positive outcome of the law reform processes in all UK jurisdictions has been a government concession that, in some instances, charitable purposes could accommodate 'prevention' as well as 'relief'; this has been particularly noticeable in all jurisdictions in respect of poverty[18] but also in relation to health.[19]

Religion A statutory definition of 'religion', first introduced by the 2006 Act in England and Wales,[20] has since been virtually replicated by an equivalent provision in Northern Ireland[21] and by something similar in Scotland.[22] This definition, which includes express reference to faiths that do not profess belief in a god as well as polytheistic religions, is a welcome outcome appropriate to the contemporary multi-culture and multi-faith populations of these jurisdictions.

Public benefit and Pemsel Another positive outcome has been the removal of a variable application of the public benefit test to the *Pemsel* heads of charity.

Additions to *Pemsel*

'Charitable purposes', as defined under the new legislation, retains but extends the common law definition given to it in *Pemsel* and subsequently interpreted by judicial precedent over many years and jurisdictions. In addition, all UK jurisdictions have committed to much the same set of '*Pemsel* plus' charitable purposes. Their respective legislative provisions list, as separate purposes, a number of activities that have gained judicial recognition over time, largely as a consequence of Charity Commission initiative (see, further, Chapter 2), including the advancement of animal welfare, the advancement of environmental protection or improvement, and the advancement of the arts, culture, heritage or science. The main exception is the promotion of amateur sport as a charitable purpose in its own right rather than as a means of advancing other existing charitable purposes.[23]

However, they also and with remarkable consistency identify clusters of new purposes which cohere around clear social policy themes, revealing the matters central to government's intended partnership arrangement with charity (see, further, Chapters 2 and 7). These are:

- the advancement of human rights, conflict resolution or reconciliation, and promotion of multiculturalism and so on
- the advancement of civil society
- the efficiency of charities
- the advancement of health and related services
- promoting the welfare of specific socially disadvantaged groups.

Reform Outcomes: Changes to the Regulatory Framework

A most important outcome of the charity law reform process in the jurisdictions of Scotland and Northern Ireland has been their decision to follow the lead given earlier by England and Wales and remove the responsibility for determining charitable status and registering and supervising charities from the tax-collecting agency and vest lead regulatory authority in a new charity-specific body. The Inland Revenue is now required to defer to the new body on matters of charitable status and interpretation of charitable purpose.

Establishing a new lead regulatory body

The new bodies vested with responsibility for determining charitable status and registering and supervising charities in Scotland and Northern Ireland are the Office of the Scottish Charity Regulator (OSCR)[24] and the Charity Commission for Northern Ireland (CCNI) respectively.[25] Armed with an extended definition of 'charitable purpose' together with access to the 'spirit and intendment' rule, these new bodies are now positioned to adopt a more expansive approach to charitable status than was feasible for the Inland Revenue to undertake. For the first time, all UK jurisdictions now have a dedicated agency with a specific brief to regulate charities, monitor their activities, protect their assets and ensure compliance with standards of practice enshrined in statute.

Register of charities

As in England and Wales, the new lead regulatory bodies in Scotland and Northern Ireland will be responsible for the establishment and maintenance of a register of charities and will oversee the reporting regimes applicable to such registered charities. Any charitable organisation operating or intending to operate in one or more of these jurisdictions will be required to register with the appropriate new regulatory body. In England and Wales, the 2006 Act has brought many more charities, both larger and smaller than those previously registered, within the scope of the Charity Commission's scrutiny and services.

The introduction of a register of charities, coupled with mandatory registration and reporting requirements, means that for the first time in these jurisdictions, as in England and Wales, there will now be reliable information as to how many charities exist, where they are located, their size, wealth and type. Registration provides an essential basis for an efficient regulatory system. The fact that the registers are accessible to the public will promote transparency.

A tighter regulatory regime
The powers and remit of the new regulatory bodies in Scotland and Northern Ireland closely follow the Charity Commission model. In all UK jurisdictions that independent, if government, agency now requires charities to register, keep proper books of account, submit annual financial and activity reports, and give an account of all fundraising activity. The supervisory powers of the agency include authority to determine charitable status, inspect charities, make cy-près schemes, remove or appoint trustees, maintain a register of disqualified trustees, de-register charities, monitor the flow of funds and share information with other agencies on both a domestic and an international basis.

Establishing an Appeals Tribunal
The creation of the Charity Tribunal for Northern Ireland[26] and the Scottish Charity Appeals Panel,[27] in addition to the Charities Appeal Tribunal already established in England and Wales, is intended to provide a cheap and swift alternative to the courts system for reviewing regulatory decisions. Given that the adjustment of charitable purposes to meet contemporary social need was for centuries dependent upon High Court rulings and emerging keystone judicial precedents regarding matters that could or could not be construed as 'charitable', a role greatly diminished in recent years, the vesting of such powers in a Tribunal would seem to offer the possibility of reviving and continuing this vital creative forum.

Adjustments to the roles of the Court and the Attorney General
The traditional role of the High Court as the forum for determining occasional points of law is retained but otherwise its adjudicatory role has passed to the Appeals Tribunal and its cy-près jurisdiction is, for

most purposes, now vested in the new regulatory agency. The Attorney General, exercising the *parens patriae* powers to protect and supervise charities, is no longer fully operational in any of the UK jurisdictions as some of the responsibilities of that office have been statutorily transferred to the new regulatory body, although the Attorney General does retain a supervisory role.[28]

Other Modernising Changes

Although UK charity reform was primarily focused on defining and encoding in statutory form certain core common law concepts and with establishing a more efficient regulatory framework, it also sought to modernise practice.

Aspects of fundraising
Improving the regulating of fundraising, thereby increasing public confidence in the sector, was among the priorities of the charity law reform processes and to a varying extent was an achieved legislative outcome in each jurisdiction. In England and Wales, fundraising provisions in the 2006 Act[29] are intended to introduce a unified system to regulate public charitable collections. These provisions have been largely replicated in the corresponding legislation for Scotland[30] and Northern Ireland.[31]

The role of trustees
In all jurisdictions, one outcome of the reform process has been the introduction of legislative provisions to strengthen the position of trustee provisions and supplement an already updated body of statute law.[32]

The use of cy-près
A further significant charity law reform outcome has been the introduction of legislative provisions to give the new lead regulatory bodies powers similar to those already held by the Charity Commission in England and Wales in respect of cy-près. All such bodies now exercise a concurrent jurisdiction with the High Court to create cy-près schemes enabling the funds of such a charity to be administered, perhaps consolidated with those of other similar defunct charities, and be directed towards a new set of similar but viable objects.

New legal structures
Another important outcome of the law reform processes was the inclusion of provisions facilitating the introduction of a new type of legal structure better suited to give effect to charitable purposes. In England and Wales,

section 34 of the Charities Act 2006 introduced the Charitable Incorporated Organisation (CIO) which can be established with limited or unlimited liability but only for charitable purposes. The Charity Commission is solely responsible for the incorporation and registration of the CIO and for assisting existing charitable companies limited by guarantee or industrial and provident societies to convert to CIOs.[33] This initiative was replicated in the charity legislation of Scotland[34] and Northern Ireland.[35]

SINGAPORE

The charitable sector in Singapore consists of a double tier: charities and Institutions of a Public Character.

Charities

There are about 1900 registered charities. To be registered, a charity must satisfy the common law definition, as stated in *Pemsel's case*[36] and confirmed by subsequent case law, namely the advancement of religion, the advancement of education, the relief of poverty or other purposes beneficial to the community. It must also meet certain registration requirements. The benefits of acquiring charitable status are automatic income tax exemption and property tax exemption on premises used for exclusively charitable purposes.

Institutions of a Public Character (IPCs)

There are about 500 IPCs in Singapore. An IPC is a status conferred on a not-for-profit organisation in respect of which donors will be granted income tax deductions for any donations made to it. They are generally required to be registered charities. An IPC must be beneficial to the community in Singapore as a whole rather than confined to sectional interests. The benefits of acquiring IPC status are a 2.5 times tax deduction for cash donations and approved in-kind donations (that is, computers, shares, artefacts, public sculptures, land and buildings).

The Impact of Recent Changes in the Regulatory Regime for Charities

Major changes in policy

The Commissioner of Charities (COC), which earlier reported to the Minister for Finance, is now focused on tax issues related to charities and IPCs. Greater powers have been given to the COC to act for the protection of charities and the public interest. These include powers to: make orders on the application of the property of a charity under certain circumstances; prohibit, stop or restrict public fundraising by a charity or person so as to protect public interest; regulate the conduct of public fundraising; tighten the registration of charities; and increase the composition sums.

The trend is towards an increase in the number and diversity of charities. There is now a greater public expectation that charities will become more transparent and accountable. In order to ensure the continued growth of the charitable sector and to maintain public confidence there is a need to go beyond tax issues to focus on the governance of charities and IPCs.

Major changes in the regulatory model (from September 2006)
The appointment of a Commissioner of Charities under the purview of the Ministry of Community Development, Youth and Sports has been a most significant development in the regulatory regime for charities. The COC is assisted by six Sector Administrators overseeing the charities and IPCs within their sectors' purviews: the Ministry of Information, Communications and the Arts overseeing charities and IPCs in arts and heritage; the Ministry of Education overseeing those in education; the Ministry of Health, those in healthcare; the National Council of Social Service overseeing those in social services or welfare; the People's Association, those in community matters; and the Singapore Sports Council overseeing those in sports.

The COC also maintains oversight of those charities and IPCs that do not fall under any of the six Sector Administrators. In addition, there is the Charity Council, led by people sector representatives. The Council's objectives are to act as promoter, by promoting good governance standards and best practices in the charity sector; as enabler, by helping to build the capabilities of charities and enable them to comply with regulatory requirements and be more accountable to the public; and as advisor, by advising the COC on key regulatory issues and proposals that have broad-ranging impact on the charity sector.

Role, Functions and Policy of the Commissioner of Charities

Principles
The office of Commissioner is informed by the following guiding principles:

- to nurture a charitable sector that remains driven by the community and is governed by a basic set of rules, with a regulatory regime that will not be onerous and stifle volunteerism but will be enforced strictly to maintain public confidence;

- to accept that boards of charities and IPCs are ultimately responsible for the charities and should take ownership to improve their governance;
- to facilitate self-regulation within the charity sector and encourage greater disclosure to promote informed giving by the public;
- to be aware that the regulatory framework should not be 'one-size-fits-all'.

Vision and strategies

The vision of the office of Commissioner is of a well-governed and thriving charity sector with strong public support. Its strategy, comprising of three strands, is:

- to ensure regulatory compliance
- to promote good governance and best practice
- to be a proactive charity advisor.

Strategy 1: ensure regulatory compliance The COC will regulate charities and IPCs, with the help of Sector Administrators. Primarily, it will:

- monitor through annual reports and financial statements to track the delivery of services, programmes, and activities to ensure that charities deliver benefits to achieve their charitable purposes and to ensure that resources are used for charitable purposes;
- audit large charities and IPCs, adopting a risk-based approach, giving priority to assessing the regulatory compliance of large charities and IPCs;
- investigate any complaints about charities that are brought to its attention.

The COC also regulates fundraising in Singapore:

- for foreign charitable causes a permit is required and conditions will be imposed to ensure proper solicitation and usage of donations;
- for local charitable causes a set of fundraising guidelines states the requirements for any persons conducting public fundraising appeals. Police permits are necessary for house-to-house and street collections and other permits may be required.

Strategy 2: promote good governance and best practice A Code of Governance has been introduced which sets out the principles and the best practice in key areas of governance and management. All registered charities and IPCs are required to file an online submission to regulators on the extent of their compliance with the Code. Field visits are conducted on a regular basis, which helps regulators to understand the charities' business and allows them to offer advice on ways to improve their governance. The COC is also in a position to offer funding support for charities from its $45million capability fund, which it can deploy to co-fund the cost of capacity-building in charities through the use of information and communication technologies, consultancy and training and so on.

Strategy 3: be a proactive charity advisory body The Charity Council acts as an important bridge between regulator and charities. It is led by people sector representatives and focuses on promoting good governance and best practice. It also advises the COC on key regulatory issues and proposals which may have broad-ranging impact on the charity sector. The Charity Council released its inaugural Charity Governance Report in February 2009.

The Charity Portal is a user-friendly mechanism for reducing the administration time and costs that burden charities. It offers a one-stop online portal to facilitate e-registration of charities and IPCs and a one-stop resource for charities, donors and the general public to obtain information on charities, charity regulations, regulatory guidance and other issues.

Positive Outcomes Achieved by the New Regulatory Regime

The indications so far show that the introduction of the Commissioner of Charities and other changes made to the regulatory regime for charities have been well received and are achieving positive outcomes. According to the Governance Evaluation Checklist, a total of 81 per cent (1500) of charities and IPCs have now filed an online submission to the Code of Governance with a median governance evaluation score of 87 per cent. Further, data from the NVPC Individual Giving Survey 2008 show that public confidence in charities has increased from 83 per cent in 2006 to 90 per cent in 2008.

Looking to the future, more changes to the Charities Act can be expected. These will:

- provide clarity on the roles and responsibilities of board members and protect them from personal liability if they have acted honestly and in good faith;
- provide power to regulate IPCs more effectively;
- enhance regulatory oversight on fundraising, including requiring any fundraisers, not just charities and IPCs, to furnish the COC with

the information necessary to conduct investigations into complaints pertaining to fundraising;

- streamline accounting standards and reports to make them more relevant for charities so as to improve their disclosure and transparency.

CANADA

The Voluntary Sector Initiative (VSI) was, arguably, the most innovative, successful and misunderstood vehicle ever devised to address issues related to Canada's voluntary sector.

As a result of work undertaken by the voluntary sector to identify issues, and the inclusion in the governing party's election policy of a commitment to re-examine its relationship with the sector, the prime minister of the day announced the creation of a programme unlike any previously used in Canada to develop public policy. The government and the sector established seven joint tables, composed of equal numbers of senior government officials and senior people from the voluntary sector, and each charged with examining an aspect of the relationship between government and the sector. For present purposes, the most relevant table was the Joint Regulatory Table (JRT).[37]

The JRT had a six-fold mandate:

- to examine ways to make the regulator more transparent and accountable;
- to recommend improvements to the appeal system applicable to charities when seeking to overturn a decision of the regulator;
- to recommend a system of intermediate sanctions, short of revocation of registration, that could be used as enforcement mechanisms in appropriate cases;
- to examine and discuss models for a charities regulator (but not to recommend a particular model);
- to advise the Charities Directorate on restructuring of the annual return required of every charity so that the administrative burden of such a return was minimised;
- to advise the Charities Directorate on amendments to its policy related to business activities by charities.

For some, the JRT was a major disappointment, but some of that disappointment seems to be based on a lack of understanding of the Table's mandate. The commentators and detractors failed to accept that the Table was bound by its mandate as established by the federal Cabinet in

consultation with a group of leaders of national voluntary sector organisations. Notwithstanding the criticism, in March 2003 the Table delivered
a report with 75 recommendations for changes. Slightly less than a year
later, the Canadian government adopted 69 of the recommendations, representing the most significant change in charity law in more than 40 years.
The following is a brief examination of the JRT's recommendations and
the government's response.

Transparency and Accountability

The JRT made a series of recommendations of characteristics or traits
that should govern a charities regulator, whatever model of regulation
was chosen. These recommendations included provisions for the publication of virtually all policy statements used by the regulator,[38] the development of educational programming about charities' obligations under the
Income Tax Act, and the development of ongoing mechanisms for dialogue including the establishment of a continuing committee to advise the
Minister of National Revenue on matters related to charities. All of these
recommendations were adopted by government.

Even during the life of the JRT, the Charities Directorate was making
more information about its policies and operations available on its
website. A granting programme was established whereby the Charities
Directorate contracts with voluntary sector organisations to educate
charities about various obligations they have under the Income Tax Act.
The Directorate began a formal process of widespread consultations on
the development of new or amended policies, providing full opportunity
for charities and others to comment before the policy was put in place. An
advisory committee was appointed by the Minister of National Revenue
and functioned effectively for almost 18 months until it was abolished by a
newly elected government of a different political stripe.

Certain other recommendations, including publication of reasons for
Directorate decisions on registration cases, were adopted by the government but have not yet been implemented. However, as a result of JRT
recommendations, the amount of information publicly available about
Directorate decisions has increased significantly. The JRT's review also
underlined the importance of the role of charity examiners in an area
where they must do more than just administer a law, but rather must help
develop it through the type of analogies called for in the common law. It
called for additional professional development and reclassification so that
examiners could make a career of working in the field, thus avoiding the
ongoing change of staff. While government accepted this recommendation
in principle, the problem has not been addressed.

Appeal System

The JRT observed that charity law could not develop without a robust set of court decisions that reflected the type of evolution identified by many common law courts, including the Supreme Court of Canada in the *Vancouver Society* case.[39] It recommended that decisions of the regulator be subject to internal reconsideration by a unit outside the Charities Directorate but staffed by people with experience in charity law. Should that reconsideration leave the matter still in contention, an appeal would lie to the Tax Court of Canada, where an appeal by re-hearing would take place. Both the organisation and the Directorate would be allowed to call witnesses and to cross-examine. An appeal would lie from the Tax Court of Canada to the Federal Court of Appeal, where the appeal would be heard on the basis of the record developed in the Tax Court. Thereafter, with leave, an appeal could be taken to the Supreme Court of Canada.

In an attempt to encourage the development and litigation of cases that were likely to further charity law in Canada, the JRT also called for the establishment of an appeal fund similar to the Court Challenges Program, which provided funding to individuals bringing court actions that engaged Canada's Constitution.[40] The federal government accepted the recommendation for an internal reconsideration process, but did not accept the remainder of the Table's proposals.

Intermediate Sanctions

Prior to the JRT's report, the only enforcement mechanism available to the Charities Directorate was revocation of charitable status.[41] This was seen by the JRT as too blunt an instrument to have as the sole vehicle for dealing with non-compliant charities. Moreover, it seemed to prevent action against certain types of charities, including universities and churches, where no Minister would ever agree to elimination of the organisation's charitable status.

The JRT therefore recommended the introduction of a system of intermediate sanctions, but significantly less complicated sanctions than those used in the United States. In adopting the recommendations, the government established a set of 'offences', such as improper issuance of donation receipts or carrying out improper business activities or the provision of an undue benefit to any person. Penalties are attached to each type of offence. The Directorate also has the option of suspending a charity's status as a qualified donee for up to one year. While allowing the charity to continue its operations, suspension prohibits it from issuing receipts to its donors, thus eliminating the tax credit to the donor. Thus far, the use of sanctions

has been minimal. This is possibly due to the Directorate's recent enforcement actions being focused on the improper use of tax shelters involving
charities.

Regulatory Models

In the period leading up to the JRT, and during its life, some people
were calling for the establishment of a new type of regulator, similar in
nature and design to the Charity Commission of England and Wales. A
model similar to the Charity Commission was examined by the JRT and
described in its report. The fundamental problem, according to the Table,
was that such a model could not exist easily within Canada's constitutional structure.

The JRT obtained legal opinions from lawyers within and outside government and concluded that it could see no way that a regulatory body
similar to the Charity Commission could be established in Canada without
constitutional challenge. The only exception would be if the federal and
provincial governments entered into contractual arrangements in which
the federal government, through the Charity Commission, would exercise
the provincial authority on behalf of the province. Given Canada's political make-up, such a model is unlikely.[42]

Administrative Policy Decisions

One of the most frequently commented-upon changes related to advocacy.
The Income Tax Act provides a 10 per cent safe-harbour provision for
charities to undertake advocacy. That is, a charity may expend up to 10
per cent of its assets on advocacy activities without being accused of failing
to use all of its resources for charitable activities. Some saw that limit as
an inappropriate vehicle to silence the voice of charities. They argued that
a charity should be allowed to undertake any amount of advocacy activity
so long as the advocacy did not become a collateral purpose.

While the Joint Regulatory Table was not mandated to deal with the
issue of advocacy (most often in Canadian law called 'political activities'), it
was instrumental in an updating of policy that clarified existing policy and
allowed some greater scope for charities to undertake advocacy activities.

The Canada Revenue Agency (CRA) has introduced or amended a
number of other policies in recent years that seek to bring charity law
somewhat closer to the 21st century. These include policies providing for
the registration of organisations assisting ethnocultural communities and
clarifying the policy on the eligibility of umbrella or peak organisations for
charitable status.

One of the more contentious policy issues relates to fundraising. The Charities Directorate issued a draft policy setting out its views on acceptable fundraising activity and reporting, to which the sector responded negatively, questioning the restrictions the CRA sought to support. A final set of guidelines – clearly delineated as representing advice, not an absolute rule – was issued later and met with greater, albeit grudging, acceptance. Far less contentious and welcomed by many is a draft policy on the potential of some sports activities to be registered as charitable which explains how an organisation might qualify for charitable registration if it positions itself so that the sports activity is ancillary and incidental to another charitable purpose, such as the promotion of health.

Judicial Decisions

In the last eight years, the Supreme Court of Canada has considered only one case dealing with the question of what is charitable at law. The Federal Court of Appeal considered nine cases dealing with the same question. It is fair to say that none of these ten decisions has changed the law of charity in Canada.[43] The Supreme Court of Canada case, *AYSA Amateur Youth Soccer Association v Canada (Revenue Agency)*,[44] reiterated that an organisation formed for the promotion of sport was not charitable. The Federal Court of Appeal cases upheld a line of cases dealing with foreign activities, business activities, political activities and use of charitable resources. No new ground was broken.

Drivers and Barriers for Reform

Drivers
With one exception, one is hard-pressed to find a major demand for change or modernisation of charity law in Canada. That exception is in the field of the social economy or social enterprise. A small, but increasing, number of people in the field are pushing government to make legislative changes that will allow the expansion of social enterprise activities. The arguments in favour of expanding the possibility of preferential tax treatment to investors in social enterprise focus on it being an alternative to government having to pay to deal with social issues. If organisations are able to entice donors with the potential of tax credits, the argument goes, they will be able to reduce their demand for government funding. The contrary view is that government should not be excused from paying to deal with social issues and that the addition of more organisations able to award tax credits to donors or investors will lead to a finite number of dollars intended to support the public good being distributed more diffusely, resulting in a reduction of service.

Barriers

While the number of drivers to reform is minimal, the barriers to modernising charity law in Canada are numerous. Moreover, they tend to be institutional or systemic in nature, which makes changing them a formidable task. The most systemic of these barriers is Canada's constitutional division of powers. While the federal government, through the CRA, is seen by most charities as their sole regulator, that is not the case. There are, effectively, at least 14 definitions of charity in Canada – that of the federal government (which most closely resembles the definition in other common law countries) and those of the ten provinces and three territories (which tend to deal with political or social demands rather than any common law). An offshoot of this constitutional divide is an inability to raise the issue of charity regulation to a political level. The opportunity for joint meetings of ministers responsible for charity regulation never arises, because each province has given that responsibility to a different ministry. Thus, there is no opportunity for these ministers to meet as peers and discuss pan-Canadian issues related to charities.

While the constitution is a significant problem, the most relevant barrier to modernising charity law is the lack of a court system that would allow for a greater number of cases to be decided. Because there are so few cases taken to the Federal Court of Appeal, due to the expense involved (mounting an appeal to that court would involve fees ranging upwards of $50 000), there is a similar dearth of decisions on charity law from the Supreme Court of Canada. That court has heard more admiralty cases than charity law cases!

The federal legislation dealing with charities is also a barrier to modernisation of charity law. While the CRA administers the provisions of the Income Tax Act, it is not responsible for the development of the legislation. That is a role jealously guarded by the Department of Finance.

But the biggest barrier to the modernisation of charity law is the very group of organisations affected by that law – Canada's charities. There is an almost total lack of understanding of, or concern about, the development of charity law amongst all but the largest charities in the country. While their requests for changes in tax treatment or support for social enterprise may invoke the law of charity, they are not seen in that vein, but rather as ways to increase fundraising mechanisms to support their work. The voluntary sector in Canada has not banded together to determine what it wants, or how it should go about getting it. It has been singularly unsuccessful in creating an awareness within government or the general public of its size and its reach. As a result, it has been unable to build the level of public support that would force legislators and regulators to pay attention to its opinions.

The Future Challenges

Canada's attempts at modernising the law of charities have constituted little more than tinkering at the edges. While substantive changes resulted from the report of the Joint Regulatory Table, those changes were limited by the scope of the Table's mandate. More important, those revisions were the first substantive changes in more than three decades.

Revisions to policies by the CRA have, for the most part, been helpful and expanded slightly the scope for charitable activity in the country. Modernising the law of charities in Canada will require a much more fundamental examination. It would require, first, a decision as to whether the law of charities was meant to be a social policy with fiscal implications or a fiscal policy alone. Government is fond of noting that it forgoes tax revenue of almost $2.7 billion as a result of the tax treatment of charitable donations.[45] Leaders of the voluntary sector respond by saying that figure needs to be offset by the (indeterminable) amount of money that government would have to spend in the absence of charities. These points and counterpoints hide the argument about whether charity law is intended, first and foremost, to address social issues or fiscal issues. It also raises questions about whether some of the barriers holding back the development of charity law are, in fact, deliberate decisions to prevent that evolution.

It is clear that the current legislative provisions, including (or perhaps particularly) the judicial oversight process, do not work. It is also clear that government will have to address the issue of social enterprise at some point in the next several years. In light of some of the people promoting the concept, and of developments in other countries, government will have to decide whether to treat these organisations as charities, like charities or as something else. That decision may open the door to consideration of a statutory definition of charity or the 'charity plus' model advocated by Arthur Drache[46] and modelled in the Charities Act 2006 in England.

Such an examination could (and should) precipitate a review of all of the charity law provisions in the Income Tax Act. Such a review could do much to address concerns that have been raised by charities and their advisors over the years. It is highly unlikely, verging on the unimaginable, to believe that the federal government would give up direct regulation of charities in favour of a charity commission or other arm's-length body. So long as the government maintains a generous tax regime available for donors to charities, it will wish to regulate those charities directly. But issues related to business activity, advocacy and the complex disbursement quota rules could be examined as a package and amended so as to make sense for charities and for Canadians.

If government were to become serious about encouraging the evolution of charity law (a premise not yet proven by any action of the federal government, whatever its political stripe), then it would immediately move to allow more cases to come before the courts through a change in the appeal process. It would recognise that it is difficult for a regulator to follow *Pemsel's* provisions for analogies to be drawn if there are no court decisions with which analogies might be drawn. All of this presupposes that government pays some attention to the advocates, another premise that might fail in analysis. It is equally possible that nothing will change and that the future of Canada's charity law will evolve not through incremental change but rather through endless tinkering.

NEW ZEALAND

In New Zealand in recent years there has been a flurry of activity at government level related to the charity and not-for-profit (NFP) sector, to an extent not seen before. Admittedly there had been half-hearted attempts to address issues of concern, such as tax compliance[47] in 1998 and the issue of a Commission for Charities[48] in 1989. Philanthropy has come of age, with organisations such as Philanthropy New Zealand now a significant part of the NFP sector. With total philanthropic funding in the 2006–07 year of NZ$742 million according to Business and Economic Research Ltd,[49] philanthropy plays a major role in New Zealand society. The economic significance of the NFP sector can be seen in that the contribution to GDP of nonprofit organisations is on a par with the tourism sector at $69 billion per annum.[50]

The Charities Act 2005

On 2 April 2005 the Charities Act 2005, which has retained the common law definition of charity as classified in the *Pemsel case*,[51] was enacted. Given that, at the time the Charities Bill was being considered in 2004, England was considering broadening the concept of charitable purposes (which it did in the Charities Act 2006), it is regrettable that the New Zealand government did not imitate the recent initiatives in England which led to the codification of a very much extended concept of charitable purposes. This was an opportunity missed.

The purpose of the Charities Act 2005 was: to establish for the first time in New Zealand's history a Charities Commission; to provide for the registration of societies, institutions and trustees of trusts as charitable entities; and to require charitable entities and certain other persons to comply with certain obligations.[52] The intent behind the Act was to regulate and to monitor the charity sector in New Zealand.

The purpose of the Charities Commission is to approve an applicant's charitable status, following which the entity will benefit from two fiscal advantages: the direct advantage is the exemption of the charitable trust from income tax; the indirect advantage relates to gifts to a registered charitable trust which will be exempt from gift duty and donations for which the donor may qualify for a tax credit. The legislation governing the fiscal advantages of charitable status is not found in the Charities Act 2005 but in specific fiscal legislation, namely the Income Tax Act 2007.

The Charities Act 2005 and Maori

The Charities Act 2005 is unique in that it gives special recognition to the contribution of Maori, the tangtata whenua[53] of Aotearoa New Zealand, to their hapu[54] or iwi[55]by stating at section 5(2)(a): 'The purpose of a trust, society or institution is a charitable purpose under this Act if the purpose would satisfy the public benefit requirement apart from the fact that the beneficiaries of the trust or the members of the society or institution are related by blood'. The Act then declares at section 5(2)(b) that:

> A marae has a charitable purpose if the physical structure of the marae[56] is situated on land that is a Maori reservation referred to in Te Ture Whenua Maori Act 1993 (Maori Land Act 1993) and the funds of the marae are not used for a purpose other than –
> (i) the administration and maintenance of the land and the physical structure of the marae;
> (ii) a purpose that is a charitable purpose other than under this paragraph.

The Charities Commission and the Inland Revenue Department (IRD): interaction of tax and charities rules

An Operational Statement dated December 2006 describes how the Charities Commission and the IRD 'will monitor and advise charitable entities of the requirements for income tax and gift duty exemptions and donee status, following the opening of the Charities Commission register on 1 February 2007'.[57] The Operational Statement also provides advice on how charities can ensure that their business income and donee status comply with the requirements for tax exemption.

Government Support for the NFP Sector

Minister for the Community and Voluntary Sector

The NFP sector in New Zealand has recently gained representation at Ministerial level, albeit outside Cabinet. The recognition due to the sector was long overdue and the initiative of the previous Labour-led government in establishing this position was warmly welcomed by the sector.

Office for the Community and Voluntary Sector

In addition, the NFP sector has its 'own' office, the Office for the Community and Voluntary Sector (OCVS), which was established in 2003. The purpose of the OCVS is 'to address overarching issues affecting the community and voluntary sector and to raise the profile of the sector within government'.[58] The OCVS has an active website with an extensive range of resources available.[59]

Government-promoted sector studies

In recent years a number of key studies of the NFP sector in New Zealand have been undertaken, including the following.

Counting for something – value added by voluntary agencies[60] The purpose of this 2004 project by the New Zealand Federation of Voluntary Welfare Organisations was to measure the work of voluntary agencies, recognising that annual accounts do not 'adequately reflect the full value these organisations add to social well-being and the economy'.[61] Having examined the voluntary inputs for ten voluntary agencies[62] the report concluded that '[t]he magnitude of the voluntary inputs of those 10 organisations is estimated to be $177.5 million'.[63] The study was the first of its kind to be undertaken in New Zealand.

Nonprofit Institutions Satellite Account In 2007, Statistics New Zealand released the results of part of the NFP study relating to the development of a Nonprofit Institutions Satellite Account.[64] The purpose of the Satellite Account is 'to measure in a consistent framework the quantity and economic value of activities undertaken by nonprofit institutions'.[65] The study is part of an inter-related work stream, the second part being a study of the sector in conjunction with Johns Hopkins University.

Study of the New Zealand nonprofit sector (Johns Hopkins) In August 2008 the results of the first comprehensive study of New Zealand's nonprofit sector were released.[66] The composition of the sector's income from philanthropy in 2004 was:[67]

Households	NZ$85 million
Businesses	NZ$216 million
Other nonprofit institutions	NZ$543 million

Total income from all sources was NZ$8,036 million and included investment income of NZ$478 million.[68]

The Promoting Generosity project   In June 2008 the OCVS released a document under the title *The Promoting Generosity Project* which addressed the question, 'How do New Zealanders give?'[69] The key points from the paper were that, of people ten years of age and over, more than 2.7 million people had supported the community and voluntary sector in the preceding 12 months through gifts of time and donations and purchasing products. It is estimated that:

- 1 217 000 people volunteered their time;
- 1 709 000 people donated money or goods to an appeal;
- 1 213 000 people donated to or sponsored an organisation;
- 969 000 people both volunteered and donated to an organisation;
- 829 000 people purchased products;
- 47.3 per cent of New Zealanders supported three or more subsectors through time, donations, sponsorship or purchasing products.[70]

Financial Incentives

In 2001, a government discussion document, *Tax and Charities*, was released.[71] Many matters raised in this document have yet to be debated, such as the definition of 'charitable purpose', particularly with respect to public benefit and fee-charging charities. In October 2006 the NZ government released a discussion document, *Tax Incentives for Giving to Charities and Other Nonprofit Organisations*.[72] This led to significant changes being made to the tax rules regarding charitable giving from 1 April 2008, which were expected 'to encourage a stronger culture of giving and generosity'.[73]

Income Tax Act 2007

Following the enactment of the Charities Act 2005, the Income Tax Act 2004 was amended to ensure that only charities registered with the Charities Commission will be exempt from income tax.[74] The responsibility for assessing donee status remains with Inland Revenue, for entities operating domestically, and with Parliament, for entities with overseas charitable purposes.[75] The relevant sections of the Income Tax Act 2007 relating to government initiatives to encourage charitable and philanthropic giving are the following.

Section DB 41 (companies)
Under this section, companies can now claim deductions for donations for charitable and other public benefits up to the level of that tax year's annual net income. GST input cannot be claimed for any donations made.

Section DV 12   Maori authorities[76]
In 2002 the right of Maori authorities to claim a deduction for donations made to Maori associations[77] was extended to include gifts of money to organisations with approved donee status.[78] The 5 per cent limit on deductions that Maori authorities can claim for cash donations to donee organisations and Maori associations for charitable or other public benefit has been removed and the amount to be deducted for donations is now up to the level of their annual net income.[79]

Section LD (individuals)
From 2008 to 2009 and for subsequent years, individuals are able to claim a rebate of one third of all donations made, limited only by the level of their annual taxable income.

Recent Initiatives

The government is encouraging people to apply their tax cuts, which were effective from 1 April 2009, to donations for charitable and other public benefit. The government released two discussion papers exploring proposals for 'clarifying and simplifying the tax law on how reimbursements and honoraria paid to volunteers in the non-profit sector are to be treated; and exploring whether New Zealand should introduce a pre-tax payroll giving scheme'.[80]

These initiatives were promoted in the Taxation (International Taxation Life Insurance and Remedial Matters) Bill in July 2008.[81] The government is also exploring the refund of imputation credits on charity investments. In April 2008 the Labour-led government suggested that the government consider the idea of people being able to claim tax deductions for non-monetary contributions.[82] The Prime Minister announced recently that the government is also investigating the concept of gift aid, where donors can gift the tax rebate on their donations to the organisation to which the donation was made.[83]

AUSTRALIA

In 1995, a federal government policy unit known as the Industry Commission completed a two-year study of charitable organisations.[84] Its 31 recommendations for the reform of the charitable sector including its regulation, legal structures, taxation, resourcing and relationship with government were left largely unimplemented because of an intervening change of federal government. As a result of the introduction of a broad-based goods and services tax which had to deal with a definition of charitable entities, the then Prime Minister, John Howard, announced in 2000 the establishment of an inquiry into definitional issues relating to charitable, religious and community service not-for-profit organisations. He said:

> We need to ensure that the legislative and administrative framework in which they operate is appropriate to the modern social and economic environment. Yet the common law definition of a charity, which is based on a legal concept dating back to 1601, has resulted in a number of legal definitions and often gives rise to legal disputes. The Inquiry will provide the government with options for enhancing the clarity and consistency of the existing definitions with respect to Commonwealth law and administrative practice. These should lead to legislative and administrative frameworks appropriate for Australia's social and economic environment in the 21st Century.[85]

The Inquiry reported on 30 June 2001 to the Federal Treasurer.[86] The report made 27 recommendations, among which was the introduction of a statutory definition of 'charity' with an independent administrative body for federal law. On 22 July 2003, after considering the Inquiry report, the Federal Treasurer released a draft Bill which took the traditional four heads of charity and divided them into seven heads, following the spirit of the Inquiry's recommendations, and this reform raised only minor public comment. Other provisions in the Draft Bill did, however, cause significant public discussion and submissions by a number of organisations argued that the draft Bill was an attack on their ability to advocate for a political cause or attempt to change the law or government policy. When that was combined with uncertainty about how regulators, mainly the Australian Taxation Office (ATO), would actually decide whether a disqualifying purpose is more than ancillary or incidental to the other purposes of the entity concerned, it created a deep sense of foreboding in the nonprofit sector. These debates were occurring at the same time as federal government funding contracts for community services were increasingly containing 'gag' clauses which, to varying degrees, prevented a funded organisation from speaking publicly on an issue unless it had prior government approval.

Further, there was concern about how the ATO would determine what the 'purposes' of an organisation were and what was merely an 'activity to achieve a purpose'. The draft Bill also sought to prevent any organisation that had engaged in a serious criminal offence (judged retrospectively and with no recording of a conviction required) from having charitable status, with no means of rehabilitation. It also sought to alter the public benefit element of the common law definition, leading some, such as private schools and religious bodies, to share the concern of their counterparts in the UK over similar provisions.

The draft Bill only applied to the federal jurisdiction; the state jurisdictions did not show any enthusiasm to adopt the proposals. The Board of Taxation was established after the significant tax changes for the introduction of a national goods and services tax, to advise the government on technical aspects of proposed taxation measures, and was given a reference by the Treasurer to comment on the draft Bill. It handed its report on the workability of the proposed definition to the Treasurer in late December 2003 and was critical of the Bill's drafting and reported the widespread community concerns about the consequences of the non-core definition provisions. On 11 May 2004 the Federal Treasurer announced that 'the common law meaning of a charity will continue to apply, but the definition will be extended to include certain child care and self-help groups, and closed or contemplative religious orders. The Government has decided not to proceed with the draft Charities Bill.'[87]

The Extension of Charitable Purpose Act 2004

Instead the government enacted the Extension of Charitable Purpose Act 2004 (Cth), proposed as part of the Tax Laws Amendment (2005 Measures No. 3) Act 2005. As indicated, it confined itself to enlarging the charity law definition for federal purposes to include child care, self-help groups and closed religious orders. These three extensions were relatively uncontroversial and all federal statutes (not just taxing acts) are now modified by this legislation. Only the inclusion of self-help groups could be claimed as any type of significant reform. These provisions have not been taken up by any state jurisdiction to reform its definition of charity.

Senate Economics Committee 2008

In 2007 the Australian Labor Party was elected into power federally, for the first time since the 1995 Industry Commission Inquiry, and had a platform of nonprofit sector reform.[88] On 18 June 2008, Senator Allison (Democrats)[89] moved that the Senate note the recent report on charities by the consumer organisation CHOICE concerning the transparency of charities' annual reports.[90] The Senate sent the matter to the Senate Standing Committee on Economics, which published its report in December 2008.[91] It contained 15 recommendations and its central theme was that the nonprofit sector required a single, independent national regulator overseeing national legislation in respect of fundraising, annual reporting and simplified legal structures. It recommended strongly that the new national regulator develop a Guidestar-type system in Australia for nonprofit financial returns. It proposed that the Government should convene a taskforce to develop such reforms together with a new unit within the Department of Prime Minister and Cabinet reporting to a Minister for the Third Sector. The Government made a holding response until it had considered the final reports of the Productivity Commission (see discussion below) and the Henry tax review[92] which was submitted at the end of 2009.

Productivity Commission Research Report

In 2009, the state and federal governments agreed on the terms of a research project for the Productivity Commission (PC). The PC is the successor to the Industry Commission which had reported on charities in 1995,[93] and is the Australian Government's independent research and advisory body on a range of economic, social and environmental issues affecting the welfare of Australians. The terms of reference were again to examine how governments could engage the sector more effectively and efficiently in the provision of human services, but also to consider the contribution of the broader nonprofit sector and how this could be measured, to identify regulatory burdens and impediments and to consider some taxation issues.

The 500-page draft report of the Commission was released for public comment in October 2009.[94] The draft report contained 32 recommendations, the main planks being: a national regulator for the whole sector, not just charities; a coordinated plan for the collection of data; new legal forms; fundraising legislation; tax simplification; and sustainable funding and innovation models. Importantly, it recommends adoption of the 2001 Charities Definition Inquiry recommendations in their original form. Sector response is generally positive but, like the government, awaits the Henry tax review contribution to the reform proposals.

Superior Court Cases and Charity

Since the ATO's public ruling on the definition of charity[95] there have been a number of cases on the issue in the superior courts and two well-argued

High Court decisions.[96] In the lower courts there has been a mixed bag of decisions around the definition of charity, some of which will probably merely stand on their individual facts and findings, such as those relating to the yacht club[97] and the women lawyers' association,[98] which were found to be charitable.

Central Bayside Division of General Practice Ltd v Commissioner of State Revenue[99] was a High Court case which concerned the degree of independence from government control required for an organisation to be regarded as charitable. Central Bayside was a nonprofit company limited by guarantee whose members were general medical practitioners in the Central Bayside area of Melbourne. The directors were appointed by the members, without government interference, and the government had no power to dismiss them. Central Bayside was part of a nationwide scheme designed by the Commonwealth government to promote healthcare at a local level through the Divisions of General Practice Program. It was agreed or assumed by all judges that its constitutional objects were charitable, falling within the head of 'purposes beneficial to the community'. About 93 per cent of Central Bayside's income was from government grants, with about 43 per cent being an 'outcomes based funding' grant from the Commonwealth.

All five judges of the High Court arrived at the conclusion that Central Bayside was a 'charitable body'. A majority agreed that the funding agreements did not take independence away from Central Bayside. The Company could decide whether to accept or reject the funding, as it had an independently formed board which made its own decisions. The fact that a charity has the same goals as government does not mean, without more, that it is not independent of government.

The other High Court case, *Commissioner of Taxation of the Commonwealth of Australia v Word Investments Ltd*,[100] concerned Word (a nonprofit company limited by guarantee), which was founded by members closely associated with Wycliffe (a religious charity). In the period 1996 to 2002, Word operated a business of conducting funerals, not all Christian, for profit. The profits generated from the investment business and the funeral business were used to support Christian activities in the form of Bible translation and missionary work largely carried out by Wycliffe and other bodies. In rejecting the Word application for endorsement as exempt from income tax, the Commissioner said, 'Commercial enterprise entities are not considered to be charities. This is the case irrespective of whether charitable consequences flow from the entity's activities.'[101]

However, the majority of the High Court found that the Word company's constitutional objective, although containing 'powers', was still charitable, being that of advancing religious charitable purposes. The court went on to endorse the approach taken in *Inland Revenue Commissioners v Helen Slater Charitable Trust Ltd*,[102] stating that 'it is likely that the position in Australia is similar'. The majority also found that Word was not prevented from being a 'charitable institution' by reason of the fact that the institutions to which it gave its profits 'were not confined as to the use to which they may put the funds distributed to them', stating that 'Wycliffe was at liberty to select any method it chose for the purpose of effectuating translations of the Christian Scriptures'.[103] It further ruled that Word did comply with section 50–50(a) Income Tax Assessment Act 1997 (Cth) in that it could be said to have a physical presence in Australia and, to that extent, incurred its expenditure and pursued its objectives principally in Australia.

Challenges and Opportunities

National law reform is not a simple or quick undertaking in Australia with its federal structure. The constitutional barrier of the States having primary responsibility for the supervision of legal 'charities' is a significant issue. For a truly national regulatory system and one that includes trusts, some referral of state powers would be necessary or a harmonising co-operation such as existed during the long journey to corporate law reform. It is very likely that any attempt at a national regulatory scheme for charities or the nonprofit sector more broadly, either under existing constitutional arrangements or by referral of powers, would result in a High Court challenge.

The second issue is the political agreement necessary for a national regulatory scheme. It is beside the point whether it should be based on a single, independent federal regulator or other models, such as a central unit (Treasury or ATO) or coalition of line department regulators, or a more incremental policy development around mutual recognition or harmonisation. For an agreement across all governments there needs to be, firstly, a sense that this issue is important as against other competing issues for national regulatory reform, and secondly, political champions who are willing to broker the inevitable political compromises between the different governments and other players. The recurrent cost of regulators will also be a potential stumbling block as little is expended in direct regulation at present.

The sector is still being 'invented' in Australia. Progress has been made in creating a dialogue which recognises that community welfare organisations do have considerable matters in common with poker machine clubs, sporting clubs, cultural organisations, rural produce co-operatives and professional associations. The work of the Australian Bureau of Statistics and its adoption of internationally recognised definitions and language, as well as its insights as to the contribution of the sector to the national economy and social life, are critical. However, the interest of governments at all levels is presently overshadowed by 'getting a better bang for the buck' from their contracting-out of human services such as health, housing and employment services.

The nonprofit sector can also exercise considerable political power and, if the sector is nervous about potentially adverse consequences, it will bring political pressure to bear. There is also limited capacity for internal dialogue across the whole of the sector as to an 'agreed position' and there are relatively strong pockets of special interest groups: specific industry umbrella groups, large religious coalitions, and professional associations. If national regulatory reform is to occur, then this capacity issue at a sector level needs to be addressed.

Finally, there are the actual technical discussions about the form of government and/or sector arrangements for regulation, whatever the balance is between self-regulation, market regulation and state regulation. All players require, among other things, an informed evidence-based understanding of the sector, its internal and external environment and its role and function. Australia lags behind other jurisdictions in progressing a strategic research agenda and the dissemination and critical evaluation of the research that is becoming available.

CONCLUSION

Since 2001, charity law reform has proceeded at a variable pace, producing varying outcomes, in all the above jurisdictions except Canada, where the process stalled, and Australia, where it collapsed, was revived and is now ongoing. All embarked on reform with the basic objectives of strengthening regulatory processes and statutorily defining common law concepts. The results achieved differ considerably on a spectrum that runs from the sophisticated and comprehensive changes introduced in the UK jurisdictions to little progress in Canada, with the presently anodyne statutory improvements in Singapore and New Zealand somewhere in the middle, and potentially far-reaching changes promised in Australia. It may well be the case that the degree of progress made reflects the relative strength of the partnership cultivated between government and the sector in each jurisdiction – a process which is inevitably more complicated in federated jurisdictions.

Following the lead given in England and Wales, Scotland, Northern Ireland, Singapore and to a lesser extent New Zealand have moved to decouple the regulatory mechanisms for charities and for determining charitable status from those traditionally used to regulate tax liability. These jurisdictions have now introduced new charity legislation which has established relatively independent, charity specific, lead regulatory bodies statutorily responsible for: sector support; maintaining a register of charities; determining charitable status; providing advice and improving governance; monitoring through annual reports and financial statements; conducting audits and investigations. This more rigorous regulatory regime should bring greater transparency, promote accountability and generate more public confidence in relation to charities.

The lead given by England and Wales in respect of extending the list of *Pemsel* charitable purposes has been followed by the other UK jurisdictions (and, indeed, by Ireland) but not by any other nation. Moreover, while those jurisdictions have also reversed the public benefit presumption traditionally granted to the first three *Pemsel* heads, again this initiative has not been adopted elsewhere. Consequently, the common law conceptual basis of charity has been left in considerable disarray. Arguably, although this phase of charity law reform has largely run its course – except as regards Canada and Australia, where the complexities of federated jurisdictions have hindered progress – a further phase may be called for if charity law is to regain its coherence.

NOTES

1. 43 Eliz. 1, Cap. 4. In Ireland, the Statute of Pious Uses 1634 (10 Car. 1, Sess. 3, Cap. 1) was also relevant.
2. *Commissioners for Special Purposes of Income Tax v Pemsel* [1891] AC 531.
3. Broadly speaking, this rule holds that even if a purpose cannot be defined as coming under one of the established heads of charity, it will nonetheless be construed as charitable if it can be interpreted as falling within the 'spirit and intendment' of the Preamble to the 1601 Act.
4. The concept of bodies established in the public interest has long existed in this jurisdiction under the common law concept of a 'public trust', which is a trust formed for the benefit of either the public at large or a section of the public. The term 'public trust' is not synonymous with the term 'charitable trust'.
5. See the Charities Act 2006.
6. See the Charities and Trustee Investment (Scotland) Act 2005.
7. See the Charities Act (Northern Ireland) 2008.
8. The Charities Act (Northern Ireland) 2008, s. 3(1).
9. The Charities and Trustee Investment (Scotland) Act 2005, s. 7(1).
10. In England and Wales, s. 1 of the Charities Act 2006; in Scotland, s. 7 of the Charities and Trustee Investment (Scotland) Act 2005; and in Northern Ireland, s. 1(1) of the Charities Act (Northern Ireland) 2008.
11. See the Charities Act 2006, s. 3(1) and s. 3(2).
12. See s. 7(1)(b) of the Charities and Trustee Investment (Scotland) Act 2005.
13. Section 3(2) of the Charities Act (Northern Ireland) 2008.

14. 'Disbenefit' under the Charities and Trustee Investment (Scotland) Act 2005, s. 8(2)(a) (ii) and 'detriment' under the Charities Act (Northern Ireland) 2008, s. 3(3)(a)(ii).
15. See: the Charities Act 2006, s. 3(2); the Charities Act (Northern Ireland) 2008, s. 3(7); and the Charities and Trustee Investment (Scotland) Act 2005, s. 8(2).
16. This, presumably, being left to the Charity Commission to address in the form of guidance.
17. See the Charities Act 2006, s. 2(4)(b) and (c) and similar wording in the Charities and Trustee Investment (Scotland) Act 2005, s. 7(2)(p) and the Charities Act (Northern Ireland) 2008, s. 2(4)(b).
18. See the Charities Act 2006, s. 2, as replicated in the Charities and Trustee Investment (Scotland) Act 2005, s. 7(2)(a) and the Charities Act (Northern Ireland) 2008, s. 2(2) (a).
19. See for example the Charities Act (Northern Ireland) 2008, s. 2(3)(b) and the Charities and Trustee Investment (Scotland) Act 2005, s. 7(3)(a).
20. The Charities Act 2006, s. 2(3)(a).
21. The Charities Act (Northern Ireland) 2008, s. 2(3)(a).
22. The Charities and Trustee Investment (Scotland) Act 2005, s. 7(3)(f).
23. The provision of recreational facilities in the interests of social welfare will continue to be recognised as charitable under the Recreational Charities Act 1958.
24. The Charities and Trustee Investment (Scotland) Act 2005, s. 1.
25. The Charities Act (Northern Ireland) 2008, s. 6(1).
26. The Charities Act (Northern Ireland) 2008, Part 3, ss 12–15.
27. The Charities and Trustee Investment (Scotland) Act 2005, s. 75.
28. The Charities Act (Northern Ireland) 2008, s. 15.
29. The Charities Act 2006, ss 45–69.
30. The Charities and Trustee Investment (Scotland) Act 2005, ss 79–92.
31. The Charities Act (Northern Ireland) 2008, ss 131–59.
32. In England and Wales, the Trustees Act 2000. In Northern Ireland, the Trustee Act (Northern Ireland) 2001.
33. In addition, the government is proposing to introduce the community interest company, which will provide an alternative to charitable status.
34. The Charities and Trustee Investment (Scotland) Act 2005, s. 49.
35. The Charities Act (Northern Ireland) 2008, s. 105 ff.
36. *Commissioners for Special Purposes of Income Tax v Pemsel* [1891] AC 531.
37. In the interest of full disclosure, the author was the co-chair of the Joint Regulatory Table.
38. Policies related to enforcement were excluded.
39. *Vancouver Society for Immigrant and Visible Minority Women v Minister of National Revenue* (1999) 169 DLR (4th) 34.
40. The Court Challenges Program was disbanded in 2006.
41. The Directorate could (and still does) use undertakings or compliance agreements voluntarily entered into by a charity, but could not take such steps unilaterally. This was not usually a problem, given that the alternative was the threat of loss of charitable status.
42. An analogous situation exists within the field of regulators of the stock markets. Successive federal governments have called for a single national regulator, a call that is just as routinely rebuffed by the provinces.
43. One could argue that one case changed the law: *Earth Fund v Canada (Minister of National Revenue)* [2002] FCA 498 clarified that the 'destination-of-funds' test was not a part of Canadian law. Some members of the charity bar had long held that *Alberta Institute on Mental Retardation v Canada* [1987] 3 FC 286 (leave to appeal dismissed, [1988] SCCA No. 32) stood for the proposition that any business activity by a charity was acceptable so long as the proceeds of that business activity were used by the charity for charitable purposes. The CRA had never accepted that proposition. The *Earth Fund* case resolved the question.

44. [2007] SCC 42.
45. Canada, Department of Finance (2008), *Tax Expenditures and Evaluations 2008*, Ottawa: Government of Canada.
46. See e.g. Drache, A. (2002), 'Hostage to History: the Canadian Struggle to Modernize the Meaning of Charity', *Third Sector Review*, 8(1), 39–65.
47. New Zealand, Committee of Experts on Tax Compliance (1998), *Tax Compliance: Report to the Treasurer and Minister of Revenue*, Wellington: Inland Revenue Department.
48. New Zealand, Working Party on Charities and Sporting Bodies (1989), *Report to the Minister of Finance and the Minister of Social Welfare by the Working Party on Charities and Sporting Bodies*, Wellington: Treasury.
49. 'Key Considers Tax Breaks for Donations to Charities', *The Press*, 19 March 2009, B4.
50. New Zealand Federation of Voluntary Welfare Organisations (2007), 'GDP Contribution of Non-profit Organisations on a Par with Tourism Sector's $69 Billion Per Annum', *Media Release*, 28 August.
51. *Commissioners for Special Purposes of Income Tax v Pemsel* [1891] AC 531.
52. Charities Act 2005, s. 3.
53. 'People belonging to New Zealand': Williams, H.W. (2000), *Dictionary of the Maori Language*, 7th edn, Wellington, NZ: Legislation Direct, 494.
54. 'Section of a large tribe, clan, secondary tribe': Williams, above n 53 at 36.
55. 'Nation, People': Williams, above n 53 at 80.
56. 'Enclosed space in front of a house, courtyard, village common': Williams, above n 53 at 180.
57. New Zealand, Inland Revenue Department (2006), *Interaction of Tax and Charities Rules, Covering Tax Exemption and Donee Status*, Operational Statement OS 6/2, IRD, available at http://www.ird.govt.nz/technical-tax/op-statements/os-interaction-tax-charities-rules.html (accessed 9 December 2009).
58. See http://www.ocvs.govt.nz/about-us/index.html#Ourrole1 (accessed 9 December 2009).
59. See http://www.ocvs.govt.nz (accessed 9 December 2009).
60. New Zealand Federation of Voluntary Welfare Organisations (2004), *Counting for Something: Value Added by Voluntary Agencies*, NZFWO.
61. Ibid, 16.
62. Ibid, iii.
63. Ibid, 32.
64. Statistics New Zealand (2007), *Nonprofit Institutions Satellite Account: 2*, Wellington: Statistics New Zealand.
65. Ibid, iii.
66. Sanders, J. et al (2008), *The New Zealand Nonprofit Sector in Comparative Perspective*, Wellington: OCVS and Johns Hopkins Institute for Policy Studies, available at http://www.ocvs.govt.nz/publications/index.html#Reportsandpapersaboutthecommunitysector3 (accessed 9 December 2009).
67. Ibid, 18.
68. Ibid.
69. Office for the Community and Voluntary Sector (2008), *How Do New Zealanders Give? Towards an Understanding of Generosity in Aotearoa New Zealand*, Wellington: OCVS, http://www.ocvs.govt.nz / documents / publications / papers-and-reports / quickstats-reports-june-08.pdf; *Generosity Hub* at http://www.ocvs.govt.nz/work-programme/promoting-generosity.html (accessed 9 December 2009).
70. Ibid. The data were sourced from Nielsen Media Research Panorama (Jan–Dec 2007) and Nick Jones & Associates Ltd, Consumer Who Cares Service, which surveyed 12,000 people aged 10 years and over: see 'Panorama' at http://www.nielsenmedia.co.nz/product.asp?ProductID=18&Go.x=10&Go.y=7 (accessed 9 December 2009).
71. Cullen, M. P. Swain and J. Wright (2001), *Tax and Charities: A Government Discussion*

Document on Taxation Issues Relating to Charities and Non-profit Bodies, Wellington: Policy Advice Division, Inland Revenue Department.

72. Cullen, M. and P. Dunne (2006), *Tax Incentives for Giving to Charities and Other Non-profit Organisations: A Government Discussion Document*, Wellington: Policy Advice Division, Inland Revenue Department.

73. See Philanthropy New Zealand (undated), 'Giving is Now Worth More!', available at http://www.ocvs.govt.nz/documents/work-programme/promoting-generosity/info-sheet-tax-changes-making-giving-easier-4-.pdf (accessed 18 December 2009).

74. Inland Revenue Department (2005), 'The Charities Act 2005 – Tax Implications', *Tax Information Bulletin*, 17(7), 59. Note that the Income Tax Act 2004 was re-written and subsequently became the Income Tax Act 2007.

75. Ibid, 6.

76. See Edward, C. and A. Sharp (2003), 'The Taxation of Maori Authorities', *New Zealand Journal of Taxation Law and Policy*, 9, 286, for a discussion of the history of the rules applying to Maori authorities.

77. Ibid.

78. Ibid.

79. Ibid.

80. New Zealand, Office for the Community and Voluntary Sector (2008), 'Case Study: Tax Incentives for Charitable Giving Reference Group', Wellington: OCVS, available at http://www.goodpracticeparticipate.govt.nz/levels-of-participation/one-off-consultation/irdcasestudy.html (accessed 10 December 2009).

81. New Zealand, Inland Revenue Department, Policy Advice Division (2008), *Tax Matters*, 2 July, available at http://www.taxpolicy.ird.govt.nz/news/archive.php?year=2008&view=613 (accessed 10 December 2009).

82. New Zealand, Inland Revenue Department, Policy Advice Division (2008) *Tax Matters*, 17 April, statement by Hon Peter Dunne, Minister for Revenue, in which the proposal was referred to, available at http://www.taxpolicy.ird.govt.nz/news/archive.php?year=2008&view=591 (accessed 10 December 2009).

83. Key, J., Prime Minister of New Zealand (2009), 'Speech to Philanthropy New Zealand Annual Conference', 18 March, available at http://www.scoop.co.nz/stories/PA0903/S00267.htm (accessed 10 December 2009).

84. Australia, Industry Commission (1995), *Charitable Organisations in Australia*, Melbourne: Australian Government Publishing Service.

85. Howard, J., Prime Minister of Australia (2000), 'Inquiry into Charitable and Related Organisations', Media Release, 18 September, available at National Library of Australia, Pandora Archive, http://pandora.nla.gov.au/pan/10052/20010821-0000/www.pm.gov.au/news/media_releases/2000/media_release456.htm (accessed 10 December 2009).

86. Australia, Inquiry into the Definition of Charities and Related Organisations (2001), *Report of the Inquiry into the Definition of Charities and Related Organisations*, Canberra: Treasury. The Report is available at http://www.cdi.gov.au/html/report.htm (accessed 10 December 2009).

87. Costello, P. (2004), 'Final Response to the Charities Definition Inquiry', Press Release, No. 31, 11 May, available from National Library of Australia, Pandora Archive, http://pandora.nla.gov.au/pan/36695/20080512-0001/www.treasurer.gov.au/DisplayDocs6327.html (accessed 10 December 2009).

88. See for example: Rudd, K., J. Gillard and U. Stephens (2007), *New Directions: Transforming the Social Economy*, Australian Labor Party; and Gillard, J. and P. Wong (2007), *An Australian Social Inclusion Agenda*, Australian Labor Party.

89. The Democrats had been the minor party that forced the then government into conducting the Charitites Definition Inquiry (above n 82), but since none of the party's candidates was successful in the 2007 election, they would shortly cease to have any senators in the Parliament.

90. CHOICE (2008), *Guide to Donating to Charities*, available at http://www.choice.com.

au/viewArticle.aspx?id=106240&catId=100268&tid=100008 (accessed 10 December 2009).

91. Australia, Senate, Standing Committee on Economics (2008), *Disclosure Regimes for Charities and Not-for-Profit Organisations*, Canberra: the Senate, available at http://www.aph.gov.au/senate/committee/economics_ctte/charities_08/report/report.pdf (accessed 10 December 2009).

92. On 13 May 2008, the Treasurer announced the 'Australia's Future Tax System Review' chaired by Dr Ken Henry, Secretary to the Treasury; it is due to deliver its final report in December 2009.

93. Industry Commission, above n 84.

94. Australia, Productivity Commission (2009), *Contribution of the Not for Profit Sector: Draft Research Report*, Canberra: Productivity Commission.

95. The Australian Taxation Office issued *Draft Taxation Ruling* TR 2005/D6 on charities on 11 May 2005, although the draft ruling does not redefine the meaning of a charity or charitable purpose or the characteristics of a charity. It updates the previous draft ruling issued in 1999.

96. *Central Bayside Division of General Practice Ltd v Commissioner of State Revenue* [2006] HCA 43; *Commissioner of Taxation of the Commonwealth of Australia v Word Investments Ltd* (2008) 236 CLR 204.

97. *Re Yachting Australia Incorporated and Chief Commissioner of State Revenue* (2005) 61 ATR 104.

98. *Victorian Women Lawyers' Association Inc v Commissioner of Taxation* (2008) 170 FCR 3.

99. [2006] HCA 43.

100. (2008) 236 CLR 204.

101. Ibid, para 7.

102. [1982] Ch 49 at 52.

103. (2008) 236 CLR 204 at para 43.

2. England and Wales: *Pemsel* plus

Lindsay Driscoll

INTRODUCTION – HISTORY

There is a long history of attempts at reform of charity law and proposals for a statutory definition in England and Wales. As far back as 1952 the Nathan Committee recommended a statutory definition of charity based on the *Pemsel* categories which preserved the existing case law[1] but the legislation that followed, the Charities Act 1960, which introduced charity registration, omitted this recommendation. The next major report on charity law was the Goodman Committee Report[2] of 1976, which recommended an updated list of the objects contained in the 1601 Preamble, but no action was taken on this. The Charities Act 1992, which followed the White Paper *Charities: a Framework for the Future*, introduced major reforms of charity law, mainly with regard to the regulation and accountability of charities, but again omitted any reference to definition. In each case there was a reluctance on the part of government to open the floodgates of debate on problem cases within existing charitable purposes and calls for new ones from a wide range of interest groups.

Over fifty years after the first recommendation, the statutory definition finally reached the statute book in 2006 but in all the debates and press coverage this has been totally overshadowed by discussion of the new emphasis on public benefit, particularly how this will affect fee-charging charitable schools and religious charities. It is the public benefit aspect rather than any extension of charitable purposes which is seen to be the modernising element.

It has been said that the Charities Act 2006 was subject to more consultation and more parliamentary scrutiny than any other piece of legislation in the United Kingdom.

The initiative for this charity law reform started with the voluntary sector itself and was then embraced and taken on by government but included extensive consultation with the sector. The origins of the reform go back to 1996 and the Report of the Commission on the Future of the Voluntary Sector, usually referred to as the Deakin Report.[3]

48

The Commission was set up by the National Council for Voluntary Organisations (NCVO), the leading generalist umbrella body in England, with support from two foundations, to carry out a wide-ranging review of the voluntary sector and its relationship with government. The Report made several recommendations, most of which have now been implemented, including the drawing up of a concordat or compact between government and the sector. Another recommendation was that the common law definition of charity should be reformed with a single definition based on a new concept of public benefit and there should be an independent Charity Appeal Tribunal to review decisions by the Charity Commission on the registration of charities. A review of the developments since the Deakin Report was undertaken in 2001.[4]

The Deakin recommendation for reform of the definition of charity was taken forward by the Charity Law Reform Advisory Group, which was established in 1998 by NCVO and chaired by Winifred Tumin to look at whether the law on charitable status should be reformed to bring it in line with modern circumstances. This was preceded by some initial work and a conference called 'The Foundations of Charity'[5] carried out in collaboration with King's College London. The terms of reference and membership of the group are included in the final report *For the Public Benefit?*.[6]

The Group considered seven options:

- abolishing the category charity;
- adding to the existing objects test an activities test and possible outcomes test;
- codifying charity law;
- re-classifying charity law;
- extending the same positive public benefit test that currently applies to 'fourth head' charities across all of the heads;
- restricting charitable status to organisations relieving poverty;
- liberalising the law on political activities and campaigning.

The chosen option, which was probably the most conservative, was to extend the same positive public benefit test to all purposes, that is to remove the presumption of public benefit from the first three heads of charity under the *Pemsel* classification.[7] This proposal, which was informed by an opinion from Francesca Quint, a leading charity lawyer,[8] would be grafted on to the existing law by means of new legislation so as to keep change to the substantive law to a minimum. The reason expressed for the rejection of the option of a statutory definition was that this would introduce inflexibility and render existing case law irrelevant. During this

period there was substantial discussion on the merits of reform or evolution of the definition of charity.

Those who opposed the proposed modernisation were mainly concerned about the loss of flexibility, loss of existing case law and the scope
for government interference. At a Charity Law Association Conference
on the subject in Bristol in 1997, Lord Phillips of Sudbury said that he
understood the desire to have an easily understood definition of charity
but believed it to be 'fool's gold'.

The period of consultation on the NCVO Report ended in July 2001,
and even before this the Prime Minister commissioned a review of the
law and regulation of charities by the Performance and Innovation Unit
(later renamed the Strategy Unit). The Review was part of a wider agenda
of partnership with the voluntary sector. It continued the work started in
the Compact and the Getting Britain Giving Initiative[9] the year before,
to increase the effectiveness of charities in the context of their enhanced
role in public service delivery, and other forms of partnership, to deliver
the government's objectives. Another complementary review undertaken
in this period covered the role of the voluntary sector in public service
delivery.[10] The very broad concerns behind the Strategy Unit Review as set
out in Tony Blair's Foreword to the Report were the need to modernise
the legal framework for charities, to decrease some of the red tape and to
increase public confidence.

The Strategy Unit is a unit attached to the No. 10 Policy Unit in the
Prime Minister's Office which carries out a study of a topic with recommendations for legislation. The process is to set up a small team, mainly
seconded from the public, private and voluntary sectors, and to carry out
extensive consultations. In this case the team was made up of persons seconded from bodies that included NCVO, a charity law firm, the Charity
Commission and the *Financial Times*. The team invited comments from a
wide range of organisations and held a number of workshops and attended
conferences to elicit views. Very detailed submissions were received from
such bodies as the Charity Law Association.

The Strategy Unit Report *Private Action, Public Benefit* was published
in September 2002.[11] It included a number of recommendations including
calls for reform of the Charity Commission, liberalisation of the rules on
trading by charities, the introduction of a Charity Appeals Tribunal and
the introduction of a new incorporated legal structure for charities. On
the question of definition, the Report repeated the recommendation of the
NCVO Report to introduce the single public benefit test for all charities
but it also included a proposed new statutory definition setting out a list
of charitable purposes.[12] These purposes were broadly those already recognised as charitable by the court and the Charity Commission with some

extensions. The longer list was intended to give a clearer picture of what is charitable today under charity law.

The Report stated the objectives for reforming charitable status to be:

- to clarify what constitutes charity in the 21st century;
- to change the parameters of charitable status to include organisations which provide a clear public benefit but which are currently either on the borderlines of recognition as charities or are denied it at present;
- to retain the flexibility of charity law to evolve as social and economic circumstances change and to provide better ways of keeping the law up to date;
- to emphasise the public character of charity.

The government's response to the Strategy Unit Report was published in July 2003.[13] This accepted all the recommendations of the Strategy Unit Report other than the liberalisation of trading by charities and on the issue of definition added two additional purposes, the promotion of animal welfare and the provision of social housing. The next stage was the publication of the draft Charities Bill. This was announced in the Queen's Speech on 26 November 2003 and published in May 2004. The draft Bill included the proposals for the removal of the presumption of public benefit and the proposed list of charitable purposes set out in the Strategy Unit Report with some additional purposes.

The draft Bill then went to Parliament for scrutiny. This is a fairly new procedure whereby a draft Bill goes to a joint committee of both houses with about a dozen members. The committee takes both oral and written evidence and may decide on the exact procedures. The Joint Committee on the Draft Charities Bill was composed of peers and MPs with a particular interest in charities. At the oral hearings the Committee took evidence on specific issues in the draft Bill from a wide range of charities. All the written submissions and a record of the oral hearings were published.[14] Much of the debate was taken up with discussion on public benefit, particularly as regards charities which charged high fees, but there was also debate about the role and independence of the Charity Commission and the need to reduce the regulatory burden for small charities. The proposed statutory definition of charity did not attract a large number of responses and was not the subject of much debate.

The Charities Bill was amended in the light of the Joint Committee's recommendations and came to the House of Lords in December 2004. It was debated in the Lords until it was timed out by the general election in May 2005. The Bill was reintroduced following the election on 18

May 2005 and was subject to more debate until it completed its passage through the Lords in November 2005 and the Commons in October 2006. It received its final debate in the Lords on 7 November 2006.[15] As with the debates on the draft Bill, much of the discussion was on public benefit and independent schools (to the extent that it was sometimes referred to in the press as 'the Schools Bill') and the effect of the decision in *Re Resch*.[16] The debates on definition were largely around religion and sport and the inclusion of additional existing charitable purposes on the face of the Bill.

The Charities Act 2006 has been implemented in stages. The high-level guidance on the public benefit required by the Charities Act was published in January 2008.[17] The sections on definition were introduced in April 2008.

SHAPING CHARITABLE PURPOSES

To understand the impact of the statutory definition and the introduction of new charitable purposes in the Charities Act 2006 it is necessary to understand the role of the Charity Commission in the determination of charitable status and the interpretation and application of the law. The role of the Charity Tribunal (now known as the 'First-tier Tribunal (Charity)' although referred to in this chapter by its original name for the sake of brevity) also has some potential to influence the future development of charitable purposes.

Role of the Charity Commission

The Charity Commission of England and Wales is a non-ministerial government department with functions to register, regulate and support charities. It also has a quasi-judicial role that allows for concurrent jurisdiction with the High Court in such matters as schemes and with the Attorney General in such matters as the approval of ex-gratia payments by charities. Great importance is placed on the independence of the Commission in all its functions. During scrutiny of the Charities Bill by the Joint Committee and the passage of the Bill through both Houses there was much debate about the need for the independence of the Commission, particularly in the light of its role in the determination of charitable status and the public benefit test. Various new structures for the Commission were considered and discarded but the question of independence was finally addressed by a provision in the Act that in the exercise of its functions the Commission shall not be 'subject to the direction or control of any Minister of the Crown or other government department'.[18]

The Commission's powers when determining charitable status are not set out expressly in the statute. The only statutory reference is the requirement that every charity must be entered in the register of charities.[19] The Commission considers that it has the following powers when determining whether an organisation has charitable status:[20]

> We have the same powers as the court when determining whether an organisation has charitable status and the same powers to take into account changing social and economic circumstances – whether to recognise a purpose as charitable for the first time or to recognise that a purpose has ceased to be charitable. We interpret and apply the law as to charitable status in accordance with the principles laid down by the courts. Faced with conflicting approaches by the courts we take a constructive approach in adapting the concept of charity to meeting the constantly evolving needs of society. The Register of Charities is therefore a reflection of the decisions made by the courts and our decisions following the example of the courts.

The Commission has adopted this approach when considering applications for charity registration, particularly when cases come to be considered under the Commission's internal review process. This process was amended in 2008 and there is now a single stage of the review process when cases are referred to a panel. Where the review will set a precedent the panel will include a member or members of the Board of the Commission. An appeal from the decision of the Commission to refuse registration now lies, in the first instance, to the Charity Tribunal. The Charity Tribunal was introduced by the Charities Act 2006. Prior to this an appeal lay direct to the High Court.

In the last few years the Commission has accepted a number of new charitable purposes and extended existing purposes using the powers set out above. These include the advancement of conflict resolution, the promotion of sustainable development, the promotion of religious and racial harmony and the promotion of equality and diversity. A more systematic process to consider whether there was scope for the recognition of new charitable purposes was undertaken in the Review of the Register which was launched in April 1998. In *The Review of the Register*, the Commissioners set out their approach to the Review and the principles adopted. They stated that they 'take a constructive approach to the analogy principle to ensure that the Preamble to the Charitable Uses Act 1601 and subsequent legal cases are interpreted in a modern context'.[21] The Commission described the process of the Review as being about 'whether within the law and by the flexible use of the Commissioners' powers there is scope to develop further the boundaries of charitable status and whether those organisations that currently benefit from charitable status should continue to do so'.[22]

The procedure adopted in the Review of the Register was to develop a proposed new charitable purpose by way of analogy to existing purposes and then draft a paper which set out the legal argument and proposed model wording for an objects clause. This then went out for consultation. New charitable purposes adopted under the Review of the Register included the relief of unemployment, the promotion of urban and rural regeneration, the promotion of community capacity building, the promotion of community participation in healthy recreation by providing facilities for playing particular sports, the promotion of the voluntary sector for the benefit of the public and promoting the efficiency and effectiveness of charities.[23] The process was halted in 2003 with the introduction of the draft Charities Bill.

Role of the Charity Tribunal

The Charity Tribunal was established under the Charities Act 2006 to hear appeals from decisions of the Charity Commission. There is also a power to review certain decisions of the Commission in a process similar to judicial review and a power for the Charity Commission, with the consent of the Attorney General, or the latter alone, to refer matters to the Tribunal for decision.[24] The call for a Charity Appeal Tribunal goes right back to 1975[25] and it was recommended by the Goodman Committee, although that Committee did not think that it should be the final arbiter of whether the objects of an institution were charitable or not. One reason for setting up the Tribunal was that in recent years there have been very few appeals to the High Court from decisions of the Charity Commission on charitable status and it was felt that a tribunal with simpler, cheaper, faster procedures would assist in the development of the law on the definition of charity, particularly in the light of the new statutory definition. An alternative suggestion was for a Suitors' Fund to finance test cases on charitable status.

One reason for the lack of cases is probably that in the last few years the Commission has adopted a progressive attitude to the authorities in the application of case law as discussed above. Other reasons include the expense of litigation and the fact that in practice legal practitioners will usually take a pragmatic approach to charity registration. It remains to be seen how many cases on charitable status will go to the Tribunal.[26] In its first year of operation there have only been three cases, none of them directly related to charitable status, but in all the cases all parties have been represented by QCs, so the costs are not as low as predicted.

Decisions of the Charity Tribunal do not set a binding precedent and it is not a Court of Record. As part of the reform of the Tribunal system, in September 2009 the Charity Tribunal transferred into the General Regulatory Chamber of the First-tier Tribunal along with several other tribunals and was renamed the First-tier Tribunal (Charity). Appeals from this Tribunal now lie to the Tax and Chancery Chamber of the Upper Tribunal, which includes High Court Judiciary and is a Superior Court of Record. Appeals will lie from the Upper Tribunal to the Court of Appeal. If it is desirable to set a precedent, such as in a public benefit case or one involving the interpretation of the statutory definition, proceedings could go straight to the Upper Tribunal with an appeal lying to the Court of Appeal.[27] A case on definition could go straight to the Upper Tribunal either by way of an appeal against a final decision of the Commission refusing charity registration or by way of referral from the Attorney General or by the Charity Commission with the consent of the Attorney General.

DEFINITION OF CHARITY UNDER THE CHARITIES ACT 2006

Under section 2(1) of the Charities Act 2006 (the Act) a charitable purpose is defined as one that '(a) falls within the list of descriptions of charitable purposes set out in section 2(2) and (b) is for the public benefit'. Section 2(2) sets out 12 specific descriptions of charitable purposes[28] and one 'catch-all' description in section 2(2)(m). The effect of the catch-all provision is to include:

- any purpose recognised as a charitable purpose under existing charity law or by virtue of the Recreational Charities Act 1958 which is not included specifically in the list;
- any purpose that may reasonably be regarded as analogous to or within the spirit of any of those purposes included in the list; and
- by the 'stepping stone' approach, any purpose which may reasonably be regarded as analogous to or within the spirit of any purpose recognised under charity law in accordance with this process.

Section 2(5) retains existing case law by providing that 'where a term used in the list of descriptions of purposes has a particular meaning under charity law that meaning shall be applied'. Case law is also retained for the interpretation of the meaning of public benefit.[29]

Overview

The list of descriptions of charitable purposes set out in the Act is largely a restatement of purposes which have been accepted as charitable by the courts or by the Charity Commission. There are some extensions, as in the case of the new first head for the prevention and relief of poverty; some partial definitions, as in the case of the advancement of religion and the advancement of amateur sport; and some re-wording, as in the case of the advancement of amateur sport and the advancement of animal welfare. However, this is subject to the provision that the wording of the purposes is to be construed in accordance with existing charity law. It is the interpretation of this provision that will prove to be important, particularly in the case of charitable purposes which have been recognised by the Charity Commission rather than the courts.

During the parliamentary debates, the Minister assured the House that no purpose which had been recognised as charitable prior to the Act would cease to be charitable. The effect of section 2 of the Act is therefore probably closest to the option of codification of charity law discarded by the Charity Law Advisory Group in 2001. The main criticism of this approach discussed by the Group was that codification would reduce the flexibility of the common law definition. This issue has been addressed in the Act by the continuation of the ability to recognise new charitable purposes where they are analogous to or within the spirit of an existing purpose, and by the retention of existing charity law to interpret the descriptions of charitable purposes set out in the Act. The Charity Commission has published a Commentary on the Descriptions of Charitable Purposes in the Act, which sets out the existing purposes which come under each heading.[30]

Description or Purpose?

The list contained in section 2(2) is referred to as 'descriptions of charitable purposes' and a charitable purpose must fall within one of the descriptions. In some cases these descriptions are very broad headings. The Charity Commission takes the view that although some of the descriptions of purposes are charitable purposes in their own right, some are not and so an objects clause which merely repeats all the wording of the list of descriptions of purposes as set out in the Act will not be accepted as being charitable. This is an issue which has been disputed by some members of the Charity Law Association. The descriptions which are not accepted as charitable purposes in their own right include 'the promotion of community development' and the 'relief of other disadvantage'.

Descriptions of Purposes Under Section 2(2) of the Charities Act 2006

Section 2(2)(a)   The prevention and the relief of poverty
As far back as 1976 the Report of the Goodman Committee recommended that the definition of charity should include the prevention as well as

the relief of poverty. The Strategy Unit Report included this in its list of purposes to address the concerns, particularly of development charities, that a charity should be able to address the causes as well as the effects of poverty. In February 2008, the Charity Commission published draft guidance on 'the Prevention or Relief of Poverty for the Public Benefit', which looked at both the definition and public benefit aspects. This went out for consultation and the final guidance was published in December 2008 along with the Legal Analysis and the summary of consultation responses.[31] The Summary reported that:

> Although the Charities Act now allows charities to focus on the prevention of poverty (tackling its root causes) without also having to relieve it or its consequences, there seems to be a general view that it is difficult in practice to distinguish between the prevention of poverty and the relief of poverty.

The responses also recognised that there were many ways of preventing and relieving poverty which were not confined to the provision of financial assistance. These could include the provision of education and addressing human rights, environmental or governance issues. In the final Guidance the Commission states: 'we think it would be unhelpful to regard preventing poverty as necessarily separate from relieving poverty; they are just different points along a continuum of financial need'. It goes on to say that 'we have long accepted that charities concerned with the relief of poverty can also prevent poverty. It is not therefore necessary for charities for the relief of poverty to extend their objects to refer specifically to the prevention of poverty'.[32]

This very much reflects the position of the Charity Commission over a long period. Charities with relief of poverty purposes have been able to work for the eradication of the causes of poverty through a wide range of activities including campaigning and political activities as far as permitted by the law.[33] Charities such as Oxfam and Christian Aid have been effective in the field of overseas development and charities such as the Child Poverty Action Group have campaigned successfully for many years on such issues as the reform of welfare benefits. Another example of a case previously accepted by the Charity Commission as under the relief of poverty was the Fairtrade Foundation, which was set up to promote a 'fair trade mark'.

Any limitations on the powers of charities established under the relief of poverty head have been imposed by the restrictions on political activities rather than any limitation imposed by the construction of the term 'relief'. The Commission's Legal Analysis on its Guidance confirms that this position will be unaltered as a result of the extension to the prevention of poverty: 'The inclusion of prevention of poverty does not mean that Parliament has accepted that a purpose of campaigning for legislative change to tackle poverty or for changes in government policy to tackle these issues is established for public benefit'.[34]

This view is not necessarily shared by all international development charities. The report of the Advisory Group on Campaigning and the Voluntary Sector includes a section by Bond, the umbrella body for inter-national development charities, which argues that 'the fact that under the Charities Act 2006 it is explicitly enshrined that charities can prevent as well as relieve poverty does, it seems to us, require charities to be more political'.[35]

The prevention of poverty is one of several of the new charitable heads where in individual cases there may be issues as to whether there is a politi-cal purpose, as it can be argued that the purpose is inherently political. Others include the promotion of human rights, the promotion of citizen-ship and the advancement of environmental protection. Examples given in the Guidance of ways in which charities might prevent or relieve poverty include:

- providing debt advice;
- advising poor farmers in developing countries about more effective farming;
- working with women's groups who are concerned about a lack of equitable conditions for women workers;
- establishing a micro credit scheme;
- providing a grant to a local business to enable them to employ an unemployed person.

It is interesting that, in line with the text, no attempt is made to distinguish between those examples which may prevent and those which may relieve poverty.

Possibly a more difficult issue with relation to the prevention of poverty is one of remoteness. The Guidance states that the beneficiary must be 'either poor or at risk of being poor' and there could be issues of interpre-tation as to when someone becomes at risk of being poor. This question could arise in the case of the provision of advice on pensions or other financial advice. At what stage does this become charitable? It would seem that it would not be charitable under this head to give advice on pensions to the public at large but what criteria would need to be adopted to define the potential class of beneficiaries? Throughout the guidance 'the poor' are referred to as people in poverty and it is confirmed that people in poverty does not just include people who are destitute but also those who cannot satisfy a basic need.

Section 2(2)(b)   Advancement of education

The statutory definition does not extend the former head, which will be interpreted in accordance with case law. The Commission's Guidance on the advancement of education for the public benefit covers issues considered in case law such as: how far all experience is educational; whether there is a difference between education and the mere increase in knowledge; the difference between advancing education and promoting a particular point of view; and whether unstructured information can be educational. It also includes a detailed list of the different ways in which education can be advanced. The Commission has confirmed that it will publish additional guidance on professional bodies, bodies that provide professional education and think tanks, which are the three most problematic areas, the first two in terms of private benefit and the third in terms of political activities.

Section 2(2)(c)   Advancement of religion

Advancement of religion was the purpose which attracted most debate during the passage of the Bill through Parliament. The debate focused on two issues: whether this purpose should be extended to include other non-religious beliefs; and whether the definition should be expressly extended to polytheistic and non-theistic religions. Amendments were introduced to address both these issues but the attempt to extend the purpose to include non-theistic beliefs was not successful. This was despite a Report of the Joint Committee on Human Rights which raised concerns about the differential treatment of religious and non-religious beliefs in the light of the European Convention on Human Rights (ECHR), Article 9 (right to freedom of religion or belief) and Article 14 (freedom from discrimination). The Minister confirmed in the Parliamentary debate that organisations concerned with non-religious beliefs were already recognised as charitable under the advancement of education or the promotion of health or the promotion of citizenship or as subsumed within purposes for the promotion of mental improvement or the promotion of the moral or spiritual welfare or improvement of society. There was also a commitment that the public benefit test for charities for the advancement of religion and that for charities concerned with non-religious belief systems would be similar.

In September 2008, the Commission published a consultation paper on public benefit and the advancement of moral or ethical belief systems.[36] In its response the Charity Law Association Working Party[37] criticised the attempt to define a moral or ethical belief system on the grounds that this was not an existing charitable purpose and any attempt to provide a definition would add to the confusion. The Charity Law Association also queried the use of much of the language in the draft Guidance as being quasi-religious and not appropriate for the very wide range of organisations covered by the Guidance. It also raised the question of whether an organisation needed to be established for a formal belief system to bring it within the scope of Article 9 of the ECHR, particularly in view of the fact that single-issue beliefs such as pacifism had been held by the European Court of Human Rights to be covered by Article 9. The Consultation Paper has now been withdrawn.

The other main issue raised in the debates, as to the scope of religion, was addressed by a new partial definition included in the Act which confirmed that the term religion includes:

- a religion which involves belief in more than one god
- a religion which does not involve belief in a god.

This amendment was made to clarify the fact that polytheistic religions such as Hinduism and non-theistic religions such as some forms of Buddhism and Jainism were charitable. These religions had been accepted as charitable by the Commission, but it was thought desirable to confirm the position on the face of the Act in view of the Commission's decision in the *Scientology* case,[38] which defined 'belief' in terms of belief in a Supreme Being. In that decision the Commissioners had stated that 'they did not think that it would be proper to specify the nature of that supreme being or to require it to be analogous to the Deity or Supreme Being of a particular religion'.[39]

However the use of the term 'Supreme Being', which had connotations of a single transcendental being, had led some lawyers to query whether it extended to polytheistic and non-theistic religions. The Act does not include a definition of what constitutes a religion. In their guidance on the advancement of religion for the public benefit[40] the Commissioners set out their definition of religion, which is based on the common law position as set out in their decision in the *Scientology* case. They state that a religion must have the following characteristics:

- belief in a god (or gods) or supreme being, or divine or transcendental being or entity or spiritual principle which is the object or focus of the religion;
- a relationship between the believer and the supreme being or entity by showing worship of, reverence for, or veneration of the supreme being or entity;
- a degree of cogency, cohesion, seriousness and importance;
- an identifiable positive beneficial, moral or ethical framework.

The Guidance includes examples of different ways in which charities can advance religion for the public benefit and confirms the common law position that closed religious orders that do not give the wider community the opportunity to benefit in a demonstrable way are not charitable.

Section 2(2)(d) Advancement of health and saving of lives

The 2006 Act includes a partial definition of advancement of health which states that 'the advancement of health includes the prevention of sickness, disease or human suffering'. Purposes accommodated under this head include those formerly found under the old first head of the relief of sickness and the old fourth head including the preservation and protection of health and the protection of life and property. The Commission's Guidance has as examples: medical research charities, the General Medical Council, mountain rescue services and blood transfusion services.

Section 2(2)(e) Advancement of citizenship and community development

This is a case where community development is not itself a charitable purpose but the description covers a number of purposes which are directed at support for social and community infrastructure rather than individuals. The Act provides that this description includes:

- rural or urban regeneration
- the promotion of civic responsibility, volunteering, the voluntary sector or the effectiveness or efficiency of charities.[41]

All these purposes had been accepted as charitable by the Commission prior to the Act. Another purpose, not expressly referred to in the Act, which would come under this description is community capacity building. The promotion of urban and rural regeneration[42] and community capacity building[43] were developed as new purposes by analogy with existing charitable purposes in the Review of the Register and there are a number of criteria and tests to be met to come within the purpose. The promotion of the voluntary sector[44] and promoting the efficiency and the effectiveness of charities[45] were also recognised as charitable at the end of the Review process.

The promotion of urban and rural regeneration has only been accepted by the Charity Commission as charitable in its own right if it is carried out for the public benefit in an area of social and economic deprivation. The purposes must be advanced by three or four of a menu of activities which are all existing charitable purposes. The activities must be included in the objects clause. The activities include the relief of poverty, the relief of unemployment, the preservation of buildings of historic interest and the provision of housing for those who are in conditions of need.

The promotion of community capacity building is described in the Commission's Guidance as being concerned with providing opportunities for people to learn through experience and involving people in collective effort. For this purpose, 'community' means a group of people who share a position of social and economic disadvantage or social advantage only.[46] The 'community' may be a geographical community or a community of interest.

The promotion of the voluntary sector for the benefit of the public was recognised as being charitable by the Commission by analogy with the promotion of commerce and industry and the promotion of agriculture and horticulture and also the promotion of the mental and moral welfare and improvement of the community. It will mainly be applicable for voluntary sector umbrella bodies which were previously registered with broad charitable purposes.

The promotion of the efficiency and effectiveness of charities and the effective use of charitable resources was accepted as charitable several years before the Review and was based on *Re White's Wills Trusts*,[47] where the provision of services directly related to an accepted charitable purpose may also be charitable. Charities which provide fundraising, media or website services, as well as those which provide accommodation for other charities, come within this purpose.

The advancement of citizenship has long been accepted as charitable in the context of young people such as Scouts. In 2009 the Commission registered a charity for the advancement of citizenship without it being limited to young people. It would seem that there is scope for further development of this purpose. It could be extended by analogy with the promotion of good governance or democracy but so far applications for registration under this latter purpose have not been successful.

Section 2(2)(f)   Advancement of the arts, culture, heritage or science

Many of the purposes which fall within this description would have formerly come under the head of the advancement of education, although the promotion of arts was accepted by the Commission as a charitable purpose in its own right in 1991. The new description would include art galleries and arts councils, which are considered by the Commission in its Review of the Register.[48] It would also cover charities for the performing arts,[49] local arts societies and so on. The advancement of heritage would cover charities to preserve historic buildings or land, again considered during the Review of the Register,[50] together with for the preservation of historical traditions, such as country dancing societies. All of these have been accepted as charitable. The advancement of science covers learned societies such as the Royal College of Surgeons,[51] the Zoological Society of London[52] and scientific research projects.

One question which remains to be answered is how far the advancement of culture can be construed disjunctively as, in the past, all charitable purposes recognised as charitable that included culture have been linked to heritage or the arts. There seems to be no clear definition of culture in this context. Heritage purposes will often raise questions as to public benefit with regard to both the historical or architectural significance and private benefit and public access issues.

Section 2(2)(g)   Advancement of amateur sport

Before 2006, charity law did not recognise the advancement of mere sport as charitable.[53] However, sporting organisations have often been able to register under other charitable purposes; for example, under education for sport and recreation for children and young people,[54] under the relief of disability, under the relief of the aged and under the Recreational Charities Act 1958. The Commission also recognised as charitable 'the promotion of community participation in healthy recreation by providing facilities for playing particular sports'.[55] This was mainly aimed at community amateur sports clubs (CASCs) but as these clubs now have their own tax status under the Finance Act 2002, with much of the tax relief available to charities and less regulation, few CASCs now seek charitable status. Sports clubs registered under the provisions of the Finance Act 2002 and receiving tax benefits under that Act are now precluded by the 2006 Act from being charities, even if established for charitable purposes. The organisations most interested in registering under the new purpose are the governing bodies of single sports, as CASC tax status is not available to them.

The 2006 Act includes a partial definition of the advancement of amateur sport which states: 'Sport means sports or games which promote health by involving physical or mental skill or exertion'.[56] The extension to mental skill or exertion was introduced by an amendment to the Bill during its passage through Parliament as a result of effective lobbying by chess enthusiasts. The definition appears to build on, but extend, the purpose accepted by the Charity Commission as there is still the linkage to health, but the reference to community participation is omitted. Guidance from the Commission on the new head has not yet been issued but is expected shortly and will go out for consultation.

There are a number of unresolved issues. Firstly, what sports and games will be considered to promote physical and mental health to come within the definition? In RR11 the Commission did not accept such sports as angling, gliding, billiards, pool and snooker, motor sports, parachuting, flying and crossbow[57] as promoting health and it is likely that in the forthcoming consultation the health benefits of the different sports which were not previously accepted will be advanced. How high is the threshold for health benefits? It would seem that almost all sport could have some benefit to physical or mental health. Will proof of health benefit be required? There will also need to be consideration of what sports or games can be construed as involving mental skill or exertion. Chess clubs have already been accommodated under the advancement of education and it seems likely that they will be accepted as promoting health through mental skill and exertion, but how far should this be extended? Arguments can be put forward that pursuits such as Sudoku and Scrabble also exercise the mind and may assist in the prevention of Alzheimer's disease and other illnesses.

Apart from identification of the sports which may promote health, there are several public benefit issues involved in this purpose. These include whether a charitable sports club can have a social membership; whether it can concentrate on competitive success as its main activity to the exclusion of community participation; whether it could promote elite competitors: for example, could it make grants to support individual Olympic competitors? All of these issues were previously addressed in the Commission's Guidance in RR11.

Section 2(2)(h)   Advancement of human rights, conflict resolution or reconciliation or the promotion of religious or racial harmony or equality and diversity

Advancement of human rights   The Charity Commission first accepted the advancement of human rights as a charitable purpose in 2002 and published a paper setting out the legal basis of the decision, including the impact of the Human Rights Act and the interrelation with the law on political purposes and political activities. The paper suggested that the promotion of human rights is charitable by analogy with existing charitable purposes for moral and mental improvement. The Commission also considered that the incorporation into domestic law of many of the rights guaranteed under the European Convention for the Protection of Human Rights and Fundamental Freedoms meant that promoting human rights in the UK is no longer a political purpose.[58] This paper was widely seen as not being very helpful on the grounds that it was too restrictive and difficult to understand. Following the Strategy Unit Report, which recommended that the promotion of human rights should become one of the new charitable purposes and that the Guidelines on Political Activities should be revised to adopt a less cautionary and a more positive approach, the 'Guidance on the Promotion of Human Rights' was revised and circulated for consultation.

The revised Guidance was published in January 2005[59] and enlarged the scope of the organisations which might be charitable in this area and the activities which might be carried out. It includes a model object clause which refers to the specific code of human rights the organisation is seeking to promote and a list of the accepted means to carry out the purpose. The current practice of the Commission is to require an organisation seeking a human rights purpose to have an objects clause framed on these lines.

The most difficult area addressed in the Guidance is the relationship between the parameters of the charitable purpose for the promotion of human rights and the law on political purposes as set out in the Amnesty case[60] and the Guidelines issued by the Charity Commission on political activities. These were revised in 2004 in response to the Strategy Unit's recommendation that they should be more positive in their approach. But they were challenged again in 2007 by an Advisory Group, chaired by Baroness Helena Kennedy, which looked at the constraints imposed on political activities by charity law and called for a change in the interpretation of the law to remove the 'dominant and ancillary rule'.[61] In response to this the Commission had a further look at the underlying common law principles and came up with revised Guidelines.[62] These went further than before to stress that although charities could not have a political purpose they could carry out political activities to support a charitable purpose. The dominant/ancillary test was dropped and the new test was that the political activity must not become the reason for the charity's existence. Subject to this, there could be circumstances where the trustees could resolve to devote all the charity's resources to political activity for a limited period. The guidance also acknowledged that there were some charitable purposes such as the promotion of human rights which were more likely than others to involve campaigning and political activities.

The Commission's Guidance confirms that a charity with a human rights purpose may only engage in political activities insofar as they do not constitute a political purpose. During the consultation in 2004 several human rights organisations and lawyers advanced the view that upholding international human rights norms as established in various human rights instruments and advocating for their inclusion into domestic law is now a charitable rather than a political purpose, on the grounds that promoting the upholding and enforcement of international law as well as domestic law is charitable. This argument was considered and rejected in the Amnesty case but it is considered by many lawyers that the understanding of international human rights norms has developed since the Amnesty case was heard in 1981. There is also a suggestion that a distinction can be made between absolute and qualified human rights. This is still a contentious area and the Commission has announced that it will have a further review of the Guidelines for Human Rights as a charitable purpose.

In its response to the 2004 consultation on the Commission's guidance on human rights the Charity Law Association expressed the hope that 'ministers will say what they consider the promotion of human rights to mean and the Commission's role will be that of interpretation not determination'. This hope was not realised. The Charities Act includes no clarification of this purpose and there was little discussion in the debates to provide clarification. The wording therefore falls to be determined in accordance with case law.

In 2008 the Commission considered the first review of a registration decision concerning a human rights purpose since the 2006 Act came into force. This was the case of *English Pen*,[63] which was interesting as it concerned letter-writing activities to secure the release of prisoners of conscience, which were very similar to those which were the subject of the Amnesty case.[64] The question of whether upholding international human rights may now be charitable was not expressly addressed but the Amnesty case was distinguished on the grounds that the political activities in the *English Pen* case were ancillary as they only constituted a small part of the human rights activities. Unlike the Amnesty case, there was a charitable purpose and the English Pen charity accepted that individual states may have legitimate reasons for limiting the exercise of human rights. Before English Pen was accepted for registration the trustees gave assurances accepting that some constraints on the right to freedom of speech are necessary and appropriate, as evidenced in their Campaign Criteria on their website, and the Campaign Criteria would form the basis of internal procedures to identify beneficiaries.

The advancement of conflict resolution or reconciliation   The promotion of conflict resolution and mediation amongst individuals and groups has been accepted as charitable by the Commission for several years as analogous to the sound administration of the law and the preservation of public order. In 2003, in the *Concordis* case, the Commission accepted the promotion of national and international conflict resolution and reconciliation as charitable.[65] In this it distinguished the *Anglo-Swedish Society* case,[66] where the court decided that international friendship or understanding was not charitable. This definition would also cover restorative justice, which was recognised as charitable by the Commission in 2003.[67]

The promotion of religious or racial harmony or equality and diversity   In 1983 the Commission recognised racial harmony and good relations as capable of being a charitable purpose. It was influenced by the existence of the Race Relations Act 1976 and by the analogies of preservation of public order, mental and moral improvement and the promotion of equality between women and men. Previously in 1949 in *Re Strakosh*[68] a trust to appease racial feeling was held to be political and not charitable. The Commission later recognised 'the promotion of equality and diversity'[69] using as its analogies the promotion of gender equality, mental and moral improvement, the promotion of religious harmony and the promotion of human rights.

Section 2(2)(i)   Advancement of environmental protection or improvement

This covers purposes concerned with conservation of the environment generally or a particular species or habitat or zoos. It also covers charities concerned with sustainable development and biodiversity, the promotion of recycling and research projects into renewable energy sources. All of these were recognised as being charitable before the 2006 Act. Some were registered under the advancement of education and others were later accepted under the conservation of the environment. The Commission carried out a consultation and published guidance on the advancement of environmental protection or improvement under the Review of the Register.[70]

This is another of the heads which include purposes that, in the past, have often given rise to issues around political activities and whether there is an unstated political purpose. Up until now most of the main campaigning environmental organisations in the UK have had both a charitable and a not-for-profit organisation, for example Greenpeace and Friends of the Earth. Another public benefit issue which may arise under this head is the question of harm which could arise where there are competing interests such as conservation versus new housing or the preservation of animals which may threaten the livelihood of a local farming community.

Section 2(2)(j)   The relief of those in need by reason of youth, age, ill-health, disability, financial hardship or other disadvantage

The Act clarifies that this 'includes relief given by the provision of accommodation or care to the persons mentioned'.[71] In the Charity Law Association's publication *For the Public Benefit*[72] the essay on this head makes the point that the wording is similar to that in the Recreational Charities Act 1958 and extends the approach in the Act to a wider category of charitable purposes.

The relief of those in need by reason of youth, age, ill-health or disability has long been recognised as charitable. There seems to be considerable overlap between the relief of financial hardship under this head and
the relief of poverty. In its guidance on the relief of poverty and public
benefit,[73] the Commission accepts that there may be circumstances where
someone who is not poor is in financial hardship. An example would be
the case of an elderly person who owns a house and might be asset rich
but has insufficient income to meet the costs of a heating bill and so might
experience temporary financial hardship. Similarly a person might suffer
a temporary financial hardship due to a sudden change in circumstances
such as illness. In its guidance the Commission says that in most cases
it will treat the relief of financial hardship and the relief of poverty the
same.

With regard to the relief of other disadvantage it would seem that other
needs already recognised as charitable, such as the relief of victims of
disasters, would come within this head. As mentioned above, as a matter
of practice the Commission requires the specific needs to be set out in the
objects clause and will not accept the wording as set out in the description.
There would seem to be scope for the development of this head by way of
analogy.

Section 2(2)(k)   Advancement of animal welfare

Advancement of the welfare of animals in general was probably not a
charitable purpose under pre-2006 law. Purposes recognised before 2006
related to the prevention or suppression of cruelty to animals or the prevention or relief of suffering of animals. The nature of the benefit to the
public has been held to be indirect as it led to 'a manifestation of the finer
side of human nature'[74] or tended to 'stimulate humane and generous
sentiments in man towards the lower animals and by these means promote
feelings of humanity and morality generally, repress brutality and thus
elevate the human race'.[75]

The emphasis was therefore on the benefit to humans in terms of their
moral improvement rather than to the welfare of the animals themselves:
'welfare' is a wide term which has been held to be too wide a concept to
be exclusively charitable. It will be interesting to see whether this description will be interpreted by the courts to extend beyond the prevention of
cruelty or suffering of animals. The public benefit requirement will mean
that there will still have to be either a direct or indirect benefit to humans
and benefit to animals alone would not be sufficient. As in the *National
Anti-Vivisection Society* case,[76] any harm to humans would need to be balanced against the benefits.

The Charity Commission's 'Commentary on the Descriptions' confirms the common law position and says of this description that it includes any purposes directed towards the prevention or suppression of cruelty to animals or the prevention or relief of suffering by animals.

Section 2(2)(l) The promotion of the efficiency of the armed forces of the Crown, or of the efficiency of the police, fire and rescue services or ambulance services

This description was introduced by amendment during the passage of the Bill as a result of effective lobbying by the armed forces charities. Organisations for the welfare of the armed forces have long been charitable as being for the defence of the realm. A very wide range of activities comes within this heading. They include supporting officers' messes, increasing the physical fitness of members of the services, encouraging esprit de corps and benevolent societies. It has also long been held to be charitable to promote the efficiency of the police, fire, rescue or ambulance services as they exist for the prevention and detection of crime, the preservation of public order and to protect the public.

Section 2(2)(m) Other purposes currently recognised as charitable and any new charitable purposes which are similar to another charitable purpose

In its 'Commentary on the Description of Charitable Purposes', the Charity Commission lists the following purposes which would come under this head:

- the provision of facilities for recreation and other leisure-time occupation in the interests of social welfare with the object of improving the conditions of life;[77]
- the provision of public works and services;[78]
- the relief of unemployment;[79]
- the promotion of certain patriotic purposes such as war memorials;
- the social relief, resettlement or rehabilitation of persons under a disability or deprivation including disaster funds;
- the promotion of industry and commerce;
- the promotion of agriculture and horticulture;
- gifts for the benefit of a particular locality, the beatification of a town, civic societies;
- the promotion of mental or moral improvement;
- the promotion of the moral or spiritual welfare or improvement of the community;
- the preservation of public order;
- promoting the sound administration and development of the law;

- the promotion of ethical standards of conduct and compliance with the law in the public and private sectors;
- the rehabilitation of ex-offenders and the prevention of crime.

CONCLUSION

The question of a statutory definition of charity has been the subject of much debate over the last fifty years. After rounds of consultation and parliamentary debate, the Charities Act 2006 finally received the royal assent and the new statutory definition of charity came into force in April 2008. Although the new extended list of charitable purposes suggests several potential changes and extensions to the common law definition, the list is mainly a restatement of the existing position and the initial guidance from the Charity Commission suggests that, in its view, the extensions are limited. As yet, the definition has not been tested in the new Tribunal or the courts, and cases are eagerly awaited.

NOTES

1. Great Britain, Committee on the Law and Practice Relating to Charitable Trusts (1952), *Report of the Committee on the Law and Practice Relating to Charitable Trusts*, London: HMSO, Cmnd 876.
2. National Council of Social Service, Committee of Inquiry into the Effect of Charity Law and Practice on Voluntary Organisations (Chairman: Lord Goodman) (1976), *Charity Law and Voluntary Organisations: Report of an Independent Committee of Inquiry*, London: National Council of Social Service.
3. National Council for Voluntary Organisations, Commission on the Future of the Voluntary Sector (1996), *Meeting the Challenge of Change: Voluntary Action into the 21st Century*, London: NCVO (the Deakin Report).
4. Centre for Civil Society (UK) (2001), *Next Steps in Voluntary Action*, London: NCVO.
5. Papers published as: Mitchell, C. and S. Moody (eds) (2000), *Foundations of Charity*, Oxford: Hart Publishing.
6. National Council for Voluntary Organisations, Charity Law Reform Advisory Group (2001), *For the Public Benefit? – A Consultation Document on Charity Law Reform*, London: NCVO.
7. See Luxton, P. (2007), 'Public Benefit and Charities: The Impact of the Charities Act 2006 on Independent Schools and Private Hospitals', in Dixon, M. and G.L.H. Griffiths, *Contemporary Perspectives on Property, Equity and Trust Law*, Oxford: Oxford University Press.
8. National Council for Voluntary Organisations, Charity Law Reform Advisory Group, above n 6.
9. HM Treasury (2000), *Getting Britain Giving in the 21st Century*, announced in Budget, 21 March.
10. HM Treasury and Home Office (2002), *Cross Cutting Review of the Role of the Voluntary and Community Sector in Service Delivery*, London: HMSO.

11. Strategy Unit (2002), *Private Action, Public Benefit*, London: HMSO.
12. See Schedule 1.
13. Home Office (2003), *Charities and Not for Profits: A Modern Legal Framework*, London: HMSO.
14. UK Parliament, Joint Committee on the Draft Charities Bill (2003–04), available at http://www.publications.parliament.uk/pa/jt/jtchar.htm (accessed 4 December 2009).
15. A good collection of links to debates and timeline for the passage of the Charities Bill is available from the Charity Commission at http://www.charitycommission.gov.uk/spr/charbillprog2.asp (accessed 4 December 2009).
16. *In Re Resch's Will Trusts* [1969] 1 AC 514. In the debates in the House of Lords, Lord Philips of Sudbury referred to *Re Resch* as a 'blancmange'.
17. Charity Commission (2008), *Charities and Public Benefit: The Charity Commission's General Guidance on Public Benefit*, London: Charity Commission. This was published in accordance with s. 4(1) of the Charities Act 2006. Under s. 4(6) charity trustees must have regard to such guidance.
18. Charities Act 2006, s. 6(1).
19. Charities Act 2006, s. 3(A)1.
20. Charity Commission (2001), *RR1a – Recognising New Charitable Purposes*, London: Charity Commission, para 8, available at http://www.charitycommission.gov.uk/publications/RR1a.asp (accessed 4 December 2009).
21. Charity Commission (2001), *RR1 – The Review of the Register of Charities*, London: Charity Commission, para 9, available at http://www.charitycommission.gov.uk/publications/rr1.asp (accessed 4 December 2009).
22. Charity Commission (2000), *RR5 – The Promotion of Community Capacity Building*, London: Charity Commission, para 4, available at http://www.charitycommission.gov.uk/publications/rr5.asp (accessed 4 December 2009).
23. See the Charity Commission's 'Review of the Register of Charities' webpage for relevant papers: http://www.charitycommission.gov.uk/registeredcharities/rorpubs.asp (accessed 4 December 2009).
24. Charities Act 2006, Sched. 1D.
25. House of Commons Expenditure Committee (1975), *Charity Commissioners and their Accountability, 10th Report*, London: HMSO.
26. The establishment and staffing of the Charity Tribunal was done on the estimate of 50 cases a year. This would include appeals from all decisions including the exercise of regulatory powers such as the removal of trustees.
27. Information about how the Charity Tribunal works and reports, details of cases, and discussion of how the Tribunal will be affected by the Reform of the Tribunal System are available from the First-tier Tribunal (Charity) website, http://www.charity.tribunals.gov.uk/ (accessed 4 December 2009).
28. See Schedule 2.
29. Charities Act 2006, s. 3(3).
30. Charity Commission (2009), *Commentary on the Descriptions of Charitable Purposes in the Charities Act 2006*, London: Charity Commission, available at http://www.charitycommission.gov.uk/spr/corcom1.asp (accessed 4 December 2009).
31. See Charity Commission (2008), *The Prevention or Relief of Poverty for the Public Benefit*, London: Charity Commission, available at http://www.charitycommission.gov.uk/publicbenefit/pbpoverty.asp (accessed 4 December 2009).
32. Ibid, para C2.
33. Charity Commission (2008), *CC9 – Speaking Out – Guidance on Campaigning and Political Activity by Charities*, London: Charity Commission, available at http://www.charitycommission.gov.uk/publications/cc9.asp (accessed 4 December 2009). See also Charity Commission (2009), *Charities and Political Donations*, available at http://www.charitycommission.gov.uk/Library/supportingcharities/pdfs/gucharpol.pdf (accessed 4 December 2009).
34. Charity Commission (2008), *Analysis of the Law Underpinning Prevention or Relief*

of Poverty for the Public Benefit, London: Charity Commission, para 27, available at http://www.charitycommission.gov.uk/Library/publicbenefit/pdfs/lawpov1208.pdf.

35. Advisory Group on Campaigning and the Voluntary Sector (UK) (2007), *Report*, London: The Advisory Group, p. 25, available at: http://peopleandplanet.org/dl/campaigninglaw1.pdf (accessed 4 December 2009).

36. Charity Commission (2008), *Consultation on Draft Supplementary Guidance on Public Benefit and the Advancement of Moral or Ethical Belief Systems*, London: Charity Commission, available at http://www.charitycommission.gov.uk/publicbenefit/pbmor.asp (accessed 4 December 2009).

37. See http://www.charitylawassociation.org.uk/en/default.aspx (Working Party Reports available to members).

38. *Application for Registration as a Charity by the Church of Scientology (England and Wales) Decision of the Charity Commissioners for England and Wales*, 17 November 1999, available at: http://www.charitycommission.gov.uk/Library/registration/pdfs/cosfulldoc.pdf (accessed 4 December 2009).

39. Ibid, 21.

40. Charity Commission (2008), *The Advancement of Religion for the Public Benefit*, London: Charity Commission, available at http://www.charitycommission.gov.uk/publicbenefit/pbreligion.asp (accessed 4 December 2009).

41. Charities Act 2006, s. 2(2)(3)(c).

42. Charity Commission (1999), *RR2 – Promotion of Urban and Rural Regeneration*, London: Charity Commission, available at http://www.charitycommission.gov.uk/publications/rr2.asp (accessed 4 December 2009).

43. Charity Commission (2000), *RR5 – The Promotion of Community Capacity Building*, London: Charity Commission, available at http://www.charitycommission.gov.uk/publications/rr5.asp (accessed 4 December 2009).

44. Charity Commission (2004), *RR13 – Promotion of the Voluntary Sector for the Benefit of the Public*, London: Charity Commission, available at http://www.charitycommission.gov.uk/publications/rr13.asp (accessed 4 December 2009).

45. Charity Commission (2004), *RR14 – Promoting the Efficiency and Effectiveness of Charities and the Effective Use of Charitable Resources for the Benefit of the Public*, London: Charity Commission, available at http://www.charitycommission.gov.uk/publications/rr14.asp (accessed 4 December 2009).

46. Charity Commission (2000), above n 43 at para 9.

47. *Re White's Will Trusts* [1951] 1 All ER 518 (rest home for nurses).

48. Charity Commission (2002), *RR10 – Museums and Art Galleries*, London: Charity Commission, available at http://www.charitycommission.gov.uk/publications/rr10.asp (accessed 4 December 2009).

49. *Royal Choral Society v IRC* [1943] 3All ER 101.

50. Charity Commission (2001), *RR9 – Preservation and Conservation*, London: Charity Commission, available at http://www.charitycommission.gov.uk/publications/rr9.asp (accessed 4 December 2009).

51. *Royal College of Surgeons of England v National Provincial Bank Ltd* [1952] 1 All ER 984.

52. *Re Lopes* [1930] All ER 45.

53. *Re Nottage* [1895] 2 Ch 649.

54. *IRC v McMullen* [1981] AC 1; *Re Mariette* [1914] All ER 794.

55. Charity Commission (2003), *RR11 – Charitable Status and Sport*, London: Charity Commission, available at http://www.charitycommission.gov.uk/publications/rr11.asp (accessed 4 December 2009).

56. Charities Act 2006, s. 2(3)(d).

57. Charity Commission, above n 55 at para 11.

58. Human Rights Act 1998.

59. Charity Commission (2005), *RR12 – The Promotion of Human Rights*, London: Charity Commission, available at http://www.charitycommission.gov.uk/publications/rr12.asp (accessed 4 December 2009).

60. *McGovern v AG* [1981] 3 All ER 493.
61. Advisory Group on Campaigning and the Voluntary Sector (UK) (2007), *Report*, London: The Advisory Group, p. 24, available at http://peopleandplanet.org/dl/campaigninglaw1.pdf (accessed 4 December 2009).
62. Charity Commission (2008), *CC9 – Speaking Out – Guidance on Campaigning and Political Activity by Charities*, London: Charity Commission, available at http://www.charitycommission.gov.uk/publications/cc9.asp (accessed 4 December 2009).
63. *Application for Registration of English Pen*, Decisions of the Charity Commission for England and Wales, 21 July 2008, available at http://www.charitycommission.gov.uk/Library/registration/pdfs/englishpendec.pdf (accessed 4 December 2009).
64. *McGovern v AG* [1981] 3 All ER 493.
65. *Application for Registration of Concordis International Trust*, Decisions of the Charity Commission for England and Wales, 23 July 2003, available at http://www.charitycommission.gov.uk/Library/registration/pdfs/concordisdecision.pdf (accessed 4 December 2009).
66. *Anglo-Swedish Society v IRC* (1931) 47 TLR 295.
67. *Application for Registration of Restorative Justice Consortium Limited*, Decisions of the Charity Commission for England and Wales, 15 January 2003, available at http://www.charitycommission.gov.uk/Library/registration/pdfs/rjcdecision.pdf (accessed 4 December 2009).
68. *Re Strakosh* [1949] Ch 529.
69. Charity Commission (undated), *Promotion of Equality and Diversity for the Benefit of the Public*, London: Charity Commission, available at http://www.charitycommission.gov.uk/registeredcharities/ped.asp.
70. Charity Commission (2001), *RR9 – Preservation and Conservation*, London: Charity Commission, available at http://www.charitycommission.gov.uk/publications/rr9.asp (accessed 4 December 2009).
71. Charities Act 2006, s. 2(3)(e). This refers back to the wording in the original list in the Strategy Unit Report.
72. Charity Law Association (2007), *For the Public Benefit: Essays Written Following the Charity Law Association's Conference on the Charities Act 2006*, London: Plaza.
73. Charity Commission, above n 31.
74. *Re Moss* [1949] 1 All ER 495 (work with cats and kittens).
75. *Re Wedgewood* [1915] 1 Ch 113.
76. *National Anti-Vivisection Society v IRC* [1948] AC 31.
77. Charity Commission (2000), *RR4 – The Recreational Charities Act 1958*, London: Charity Commission, available at http://www.charitycommission.gov.uk/publications/rr4.asp (accessed 4 December 2009).
78. Including the repair of bridges, the provision of water and lighting, a cemetery or crematorium, the provision of a library, reading rooms.
79. Charity Commission (1999), *RR3 – Charities for the Relief of Unemployment*, London: Charity Commission, available at http://www.charitycommission.gov.uk/publications/rr3.asp (accessed 4 December 2009).

3. Ireland: *Pemsel* plus

Oonagh B. Breen

INTRODUCTION – THE DRIVERS OF CHARITABLE CHANGE

> While the essential characteristics of charitable purposes do not change, what will satisfy those purposes changes with society . . . What is charitable is to be determined in accordance with contemporary community values. A contemporary activity may be charitable now, though it would not have been charitable a century ago, or less . . . Rules established a century ago relating to what is charitable need to be revisited in this light.[1]

The introduction of a new charity statute affords a state an opportunity to revise its policy approach on charities and in so doing to redraw the boundaries between the state, the market and the nonprofit sector. At its core, the power to determine what constitutes a charitable purpose is – and always has been – a political one. As history reveals, it matters not that definitional classification is not always to the fore of political intent or deliberation. The Statute of Charitable Uses 1601, although primarily intended as an accountability tool to ensure that charitable assets were applied to charitable ends, is today best and perhaps only remembered for its Preamble setting out the parameters of 17th-century charity.[2] It is somewhat less surprising then that history is once more repeating itself: whereas the political motivation for new charity legislation in Ireland springs primarily from concerns relating to transparency and accountability, the focus of popular, political (and most likely future legal) debate rests on the scope of the definition of charity.

In Ireland, the need for charitable change had existed for many years, driven by a lack of judicial opportunity to keep the common law definition current and the absence of a charities regulator with responsibility for pronouncing regularly (and publicly) on the evolution and status of charitable purposes in modern Ireland. Almost a decade ago, a coincidence of events provided the necessary driver for the reform of charity law in Ireland and with it the revision of the common law definition from *Pemsel's case*.[3] In June 2002, the then newly elected coalition government made an express commitment that 'A comprehensive reform of the law relating to charities

74

will be enacted to ensure accountability and to protect against abuse of charitable status and fraud'.[4] The driver for this reform sprang, in large part,[5] from earlier Irish government commitments to the United Nations Security Council's Counter-Terrorism Committee to strengthen charity regulation amidst general fears that absence of effective regulation in Ireland (among a number of other countries) provided a haven for terrorist organisations that wished to launder money through nonprofit and charitable entities.[6] Thus, international pressure served as an external catalyst in the prioritisation of charity law reform where earlier domestic pressure had failed, resulting in the government's new-found commitment to new legislation.

Legislation however provides only a framework into which content must be added and luck was with the Irish government in the timing of its policy agenda. A month after the government's public commitment to charity law reform, the Law Society of Ireland published a 284-page report on the need for charity law reform in Ireland.[7] The report was influential and wide-ranging, covering substantive issues relating to registration and regulation, legal structures for charities and legal requirements for charity trustees. Many of the Law Society's recommendations relating to charitable purpose find expression today in the new Charities Act 2009.[8] The report received a broad welcome from both charities and the government alike.

When the government department in charge of charity law reform published its Consultation Paper in 2003, it cited as one of its main aims the need to 'give clear statutory guidance regarding the *definition of charity*, thereby bringing the definition of charitable purposes into line with a modern perspective of what constitutes charity and protecting against abuse of charitable status'.[9] The Consultation Paper, acknowledging the root problems of lack of judicial opportunity to update the common law definition and the ensuing dissatisfaction with the test, recommended that '[a] statutory definition could codify and replace the current common law interpretation, setting out clear charitable purposes of public benefit'.[10]

The suggested heads put forward by the Department of Community, Rural and Gaeltacht Affairs for consultation purposes drew heavily on the Law Society of Ireland Report and its proposed definition of charity, which in turn had been influenced by the Australian Charities Definition Inquiry's proposals[11] with one exception: the Consultation Paper did not include the advancement of human rights as a proposed head of charity. This omission drew much adverse comment from charities and the public – so much so that the external Consultation Evaluation Report subsequently recommended its specific inclusion.[12] When published in March 2006, the draft Charities Bill's definitional provision parsed out

11 categories of activity under the heading 'other purposes beneficial to
the community' that included express reference to 'the advancement of
human rights'.[13] Three years later, Ireland finds itself endowed with a new
statutory definition consisting of four main heads of charity and 12 subheads, albeit one that again omits reference to the advancement of human
rights, an issue discussed further below. This chapter outlines the changes
wrought by the new statutory definition, detailing in so far as is possible
the likely coverage of each new subsection. The chapter then discusses
those areas excluded either expressly or implicitly from the new statutory
definition before concluding by briefly examining the effect of the new
Charities Act on the concept of charitable purposes in Ireland.

THE NEW STATUTORY DEFINITION OF CHARITABLE PURPOSE

Until 2009, the definition of charitable purpose in Ireland has been a matter
of common law and the Irish courts have applied Lord Macnaghten's four
heads of charity set out in *Pemsel*.[14] The Charities Act 2009 updates the
Charities Acts 1961–73 and the regulatory regime instituted under those
Acts. For the first time in Ireland, the 2009 Act introduces a statutory
definition of charitable purposes. To qualify as charitable, a purpose must
fall within one of the headings set out in section 3 of the Act and it must be
for the public benefit.[15] To the casual observer, section 3(1) retains (with
some expansion) the language of the common law *Pemsel* headings with
the last heading of 'other purposes beneficial to the community' receiving
its own expansive elaboration in section 3(11). The statutory definitions
of charity enacted recently in Scotland,[16] Northern Ireland[17] and England
and Wales[18] resemble but are not identical to the language found in the
Irish Act. And, as every good lawyer knows, the devil lies in such detail.

Section 3 of the Charities Act 2009 – the New Meaning of Charity in Ireland

Section 3 of the Charities Act 2009 sets out a new baseline for determining what constitutes 'charitable' in Ireland. It breaks the link with the
common law by replacing and expanding the *Pemsel* heads of charity with
a codified statutory version of 'charitable purpose'. Section 3(1) retains
unchanged the charitable heads of advancement of education, advancement of religion and the advancement of any other purposes beneficial to
the community; and section 3(11) expands upon the meaning of purposes
beneficial to the community (the fourth head) in a series of 12 subheads.

There was much debate in the Oireachtas (the Irish Parliament) during the passage of the Bill as to the political choices underlying the new definition. Whereas the opposition parties felt that the new statutory definition should update and, where possible, improve upon the existing common law definition,[19] the government was adamant that the statutory definition was intended only to clarify – and not to expand upon – the existing common law meaning of charitable purpose in Ireland.[20]

The government's position is not without difficulty: the decision to enshrine an existing common law position in statute is of itself a political choice. By abrogating its power to review the contents of charitable purpose in certain instances, the government nonetheless makes a political choice regarding charity's scope and thereby influences the future direction of charitable giving. Moreover, some of the new statutory heads do indeed constitute legislative expansions of the common law concept of charity, resulting in inconsistency in the government's stance on the basis for its definition.

Poverty: Section 3(1)(a) The prevention or relief of poverty or economic hardship

Both the Australian Charitable Definition Inquiry and the Irish Law Society in their respective reports on charity law reform[21] recommended that reference to poverty should tackle not only the symptoms of poverty (via relief) but also its causes (via the introduction of reference to prevention). The newly expanded poverty head in subsection (1) refers now to '*the prevention* or relief of poverty *or economic hardship*' (emphasis added). In the context of poverty, 'prevention' is normally conceived of as the power to question or challenge systems that are responsible for the beneficiaries' poverty. The beneficiary class is normally given a broad interpretation to include amongst its number those who, without assistance, may become poor in future.[22]

As to the range of activities that a charity may be able to engage in under this new heading, advocacy will be possible provided it directly furthers the charitable purpose of preventing poverty.[23] Thus, the need to engage in informed debate (as opposed to propaganda) and the onus on the charity trustees to ensure that any lobbying or campaigning is proportionate and does not detract from the charity's focus on mission or the ongoing needs of its beneficiaries will remain. As such, it is unlikely that this amendment would go so far as to enable any future 'Make Poverty History' campaign to be charitable in its own right although poverty charities could affiliate to the campaign without risk of losing their charitable status.[24]

At common law, poverty is construed as a relative concept, which does not require proof of destitution.[25] The addition of the descriptive term 'economic hardship' to section 3(1)(a) may be a statutory reinforcement of this common law principle. A person whose standard of living declines dramatically might experience 'economic hardship' without necessarily falling within the popular conception of poverty. The focus here would appear to be on income poverty rather than poverty resulting from social exclusion. The UK also picks up on the notion of impecuniosity with all three statutes making similar reference to the concept of 'financial hardship'. Interestingly, the reference to such hardship in each of those statutes arises not in the context of the poverty heading but under the broader community welfare heading of the expanded fourth *Pemsel* head.[26] Moreover, 'financial hardship' in all three Acts expressly includes relief through the provision of accommodation or care, presumably covering childcare centres and housing associations.[27]

Education: Section 3(1)(b)   The advancement of education

The advancement of education has been the workhorse of the common law definition in Ireland, encompassing school and university education, research of all types (from literary to scientific), sports-related activities, theatre, the arts, and cultural activities.[28] To a degree, the new statutory definition parses out these multiple spokes by creating specific subheadings for them under 'other purposes beneficial to the community' and thus freeing advancement of education to focus once more on the meaning of 'education'.[29]

Advancement of education will continue to cover both formal education (for example, schools and universities) and informal education (for example, adult education, vocational training, and playgroups). In terms of the former, although the statutory definition of education extends to the activities of education bodies, schools and universities, these bodies will not be fully subject to the rigours of the Charities Act 2009, particularly with regard to accountability. Thus, such educational bodies will neither be required to submit their annual statements of accounts to the Charities Regulatory Authority (CRA) under section 48, nor will they be subject to the audit requirements of section 50. At present, the Revenue Commissioners recognise private fee-paying schools as charitable. There has not been the same level of debate to date in Ireland as has occurred in the UK over whether such institutions provide sufficient public benefit to warrant their charitable status.[30]

Notwithstanding the government's deliberate decision to exclude sport as a charitable heading in its own right, it is likely that sport will continue to find a home under the advancement of education heading provided that it is sufficiently integrated with educational purposes.

Religion: Section 3(1)(c)   The advancement of religion

Since the early 20th century, Irish law has treated the advancement of religion differently from its common law neighbours. The differences, attributable to the socio-cultural differences that exist between Ireland and the UK, have long been recognised in both the statutory provisions[31] and case law.[32] The 2009 Act carries over and updates the basic law relating to religious advancement and charities in Ireland. The Irish Act does not set out a statutory definition of religion, thus leaving intact the common law definition based upon there being worship of a Supreme Being. In determining whether a gift advances religion, section 3(6) of the 2009 Act reiterates the test from the 1961 Act, to the effect that 'A charitable gift for the purpose of the advancement of religion shall have effect, and the terms upon which it is given shall be construed, in accordance with the laws, canons, ordinances and tenets of the religion concerned'.

The new Act also retains the presumption that a gift for the advancement of religion is for the public benefit. Whereas this presumption was conclusive under section 45 of the 1961 Act, section 3(4) of the 2009 Act makes it rebuttable. In other words, once an entity proves to the CRA that the gift is in support of a recognised religion and the gift's purpose is to advance worship within the context of that religion, then public benefit is presumed to flow without further need for demonstrable proof. If the CRA concludes that the evidence before it rebuts the presumption of public benefit in favour of a particular religion, it cannot decide against the gift without the consent of the Attorney General.

The Attorney General's power in this respect is unusual in the new statutory regime since section 38 of the 2009 Act more generally divests the Attorney General of all his previous powers and functions in relation to charities, transferring them to the CRA.[33] Upon receipt of the Attorney General's consent and the CRA's issuance of its determination that a gift does not advance religion, section 3(5) closes off the avenue of an appeal to the Charities Appeal Tribunal for the disappointed applicant. Thus, the only recourse upon refusal of recognition as a charitable gift for religious purposes will be an application to the High Court.

The statutory presumption in favour of religious charities is not found elsewhere in the British Isles. Thus, whereas Northern Ireland takes a broader statutory view of what constitutes religion (including polytheistic and non-theistic religions in addition to 'any analogous philosophical beliefs'), it is more demanding of the public benefit in that it requires the gift to be charitable. In contrast, the narrower common law definition of religion used in Ireland is enhanced by the presumption of public benefit and the fact that advancement of any religion is determined on the religion's own terms and not objectively. The case law speaks to the State's accordance of equal recognition for all theistic religions[34] and there is some circumstantial evidence that the Revenue Commissioners do not discriminate between monotheistic and polytheistic religions in granting charitable tax-exempt status.[35]

A last-minute amendment to the Charities Bill at the Seanad Report Stage hearings sought to prevent religious cults availing themselves of Ireland's more lenient public benefit provisions for religion. In this regard, section 3(10) provides that a gift is not a gift for the advancement of religion if it is made to or for the benefit of an organisation or cult –

    (a) the principal object of which is the making of profit, or
    (b) that employs oppressive psychological manipulation –
        (i) of its followers, or
        (ii) for the purpose of gaining new followers.

It remains to be seen how section 3(10), which employs an objective test as to the purposes and effect of an organisation, will be reconciled with section 3(6), which adopts an inherently subjective approach in determining the manner in which a gift advances the religion in question.

On a comparative note, the Irish statutory presumption of public benefit in favour of the advancement of religion finds echoes, albeit on a narrower basis, in section 5 of the Extension of Charitable Purpose Act 2004 of Australia. Section 5 deems an institution's purpose to have public benefit to the extent that the institution is a closed or contemplative religious order that regularly undertakes prayerful intervention at the request of members of the public. The effect of both the Irish and Australian provisions is the same. Underlying both is a policy choice that runs contrary to the House of Lords decision in *Gilmour v Coats*[36] and which says that if public benefit depends on a matter of religious faith, to require tangible proof may neither be logical nor just.

Secular philosophical beliefs

There is no provision in the Irish statutory definition of charitable purposes for the advancement of philosophical beliefs to be charitable. Attempts to include reference to humanism as a charitable purpose failed. Refusing to contemplate the introduction of a broad statutory definition of religion that would cater to secular beliefs, the Minister thought that religion, like poverty and education, is best left undefined,[37] and hence subject to existing common law constraints.

Sections 3(1)(d) and 3(11)   Any other purpose that is of benefit to the community

A statutory expansion of the fourth head of charity occurs in section 3(11).[38] This elaboration is significant since, according to Revenue records, more than 50 per cent of tax-exempt charities were registered with the Revenue Commissioners under this heading.[39] The scope of section 3(11) is intended to be non-exhaustive. The wording of subsection (11) reads that 'other purposes beneficial to the community' *includes* the 12 categories of activity listed there but presumably is not limited to these. Nonetheless, there is no express provision, as there is in section 2(4) of the English Charities Act 2006, to allow for continued use of common law precedent in conjunction with future analogous extensions of the statutory definition when determining whether a purpose is charitable.[40]

In the absence of such enabling language, it would be open to the Irish courts to hold that only those purposes falling within the four corners of the statutory provision can be construed as charitable. When combined with the mandatory legislative five-year review of the Act,[41] the Oireachtas' deliberate exclusion of certain purposes from the statutory list might be further interpreted as making the legislature solely responsible for future organic growth within the statutory heads[42] thereby inhibiting such development by the courts or the charities regulator.

With regard to the substantive list that now comprises section 3(11), there was little discussion in the Houses of the Oireachtas on the merits of the various sub-categories, most likely because Revenue already grants tax-exempt status to these activities. Thus, while the lack of parliamentary debate is explicable, it is nonetheless unhelpful since Revenue does not publish its decisions and therefore no precedents exist regarding the application of these sub-categories in Ireland.

Section 3(11)(a)   The advancement of community welfare including the relief of those in need by reason of youth, age, ill-health, or disability

This heading elaborates on the traditional *Pemsel* heading of relief of poverty and many organisations currently enjoy tax exemption under each of these subheadings encompassed by the new wording. One would, of course, still have to demonstrate that sufficient public benefit exists with regard to the activity or purpose at hand before the charity test would be satisfied.[43]

Section 3(11)(b)   The advancement of community development, including rural or urban regeneration

In their 2001 Manual on Charities (issued under section 16 of the Freedom of Information Act 1997), the Revenue Commissioners identify 'improvements to an area' as a classical example of charitable purpose. Given the large numbers of partnerships/leader groups and enterprise boards registered with Revenue, whose role it is to act as a conduit for distributing national grants as well as EU funding to regeneration projects and enterprise schemes in disadvantaged areas, it is not surprising from a policy perspective to see specific reference to rural or urban regeneration in section 3(11)(b).

Since most of the funding for existing bodies under this heading comes from the public purse, the relationship between the state and the voluntary sector and the degree to which partnership is possible will be crucial to the charitable outcomes under this heading.[44]

Section 3(11)(c)   The promotion of civic responsibility or voluntary work

Traditionally, Revenue has granted charitable tax-exempt status to volunteer centres, on both a local and a national level. Moreover, in 2006 the Irish government convened a taskforce on active citizenship to carry on a 'national conversation' on what it means to participate fully in one's community in modern Ireland. The taskforce delivered its final report to government in March 2007.[45] Although there are no express references to the taskforce's work, the government accepted its recommendations and a provision in the Charity Act recognising the importance of civic responsibility would constitute a cost-free form of implementation of its proposals.

Section 3(11)(d)   The promotion of health, including the prevention or relief of sickness, disease or human suffering

The substance of this heading is unlikely to be controversial in its statutory format, as there are many examples on the Revenue listing of organisations falling under these headings. The government has argued that the reference to 'relief or prevention of human suffering' will enable human rights organisations to register as charities notwithstanding the deliberate political choice to exclude reference to the advancement of human rights as charitable per se. It is unclear whether this amounts to an invitation to human rights organisations to re-word their human rights activities in the language of relief of suffering in return for charitable status or whether an organisation that professes both missions (that is, to advance human rights and to relieve human suffering) would be viewed as being charitable. There is a certain overlap between this heading and section 3(11)(a) 'the advancement of community welfare including the relief of those in need by reason of . . . ill-health, or disability' so one would assume that the organisations qualifying as promoting health under this heading will equally qualify as relieving those in need by reason of ill-health.

Section 3(11)(e)   The advancement of conflict resolution or reconciliation

When this heading first appeared in the draft Charities Bill 2006 it took the more inclusive form of 'the advancement of human rights, social justice, conflict resolution or reconciliation or the promotion of religious or racial harmony or equality and diversity'. In its enacted form, 'conflict resolution or reconciliation' has been separated from the promotion of religious or racial harmony (which now forms section 3(11)(f)). References to the advancement of human rights, social justice, equality and diversity disappear entirely. No official explanation has been offered for this change in policy direction.

The deletion of the references to equality and diversity in the Charities Bill coincided with a Government decision to cut funding to and to merge a number of state-sponsored bodies dealing in the areas of equality and poverty. Commentators claimed that the Irish government was using the cover of the economic recession to dismantle equality and human rights frameworks in Ireland.[46] The exclusion of human rights engendered the most controversy during the Bill's passage, an omission discussed in more detail below.

As to the meaning of conflict resolution and reconciliation, the exact scope of this heading remains to be determined. Advancement of conflict resolution or reconciliation would seem to be distinct from the promotion of peace, which is charitable only under the Charities Act (Northern Ireland) 2008. Given the nature of conflict, its resolution may often involve political considerations such that the activities advanced under this heading may come close to the line drawn in section 2 of the Charities Act, precluding from charitable status organisations promoting political causes unless those causes are in furtherance of an existing charitable purpose. The potential for circular reasoning here is evident and it may be that the CRA will need to issue guidance on acceptable charitable activities under this heading.

Section 3(11)(f) The promotion of religious or racial harmony and harmonious community relations

There are no identifiable Revenue precedents in the Revenue Listings that fall naturally under this particular heading. The inclusion of this heading therefore rebuts the government's claim that it is not broadening the definition. As recently as 15 years ago, Ireland was a homogenous nation still experiencing negative migration. In 1996, Ireland reached its migration 'turning point', making it the last EU member state to become a country of net immigration. This change was due largely to the Celtic Tiger, which saw rapid economic growth create an unprecedented demand for labour.

When these changing demographics are plotted against the Supreme Court's 2003 decision removing the automatic right to permanent residence for non-national parents of Irish-born children[47] and a successful Constitutional referendum in 2004 to eliminate an Irish-born child's automatic right to citizenship when the parents are not Irish nationals,[48] the need for positive policy statements on racial harmony and harmonious community relations may be more readily understood. The stated aspirations of the racial harmony clause, however, must be balanced against the government's recent actions in disbanding the National Consultative Committee on Racism and Interculturalism, which when coupled with a lack of strategy to build on the work of the National Action Plan Against Racism (which completed its four-year mandate in January 2009) 'leave[s] a void at the heart of the government's efforts in tackling racism'.[49]

Section 3(11)(g)   The protection of the natural environment, and 3(11)(h) The advancement of environmental sustainability

The Revenue lists include a number of environmental organisations engaged in conservation, environmental improvement, education and overseas development. The protection of the natural environment, first suggested by the CDI Report and adopted by the Irish Law Society, would not seem to extend to conservation of the built environment, which presumably will find a charitable home under the advancement of heritage.

Section 3(11)(i)   The advancement of the efficient and effective use of the property of charitable organisations

The purpose of this heading, it would appear, is to deliver on government commitments set out in the national social partnership agreement, *Towards 2016*, in which the government recognised the need for capacity building within the charity sector generally to enable it to meet the challenges of the pending regulatory regime.[50]

The inclusion of this provision recognises an existing weakness in Irish voluntary sector development, namely the lack of an indigenous foundation sector. Reasons proffered for this absence are many: historically, a lack of indigenous wealth in Ireland to endow such entities and, culturally, a preference for ad hoc giving as opposed to strategic planned giving have meant that it is only in very recent years that philanthropic spirit has begun to sprout in Ireland.[51] That Revenue are happy to encourage such development is clear from the inclusion on the tax-exempt listing of social investment funds that provide both loan finance and, occasionally, direct investment to charities that find it hard to access funding from mainstream lending institutions.[52] More recently, the government established the Social Finance Foundation[53] under its Social Finance Initiative, with a seed funding grant of €25 million from the Irish banking sector to enable charities to access social finance capital at wholesale rates.

Aside from financial support, section 3(11)(i) may also provide a charitable home to third-tier support organisations, such as Boardmatch Ireland, which aims to build the governance skill sets of nonprofit boards by linking qualified professionals seeking volunteering opportunities with nonprofits seeking assistance in a variety of fields. In other words, support organisations that assist charities in achieving their charitable purposes may also be charitable.

Section 3(11)(j)   The prevention or relief of suffering of animals
This heading has long been accepted in Ireland as a charitable purpose both in the case law and by the Revenue Commissioners. Traditionally, the Irish courts view the prevention or relief of suffering of animals as a charitable purpose in its own right,[54] unlike the English courts, where the validity of such gifts depended heavily upon whether they produced a benefit to humankind.[55]

Section 3(11)(k)   The advancement of the arts, culture, heritage or sciences
Section 3(11)(k) is possibly the least controversial subsection in that the Revenue Commissioners have previously accepted each of the constituent elements contained there as worthy of charitable tax-exempt status under the heading of advancement of education. The specific listing of arts, culture, heritage and sciences breaks the link between advancement of education and these purposes, which are of benefit to the community. Substantively, this clarification does not change the law and public benefit will still be required for charitable status to be granted.

Section 3(11)(l)   The integration of those who are disadvantaged, and the promotion of their full participation in society
Section 3(11)(l) lacks a comparator in neighbouring charities legislation. In essence, it ensures that an Irish court could not reach a decision similar to that reached by the Canadian Supreme Court in 1999 in *Vancouver Society of Immigrant and Visible Minority Women v MNR* when a 4–3 majority held that assisting immigrant women to integrate into society through helping them to obtain employment was not a charitable purpose under the fourth head of charity.[56] One would hope that this heading would provide a charitable home to victims of social exclusion that may not fit as easily within the Irish definition of poverty.

THE EXCLUSION ZONE – WHAT FALLS OUTSIDE THE DEFINITION AND WHAT ARE THE CONSEQUENCES OF EXCLUSION?

> [T]he duty of the court is to the law. If a valid statute is enacted with relevant effect, that duty extends to giving effect to the statute, not ignoring it. No principle of the common law can retain its authority in the face of a legislative prescription that enters its orbit with relevant effect. The proper starting point for the ascertainment of legal duties . . . is the statute.[57]

Under the provisions of the Charities Act 2009, it will be a criminal offence for a body to hold itself out as a charity in Ireland without registering with the Charities Regulatory Authority.[58] An organisation wishing to use the charity moniker must therefore register and in so doing will be obliged to file an annual report on its charitable activities as well as making annual returns either directly to the CRA or the Companies Registration Office, as appropriate. Notwithstanding the broad nature of many of the headings in section 3, the Act specifically excludes the following bodies from having charitable status:[59]

- a political party, or a body that promotes a political party or candidate;
- a body that promotes a political cause, unless the promotion of that cause relates directly to the advancement of the charitable purposes of the body;
- a body established for the promotion of athletic or amateur games or sports;
- a trade union or a representative body of employers;
- a chamber of commerce;
- a body that promotes purposes that are – (i) unlawful, (ii) contrary to public morality, (iii) contrary to public policy, (iv) in support of terrorism or terrorist activities, whether in the State or outside the State, (v) for the benefit of an organisation membership of which is unlawful.

The exclusion of political, trade union and business parties is not out of line with social expectations. More striking is the exclusion of amateur sports bodies and bodies 'that promote a political cause, unless the promotion of that cause relates directly to the advancement of the charitable purposes of the body'. In addition to these express exclusions, no provision is made for human rights organisations, social and recreational organisations, defence force related and peace-related activities, all of which are discussed below.

Sporting Activities

Historically, the charitable hook for sporting organisations has been advancement of education, thus limiting the beneficiaries of charitable sporting activities predominantly to students at school and university.[60] As global perceptions of health have developed to incorporate exercise as a constituent element, some charity regulators developed policies that looked kindly upon non-educationally related participation in amateur sports.[61]

The Irish government made a political choice to exclude sport from the list in section 3(11).[62] The effect of such exclusion is that sporting bodies will not be required to register with the CRA but it also prohibits such bodies from registering as charities if they so wished.[63] Those sports-related charities currently on the Revenue list of charitable tax-exempt bodies will be deemed 'charities' under the new regime[64] and one must assume that their purposes relate to the advancement of education or that sport is simply an ancillary means to the achievement of a broader charitable purpose.[65] Amateur sporting bodies in Ireland currently enjoy certain tax relief under the tax code separate from the exempt charitable purpose provisions that is not as extensive as the relief granted to charitable organisations.[66]

Recreational and Social Activities

Ireland does not have an equivalent statute to the UK's Recreational Charities Act 1958. Activities that are purely recreational or social are thus not viewed as 'exclusively charitable' unless the recreational or social element is ancillary to a broader charitable purpose that benefits the community.[67] This position is unlikely to change even with the introduction of the new statutory definition of charity in Ireland.

Promotion of Peace

One must assume, in the absence of a broad interpretation of the promotion of conflict resolution/reconciliation that promotion of peace *per se* is not exclusively charitable but would rather be viewed as a private purpose and thus suffer the same fate as the trusts in *Re Astor*.[68] It remains to be seen, however, whether one can truly distinguish between a body that has as its objects the promotion of reconciliation and all that presumably entails and the promotion of peace.

Promotion of the Defence Forces

There was no discussion in Ireland over whether promotion of the defence forces should be listed as charitable, presumably based on the relatively small size of the Irish defence forces. A search of the Revenue Listings of organisations enjoying charitable tax-exempt status reveals one defence-related entity – the Army Benevolent Fund – that will be deemed to maintain its charitable status upon the coming into force of the Charities Act.[69]

Promotion of Human Rights

One of the more controversial elements is the exclusion of the promotion of human rights from the definition of 'charitable purposes'. Although originally included in the draft Charities Bill 2006, the Charities Bill 2007 omitted reference to this purpose. Despite the strenuous efforts of human rights organisations,[70] scholars[71] and politicians,[72] the government resolutely refused to re-insert any reference to human rights in the Bill, yet declined to explain the reason for its deletion.

Revenue's objections to human rights organisations gaining charitable status most likely stems from a strict application of the principles set out by the English High Court in *McGovern v Attorney General*.[73] In *McGovern* Slade J refused to grant charitable status to a human rights trust which included among its educational and poverty relief objectives securing the release of prisoners of conscience by procuring the reversal of governmental policy or decisions by lawful persuasion. This object was held to be political in nature and thus tainted all of the objects, making the trust non-charitable. In its 2001 Charities Manual, Revenue made specific reference to *McGovern* in its section on non-charitable political purposes, citing the case as authority for the proposition that 'The Amnesty International Trust was founded with the object of securing world-wide observance of the Universal Declaration of Human Rights – exemption refused'. Notwithstanding the Revenue Commissioners' philosophically rigid approach to human rights organisations, in general these organisations appear to be no worse off than any other charitable organisation from a tax-liability perspective for two reasons.

First, some human rights bodies reorganise their legal structures to ensure that an affiliate or parent organisation does in fact qualify for charitable status while they run their 'non-charitable' human rights activities typically through a non-charitable company limited by guarantee. Thus, to take one excellent example: Amnesty International Ireland has a charitable trust, Amnesty International Ireland Foundation, which is recognised by Revenue as tax-exempt for charitable purposes. This trust is legally separate from Amnesty International Irish Section, a non-charitable company limited by guarantee which campaigns to promote respect for all the human rights set out in the Universal Declaration of Human Rights.

Second, for tax purposes, the Revenue Commissioners operate a separate exemption for human rights bodies. Under section 209 of the Taxes Consolidation Act 1997, where a body (a) enjoys consultative status with either the United Nations or the Council of Europe and has as its sole or main object the promotion of observance of the Universal Declaration of Human Rights or the implementation of the European Convention for the Protection of Human Rights and Fundamental Freedoms and (b) is precluded by its rules or constitution from the distribution of its assets to any of its members, that body will be granted similar income tax exemptions to those of bodies that qualify for charitable tax exemption.

However, the introduction of the Charities Act 2009 changes the focus of charity regulation in Ireland. A human rights organisation that is not registered with the CRA cannot claim to be a charity in any of its dealings with the public without committing an offence.

Whereas existing human rights organisations that have charitable tax-exempt status will be deemed to be registered on the new register subject to section 40 of the 2009 Act, new human rights bodies may be the most affected under the new regime. If an organisation's primary purpose is 'to advance human rights' the new CRA will have to decide whether that body satisfies section 3 of the Act. The Charities Act requires that charities have 'exclusively' charitable objects, so the CRA will be called to adjudicate upon a body professing mixed human rights and more recognisable charitable purposes. How will it treat an organisation that seeks in its objectives to relieve poverty, advance education *and* advance human rights? If it applies the Revenue's interpretation of *McGovern* the body is unlikely to be charitable. If the CRA turns to legislative history, the outcome will be no different since the clear intent of the legislature was to exclude human rights as a charitable purpose. If it turns instead to first principles and seeks to unpack what is meant by 'advancing or promoting human rights', it may or may not conclude that the promotion of human rights entails the promotion of a political cause, resulting in the body being statutorily ineligible for registration as an 'excluded body' under section 2(1).

In a nutshell, excluding the promotion of human rights as a charitable purpose leaves human rights organisations with no ready hook upon which to hang their case for charitable status. Ineligibility to register, although separate from matters of taxation relief, will deny an organisation the right to hold itself out as a charity in a new legal environment in which that claim will now actually have some meaning. Ineligibility to register will also mean that human rights organisations will not be subject to the transparency and accountability requirements of the Charities Act. This may cause the greatest disservice to those organisations that wish to use this mechanism to demonstrate their charitable efficiency and governance standards. Donors and the general public will also be deprived of a statutory oversight mechanism for monitoring what human rights organisations do with their money.

Promotion of Political Causes

The final exclusion in the Charities Act 2009 relates to bodies 'that promote a political cause, unless the promotion of that cause relates directly to the advancement of the charitable purposes of the body'. Traditionally, the common law has stopped short of deeming the promotion of 'political purposes' as charitable *per se*.[74] The courts have interpreted 'political purposes' broadly to encompass not just direct support for a political party or political candidate but also any activities that retain, oppose or change the law, policy or decision of any level of government domestically or in a foreign country.[75] The courts refuse to recognise political purposes as charitable because judges cannot determine whether such purposes would be for the public benefit.[76] The Charity Commission for England and Wales, however, has permitted charities – including human rights charities[77] – to lobby and to engage in political campaigning when these activities could be said to be an ancillary means for the achievement of the bodies' greater charitable objectives.[78]

With limited Irish judicial guidance available,[79] the Revenue Commissioners have applied the English judicial authorities up to and including *McGovern*[80] and refused charitable tax-exempt status in at least two documented cases in which applicant organisations had undefined political activities and the stated purpose of changing the law.[81] Section 2 of the Charities Act 2009 includes under the definition of 'excluded body' (which cannot be a charitable organisation) one that promotes a political cause – unless promotion of that political cause 'relates directly to the advancement of the charitable purposes of the body'. Section 2 gives rise to three issues that require further consideration: (a) what constitutes a 'political cause'?; (b) are there any limits on the extent to which a charity can devote itself to political causes without endangering its charitable status?; and (c) to what extent is the CRA's treatment of political causes under the Charities Act likely to resemble the Revenue Commissioners' treatment of political activity under the tax provisions?

What constitutes a 'political cause'?
The term 'political cause', as used in section 2 of the Charities Act 2009, is not defined further. Does having a political cause, for instance, equate with having a political purpose or a political end? In *Colgan v Independent Radio and Television Commission*, the Irish High Court defined a 'political end' within the context of the Radio and Television Act 1988, as being an activity that is

> directed towards furthering the interests of a particular political party or towards procuring changes in the laws of this country or . . . countering suggested changes in those laws, or towards procuring changes in the laws of a foreign country or countering suggested changes in those laws or procuring a reversal of government policy or of particular decisions of governmental authorities in this country or . . . countering suggested reversals thereof or procuring a reversal of governmental policy or of particular decisions of governmental authorities in a foreign country or countering suggested reversals thereof.[82]

In reaching this conclusion, O'Sullivan J also drew heavily upon the English authority of *McGovern v Attorney General*. Thus if 'political cause' equates with 'political end' then a body can only engage in such activities if they relate directly to the body's other charitable purposes. To the extent that a body enjoys charitable status, section 2 brings some comfort that political activities aimed directly at achieving its charitable purposes will be permitted. Thus, for existing charities, it is clear that advocacy in support of valid charitable purposes is entirely permissible. Poverty charities could thus legitimately engage in a 'Make Poverty History' type campaign without endangering their charitable status. However, human rights organisations wishing to register as charities cannot make the argument that advancement of human rights is charitable *per se*. And without this baseline, even if these bodies qualify as charities under one of the other permissible heads, such as education or relief of poverty, any advocacy directly relating to their human rights activities will not enjoy immunity from the 'no political cause' clause.

Therefore, even if the Minister is correct and human rights organisations that relieve human suffering or poverty or engage in education will not be prejudiced by the omission of human rights as a charitable purpose but will find another suitable home in the Act's purposes, any political activity undertaken by these organisations must be directly related back to these particular charitable purposes or it will fall outside the protection of section 2 of the Act.

Are there any limits on the extent to which a charity can devote itself to political causes without endangering its charitable status?

It is also unclear from the Charities Act whether there is any limit on the extent to which any charity can devote itself to political activity without endangering its charitable status. The draft Charities Bill 2006 had a dominant activity or ancillary activity test, which provided that a charity could engage in advocacy-related activities so long as they did not become the *raison d'être* of the organisation.[83] The removal of this provision would seem to imply a departure from this approach but no policy guidance is provided as to how charities are to operate in this new environment.

Will the CRA's treatment of political causes tally with that of the Revenue Commissioners?

It remains to be seen whether the CRA, when established, will issue guidance on charities and political activity, along the lines of the English Charity Commission. The publication of such guidance would bring welcome clarity and transparency to this area of law and would make it easier to compare the approaches of the CRA and the Revenue should their views on 'political causes' diverge in the future. Since, under section 7 of the Charities Act, it will be possible for the Revenue Commissioners to continue to apply their strict interpretation of *McGovern*, the likely extent to which there may be interpretative differences will depend upon the autonomy of the newly appointed CRA. In anticipation of such differences arising between regulators it is hoped that when established the CRA will follow the example of its Scottish counterpart, the Office of the Scottish Charity Regulator (OSCR), and enter into a memorandum of understanding with Revenue.[84]

THE EFFECT OF THE CHARITIES ACT ON THE DEFINITION OF CHARITY – DILUTION, ALIGNMENT OR CONFUSION?

The likely effect of the new Irish definition of charity – namely, whether it is more likely to dilute the guiding principles of charity or align those principles with social expectations – depends upon two factors: (a) the status of the guiding principles of charity in Ireland before the 2009 Act; and (b) the state of current social expectations.

As to the first issue, this chapter argues that the lack of publicly available authoritative material, caused by the dearth of Irish case law,[85] makes clarity on Irish charity law principles extremely difficult. In the absence of judicial authority, those who comment on the topic of charity law in Ireland must assume that the common law decisions (and indeed sometimes the regulatory guidance) of foreign jurisdictions is more than just persuasive precedent.[86]

Until now, the development of the common law definition of charitable purpose in Ireland has occurred on a case-by-case basis in the context of revenue law rather than charity law. The Revenue Commissioners adjudicate on applications for charitable tax-exempt status, applying the Macnaghten heads of charity from *Pemsel's case*. Although Revenue publishes a list of tax-exempt entities and some basic contact details,[87] it does not publicise the grounds for its decisions nor does it specify under which *Pemsel* category the applications were successfully made. The closest that one comes to ascertaining the guiding principles of charity in Ireland is through Revenue's 2001 Charities Manual, issued under section 16 of the Freedom of Information Act 1997, which gives a broad indication of categories that Revenue is happy to approve for charitable purposes. Aside from the Revenue listings, if a charity is incorporated, one can obtain a copy of its memorandum and articles of association from the Companies

Registration Office and therefore glean some insight as to what type of objects are acceptable to Revenue. If, however, the organisation is unincorporated, it is under no obligation to share its governing instruments with any interested member of the public.

The existence of such information asymmetries makes it even more difficult in Ireland than in most countries to say whether the social or popular conception of charity is now aligned with the political version enshrined in the Act. To be sure, the express inclusion of human rights in neighbouring jurisdictions places the Irish legal position at odds with the legal position in the UK. Depending upon the approach adopted by the CRA, difficulties may arise for human rights charities registered in the UK but operating in Ireland that will need to register with the CRA. Charities that qualify for registration in the UK on the basis of human rights advancement may need to amend their constitutions in order to register in Ireland, with the attendant trustee and home regulator difficulties that this causes.

Given the express decoupling of the legal definition of charity and the taxation definition, the Charities Act 2009 provided the ideal opening for a more coherent definition of the former. For the most part, the Government decided not to take advantage of this opportunity. In some respects, section 3 of the 2009 Act clearly enlarges on the common law definition of charity: making it charitable for the first time to act as a support organisation to other charities, thereby increasing their efficiency and effectiveness;[88] including environmental sustainability as a new charitable heading; and expanding the concept of relief of poverty to include its prevention.[89] Yet, even in these respects, the government claims only codification as opposed to expansion – a non sequitur surely. Until the CRA is established and the register of charities set up, one can only speculate on the likely effects of the new statutory definition. Much will depend on the calibre of appointments made to the CRA and the level of resources (in terms of both financial and human capital) provided by government.

On a positive note, the Charities Act 2009 provides a welcome space in which we can begin to develop a public sense of what constitutes charity. The creation of the register, the provision of details on the activities of registered charities and the publication by CRA of reasoned decisions relating to the grant or refusal of charitable status will help to create a necessary awareness of what it means to be charitable in Ireland. It is hoped that by the time of the mandatory five-year review of the Act's operation, we will be in a more informed position to begin the real challenge of modernising charity law in Ireland.

CONCLUSION: THE USE OF STATUTORY DEFINITIONS AS POLICY TOOLS

If Osborne and Gaebler[90] are right and the political economy works best when government sticks to 'steering' and stops trying to 'row', then the regulatory indicators would suggest that in reforming charity law governments should concentrate more on developing mechanisms for good oversight, monitoring and ensuring accountability of charities and less on channelling the direction of private benevolence. And yet, of all areas, the decision as to what is charity is essentially political. It is no mere coincidence that there is frequently a lien between the accordance of charitable status to a particular activity or purpose and a lightening of financial burden on the public purse.[91] The power to define 'charity' thus carries with it unavoidable fiscal implications, which colours the final definition chosen. As Lord Cross noted in his leading judgment in *Dingle v Turner*, nearly 40 years ago:

> It is, of course, unfortunate that the recognition of any trust as a valid charitable trust should automatically attract fiscal privileges, for the question whether a trust to further some purpose is so little likely to benefit the public that it ought to be declared invalid and the question whether it is likely to confer such great benefits on the public that it should enjoy fiscal immunity are really two quite different questions.[92]

In Ireland, the strong ties between charitable purpose and tax-exempt status have influenced the working definition of charity in the past. With the new Charities Act 2009, a legislative break in that link has occurred. Whether the separation of tax exemption from charitable status will be sufficient to liberate the concept of 'charitable purpose' remains to be seen.

NOTES

1. *Aid/Watch Incorporated v Commissioner of Taxes* [2008] AATA 652, per Downes P at paras 16–17.
2. See Fishman, J. (2005), 'Encouraging Charity in a Time of Crisis: The Poor Laws and the Statute of Charitable Uses of 1601', available at SSRN: http://ssrn.com/abstract=868394 (accessed 11 December 2009).
3. *Commissioners for Special Purposes of Income Tax v Pemsel* [1891] AC 531.
4. Agreed Programme for Government between Fianna Fáil and the Progressive Democrats, June 2002, available at http://www.taoiseach.gov.ie/attached_files/Pdf%20files/AgreedProgForGovernment.pdf (accessed 9 February 2009).
5. The recommendations of previous government-sponsored reviews of charity law, although welcomed, had not been implemented by a succession of governments. See Costello, Mr Justice D. (1990), *Report of the Committee on Fundraising Activities for Charitable and other Purposes*, Dublin: The Stationery Office; Department of Justice

(1996), *Report of the Advisory Group on Charities/Fundraising Legislation*, Dublin: The Stationery Office.

6. See further Ireland's Third Report to the Counter-Terrorism Committee established pursuant to paragraph 6 of resolution 1373 (2001), S/2003/816. In 2004, the Irish Minister of State for charity law reform confirmed that the UN Security Council's Counter-Terrorism Committee had requested Ireland to consider and update its charity legislation. See *Dáil Debates*, Vol. 589, Col 899 (Tuesday, 5 October 2004), Priority Questions: Charity Regulation. A similar request by the Counter-Terrorism Committee to the New Zealand government provided a catalyst for new charity legislation in that country too. See New Zealand Ministry of Foreign Affairs and Trade, *New Zealand Response to the United Nations Security Council Counter-Terrorism Committee, Questions for Response by 30 April 2004*, available at http://www.mfat.govt.nz/Foreign-Relations/1-Global-Issues/International-Security/0-NZ-UN-Counter-Terrorism-April-04.php (accessed 7 December 2009).

7. Law Society of Ireland (2002), *Charity Law: The Case for Reform*, Dublin: the Law Society.

8. Successful proposals include: the inclusion of prevention of poverty as well as relief; the inclusion of advancement of culture; the inclusion of advancement of health; new references to social inclusion and community welfare; the express inclusion of promotion of the natural environment; the continuation of a presumption of public benefit in respect of gifts to advance religion.

9. Ireland, Department of Community, Rural and Gaeltacht Affairs (2003), *Consultation Paper on Establishing a Modern Statutory Framework for Charities*, Dublin: The Stationery Office, chap 4 at 6.

10. Ibid, 7.

11. Australia, Inquiry into the Definition of Charities and Related Organisations (2001), *Report of the Inquiry into the Definition of Charities and Related Organisations*, Canberra: Treasury (CDI or CDI Report).

12. Breen, O.B. (2004), *Establishing a Modern Framework for Charities: Report on the Public Consultation for Department of Community, Rural and Gaeltacht Affairs*, Dublin.

13. 2006 Draft Bill, Head 3(1)(v).

14. *Commissioners for Special Purposes of Income Tax v Pemsel* [1891] AC 531 (HL).

15. On the issue of public benefit see 2009 Act, s. 3(2) ('A purpose shall not be a charitable purpose unless it is of public benefit'); s. 3(3) ('Subject to *subsection (4)*, a gift shall not be of public benefit unless – (a) it is intended to benefit the public or a section of the public, and (b) in a case where it confers a benefit on a person other than in his or her capacity as a member of the public or a section of the public, any such benefit is reasonable in all of the circumstances, and is ancillary to, and necessary, for the furtherance of the public benefit') and s. 3(7) ('In determining whether a gift is of public benefit or not, account shall be taken of – (a) any limitation imposed by the donor of the gift on the class of persons who may benefit from the gift and whether or not such limitation is justified and reasonable, having regard to the nature of the purpose of the gift, and (b) the amount of any charge payable for any service provided in furtherance of the purpose for which the gift is given and whether it is likely to limit the number of persons or classes of person who will benefit from the gift').

16. Charities Trustee and Investment (Scotland) Act 2005, s. 7 (the Scotland Act).

17. Charities Act (Northern Ireland) 2008, s. 2 (the NI Act).

18. Charities Act 2006, s. 2 (the Eng & Wales Act).

19. See the comments of Senator David Norris speaking during the Committee Stage of the Charities Bill 2007 to the effect that 'The Minister of State has fundamentally misunderstood the purpose and function of Seanad Éireann under the Constitution. We are here to amend and improve legislation, not maintain the status quo, which is an absurd position', *Seanad Debates*, Vol. 192 No. 12, p. 758 (4 December 2008).

20. Minister Curran addressing the Committee Stage hearings of the Charities Bill 2007 in Seanad Éireann to the effect that 'I have outlined that it was a policy decision to

reflect the practices. Revenue was consulted as to what the practices were. It is a policy decision to introduce this legislation to regulate charities. I know it is not what people want and they are looking to go somewhere else. That was not the policy decision. The decision was that we would reflect on what was happening', *Seanad Debates*, Vol. 192 No. 12, p. 760 (4 December 2008).

21. CDI Report, above n 11; Law Society of Ireland, above n 7.
22. *Re Segalman* [1996] Ch 171.
23. 2009 Act, s. 2 (providing that a body will not be charitable if it promotes a political cause, unless the promotion of that cause relates directly to the advancement of the charitable purposes of the body).
24. Ibid.
25. *Re Coulthurst* [1951] Ch 661.
26. See Eng & Wales Act, s. 2(2)(j) ('the relief of those in need by reason of youth, age, ill-health, disability, financial hardship or other disadvantage'); similar language is found in NI Act, s. 2(2)(j). See also Scotland Act, s. 7(2)(n) ('the relief of those in need by reason of age, ill-health, disability, financial hardship or other disadvantage').
27. Scotland Act, s. 7(3)(e); Eng & Wales Act, s. 2(3)(e); NI Act, s. 2(3)(f).
28. In 2001, Revenue figures revealed that 26% of organisations enjoying charitable tax-exempt status were registered under the advancement of education heading. See also *Dáil Debates*, 12 November 1997.
29. Some judicial authority does exist in the context of advancement of education. In *Re Worth Library* [1995] 2 IR 301, Keane J, as he then was, distinguished advancement of education from the broader concept of advancement of learning, arising under the fourth head of charity. In the words of Keane J, 'A gift for the advancement of scholarship or academic research, and thus for the advancement of learning, which might reasonably be regarded as for the public benefit, did not lose its charitable object merely because such scholarship or research was not combined with teaching or education'.
30. See Charity Commission for England and Wales (2008), *Charities and Public Benefit*, London: Charity Commission, available at http://www.charitycommission.gov.uk/publicbenefit/publicbenefit.asp (accessed 7 December 2009). See also Frean, A., N. Woolcock and R. Bennett (2008), 'Five independent schools face investigation by government's Charity Commission', *The Times*, London, 7 October.
31. Charities Act 1961, s. 45.
32. *O'Hanlon v Logue* [1906] 1 IR 247; *Maguire v Attorney General* [1943] IR 238 (HC).
33. Cf. the position of the Attorney General as residual *parens patriae* under neighbouring common law systems of England & Wales and Northern Ireland, respectively: ss 2C and 2D Charities Act 1993 (as inserted by s. 8 Charities Act 2006); s. 15 Charities Act (Northern Ireland) 2008.
34. See *Corway v Independent Newspapers (Ireland) Ltd* [1999] 4 IR 484 at 502 (SC), Barrington J commenting on the standing of the Muslim, Hindu and Jewish religions under Art. 44 of the Constitution, to the effect that Art. 44 'is an express recognition of the separate co-existence of the religious denominations, named and unnamed. It does not prefer one to the other and it does not confer any privilege or impose any disability or diminution of status upon any religious denomination, and it does not permit the State to do so'.
35. The evidence based on the registration of polytheistic religious organisations in Ireland is at best circumstantial since the Revenue Commissioners are not obliged to indicate the charitable heading under which a registered organisation is granted charitable tax-exempt status. Thus it is quite possible that some of the polytheistic religious groups listed may have charitable status based on advancement of education rather than advancement of religion. See further Breen, O.B. (2008), 'Neighbouring Perspectives: Legal and Practical Implications of Charity Regulatory Reform in Ireland and Northern Ireland', *Northern Ireland Legal Quarterly*, 59(2), 223–43 (Breen, 'Neighbouring Perspectives').
36. [1949] AC 426 (HL).

37. Minister Curran speaking in the Report Stage Debates of the Charities Bill 2007: *Seanad Debates* Vol. 192 No. 16, p. 1059.

38. The 12 categories of activities listed in s. 3(11) are similar, though not identical, to the heads of charity approved by the relevant statutes in Scotland, Northern Ireland, and England and Wales.

39. *Dáil Debates*, 12 November 1997, Minister for Finance, Mr Charlie McCreevy speaking during Private Members Business: Tax Relief on Charitable Donations: Motion (to the effect that 'The data on bodies granted exemption between 1992 and 1996, inclusive, show that 7% of the applications approved were for religious purposes, 12% were for poverty, 24% for educational purposes and 57% for purposes beneficial to the community. It is significant that most of the recently exempt bodies fall into the "beneficial to the community" category'). By 2001, these figures had changed only marginally with Revenue figures indicating that the relief of poverty accounted for 3% of new registrations, the advancement of education for 26%, the advancement of religion for 7% and other purposes beneficial to the community for 54%.

40. Eng & Wales Act, s. 2(4) provides, 'The purposes within this subsection [subsection (2)(m)] are – (a) any purposes not within paragraphs (a) to (l) of subsection (2) but recognised as charitable purposes under existing charity law or by virtue of section 1 of the Recreational Charities Act 1958 (c. 17); (b) any purposes that may reasonably be regarded as analogous to, or within the spirit of, any purposes falling within any of those paragraphs or paragraph (a) above; and (c) any purposes that may reasonably be regarded as analogous to, or within the spirit of, any purposes which have been recognised under charity law as falling within paragraph (b) above or this paragraph'.

41. 2009 Act, s. 6.

42. A role that the government vehemently eschewed during the debates on the Charities Bill.

43. On the public benefit requirements see ss 3(2), 3(7) and 3(8) Charities Act 2009.

44. In this regard, see Department of Community, Rural and Gaeltacht Affairs (2007), *Guidelines on the Governance of Integrated Local Development Companies and Urban Based Partnerships*, Dublin: The Stationery Office.

45. Taskforce on Active Citizenship (2007), *Report*, Dublin, available at http://www.activecitizenship.ie/index.asp (accessed February 2009).

46. Zappone, K. and M. Farrell (2009), 'Cutbacks in the area of human rights are excessive and unfair', *The Irish Times*, Dublin, 10 February.

47. *Lobe and Osayande v The Minister for Justice, Equality and Law Reform* [2003] IESC 3 (SC).

48. See now Irish Nationality and Citizenship Act 2004.

49. See the comments of the Chairwoman of the National Plan Against Racism, Lucy Gaffney, reported in Carbery, G. (2008), 'Winding up of integration groups makes policy weaker', *The Irish Times*, Dublin, 28 November. See also MacCormaic, R. (2009), 'Minister Says Efforts to Avoid Racial Discrimination Crucial in Time of Recession', *The Irish Times*, Dublin, 21 March.

50. Department of An Taoiseach (2006), *Towards 2016: Ten-Year Framework Social Partnership Agreement 2006–2015*, Dublin: The Stationery Office, paras 34.1 and 34.2.

51. See generally Centre for Voluntary Action Studies (2003), *Two Paths, One Purpose: Voluntary Action in Ireland, North and South: A Report to the Royal Irish Academy Third Sector Research Programme*, Dublin: CVAS.

52. See e.g. the listing of the Community Foundation for Ireland (http://www.foundation.ie), which was established in 2000 with the help of the Irish Government and the Irish business sector as a donor services and grant-making organisation, and Philanthropy Ireland (http://philanthropy.ie), established in 2004 with the objective 'to contribute to and inspire an effective and robust philanthropic sector in Ireland by promoting philanthropy, advocating for an encouraging environment for giving and providing an effective network and quality services to members and those with an interest in philanthropy'.

53. Which itself now has charitable tax-exempt status.
54. *Armstrong v Reeves* (1890) 25 LR Ir 325 (Ch D).
55. *Re Grove-Grady* [1929] 1 Ch 557 at 582. See also *National Anti-Vivisection Society v IRC* [1948] AC 31 at 45 (HL).
56. [1999] 1 SCR 10. The dissenting judges (L'Heureux-Dubé, Gonthier and McLachlin JJ) found that immigrants are often in special need of assistance in their efforts to integrate into their new home. The applicant provided assistance, guidance, and learning opportunities. It helped immigrants in developing and acquiring vocational skills, so that they might obtain employment. The dissenters held that an organisation, such as the applicant, which assisted immigrants through a difficult transition was directed towards a charitable purpose.
57. Kirby J in *Brodie v Singleton Shire Council* (2001) 206 CLR 512 at 602.
58. 2009 Act, s. 46, subject to a limited exception in s. 46(6) for foreign charities.
59. 2009 Act, s. 2(1).
60. See e.g. the English authority of *Inland Revenue Commissioners v McMullin* [1981] AC 31 (HL).
61. Breen, O.B. (2001), 'Taxing Considerations – Levelling the Playing Fields of Charity', *Conveyancing and Property Law Journal*, 6(4), 76–83.
62. 2009 Act, s. 2(1). The Charities Bill 2007: Report Stage, *Seanad Debates*, 11 December 2008, per Minister Curran, 'Sport is not regarded as a charitable purpose. Therefore [amateur sports bodies] cannot become charitable organisations. I do not believe that considering the inclusion of sporting bodies as charities on the principled basis that a particular advantage might accrue to them under the taxation system is a sound approach. Revenue will still retain the absolute right to make its own determination on eligibility for tax exemptions for any body on or not on the register of charities. Therefore, I cannot accept the Opposition amendments before the House on this matter as they are directly contrary to the intent of the Bill and they also involve amendments to tax law, which is not within my remit'.
63. A similar problem exists in England and Wales under the Charities Act 2006 in relation to community amateur sports clubs, which under the Finance Act 2002 were given favourable tax treatment if they met certain requirements and registered with Her Majesty's Revenue and Customs (HMRC). According to Lloyd, it was feared that the introduction of the promotion of amateur sport as charitable in its own right would result in such community clubs being forced to register as charities: Lloyd, S. (2007), *Charities: The New Law 2006, A Practical Guide to the Charities Acts*, Bristol: Jordans, 29. Hence ss 5(4) and (5) of the Eng & Wales Act expressly exclude such bodies from being charitable, whether they wish to or not.
64. 2009 Act, s. 40.
65. See e.g. Cooneal Resource & Sports Centre Limited (CHY 17186), Irish Adventure Sports Training Trust (CHY 133324) and Sligo Regional Sports Centre Limited (CHY 8477) aside from the many educationally related sports charities such as Cork County Primary School Sports (CHY 8216) and Irish Blind Sports Ltd (CHY 10793). Source: Revenue List of 7,438 bodies who have been granted charitable tax exemption at 27th January 2009 under Taxes Consolidation Act 1997, s. 207.
66. See Taxes Consolidation Act 1997, s. 235, which allows approved sporting bodies to obtain tax relief on money spent on capital projects. However, one cannot claim tax back for example for hiring instructors or coaches.
67. *Clancy v Commissioner of Valuation* [1911] 2 IR 173 (KB Div) (holding that a hall used to promote temperance among the poor and labouring classes by providing recreational activities ranging from billiards and card games to taking baths had the primary charitable purpose of the moral and educational improvement of its users but finding the trust not exclusively charitable on other unrelated grounds).
68. [1952] Ch 534 (Roxburgh J holding that a trust for 'the establishment, maintenance and improvement of good understanding, sympathy and co-operation between nations, especially the nations of the English speaking world and also between

different sections of people in any nation or community' was non-charitable and void for uncertainty).

69. 2009 Act, s. 40.

70. Politicians received petitions from many human rights organisations, including Amnesty International, Free Legal Advice Centres, Trocaire, Human Rights Watch, Frontline, and the Irish Council for Civil Liberties in addition to the Law Society of Ireland's Human Rights Committee.

71. See Breen, 'Neighbouring perspectives', above n 35.

72. See in particular the contributions of Senators David Norris and Ivana Bacik at the Report Stage of the Bill, *Seanad Debates*, 11 December 2008, and the contribution of Deputies Wall and Costello, *Dail Debates*, Vol. 674 No. 2, 11 February 2009.

73. *McGovern v Attorney General* [1982] Ch 321, applying *Bowman v Secular Society Ltd* [1917] AC 406 (HL) and *National Anti-Vivisection Society v Inland Revenue Commissioners* [1948] AC 31 (HL).

74. See e.g. *Bowman v Secular Society* [1917] AC 406 (CA); *National Anti-Vivisection Society v Inland Revenue Commissioners* [1948] AC 31 (HL); *McGovern v Attorney General* [1982] Ch 321 (Ch D) applied in *Wolf Trust's Application for Registration as a Charity* [2006] WTLR 1467 (CCEW).

75. *McGovern v Attorney General* [1982] Ch 321 (Ch D); *Webb v O'Doherty* (1991) 3 Admin LR 731 (Ch D); *Southwood v Attorney General* (2000) 80 P&CR D34 (CA). In Ireland see *Re Ni Brudair* (unreported High Court, Gannon J, 5 February 1979). Cf. *Public Trustee v Attorney General (NSW) and Ors* (NSW Supreme Court, 30 September 1997) (Santow J noting that 'if persuasion towards legislative change were never permissible, this would severely undermine the efforts of those trusts devoted to charitable ends that ultimately depend on legislative change for their effective achievement').

76. See Lord Parker in *Bowman v Secular Society* [1917] AC 406 at 442: 'a trust for the attainment of political objects has always been held invalid, not because it is illegal, for everyone is at liberty to advocate or promote by any lawful means a change in the law, but because the court has no means of judging whether a proposed change in the law will or will not be for the public benefit, and therefore cannot say that a gift to secure the change is a charitable gift'.

77. See Charity Commission for England and Wales (2005), *RR12 – The Promotion of Human Rights*, London: Charity Commission.

78. The Charity Commission for England and Wales (2008), *CC9 – Speaking Out: Guidance on Campaigning and Political Activity by Charities*, London: Charity Commission, available at http://www.charitycommission.gov.uk/publications/cc9.asp (accessed 7 December 2009). This updated Guidance followed a 2007 revision in which CCEW stated that: 'We are aware from our work with charities that trustees sometimes exercise a considerable degree of self-censorship in undertaking campaigns, and may not be aware of the extent to which they can campaign and engage in political activities to achieve their objectives. We want charities to be in no doubt about this point'. The more flexible approach adopted by the CCEW in interpreting the limits on charitable political engagement has been acknowledged by the charities sector: see Advisory Group on Campaigning and the Voluntary Sector (UK) (2007), *Report*, London: the Advisory Group, at para 2.3, available at http://peopleandplanet.org/dl/campaigninglaw1.pdf (accessed 4 December 2009).

79. *Re Ni Brudair* (unreported High Court, Gannon J, 5 February 1979) (holding that a bequest for the benefit of republicans was too vague to be charitable but that had it been properly defined it would still have amounted to a broad statement of political objectives and would not have constituted a valid charitable trust); see also *Gurhy v Goff* [1980] ILRM 103 (SC) (holding that a lottery to benefit members of a political party was purely self-promotion and did not fall within the meaning of charitable or philanthropic purposes as defined by the Gaming and Lotteries Act, 1956).

80. Revenue Commissioners (2001), *Charities Manual*, Dublin, at 62–3, in which Revenue cites a number of authorities (*National Anti-Vivisection Society v Inland Revenue*

Commissioners [1948] AC 31; *Temperance Council of the Christian Churches of England and Wales v CIR*, KB 1926, 10 TC 748; *Bonar Law Memorial Trust v CIR* (1933) 49 TLR 220; *Keren Kayemeth Le Jisroel Ltd v CIR* [1932] AC 650 (HL) and *McGovern v Attorney General* [1982] Ch 321) to the effect that an organisation with political aims such as law reform or which engages in lobbying will not qualify for charitable status.

81. The *Charities Manual 2001*, above n 80, at 63, noting that in APP 12317 exemption was refused as the main objects of the body included political activities and that in APP 6837 the objects involved changing legislation such that tax-exempt status was also refused.

82. [2000] 2 IR 490 at 504 (HC) per O'Sullivan J.

83. See Breen, 'Neighbouring Perspectives', above n 35.

84. Power for the CRA to enter into such understandings is provided in s. 33 of the 2009 Act. Cf. Memorandum of Understanding between the Office of the Scottish Charity Regulator and HM Revenue & Customs (Charities) (2006).

85. See e.g. *In re Worth Library* [1995] 2 IR 301, one of the few decisions handed down since 1961 that touches on the meaning and scope of 'charitable purpose'. It is noteworthy that Counsel on both sides were willing to concede that the bequest at issue was charitable and it was only upon the court's insistence that this matter was argued.

86. See Delany, H. (2006), *Equity and the Law of Trusts in Ireland*, 4th edn, Dublin: Roundhall Sweet & Maxwell, chapter 10; Keane, R. (1988), *Equity and Trusts in the Republic of Ireland*, Dublin: Butterworths; O'Halloran, K. (2000), *Charity Law in Ireland*, Dublin: Roundhall Sweet & Maxwell.

87. See 'List of bodies who have been granted charitable tax exemption . . . under Section 207, Taxes Consolidation Act 1997', available at http://www.revenue.ie/en/index. html (accessed 11 December 2009). Publication of the names of charitable tax-exempt organisations only came about in 1999 as a result of a successful application under the Freedom of Information Act 1997. See Office of the Information Commissioner (Ireland) (1999), Case 98042: Mr John Burns of The Sunday Times newspaper and the Office of the Revenue Commissioners, *Annual Report of the Information Commissioner*, Dublin, p. 33.

88. 2009 Act, s. 3(11)(i).

89. 2009 Act, s. 3(11)(g) and (h) and s. 3(1)(a).

90. Osborne, D and T. Gaebler (1992), *Reinventing Government: How the Entrepreneurial Spirit is Transforming the Public Sector*, New York: Penguin Press.

91. See Dunn, A. (2000), 'As Cold as Charity? Poverty, Equity and the Charitable Trust', *Legal Studies* 20(2), 222–40, viewing the particular charitable purposes identified in the Statute of Charitable Uses 1601 as comprehensible more as a pragmatic attempt to reduce the financial burdens imposed on the community than necessarily a list of altruistic or philanthropic ideals.

92. [1972] AC 601 at 624 (HL).

PART II

Boundaries

4. Public benefit: the long and winding road to reforming the public benefit test for charity: a worthwhile trip or 'Is your journey really necessary?'[1]

Debra Morris

INTRODUCTION

Public benefit has always been an essential element in charities. It is this factor that distinguishes charitable trusts from private trusts, and it is the public benefit that is often said to justify the advantageous taxation treatment afforded to charities.[2] In England and Wales,[3] for example, the Charity Commission describes it as a kind of covenant that charities have with society: charities bring public benefit and, in their turn, are accorded high levels of trust and confidence and the considerable benefits of charitable status.[4] As well as significant tax advantages and certain legal privileges, charities can access funds which others – even other voluntary organisations – cannot; volunteers and donors give, respectively, time and money.

The English common law tradition has provided no statutory definition of charity. The starting point was the Preamble to the Statute of Charitable Uses 1601 (known as the Statute of Elizabeth). Though it has been repealed,[5] it has remained of significance throughout the common law world. The Preamble set out the most typical charitable purposes of the time, ranging from the 'relief of the aged, impotent and poor people' to the 'education and preferment of orphans' and it has formed the basis for modern judicial pronouncements on how to establish a charitable purpose. The courts and, in England, the Charity Commission, have been much influenced by Lord Macnaghten's attempt to distill the spirit of the Preamble by formulating it into clear guidance. In *Commissioners for Special Purposes of Income Tax v Pemsel*,[6] His Lordship said:

> charity in its legal sense comprises four principal divisions: trusts for the relief of poverty; trusts for the advancement of education; trusts for the advancement

of religion; and trusts for other purposes beneficial to the community not falling under any of the preceding heads.

Lord Macnaghten's four categories (known as the 'four heads of charity') have acquired considerable persuasive status. To be charitable, the purpose had to fall under one of these headings, it had to have an element of public benefit, and it had to be exclusively charitable. Previously, there was a presumption that purposes within the first three heads of charity were for the public benefit.[7] The effect of the presumption was that, when the charitable status of an organisation established for the relief of poverty, the advancement of education, or the advancement of religion was being considered, the organisation's purpose was presumed to be for the public benefit, unless there was evidence that it was not. By contrast, organisations established for all other purposes, which did not benefit from that presumption, were required, at the time that their status was being considered, to provide evidence that their purpose was for the public benefit.

In England, the Charities Act 2006 now provides a statutory definition of charity for the first time and what might[8] be regarded as a positive requirement for all charities to prove public benefit. Other countries in the common law world have also begun to enshrine the public benefit requirement within legislation, including Barbados,[9] Scotland,[10] New Zealand,[11] Northern Ireland[12] and Ireland.[13] By reference to the English experience of the long and ongoing process towards statutory reform, the challenges presented will now be considered.

Background to the English Charities Act 2006

In recognition of the diversity of the charitable sector and of the public interest in the law in this area, the English experience (which has been mirrored in other jurisdictions) is marked by a significant degree of public consultation at every stage of the review process. Following on from the report of the Deakin Commission,[14] which called, inter alia, for reform of charity law, the then Prime Minister, Tony Blair, commissioned a review of the legal and regulatory framework for charities and other not-for-profit organisations in England and Wales in July 2001, with a view to making proposals for reform.[15] The Prime Minister's Strategy Unit published a consultation document on charity law reform in September 2002,[16] which proposed wide-ranging changes in the law and regulation of the charitable and wider not-for-profit sector.[17] Following public consultation, the Government published its response in July 2003, with support for most of the Strategy Unit's main proposals.[18] The Charities

Bill was first published in draft in May 2004 for pre-legislative scrutiny by a Joint Committee of both Houses of Parliament, which published its report in September 2004.[19] The Government's response to that report was published in December 2004[20] alongside the Bill itself. The Bill eventually completed its passage through the House of Lords in November 2005 after more than 60 hours of scrutiny by Peers, and through the House of Commons in October 2006. It finally received royal assent on 8 November 2006. The Charities Act 2006 is being brought into force in stages and the provisions on the new definition of charity and the public benefit require- ment were brought into force in April 2008.[21]

Definition of Charity under the Charities Act 2006

For the first time, under the Charities Act 2006, 'charity' has a statu- tory definition. Charitable status is subjected to a two-stage test. To be considered charitable, under section 2 of the Act, an organisation must demonstrate that its purposes, as set out in its constitution, fall within one or more of those in the new list of 12 charitable purposes, and also that it is established for the public benefit.[22] In general terms, the list in section 2(2) covers all purposes which have, over the years, become recognised as charitable purposes, but none brings with it a presumption that public benefit is automatically provided. Whilst it is, therefore, a vital second step for all charities to prove the existence of public benefit, the key issue of defining public benefit is side-stepped[23] under the Charities Act 2006. The Government has decided that the current non-statutory approach will remain, giving flexibility and the capacity to accommodate the diver- sity of the sector.[24] Public benefit will be determined, case by case, by the Charity Commission on the basis of the law as it is.[25] Unfortunately, due to the fact that there has always been a presumption of public benefit in favour of particular charitable purposes in the past, the law as it relates to public benefit is not well developed in the case law. Another problem with the case law, which Warburton notes,[26] is that, due to the age of many of the cases, they tend to be decisions restricted very much to facts of the particular case.[27]

Throughout the parliamentary debates on the Charities Act 2006, the public benefit test was one of the most controversial issues, with much of the inquiry endeavouring to establish what the consequences of the proposed changes would be. Much has been made of the lack of clarity surrounding the new public benefit requirement. Some seek to rely on the new requirement as a way of doing away with the more controversial fee-charging charities, such as schools. Others argue that the new public benefit test will have little impact in this area. Even at the draft Charities

Bill stage, the Joint Parliamentary Committee[28] was concerned that the Home Office and the Charity Commission disagreed as to the extent to which the new provisions would impact on the existing charitable status of fee-charging bodies. The Commission appeared (initially) to be suggesting that there would be little change,[29] while the Home Office was of the view that the Act would have a real impact, with some schools, for example, losing their charitable status. The Joint Committee accepted that including a definition of public benefit in the Charities Act 2006 would stifle development of the law and perhaps lead to uncertainty. It noted that the Home Office and the Charity Commission had agreed a concordat as to how public benefit would be tested. The Joint Committee felt that the principles in the concordat could be set out either as non-exclusive criteria of public benefit in the Act, or in non-binding statutory guidance issued by the Secretary of State.[30] The Government accepted that guidance as to the operation of the public benefit requirement should be issued, but maintained that it should be published by the Charity Commission rather than the Secretary of State, in order to emphasise the independence of the Commission from Government.[31]

THE PUBLIC BENEFIT REQUIREMENT – WHAT DOES IT MEAN?

Before turning to consider the Charity Commission's new statutory role in relation to the public benefit test, and the guidance that the Commission has produced, a brief examination of the public benefit requirement, as it has been applied through the case law, will be undertaken.

There have always been two essential elements of the public benefit requirement: first, the pursuit of an organisation's purposes must be capable of producing a benefit which can be demonstrated and which is recognised by law as beneficial;[32] and, secondly, that benefit is provided for, or available to, the public or a sufficient section of the public.[33] In addition, there should be no undue private benefit.

Benefit

Whilst every charity must confer benefit on the public, the law does not adopt the same practical measures to assess public benefit in every type of case. Despite the fact that the Explanatory Notes to the Charities Act 2006 state that section 3(2) abolishes the presumption of public benefit, 'putting all charitable purposes on the same footing',[34] section 3(3) makes it clear that the term 'public benefit', wherever it occurs in sections 1 to 3, refers to the existing concept in charity law in England. That concept was explained by Lord Simonds when he said:[35]

> it would not be surprising to find that, while in every category of legal charity some element of public benefit must be present, the courts . . . have accepted one standard in regard to those gifts which are alleged to be for the advancement of education and another for those which are alleged to be for the advancement of religion and it may be yet another in regard to the relief of poverty.

This means that the ways in which benefit can be demonstrated can differ for different charitable purposes.

The benefit to the public should be capable of being proven, whether the nature of that benefit is tangible or intangible.[36] If the benefit is not immediately obvious, it will need to be demonstrated. This is a question to be determined objectively by the court, not by the founder of the alleged charity or the donor.[37] Most charitable purposes will involve direct benefits. However, indirect benefits, extending beyond the immediate beneficiaries, in many cases to the public generally, may also be taken into account in assessing whether an organisation provides sufficient benefit to the public.[38] Interestingly, whilst the accompanying legal analysis paper acknowledges the fact that benefit may be direct or indirect,[39] the final Charity Commission guidance on public benefit[40] does not refer to indirect benefit.[41]

Public

Every charity must provide a benefit which is available to either the public as a whole or a sufficient section of the public.[42] Relatively few charities provide universal public benefit – that is, most charities have a limited number of beneficiaries. What is 'sufficient' will vary from case to case depending upon the organisation's purposes as well as its activities. The courts have looked at what a sufficient section of the public is on a number of occasions. It is not merely a question of the size of the group, but of whether the group constitutes a recognisable section of the community. The courts focus on the connecting link (or common quality) which unites the people intended to benefit. If the connecting link is impersonal, the class or group may be a section of the public. But, if the connecting link is a personal one, often described as a 'personal nexus',[43] the trust will be private and not charitable. Where beneficiaries are determined only by reference to a personal relationship, family tie or contract with an individual(s) or company, these have been held to be essentially personal connections. For example, the gift in *Oppenheim v Tobacco Securities Trust Co Ltd*[44] was held to lack public benefit even though the potential beneficiaries – children of employees of a certain company – exceeded 110 000. Lord Simonds said:[45]

> These words 'section of the community' have no special sanctity, but they conveniently indicate
> (i) that the possible (I emphasize the word 'possible') beneficiaries must not be numerically negligible, and
> (ii) that the quality which distinguishes them from other members of the community, so that they form by themselves a section of it, must be a quality which does not depend on their relationship to a particular individual.

Whilst width of class will therefore not necessarily validate a charitable trust, the opposite is also true. In some cases, it might be possible to show that a benefit to a small section of the public benefits the public as a whole. The Charity Commission gives the example of an organisation directed towards relieving the suffering caused by a very rare disease.[46] Alternatively, a charity may offer benefit to all members of a specific ethnic group in a particular location, but the actual number of people who may benefit might be very small. This will provide benefit to the public and is open to the public even though few people need to avail themselves of its services. If a charity's benefits are potentially available to anyone who, falling within the (acceptable) criteria, chooses to take advantage of them, it can be considered to provide benefit to the public, even though in some cases the actual number of beneficiaries may be quite small.

In its public benefit guidance,[47] the Charity Commission adds a further requirement, which is that there must be a rational link between any restriction on who can benefit and the charitable purpose to be carried out.[48] This does not appear to be supported by the existing case law.[49] Gifts for the relief of poverty are considered to be anomalous in that the requirement of public benefit, which is vital when determining charitable status in the other three traditional heads of charity, is not applied in the same way in this category.[50] Another way of looking at it might be to accept that all relief of poverty is for the public benefit.[51] Nevertheless, however it is regarded, the cases show that the relief of poverty of a very limited class of beneficiaries, who may even be connected by some private or personal link, may be charitable.[52] The Charity Commission is not disputing that this exception remains valid,[53] thereby acknowledging (indirectly) that the law on public benefit has not changed.[54]

In some cases, access to the benefits of a charitable organisation are restricted to people who can afford to pay for them. The fact that the charitable facilities or services will be charged for, and will be provided mainly to people who can afford to pay the charges, does not necessarily mean that the organisation does not have aims that are for the public benefit.[55] It has always been accepted that charities may charge for the services they provide. If this were not the case, charitable status would be severely limited to those organisations that were sufficiently well endowed that they could provide their services free. As Sachs LJ said in *Incorporated Council of Law Reporting for England and Wales v AG*:[56]

> [I]t is clear that the mere fact that charges on a commercial scale are made for services rendered by an institution does not itself bar that institution from being held to be charitable – so long, at any rate, as all the profits must be retained for its purposes and none can enure to the benefit of its individual members.

Re Resch[57] is a Privy Council case from New South Wales, Australia, concerning a gift to a private hospital which charged fees. The hospital was established to relieve demand for admission to an adjacent public hospital by providing medical and nursing care for which there was a need. It was open to contributors under medical benefit schemes and was not conducted for profit. The Privy Council confirmed the principle that charges could be raised by a charity for the services that it provides, even if the charges produce a profit. Further, in *Joseph Rowntree Memorial Trust Housing Association Limited v AG*[58] it was held that a charity's beneficiaries could be required to pay, and that, provided that they fell within the beneficiary class,[59] their economic circumstances did not have to be modest. Relief of need in the field of charity is not limited to the relief of the poor. The elderly have needs which require relief by the provision of sheltered housing, and it would be no objection to a trust designed to meet that need that some residents would pay for their benefits because what they needed was the physical amenity, not an economic subsidy. In certain circumstances, persons may be in need of assistance in an area where charity law recognises the need for relief, but relief in exchange for payment may be the appropriate manner in which to provide that relief.

Dicta in *Re Resch* confirm that an organisation which wholly excluded 'the poor' from any benefits, direct or indirect, would not be for the benefit of the public and therefore would not be a charity.[60] Applying this approach in cases where high fees are charged for services or facilities provided, the Charity Commission has stated that if the level at which fees are set has the effect of excluding 'people in poverty'[61] from the opportunity to benefit, there will be no public benefit.[62] There are objections to this principle. For example, it has been suggested that it would be more accurate to state that people in poverty must not be expressly excluded from benefit.[63]

Any Private Benefit Must be Incidental

Whilst charity law is strict in requiring a public benefit in order for a purpose to be charitable, the converse proposition may also be relevant. Any private benefit derived from a 'charitable' purpose may detract from its charitable nature. Difficulty arises when the pursuit of a charitable purpose has the result that people who are not beneficiaries happen to reap some benefits. In order for a private benefit to be countenanced, it must be shown to be an incidental consequence of the pursuit of a public benefit. For example, in *Incorporated Council of Law Reporting for England and Wales v AG*,[64] the fact that publication of law reports supplies lawyers with tools of their trade did not destroy the charitable basis of the exercise. Buckley LJ commented that the private advantage was 'incidental to or consequential on the primary scholastic function of advancing and disseminating knowledge of the law, and [did] not detract from the exclusively charitable character of the council's objects'.[65]

In general, an acceptable private benefit is a necessary result, or by-product, of carrying out a charity's aims if it follows from some action that is taken, and is only taken, with the intention of furthering the charity's aims.[66] In addition, the amount of private benefit should be reasonable in the circumstances.[67] In the words of Rowlatt J,[68] 'the question which emerges in all these cases is: Is there so much personal benefit . . . as to be incapable of being disregarded? . . . It is a question of degree and a question of fact'.

THE ROLE OF THE CHARITY COMMISSION IN RELATION TO THE PUBLIC BENEFIT REQUIREMENT

The Charity Commission Guidance

Under the Charities Act 2006, one of the Charity Commission's statutory objectives is to promote awareness and understanding of the public benefit requirement,[69] and how it will test this.[70] It is required to consult with the public and others before issuing or revising any related guidance and to publish this guidance once agreed. Following a four-month public consultation on draft guidance,[71] which generated nearly 1000 responses, in January 2008, the Commission published its general guidance on public benefit – over 19 000 words that try to describe what public benefit is and what charity trustees should consider in order to show that their charity's aims are for the public benefit.[72] Following publication of this general guidance, the Commission launched a series of consultations on draft sup-plementary sub-sectoral guidance[73] on the public benefit of those charities most directly affected by the changes in the Act – that is, charities estab-lished for the prevention and relief of poverty, the advancement of educa-tion, the advancement of religion and also fee-charging charities, which were highlighted during debates on the Charities Bill. Finalised versions of these guidelines were published in December 2008.[74]

Under the Charities Act 2006,[75] charity trustees must have regard to the public benefit guidance when exercising any powers or duties where the guidance may be relevant. They also have a new duty to report in their Trustees' Annual Report on how they are carrying out their charity's aims for the public benefit.[76] The Annual Report will also include a statement by the charity trustees as to whether they have complied with the duty in section 4 to have due regard to public benefit guidance.

It is important to note that the Charity Commission's guidance should reflect the common law, as amended by the Charities Act 2006. It should not change the law in any other way, nor re-interpret the existing case law on public benefit, which can only be tested further by the courts or otherwise changed by further legislation. It should be remembered that section 3(3) states that 'any reference to the public benefit is a reference to the public benefit as that term is understood for the purposes of the law relating to charities in England and Wales'. This would suggest that there is no change to the public benefit test and therefore the common law, as identified through the case law, should still apply. Nevertheless, there are a number of areas of controversy which have arisen due to the Charity Commission's approach to its statutory obligations relating to public benefit.[77]

Focus on Activities

The Charity Commission has placed great emphasis in its various public benefit guidance documents on examination of a charity's activities (as opposed to its objects) when it comes to satisfying the public benefit requirement.[78] Many charity lawyers have objected to this requirement for charities to prove public benefit through their activities (as opposed to their objects), arguing that it is not in line with the existing case law on public benefit, which does not support an activities test.[79] This is the view, for example, of the Charity Law Association – an association of around 900 members, made up largely of lawyers but also of accountants and other professionals (including charity representatives) all of whom are concerned with advising in the area of charity law.[80] Whilst all would accept that it is correct for the Charity Commission to monitor activities in order to ensure trustees' compliance with their trusts, the case law (and the Charities Act 2006 itself[81]) does support the view that it is an organisation's purposes which must be for the public benefit:[82]

> Actual or proposed activities can indicate ways in which the purposes might be furthered. However, if an organisation's actual activities do not offer public benefit but the objects do, then the problem is that the activities are not furthering the objects, not that the objects themselves do not benefit the public.

It is interesting to note, by comparison, that the Scottish legislation (which is discussed below) states that 'a body meets the charity test if (a) its purposes consist only of one or more of the charitable purposes, and (b) it provides (or, in the case of an applicant, provides or intends to provide) public benefit in Scotland or elsewhere'.[83] The reference to the requirement for the provision of public benefit clearly makes a charity's activities its yardstick to measure the required public benefit: 'In Scotland, public benefit is assessed on the basis of how a body exercises its functions; in England and Wales, the issue is whether a particular charitable purpose is for the public benefit'.[84]

The Difficulty of Removing the Presumption of Public Benefit – the Disputed Effect of Section 3(2) of the Charities Act 2006

The wording of section 3(2) is as follows: 'It is not to be presumed that a purpose of a particular description is for the public benefit'. It is uncertain what effect these words have upon the law of public benefit. In its guidance documents, the Charity Commission makes clear that its view of these words is that every organisation entered in the Register of Charities will need to show positively that it is set up and operates for the public benefit. For example, churches and schools seeking the benefits of charitable status will have to demonstrate that they provide a public benefit. This would change the previous law, where a (selective) presumption of public benefit operated. However, it is not so clear cut. There are some who argue that the section effects no change at all to the substantive law on the definition of a charitable purpose: if a purpose is within one of the 12 'descriptions of purposes' enumerated within section 2(2) of the Charities Act 2006, then there is no need to prove public benefit as the section makes it clear that these purposes are charitable and of public benefit.[85] This was the case before under the first three heads of *Pemsel*, which required no proof of public benefit; the purposes were simply accepted as beneficial. This had also become the case, before the Charities Act 2006, in relation to other purposes that had been recognised as charitable since *Pemsel* under the fourth head.[86] The only issue will be to determine whether a particular purpose does in fact, for example, advance education and then whether it does so to a sufficient section of the public to give it the required public character. This question will be determined by the evidence. In the words of Hackney, for example:[87]

> there is no need to prove benefit in any different way after the coming into force of the Act than was true before: proving it falls within one of the first twelve categories will do it. It will indeed be bizarre if it is held that a disposition simply to give effect to one of the new statutory purposes, without more, is not beneficial.

Luxton reflects the same view when he says:[88]

> It therefore makes no sense to require trusts in the first three heads (or after the Charities Act 2006, any purposes listed in paragraphs (a) to (l)) [of section 2(2) of the Charities Act 2006] to show that their purposes are for the public benefit – they must necessarily be so.

The contrary view is expressed by Warburton, who, perhaps optimistically, suggests that 'common sense indicates that the present confused state of the law in relation to public benefit cannot be allowed to continue'.[89]

Nevertheless, it cannot be overlooked that section 3(3) states that 'any reference to the public benefit is a reference to the public benefit as that term is understood for the purposes of the law relating to charities in England and Wales'. 'The law relating to charities' could be said to be that the purposes now laid down in section 2(2) are charitable purposes, without the need for any consideration of public benefit, so presumption or lack thereof is irrelevant. The established charitable purposes are not neutral and necessarily contain public benefit. This is not the view that the Charity Commission is now taking of the public benefit requirement.[90] So the question arises as to what charities can do to challenge the Commission's approach to public benefit questions.

Challenging the Charity Commission's Decisions in Relation to an Organisation's Public Benefit

If a charity's trustees, or a person applying to register an organisation as a charity, or other person who is affected, disagree with a Charity Commission decision about an organisation's public benefit, there is an internal decision review process to be followed. If this process fails to bring satisfaction, an appeal may be brought to the newly established Charity Tribunal.[91] The Tribunal's role is to make judgments about the legality of the Commission's actions in exercising its statutory powers to regulate charities. The Charities Act 1993, as amended,[92] provides for specified rights of appeal to the Tribunal against specified decisions, directions or orders of the Charity Commission, prescribing, in the case of each specified decision, which persons have the right of appeal (in addition to the Attorney General, who may always appeal[93]) and what powers the Tribunal has in relation to the appeal or to the Commission's decision or action which is the subject of the appeal.[94] The Charity Commission is the respondent to such an appeal.[95] For example, the decision of the Commission to register an institution (or not) or to remove an institution from the Register (or not)[96] is subject to appeal to the Tribunal. The persons who can bring the appeal are: the persons who are or claim to be the charity trustees of the institution; (if a body corporate) the institution itself; and any other person who is or may be affected by the decision. The Tribunal has the power to quash the decision and (if appropriate) remit the matter to the Commission and direct the Commission to rectify the Register.

In determining such an appeal, the Tribunal shall consider afresh the decision, direction or order appealed against, and may take into account evidence which was not available to the Charity Commission.[97] The Tribunal can only award costs in limited circumstances[98] and it cannot award compensation. Appeals from the First-tier Tribunal are to the Upper Tribunal on points of law only.[99] If an institution is denied registration as a charity on the grounds of lack of public benefit, applying the principles in the Charity Commission guidance, the institution could use the Tribunal to challenge the decision.

Challenging the Guidance Itself

Schedule 1D of the Charities Act 1993 makes provision for references to be made to the Tribunal without a decision first having been made. This procedure is very different from the usual function carried out by most tribunals, in that the Tribunal is not being asked to reconsider a decision made by one party in relation to another party appearing before it. Rather, the Tribunal is being asked to consider a question relating to charity law. Such a reference is made before the Charity Commission has made any decision on the matter and allows the Tribunal to consider wider questions to help to clarify or to develop charity law.

The Charity Commission[100] (with the consent of the Attorney General) or the Attorney General[101] may refer to the Tribunal a question which has arisen in connection with the exercise of any of its functions and which involves either the operation of charity law[102] in any respect or its application to a particular state of affairs.[103] Both the Commission and the

Attorney General shall be parties to the proceedings. The following may also be parties with the Tribunal's permission: the charity trustees of any charity which is likely to be affected by the Tribunal's decision on the reference; any such charity which is a body corporate; and any other person who is likely to be so affected.[104]

Having the ability to make references to the Tribunal will provide the Charity Commission with a way to deal with test cases and should help to provide clarity about the operation of charity law. A proposal to initiate a reference from the Commission must be agreed by the Board[105] because any reference could have an important impact on the development of charity law.[106] The specific provisions regarding the Attorney General's powers in relation to references were introduced after concerns about access to justice and lack of public funding were repeatedly raised in evidence before the Joint Committee scrutinising the Charities Bill. Much is therefore expected of the possibility to ask the Attorney General – the protector of charities – to make a reference to the Tribunal. This possibility may provide a means of achieving justice in cases raising issues of principle, where a charity may not have the means to fund litigation, or may not want to be seen to be spending donated funds on litigation, or may not wish to be in the public eye in court as a matter of policy.

An opportunity to test the legality of the public benefit guidance could well be provided by a referral to the Tribunal by the Attorney General. Rather than dealing with the principles in a particular case, the Tribunal will be able to review the guidance generically, allowing individual charities to become parties to the reference as intervener if appropriate. The Charity Commission itself has now acknowledged that a challenge to the legality of its assessments of charities' public benefit (based on the guidance) might need to be tested in the Tribunal[107] and it is suggested that the best way for this to happen would be by way of a reference. In this way, the Tribunal will help to develop charity law. Lack of resources have hitherto led to there being limited litigation in the charity sphere (unlike in the commercial sector, for example, where well-resourced parties can fight to the end). It is hoped that charities that feel the public benefit guidance is unnecessarily limiting their activities will be able to petition the Attorney General with a view to developing the law through a Tribunal reference. This will speed up the creation of case law that will assist with the provision of legal certainty for charities. The more pessimistic view is that charities that find their activities under scrutiny, possibly as a result of falling foul of the public benefit guidance, might take the line of least resistance and choose to fall in line, rather than seek to challenge the guidance.[108] This tactic could have the unfortunate effect of stifling rather than encouraging charitable activity and innovation.

OTHER APPROACHES

It has been seen that the new statutory definition of charity has set up a
requirement – 'the public benefit requirement' – that must be met if an
organisation is to be recognised as a charity. Yet it has also been seen that
defining what public benefit means is to be left to be determined by reference to Charity Commission guidelines, reflecting the existing case law.
There are some valid arguments for keeping the 'case law' methodology
and allowing the guidelines on public benefit to continue to develop in the
light of modern social and economic conditions. This approach will ensure
that the law is flexible enough to evolve over time and to encompass the
diverse range of existing and future purposes that benefit the public in
some way. Some argue that a rigid statutory definition of public benefit
will inhibit future growth.[109] One of the characteristics of charitable status
has always been its ability to develop over the years and to adapt in order
to recognise new methods of achieving public benefit. To replace this flexible notion with a defined concept may hamper the law's development
in this area. The complexity of what constitutes public benefit may only
make any attempted definition confusing, and a more subtle qualitative
(rather than crude quantitative) assessment is indeed called for.

However, it has been seen that there are problems with the current
Charity Commission guidelines on public benefit, which could take some
time to resolve. One solution might have been to consider a statutory definition of public benefit. A number of attempts were made to include such
a definition during the passage of the Charities Bill through Parliament
and the National Council for Voluntary Organisations (NCVO)[110] was
ultimately[111] clearly in favour of strengthening the test.[112] Nevertheless, the
Government stood firm against all calls to clarify or strengthen the test.[113]
Interestingly, the Charities and Trustee Investment (Scotland) Act 2005,
which was preceded by a Scottish review of charity law,[114] does contain a
definition of public benefit, rather than wholly relying on guidance from
the Office of the Scottish Charity Regulator (OSCR) and case law, in order
to determine whether charitable status should be granted. To determine
whether a body provides or intends to provide public benefit, OSCR and
the courts must have regard to:[115]

(a) how any –
     (i)   benefit gained or likely to be gained by members of the body or any
           other persons (other than as members of the public), and
     (ii) disbenefit[116] incurred or likely to be incurred by the public, in con-
           sequence of the body exercising its functions compares with the
           benefit gained or likely to be gained by the public in that consequence,
           and

(b)   where benefit is, or is likely to be, provided to a section of the public only, whether any condition on obtaining that benefit (including any charge or fee[117]) is unduly restrictive.

The level of fees charged by a charity for the provision of its service therefore specifically forms part of the judgment of OSCR when it decides whether an organisation should be granted or retain its charitable status. The same test is laid down in the new Northern Irish charities legislation,[118] except that the word 'disbenefit' is replaced with the word 'detriment'.[119]

OSCR is responsible for keeping the Scottish Charity Register[120] and it may enter an applicant in the Register only if it considers that the applicant meets the charity test.[121] Any organisation that wishes to refer to itself as 'a charity', 'charitable body', 'registered charity' or a 'charity registered in Scotland' must apply to OSCR for registration, since a body which refers to itself in any of these ways is to be treated as representing itself as a body entered in the Register.[122] This may include organisations which are already registered as charities in another jurisdiction, for example, England. One key principle of the Scottish Act is that all significant operations by charities within Scotland should be regulated by OSCR, regardless of where that charity was first registered.[123] This will provide a level playing field for all charities operating in Scotland, ensuring fairness and consistency. A charity registered (or excepted or exempt from registration) with the Charity Commission in England (or another foreign charity) will therefore also need to register with OSCR if it wishes to call itself a charity and if it occupies land or premises in Scotland or if it carries out activities in an office, shop or similar premises in Scotland.[124]

In order to be entered in the Scottish Charity Register, and therefore to have charitable status, all charities operating in Scotland, regardless of where they were first registered, must pass the charity test, including the public benefit aspect.[125] This could well cause difficulties for cross-border charities if the Charity Commission and OSCR take different approaches to public benefit as a result of their different statutory powers. Aside from the fact that a definition of public benefit is included in the Scottish Act but not in the English counterpart, it has already been seen that the public benefit test in Scotland is clearly focused on a charity's activities, whilst the comparable statutory test in England relates to a charity's purposes.[126] While the intention is that there should be consistency of decision-making, especially in areas where there is a UK-wide application,[127] it is recognised that there are differences between the two legal frameworks in relation to charitable status.[128]

One problem has already been identified for charities that operate across the borders and which need to be registered in Scotland as well as England; it has been seen that the words 'charitable' and 'charitable purposes' do not have the same meaning under English and Scottish legislation. The governing documents of charities established under the law of England are interpreted according to English law. Therefore, where an English charity's governing documents make reference to 'charitable' or 'other charitable purposes' in its objects and/or dissolution clause (as opposed to specific individual charitable purposes), it is not guaranteed that the organisation can only use its assets for purposes which are exclusively charitable in accordance with the Scottish law. This means that an English charity with such words in its governing documents will fail the Scottish charity test. This situation is arising with some frequency and the Charity Commission has agreed a standard form of words[129] with OSCR for the amendment of governing documents so that there is compliance with the charity test.[130] The Commission notes that by amending a charity's governing document in order to pursue purposes that are charitable under both English and Scottish law, there is, in effect, a narrowing of the charity's purposes. Whilst the two sets of legislation only differ slightly, it is possible that the gap between what is charitable or what constitutes public benefit under the two jurisdictions may become wider in the future, due to diverging interpretation of the public benefit tests by the Charity Commission and OSCR.

A number of Labour backbenchers supported the Scottish statutory option for England, as did Liberal Democratic policy, and there were a number of attempts to include a provision similar to section 8 of the Scottish Act within the English Charities Act. As these attempts have failed, the specific reference to unduly restrictive fees, together with OSCR's approach to it, will clearly bring the issue into focus in Scotland in a more transparent way than in England.

In Northern Ireland, where, it has been noted,[131] a similar definition of public benefit applies to that in Scotland, there appears to be a lighter touch regime envisaged for foreign bodies already registered in other jurisdictions that operate for charitable purposes in or from Northern Ireland (which could well include such bodies registered as charities in the Republic of Ireland and England).[132] Such bodies must produce a financial statement and statement of activities relating to their operations for charitable purposes in or from Northern Ireland. Any further control of such organisations is to be dealt with by secondary legislation and the primary law hints at the possibility of the Northern Irish Charity Commission setting up some kind of parallel register for such bodies. This would presumably embrace diversity, rather than require consistency. It is therefore considered, at this stage, that the problem discussed above in relation to the incompatibility of the definitions of charitable purposes in

England and Scotland, and the problems that this has caused for cross-border charities requiring to register in both jurisdictions, will not arise in Northern Ireland.

In Ireland, the Charities Act 2009[133] also contains a 'definition' of public benefit. Having made it clear that a purpose shall not be a charitable purpose unless it is of public benefit,[134] it is stated that a gift shall not be of public benefit[135] unless:[136]

(a) it is intended to benefit the public or a section of the public, and

(b) in a case where it confers a benefit on a person other than in his or her capacity as a member of the public or a section of the public, any such benefit is reasonable in all of the circumstances, and is ancillary to, and necessary, for the furtherance of the public benefit.

Furthermore, the Irish Act provides that, in relation to fee-charging charities, in determining whether a gift is of public benefit or not, account shall be taken of:[137]

(a) any limitation[138] imposed by the donor of the gift on the class of persons who may benefit from the gift and whether or not such limitation is justified and reasonable, having regard to the nature of the purpose of the gift, and

(b) the amount of any charge payable for any service provided in furtherance of the purpose for which the gift is given and whether it is likely to limit the number of persons or classes of person who will benefit from the gift.

CONCLUSION

It has been seen that reforming the definition of charity in England, including the making of changes to the public benefit requirement, has proved to be a tremendous challenge. There is a recurring theme in this chapter, which is that the English experience has proved, so far, that it is difficult to remove certain aspects of the common law legacy, derived from the Preamble to the 1601 Act and subsequent case law.[139] Moreover, it is unclear, as yet, whether or not it would be desirable to do so. Public benefit, in particular, is a complex concept, deriving from case law decided over several centuries. There are many principles to be considered which have to be delicately balanced, and some of these apply to some heads of charity and not to others.[140]

Many would argue that the common law definition of charity, together with the public benefit component, has served society well and will continue to do so, despite legislative attempts to interfere. Perhaps a lesson to be learned is that if real substantive reform in this area is desired, this should be made clear on the face of the law. The English Charities Act 2006 obviously changes the law in this area, but due to the fact that the precise extent of those changes is as yet unclear, the attempt at reform could be regarded as somewhat half-baked. In a statement from the Charity Commission in July 2005 on how public benefit was treated in the (then) Charities Bill, it said, 'the development of the law would be enhanced if a future Charities Act included non-exclusive, high level criteria, including issues around fee-charging charities, which would clarify the general principles established by the existing law to be taken into account in assessing public benefit'.[141]

This was not forthcoming and what we have witnessed so far is the Commission's struggle to develop policy to apply to modern conditions within the framework of the common law. Whilst existing case law sets a starting point for thinking about public benefit in theory, it does not necessarily provide easy answers in practice. Robust statutory guidance might have provided a more transparent way forward than the continued reliance on opaque case law. Since the enactment of the Charities Act 2006, the Charity Commission has acknowledged, in its public benefit guidance, that 'applying principles from a small number of cases involving particular charities and situations will involve difficult judgments and interpretations of the law to be made'.[142] In a text that emphasises that 'charity' in a common law context is best viewed as a political construct, O'Halloran, McGregor-Lowndes and Simon comment on the lack of definition of this pivotal common law characteristic – public benefit – thus: 'To leave this test, and the definition of "charity", open to continued subjective interpretation raises questions as to the veracity of the political will to address social policy issues such as the charitable status of fee paying hospitals and private schools'.[143]

To conclude, the reader is invited to consider whether the requirement of 'proving' public benefit is worth the cost. The writer is mindful of a similar question asked and answered by the editor of the charity magazine *Third Sector* when reporting upon the final publication of the Charity Commission's guidance on public benefit in the context of fee-charging: 'And has the world of charities been turned upside down? Hardly. As one specialist lawyer put it, 95 per cent of them will be able to carry on pretty much as before'.[144]

So far, and it is admittedly very early days, the English journey on the road to reform has been a bumpy one, whose ultimate destination may well prove in time to be somewhere very close to its departure point. It is hoped that other jurisdictions considering their own reform process can learn from this experience and take a more straightforward route to their desired location.

NOTES

1. Taken from a World War II British propaganda poster, published by the Railway Executive in 1942.
2. See e.g. dicta of Lord Cross in *Dingle v Turner* [1972] AC 601 (HL).
3. Future references in this chapter to England or English refer to England and Wales or English and Welsh. For constitutional purposes, charity law is a devolved matter in the UK, for purposes other than tax. Reform in Scotland and Northern Ireland has been the subject of separate local initiatives. In the past, provisions for regulating charities have differed significantly in each jurisdiction, but Scotland now has a similar regulatory regime to that in England and Wales, as a result of the implementation of the Charities and Trustee Investment (Scotland) Act 2005, and it is expected that reforms in Northern Ireland, through the implementation of the Charities Act (Northern Ireland) 2008, will also result in the introduction of a similar regime. See further below.
4. Charity Commission (2008), *Charities and Public Benefit. The Charity Commission's General Guidance on Public Benefit*, London, Charity Commission, p. 3.
5. By a combination of the Mortmain and Charitable Uses Act 1882 and the Charities Act 1960, s. 38(1).
6. [1891] AC 531 (HL) at 583.
7. *National Anti-Vivisection Society v Inland Revenue Commissioners* [1948] AC 31 (HL) at 42 per Lord Wright.
8. See discussion below on the difficulty of removing the presumption of public benefit.
9. Charities Act, Cap. 243, ss 2–3.
10. Charities and Trustee Investment (Scotland) Act 2005, s. 8.
11. Charities Act 2005, s. 5(2)(a).
12. Charities Act (Northern Ireland) 2008, ss 2–3.
13. Charities Act 2009, s. 3 (not yet in force, at December 2009).
14. National Council on Voluntary Organisations, Commission on the Future of the Voluntary Sector (1996), *Meeting the Challenge of Change: Voluntary Action into the 21st Century*, London: NCVO, Volume 2 (known as the 'Deakin Report').
15. Strategy Unit (2001), 'Prime Minister Announces Voluntary Sector Review', Press Release, CAB 128/01, 3 July.
16. Strategy Unit (2002), *Private Action, Public Benefit: A Review of Charities and the Wider Not-For-Profit Sector*, London: HMSO.
17. For a discussion of the recommendations, see Morris, D. (2002), 'Strategy Unit Proposes Major Shake-up of Charity Law – Part 1', *Exempt Organization Tax Review*, 38, 459; and Morris, D. (2003), 'Strategy Unit Proposes Major Shake-up of Charity Law – Part 2', *Exempt Organization Tax Review*, 39, 201.
18. Home Office (2003), *Charities and Not-for-Profits: A Modern Legal Framework. The Government's Response to 'Private Action, Public Benefit'*, London: HMSO.
19. Great Britain, Parliament, Joint Committee on the Draft Charities Bill (2004), *The Draft Charities Bill, Vol. 1: Report*, HL 167-I/HC 660-I, London: HMSO.
20. Secretary of State for the Home Department (2004), *The Government Reply to the Report from the Joint Committee on the Draft Charities Bill*, Session 2003–04 HL Paper 167/HC 660, Cmnd 6440, London: HMSO.
21. Charities Act 2006 (Commencement No. 4, Transitional Provisions and Savings) Order 2008, SI 2008 No. 945.
22. Charities Act 2006, s. 2(1).
23. Or 'skirted around'. See the comment to this effect in O'Halloran, K., M. McGregor-Lowndes and K. Simon (2008), *Charity Law and Social Policy: National and International Perspectives on the Functions of the Law Relating to Charities*, Heidelberg: Springer, 481.
24. Secretary of State for the Home Department, above n 20 at 7.
25. Under Charities Act 2006, s. 3(3) it is stated that 'any reference to the public benefit is

a reference to the public benefit as that term is understood for the purposes of the law relating to charities in England and Wales'.

26. Warburton, J. (2008), 'Charities and Public Benefit – From Confusion to Light?', *Charity Law & Practice Review*, 10(3), 1 at 3.

27. Charity Law Association (undated), *Response to the Charity Commission's Consultation on the Draft Public Benefit Guidance* also notes at p. 6 that many of the old cases on public benefit are about charitable trusts, where one of the court's concerns is to ensure that it can enforce the trusts. Considerations may be different for charities which have the legal structure of a company.

28. Joint Committee on the Draft Charities Bill, above n 19 at 25, para 79.

29. The Charity Commission has clearly changed its view, bearing in mind the content of its voluminous guidance on public benefit that has been published since 2004. See below.

30. Joint Committee on the Draft Charities Bill, above n 19 at 33, para 102.

31. Secretary of State for the Home Department, above n 20 at 7.

32. See e.g. *Gilmour v Coats* [1949] AC 426 (HL).

33. *Verge v Somerville* [1924] AC 496 (PC).

34. Explanatory Notes to the Charities Act 2006, para 26.

35. *Gilmour v Coats* [1949] AC 426 (HL) at 449 per Lord Simonds.

36. See *National Anti-Vivisection Society v IRC* [1948] AC 31 (HL) at 49 per Lord Wright: 'I think the whole tendency of the concept of charity in a legal sense under the fourth head is towards tangible and objective benefits, and at least, that approval by the common understanding of enlightened opinion for the time being, is necessary before an intangible benefit can be taken to constitute a sufficient benefit to the community to justify admission of the object into the fourth class'.

37. *Re Hummeltenberg* [1923] 1 Ch 237 (Ch) at 242 per Russell J. For a modern example, see *Re Le Cren Clarke* [1996] 1 WLR 288 (Ch). See also Morris, D. (1996), '*Re Le Cren Clarke* – Faith Hope and Charity in Healing', *Liverpool Law Review*, 18(1), 63–71.

38. See e.g. Lord Wilberforce in *Re Resch* [1969] 1 AC 514 (PC) at 544. See however the Government's view: 'we do not believe that indirect benefit – that the claim that, for example, private schools save the state money by educating pupils – is enough to justify charitable status': Edward Miliband MP and Parliamentary Secretary, Cabinet Office (2006), Hansard, HC, vol. 448, col. 96, 26 June.

39. Charity Commission (2008), *Analysis of the Law Underpinning Charities and Public Benefit*, London: Charity Commission, para 3.59, available at http://www.charity-commission.gov.uk/Library/publicbenefit/pdfs/lawpb1208.pdf (accessed 7 December 2009).

40. See further below on the Charity Commission's role in relation to the public benefit requirement.

41. In early draft guidance, the Charity Commission provided examples, including the provision of a scanner in a hospital, which (as well as providing direct benefits to those who use it) indirectly benefits other patients in the hospital and the public at large by enabling the hospital to use its resources in other ways: Charity Commission (2007), *Consultation on Draft Public Benefit Guidance*, London: Charity Commission, 20.

42. *Verge v Somerville* [1924] AC 496 (PC).

43. For a discussion of the 'personal nexus' test and the irrational consequences it can cause in some cases, see e.g. Atiyah, P.S. (1958), 'Public Benefit in Charities', *Modern Law Review*, 21, 138 at 147.

44. [1951] AC 297 (HL).

45. [1951] AC 297 (HL) at 306.

46. Charity Commission, above n 39 at para 3.25.

47. See further below on the Charity Commission's role in relation to the public benefit requirement.

48. Charity Commission, above n 4 at 20. See also Warburton, above n 26, where there are many references to this requirement.

49. In Charity Commission, above n 39 at para 3.11; *IRC v Baddeley* [1955] AC 572 (HL) is used as authority for this point, but this is open to debate.
50. For a discussion of this aspect of the public benefit test in relation to each of the traditional four heads of charity, see Sanders, A. (2007) ,'The Mystery of Public Benefit', *Charity Law & Practice Review*, 10(2), 33–57. See also Atiyah, above n 43.
51. 'Relief of poverty is so altruistic a character that the public element may necessarily be inferred thereby': *Re Scarisbrick* [1951] Ch 622 (CA) at 639 per Evershed MR.
52. See e.g. *Dingle v Turner* [1972] AC 601 (HL) and *Re Scarisbrick* [1951] Ch 622 (CA), applied more recently in *Re Segelman* [1996] Ch 171 (Ch). Compare *Re Compton* [1945] Ch 123 (CA) where a trust for the advancement of education which was limited to the testatrix's relations was held not a valid charitable trust, due to lack of public benefit.
53. See e.g. Charity Commission, above n 4 at 20. See further below on the Charity Commission's role in relation to the public benefit requirement. For a contrary view, see Warburton, above n 26 at 16: 'It is debatable whether the exception will survive'.
54. See also, to this effect, Rahmatian, A. (2009), 'The Continued Relevance of the "Poor Relations" and the "Poor Employees" Cases under the Charities Act 2006', *Conveyancer and Property Lawyer*, 20(1), 12–20.
55. See e.g. *Scottish Burial Reform and Cremation Society Ltd v Glasgow Corporation* [1968] AC 138 (HL) where the provision of cremations did not cease to be a charitable purpose merely because fees were charged.
56. [1972] Ch 73 (CA) at 90.
57. [1969] 1 AC 514 (PC). See also *Brighton College v Marriott* [1926] AC 192 (HL) recognising the charitable status of a fee-charging school.
58. [1983] Ch 159 (Ch).
59. Effectively, in that case, elderly people with a disability or infirmity which necessitated specially adapted accommodation.
60. [1969] 1 AC 514 (PC) at 544 per Lord Wilberforce. See also Charity Commission, *Review Decision Made on the Application for Registration of Odstock Private Care Limited*, 25 September 2007.
61. The draft public benefit guidance referred to 'people on low incomes' rather than 'people in poverty': Charity Commission, above n 41 at 28. Neither phrase is a term of art. The Charity Commission suggests that, for a charity carrying out its aims in England and Wales, 'people in poverty' might typically mean households living on less than 60% of average income or people living on or below the level of 'income support'. However, even then, it is accepted that 'poverty' is a relative term that may be interpreted differently depending upon the organisation's aims.
62. Charity Commission, above n 4 at 26. See also the supplementary guidance: Charity Commission (2008), *Guidance on Public Benefit and Fee-Charging*, London: Charity Commission, which provides more detailed guidance on how the public benefit principle applies to charities that charge fees. See further on charities and fees, Morris, D. (2007), 'Fee-Paying Hospitals and Charitable Status: A New Dawn or Lost Opportunities?', *King's College Law Journal*, 18, 455–479.
63. Charity Law Association (2008), *Response to the Charity Commission's Consultation on the Draft Supplementary Guidance on Public Benefit and Fee Charging Charities*, Rainham, Kent: CLA. *See also*, Luxton, P. (2009), 'A three-part invention: Public benefit under the Charity Commission', *Charity Law & Practice Review*, **11**(2), 19–33.
64. [1972] Ch 73 (CA).
65. [1972] Ch 73 (CA) at 103.
66. See e.g. *Royal College of Nursing v St Marylebone Corporation* [1959] 1 WLR 1077 (CA). Compare, however, *General Nursing Council for England and Wales v St Marylebone Borough Council* [1959] AC 540 (HL).
67. Charity Commission, above n 4 at 27.
68. *The Midland Counties Institution of Engineers v IRC* (1928) 14 TC 285 (CA) at 293.

69. Charities Act 2006, s. 4.
70. Charities Act 2006, s. 7.
71. Charity Commission, above n 41.
72. Charity Commission, above n 4. Separate guidance that explains the legal underpinning for the principles of public benefit set out in this guidance can be found in the Charity Commission's *Analysis of the Law Underpinning Charities and Public Benefit*, above n 39. Cf., in Canada: Canada Revenue Agency (2006), *Guidelines for Registering a Charity: Meeting the Public Benefit Test*, Reference Number CPS-024, Ottawa: CRA.
73. Some have suggested that the Charity Commission's multiple documents confuse rather than clarify. See e.g. 'Too Much Public Benefit Guidance?', *Third Sector*, 16 March 2009.
74. Charity Commission (2008), *The Prevention or Relief of Poverty for the Public Benefit*, London: Charity Commission; Charity Commission (2008), *The Advancement of Education for the Public Benefit*, London: Charity Commission; Charity Commission (2008), *The Advancement of Religion for the Public Benefit* London: Charity Commission; Charity Commission (2008), *Public Benefit and Fee-Charging*, London: Charity Commission. Each consultation ran for four months and the Commission received a total of 675 responses.
75. Charities Act 2006, s. 4(6).
76. Charities Act 1993, s. 45 and The Charities (Accounts and Reports) Regulations 2008, SI 2008 No. 629, Part 5. The level of detail required will depend on whether the charity is above or below the audit threshold. An audit is required when a charity's gross income in the year exceeds £500 000, or where income exceeds £250 000 and the aggregate value of its assets exceeds £3.26 m.
77. Some of these areas have already been identified in this chapter. See text above at n 47 and at n 63.
78. See e.g. Charity Commission, above n 4 at 9.
79. This is described as an 'arguably unwarranted departure from the purposes test' in Iwobi, A. (2009), 'Out with the Old, in with the New: Religion, Charitable Status and the Charities Act 2006', *Legal Studies*, 29, 619 at 639.
80. See e.g. Charity Law Association, above n 27. Academics have also written in support of this view. See e.g. Luxton, above n 63.
81. Charities Act 2006, ss 2(1)(b) and 3(1) refer to a charity's purposes needing to be for the public benefit.
82. Charity Law Association, above n 27 at 12. See also Charity Law Association, above n 63; Buckley, C (2008), 'The Charities Act 2006: Consolidation or Reform?', *Charity Law & Practice Review*, 11(1), 1–42.
83. Charities and Trustee Investment (Scotland) Act 2005, s. 7(1).
84. Office of the Scottish Charity Regulator (2008), *Meeting the Charity Test*, Dundee: OSCR, 4.
85. See e.g. Charity Law Association, above n 27 at 3: 'trustees should be entitled to presume that each statutory head of charity will cover an area of public benefit'.
86. The advancement of animal welfare, for example: *Re Wedgwood* [1915] 1 Ch 113 (CA).
87. Hackney, J. (2008), 'Charities and Public Benefit', *Law Quarterly Review*, 124, 347 at 349.
88. Luxton, above n 63 at 23.
89. Warburton, above n 26 at 6–7.
90. See e.g. Charity Commission, above n 4.
91. Charities Act 2006, s. 8(1) provides for a new Pt 1A of the Charities Act 1993, which contains new ss 2A–2D covering, respectively: the creation of the Tribunal; its practice and procedure; appeals from the Tribunal; and the powers of the Attorney General to intervene. Since September 2009, the work of the Charity Tribunal has transferred to the First-tier Tribunal and Upper Tribunal of the General Regulatory Chamber.
92. Charities Act 1993, Sched. 1C.

93. Charities Act 1993, Sched. 1C, para 1(2)(a).
94. The details are set out in a Table in Charities Act 1993, Sched. 1C, para 5.
95. Charities Act 1993, Sched. 1C, para 1(3).
96. Under Charities Act 1993, s. 3 or s. 3A.
97. Charities Act 1993, Sched. 1C, para 1(4).
98. Tribunal Procedure (First-tier) General Regulatory Chamber Rules 2009, SI 2009 No. 1976, r. 10.
99. Tribunals, Courts and Enforcement Act 2007, s. 11.
100. Charities Act 1993, Sched. 1D, para 1.
101. Charities Act 1993, Schedule 1D, para 2.
102. 'Charity law' is defined widely in Charities Act 1993, Sched. 1D, para 7(1).
103. Any relevant matters before the Commission are put on hold until the reference proceedings are concluded: Charities Act 1993, Sched. 1D, para 3(2). Normal time limits which may apply for the Charity Commission to take any action are suspended while the reference is in progress: Charities Act 1993, Sched. 1D, para 4.
104. Charities Act 1993, Sched. 1D, para 1(3)(4) and para 2(2)(3).
105. The Board is the Members of the Charity Commission acting collectively.
106. Charity Commission (2008), 'Reference Procedure', in *The Charity Tribunal*, Operational Guidance OG 95, B4, 18 March, London: Charity Commission, para 2.1.
107. 'Andrew Hind Defends Charity Commission against Charges of Political Bias', *Third Sector*, 1 October 2009.
108. There is evidence that fee-charging charitable schools are already changing their practices: an annual benchmarking survey showed that, for the first time in 2007, such schools allocated more money to means-tested bursaries for poor pupils than to scholarships awarded to the most able: National Independent Schools' Benchmarking Survey (2008), *Guidance for Independent Schools. Benchmarking Financial Performance in Independent Schools 2008*, London: Horwath Clark Whitehill.
109. See e.g. Independent Schools Council (2004), 'ISC Welcomes Charities Bill', Press Release, 21 December.
110. The National Council for Voluntary Organisations (NCVO) is the umbrella body for the voluntary sector in England, with sister councils in Wales, Scotland and Northern Ireland. NCVO has a growing membership of over 7,500 voluntary organisations, ranging from large national bodies to community groups, volunteer bureaux, and development agencies working at a local level.
111. This is a change to its original view – see Joint Committee on the Draft Charities Bill, above n 19, at 30, para 97 where it is reported that the NCVO was strongly in favour of leaving the detailed definition of public benefit to the courts.
112. National Council for Voluntary Organisations (2006), 'Charities Call for Action on Public Benefit as MPs Consider Charities Bill', Press Release, 22 June.
113. See e.g. Lord Phillips's unsuccessful attempt during the Charity Bill's report stage in the House of Lords to introduce an amendment which would have required the Charity Commission to 'consider the effect on public benefit of the charging policy of any charity' when consulting in advance of issuing guidance to charities on public benefit: Hansard, HL, vol. 674, col. 312, 12 October 2005.
114. Scottish Charity Law Review Commission (2001), *Charity Scotland: The Report of the Scottish Charity Law Review Commission*, Edinburgh: Scottish Executive. See e.g. Ford, P. (2005), 'The Charities and Trustee Investment (Scotland) Bill: Falling Between Two Stools?', *King's College Law Journal*, 16, 1–28.
115. Charities and Trustee Investment (Scotland) Act 2005, s. 8. For a comparative discussion of the position in England and Wales, Scotland, Northern Ireland, and the Republic of Ireland, see Breen, O., P. Ford and G. Morgan (2009), 'Cross-Border Issues in the Regulation of Charities: Experiences from the UK and Ireland' *International Journal of Not-for-Profit Law*, 11(3), 5–41.
116. 'Disbenefit is the opposite to benefit. It is therefore more than the mere absence of

benefit, and, in the view of OSCR, it is equivalent to detriment or harm': Office of the Scottish Charity Regulator (2008), *Meeting the Charity Test*, Dundee: OSCR, 21.

117. On OSCR's approach to these words, see in particular OSCR, above n 116 at 25–7.
118. Previously in Northern Ireland there was no local registration of charities and only limited control of how charities were run. In the past, charities would usually apply to HM Revenue and Customs for tax benefits and receive a reference number. The Charities Act (Northern Ireland) 2008 inter alia creates a Charity Commission for Northern Ireland and establishes a compulsory charity register of all charities operating in Northern Ireland. In order to register as a charity, an organisation will have one or more of the charitable purposes as listed in the Act and it will have to provide public benefit in Northern Ireland or elsewhere.
119. Charities Act (Northern Ireland) 2008, s. 3(3).
120. Charities and Trustee Investment (Scotland) Act 2005, s. 3. Historically, the Inland Revenue has been responsible for the grant of charitable status to organisations in Scotland. Since April 2006, OSCR, as a non-Ministerial Department, has taken over the role of granting charitable status and has a statutory obligation to maintain and publish a Register of Charities.
121. Charities and Trustee Investment (Scotland) Act 2005, s. 5(1).
122. Charities and Trustee Investment (Scotland) Act 2005, s. 13(3).
123. See, in general, Office of the Scottish Charities Regulator (2009), *Seeking Charitable Status in Scotland: Guidance for England and Wales Charities on Registration with the Office of the Scottish Charity Regulator*, Dundee: OSCR.
124. Charities and Trustee Investment (Scotland) Act 2005, s. 14.
125. Office of the Scottish Charities Regulator (2009), above n 123 at para 5.
126. See text above at n 83.
127. Charity Commission and Office of the Scottish Charities Regulator (2007), *Memorandum of Understanding between the Charity Commission and the Office of the Scottish Charity Regulator*, revised May, para 4.1.
128. Ibid, Annex 3, para 2.
129. For example, where a charity is established in England and it undertakes significant activities in Scotland and its objects clause makes reference to 'charitable' or 'other charitable purposes', this form of wording will be suitable for use as an interpretation clause for the governing document: '"charitable" means charitable in accordance with the law of England and Wales provided that it will not include any purpose which is not charitable in accordance with section 7 of the Charities and Trustee Investment (Scotland) Act 2005. For the avoidance of doubt, the system of law governing the constitution of the charity is the law of England and Wales'.
130. Charity Commission (2007), *English and Welsh Charities Registering with the Office of the Scottish Charity Regulator (OSCR)*, Operational Guidance OG 32 A1, London: Charity Commission.
131. See text above at n 118.
132. Charities Act (Northern Ireland) 2008, s. 167.
133. As well as introducing a statutory definition of 'charitable purposes' and 'public benefit', the Act will inter alia provide for a new Charities Regulatory Authority. When the Authority is established, it will establish a public Register of Charities. Any organisation that wishes to operate as a charity in Ireland will be legally obliged to be in the Register of Charities.
134. Charities Act 2009, s. 3(2).
135. The law here is different in that the presumption of public benefit is retained for a gift for the advancement of religion: Charities Act 2009, s. 3(4). Cf, in Australia, the Extension of Charitable Purpose Act 2004, s. 5, which has introduced a legal presumption that self-help groups and closed or contemplative religious orders are for the public benefit.
136. Charities Act 2009, s. 3(3).

137. Charities Act 2009, s. 3(7).
138. Such a limitation shall not be justified and reasonable if all of the intended beneficiaries of the gift or a significant number of them have a personal connection with the donor of the gift: Charities Act 2009, s. 3(8).
139. For example, as early as 1767, the case of *Jones v Williams* (1767) Amb 651 emphasised the 'public' character of charity.
140. See e.g. the discussion above, at n 50, on the public benefit requirement as it applies to charities for the relief of poverty.
141. Charity Commission (2005), *Public Benefit – The Charity Commission's Position on How Public Benefit is Treated in the Charities Bill*, London: Charity Commission.
142. Charity Commission, above n 4 at para H1.
143. O'Halloran, McGregor-Lowndes and Simon, above n 23 at 481.
144. 'Editorial: We Need a Definitive Ruling on Fee-Charging Charities', *Third Sector*, 7 January 2009.

5. Developing issues in the regulation of public benefit organisations in Japan and China

Karla W. Simon[1]

INTRODUCTION

Japan and China – two civil law[2] countries – are in the process of developing new legal regimes for public benefit organisations, which are sometimes known as charities in the common law world. The designations of these new types of organisations vary in translation:

- In Japan they are called public benefit or public interest organisations; there is also a chapter on 'charitable' trusts in the Law on Trusts.
- In China the term 'public welfare' (*gong yi*) is generally used; there is a chapter on charitable trusts in the Law on Trusts; and work is being done to develop a 'charity' (*cishan*) law.[3]

What is meant in general is a subset[4] of not-for-profit legal entities that meet the definition of public benefit used in Anglo-American law.

In a civil law regime there are generally two legal forms of not-for-profit legal person – associations and foundations. Associations are groups of persons, while foundations have an endowment. Thus, for example, the German Civil Code provides for both registered and unregistered associations and for foundations. Foundations are, however, regulated under the laws of the German states (Länder).[5]

The similarities between the formal legal regime in China and that of Japan are worth emphasising to the extent of the structural elements of the Civil Codes adopted in Japan at the end of the 19th century and in Republican China at the beginning of the 20th century.[6] Regarding juristic persons, both Civil Codes required that:

1. the permissible entities be organised for public benefit;[7]
2. the organisers have permission from the government to set them up;[8]
3. public benefit foundations meet a high initial endowment requirement.[9]

Moreover, one administrative feature of the system in Japan which the Diet and the sector are now seeking to remedy is the frequent placement of retired or just former government officials in positions of importance in the civil society organisations (CSOs).[10]

Because of the party-state's continued blurring of the state and civil society, the situation in China is much more difficult to change than it was in Japan. In fact, the Japanese government itself made clear in the run-up to the 2006–08 reforms that it needed *independent* CSOs to assist it in harnessing resources to meet social and economic needs.[11] It is unlikely that stress will be laid on the independence of CSOs in China, in large part because of the fear (whether real or manufactured) of releasing uncontrollable forces that could challenge the state–party apparatus.[12] On the other hand, watching a neighbour, with similar strictures on CSOs created by legal structures in the Civil Code, reduce these requirements in order to achieve important societal purposes may prove to be instructive for the Chinese government. If the loosening of the bonds binding CSOs to the state goes well in Japan, the Chinese government may decide to experiment more fully with possible ways to allow its CSOs more freedom.

JAPAN

The developments in the decade between 1998 and 2008 with regard to the legal environment for CSOs in Japan are quite significant.[13] In an immediate response to the Kobe Earthquake, the Specified Nonprofit Corporations Act was passed by the Diet (Parliament) in 1998.[14] This legislation created the new legal form of Specified Nonprofit Corporations (SNPCs), which allows people to engage in various public benefit activities merely by registering their organisations with the local government organs.[15] In subsequent years the Diet has improved the legal environment for SNPCs while also modifying the rules with regard to the public benefit CSOs provided for in the Civil Code. Now that the new 2006–08 reforms are fully in place, the following changes will have been made:

- A new legal framework for 'general not-for-profit corporations' is now provided for in the Civil Code of Japan.[16] The present general public benefit corporations (PBCs) will fall under the new category of not-for-profit corporations, as will the mutual benefit form of organisation (*chukan hojin*),[17] and those two legal forms have now been eliminated.[18] The new General Not-for-Profit Association and

Foundation Act (General Act) contains provisions that have been incorporated in the Civil Code to apply to all organisations that seek to become legal entities irrespective of whether they wish to apply for recognition of 'charitable status'.[19]

- Under the new Civil Code provisions, there is a simplified legal process for incorporation, making it entirely non-discretionary and applying standards similar to those for for-profit corporations. Thus, the General Act permits CSOs to apply for registration at the local Registry Office, after a notary has inspected the corporate documents for conformance with the Act.[20]

- A new application system for not-for-profit corporations that seek to be classified as 'authorised public benefit corporations' (APBCs)[21] has been introduced. This status is determined by a Public Benefit Corporation Commission (*koeki nintei tou iinkai*) (PBCC).[22] The Commission has been established in the Cabinet Office,[23] and includes a mix of academics, scholars, and sector professionals.[24]

- Similar 'councils'[25] are established to carry out the authorisation and oversight functions at the local prefectural level in addition to the one at the national level.

- The new legislation contains strict rules dealing with governance and oversight, and it addresses various technical problems inherent in the PBC system prior to the reforms.

In summing up the reforms, it is important to note that the new Japanese system fully respects the freedom of association, while at the same time creating strict scrutiny for organisations that seek to be charities or public benefit entities. This is the type of fundamental reform that should be adopted in China.[26]

CHINA

The only actual laws (passed by the National People's Congress or NPC) that affect CSOs in China are the Public Welfare Donations Law (PWDL),[27] the tax laws,[28] and the Trust Law of the People's Republic of China (which governs charitable trusts).[29] At the present time, the government is working to add a 'Charity Law' to the legal system. This has been a controversial development, with various factions contending for more government control of charity and others for less. But the idea to add such a law clearly implies the need for better oversight of those organisations that receive charitable donations.

The PWDL regulates:

- which activities are considered 'public welfare' activities[30] (the activities are generally the same as those listed in the proposed Charity Law,[31] and I use the term 'public benefit' to encompass both);[32]
- relationships between donors and recipients;[33]
- ways in which donees should use and manage donated property;[34]
- what legal responsibilities apply to donors and donees.[35]

The tax laws describe the tax benefits that are available to donors and CSOs.[36] The Trust Law provides that 'charitable'[37] trusts may be formed, but it does not appear to have been used as yet.[38] All the other rules creating the legal framework within which CSOs operate are regulations. These include the 1998 Regulations on Social Organisations,[39] the 1998 Provisional Regulations on Non-enterprise Institutions (*minban fei qiye danwei*),[40] and the 2004 Regulations on Foundations.[41] Each of the regulations introduces a 'dual management' system, with organisations having to receive approval of a so-called 'mother-in-law' before being registered at the Ministry of Civil Affairs (MoCA).[42]

On the other hand, developments in China indicate that the government may be lightening its hand a bit. It has been traditional in China since Imperial times for major national changes in law and regulations to be 'tried out' first through local experiments. Indeed, in February 2009 MoCA reported at a meeting that there are now five different types of local-level experiments, in places such as Qingdao municipality and Jiamusi municipality, to get rid of the dual management system. In a report published by the Chinese Association of NGOs in its January/February Newsletter for 2009,[43] these are five different methods that were discussed:

1. getting rid of dual management altogether and moving to a registration system;
2. moving to a 'documentation system';
3. adjusting the supervisory authority's permission process;
4. reducing the oversight role of the supervisory authority;
5. making it possible to have a one-stop shop, with MoCA having both registration and supervisory powers.

The documentation system (instead of registration) is a very promising development, and it is being used for small local CSOs that provide services to the poor and other persons suffering social or economic disabilities (for example, children of migrant workers). It does not require a formal registration, but a CSO is granted 'recognition' by the local civil affairs authorities if it files papers with them. The 'one-stop shop' (no sponsor) requires registration with MoCA, and it is being used for certain types of CSOs in Shenzhen,[44] such as trade associations (these obviously do not threaten the government but assist with economic development).

What this all means for the charity law is unclear, but it is certain that the adoption of the law will help to clarify some issues and add some transparency and accountability for the CSOs in China. Several provisions of the draft 2006 law deal with such issues (article 8) but, as the Charity Law Comments suggest, other formulations would be helpful.[45] Two important issues are: ways to address the non-distribution constraint; and how to include fiduciary responsibilities.[46] It is certain that once the law is adopted, there will be additional constraints on organisations that receive charitable contributions, and that these will make them deal more appropriately with their donors.[47] It is also important to note that the way in which the tax legislation is implemented can assist in providing such controls. Recent advice from the tax authorities addresses some of those issues.[48]

The legal changes that have been made and that are being made in Japan and China represent a welcome recognition that charity or public benefit organisations are important for the development of civil society in any country. The modifications of the legal framework in each represent an attempt to in some ways emulate the Charity Commission model of regulation (in Japan more consciously than in China). It remains to be seen to what extent the reforms will create a more sector-friendly regulatory environment, such as exists in England and Wales.

NOTES

1. Karla W. Simon is Professor of Law, Columbus School of Law, Catholic University of America. She is grateful for research funds from the Law School Faculty Research Fund, which have supported her work in Japan and China. A Research Fellow at the University, Hang Gao, provided substantial and important research assistance for this chapter.
2. Whether China is truly a civil law country depends on the interpretation of various scholars. China does have an enactment called the General Principles of Civil Law (GCPL), and it is fleshing out various aspects of traditional civil codes with laws on property rights, contracts, and torts. At some time the GPCL is supposed to be developed into a real Civil Code. Thus, for practical purposes I will call it a civil law country, at least with respect to the tradition of how law is made.
3. The draft was finished and sent to the State Council by the Ministry of Civil Affairs before 11 February 2009. Some news said that the draft has not been disclosed to the public yet. The law has been put on the calendar of the State Council and the People's Congress, but without a deadline or a detailed calendar: email from Hang Gao of 22 November 2009 on file with the author.
4. This is not strictly a true statement in China – under the GPCL, all social organisations

(not-for-profit associations) must serve a public benefit purpose; mutual benefit organisations, such as alumni associations, are not permitted to be formed. See Ge, Y. (2000), 'On the Establishment of Social Organizations under Chinese Law', *International Journal of Not-for-Profit Law*, 2(3), available at http://www.icnl.org/knowledge/ijnl/vol2iss3/index.htm (accessed 5 January 2010).

5. See discussion of Germany in Hopt, K. et al (eds) (2006), *The European Foundation: A New Legal Approach*, Cambridge: Cambridge University Press.

6. See, generally, Chen, Y.-C. (2002), 'Civil Law Development: China and Taiwan', *Stanford Journal of East Asian Affairs*, 2, available at http://www.stanford.edu/group/sjeaa/journal2/china1.pdf (accessed 14 December 2009).

7. Until the *chukan hojin* or 'intermediate' NPO law was adopted in 2001, all registered associations had to be for public benefit. In that year the Diet changed the situation by adopting legislation which is now being folded into the new legal framework for all 'general' NPOs. See Simon, K.W. (2009), 'Enabling Civil Society in Japan: Reform of the Legal and Regulatory Framework for Public Benefit Organisations', *Journal of Japanese Law*, 28, 5.

8. See *Minpō*, Art. 34, translated as Japanese Civil Code, Act No. 89 of 1896, Art. 34, available at http://www.cas.go.jp/jp/seisaku/hourei/data/CC_2.pdf (accessed 15 December 2009), as it existed before the 'Drastic Reform' of the legal regime related to public benefit organisations in 2006. See Simon, above n 7.

9. See *Minpō*, Art. 34, translated as Japanese Civil Code, Act No. 89 of 1896, Art. 34, available at http://www.cas.go.jp/jp/seisaku/hourei/data/CC_2.pdf (accessed 15 December 2009).

10. This issue has received much attention. See Simon, above n 7. It is also a feature of CSOs in China. See Saich, T. (2000), 'Negotiating the State: The Development of Social Organisations in China', *The China Quarterly*, 161, 121–41, at 134.

11. The constant theme in the documents developed during the most recent reform process in Japan stresses this aspect of the need for reforms. See *Documentary Supplement: Original Cabinet Decision to Introduce Reforms: Reform of the System of Public Benefit Juristic Persons*, Cabinet Decision, 29 March 2002, available at http://www.iccsl.org/pubs/Japan_Doc_Supp.pdf (accessed 15 December 2009).

12. One of the rationales for not relaxing the dual management system for CSOs is the fear of the 'colour revolutions' experienced in Ukraine, Georgia, and other post-communist countries. See notes of Zhu Weiguo's talk at a 2005 Beijing Conference, suggesting that this was a political decision made at the top, not one with which the Ministry of Civil Affairs (MoCA) personnel were necessarily in accord (notes on file with the author). It used to be claimed that China did not want to fall apart like the Soviet Union or that it wanted to avoid the emergence of an organisation like Solidarity in Poland. See Saich, above n 10 at 133. This allowed officials to fend off Western suggestions that more independence for CSOs would be desirable.

13. See Simon, above n 7. This discussion draws extensively on the analysis in that article.

14. See Japan Center for International Exchange (2003), 'Law to Promote Specified Nonprofit Activities', *Civil Society Monitor*, 8, available at http://www.jcie.or.jp/civil-net/monitor/npo_law.html (accessed 15 December 2009).

15. Ibid.

16. There are several issues about overlapping coverage of the new laws with the SNPC legislation, but they are not explored here. See Simon, above n 7.

17. The *Chukan Hojin Ho*, Law No. 49 of 2001, was adopted on 15 June 2001, effective 1 April 2002.

18. The third piece of legislation passed in May 2006 will require amendments to the Civil Code and 300 other pieces of legislation. See Miyakawa, M. (2006), 'An Outline of the Three PBC Reform-Related Laws', *International Journal of Civil Society Law*, 4(4), 64–71, 68, available at http://www.iccsl.org/pubs/06-10-IJCSL.pdf (accessed 15 December 2009). The 2001 legislation on *chukan hojin* has been repealed and all associations and foundations, whether for public or mutual benefit, are allowed to register

themselves as legal entities without any permission or approval required. This is significant because for the first time it will bring the Japanese Civil Code into line with, e.g., the German Civil Code in regard to associations and foundations: see Hopt et al, above n 5. For a background to the reforms, see Ohta, T. (2006), 'Public Benefit Organizations in Japan: Present Situations and Remaining Challenges', *International Journal of Civil Society Law*, 4(4), 72–90.

19.	Miyakawa, above n 18 at 66.

20.	Ibid.

21.	Although the unofficial translation provided on the web at http://www.cas.go.jp/jp/ seisaku/hourei/data/AAPII.pdf (accessed 15 December 2009) refers to these organisations as 'public interest' corporations, I intend to continue using the term 'public benefit', as it is more consistent with the term used in other countries to designate organisations serving the public. The Japan Association of Charitable Organizations (JACO) had recommended that all foundations be required to be public benefit foundations under the new system, but that view did not prevail. See Ohta, above n 18 at 85–6. With the reforms in place, the Japanese situation will be much like that in Germany, where private interest foundations (*Stiftungen*) are permitted. According to a recent study, half the countries in Europe require foundations to have a public benefit purpose, while the other half permit them to have any lawful purpose. See Hopt et al, above n 5 at 62. This option is not being suggested for China, however.

22.	This is variously also translated as 'Committee'. See e.g. Miyakawa, above n 18 at 64.

23.	Technically, the authorising administrative agency is the Prime Minister's Office itself: see Art. 3, Law No. 49 of 2006. However, that office delegated the authority to the Commission pursuant to Art. 59, Law No. 49/2006. See unofficial translation provided at http://www.cas.go.jp/jp/seisaku/hourei/data/AAPII.pdf (accessed 15 December 2009).

24.	here are seven members of the Commission.

25.	The 'councils' are intended to assist the prefectural governors, who are technically the authorising administrative agencies at the local level.

26.	The type of accountability and oversight required for public benefit CSOs would be required under the proposed Charity Law. See discussion below.

27.	See 'Comments on the Draft Charity Law for the People's Republic of China' (2007), *International Journal of Civil Society Law*, 5(1), 12–27 (hereinafter, Charity Law Comments), available at http://www.iccsl.org/pubs/07-01_IJCSL.pdf (accessed 15 December 2009).

28.	A pre-2008 description of the tax laws and their applicability to CSOs can be found in Irish, L.E., J. Dongsheng and K.W. Simon (2004), *China's Tax Rules for Not-for-profit Organizations*, Beijing: World Bank, available at http://siteresources.worldbank. org/INTCHINA/1503040-1122886803058/20601839/NPO_tax_En.pdf (accessed 15 December 2009).

29.	Trust Law (*Minpō*) of the People's Republic of China (promulgated by the Standing Committee of the Ninth National People's Congress of the People's Republic of China, 28 April 2001, effective at 1 October 2001). For a discussion of the law and its history and usage, see Qu, C.Z. (2003), 'The Doctrinal Basis of the Trust Principles in China's Trust Law', *Real Property, Probate and Trust Journal*, 38(2), 345–76, at 346–57. See also Tan, Z. (2001), 'The Chinese Law of Trusts: A Compromise Between Two Legal Systems', *Bond Law Review*, 13(1), 224–38, at 224, available at http://www.austlii.edu. au/au/journals/BondLRev/2001/9.html#Heading10 (accessed 15 December 2009). The author points out various differences between the PWDL and the Trust Law with regard to charitable trusts.

30.	See PWDL, Art. 3, available at http://www.iccsl.org/pubs/China_Public_Welfare_ Donations_Law.pdf (accessed 15 December 2009).

31.	See Charity Law Comments, above n 27.

32.	The terms used in Chinese are different. 'Public welfare' is *gongyi*, while 'charity' is *cishan*. The broad interpretation of the definitions is, however, essentially the same and translates best into English terminology as 'public benefit'.

33. PWDL, Art. 4.
34. PWDL, Art. 5.
35. PWDL, Arts 6 and 7. Art. 8 refers to preferences that should be made available to organisations engaging in public welfare activities, but it does not grant such benefits on its own; they are available under other legislation, such as tax legislation.
36. See Enterprise Income Tax Law, effective 1 January 2008. The new EIT permits the same percentage limitation (12%) on the charitable contribution deduction for both foreign and domestic companies. This represents an increase from 3% to 12% for domestic companies. The language of Art. 9 of the new EIT reads as follows: 'Expenditure incurred in connection with donations for public interest may be deducted when computing taxable income if it does not exceed 12% of the year's total profits'. The upper limit on donations by individuals remains at 30% of income, which is a fairly generous amount by international standards.
37. The term used in Chinese is *gong yi.*
38. This information was disclosed during conversations with Chinese law professors. The development of the Trust Law was influenced by the creation of such laws in Japan and Taiwan, as well as Hong Kong. Even though these countries are within the civil law tradition, they have decided to use common law instruments such as the trust.
39. See *She hui tuan ti deng ji guan li tiao li* (Regulations for registration and management of social organisations) (promulgated by the State Council at the 8th Ordinary Session, 25 September 1998, effective 25 September 1998), English translation published in *China Development Brief*, available at http://www.chinadevelopmentbrief.com/node/298 (accessed 15 December 2009).
40. See *Min ban fei qi ye dan wei deng ji guan li zan xing tiao li* (Provisional Regulations on Registration and Management of Private Non-Enterprise Units) (promulgated by the State Council, 25 September 1998, effective 25 September 1998), *State Council Gazette*, Arts 5–8 (PRC), English translation published in *China Development Brief*, available at http://www.chinadevelopmentbrief.com/node/300 (accessed 15 December 2009).
41. See *Ji jin hui guan li tiao li* (Regulations for the Management of Foundations) (promulgated by the State Council, 8 March 2004, effective 1 June 2004) (hereinafter, Foundation Regulation), *State Council Gazette*, English translation published in *China Development Brief*, available at http://www.chinadevelopmentbrief.com/node/301 (accessed 15 December 2009).
42. This is described in Simon, above n 7.
43. See CANGO Newsletter, January/February 2009, at 1.
44. See China Trade Associations and Chambers of Commerce (2009), 'A Reform of Social Organization Regulation System Starts in Southern China', available at http://english.chinaassn.com/show.aspx?id=29536 (accessed 16 December 2009).
45. See Charity Law Comments, above n 27. In this regard, an important article and draft 'Public Benefit Law' and draft 'Regulations' for such a law have been prepared by a German law student named Josephine Asche. See Asche, J. (2009), 'Entwurfsarbeiten zu einer chinesischen Gemeinnuetzigkeitsgesetzgebung', *Zeitschrift fuer Chinesisches Recht (Journal of Chinese Law)*, at 276 (my translation).
46. The latter is also addressed by Josephine Asche in her paper and draft legislation. See Asche, above n 45 at 279–80.
47. For anecdotal evidence of difficulties faced by ordinary Chinese in making donations, see Liping, Y. (2008), 'Our State's Charity Looks Forwards to Legislation That is Expected to Regulate', *Legal Daily*, 5 December, available at http://www.legaldaily.com.cn/misc/2008-12/05/content_997812.htm# (accessed 16 December 2009). This short article in Chinese details the problems faced in making donations to organisations and the times when they have gone astray in many cases (Hang Gao translation).
48. See Circular 123 of 2009, 'On the Management Issues Concerning NPOs' Eligibility of Tax Deduction', available at http://www.iccsl.org/pubs/Caishui_123_(eng).pdf.

6. Holding the line: regulatory challenges in Ireland and England when business and charity collide

Oonagh B. Breen[1]

INTRODUCTION

The debate on the legitimacy of charity involvement in business activities is not new. Regardless of legal jurisdiction, similar perennial concerns regarding the mingling of the nonprofit and for-profit spheres predominate. There are advocates on both sides of the charity–business divide who argue for a complete separation of the two spheres from one another. Those concerned with the purity of charitable mission argue that forays by charities into the world of commercial activity constitute an unwarranted distraction from the focus on achievement of charitable purpose.[2] Given the risk involved with any profit-maximising venture, unregulated charitable trading has the ability to threaten the security of a charity's assets. On the business side of the line, the ability of charities to compete with for-profit entities also raises the ire of private firms. The argument is made that charities engaged in trade enjoy an unfair advantage over their for-profit counterparts because of the corporate and other tax exemptions afforded to charities. Thus, it is said that charitable forays into the business sector, if not prohibited or at least regulated, unfairly distort competition in the market place. The state, too, has an iron in this particular fire since the loss of any revenue caused by such trading, particularly when it is at the expense of tax-paying private enterprises, results in a net loss to the treasury.

And yet, there are many examples of increasing collaboration between for-profit and nonprofit entities and incursions by both into the other's territory. No single stakeholder can claim credit or blame for this mingling of commerce and charity. On the one hand, government has used its funding power to encourage charities to deliver services formerly provided by government, thereby creating an array of 'captive' nonprofits that must compete with for-profit firms in artificially created service markets.[3]

In some instances, states have even created their own charities to deliver statutory services, for example in the provision of health and library facilities.[4]

From a business perspective, there is a growing realisation of the opportunities for charities and businesses to work together. Nonprofit businesses can be more attractive partners than commercial businesses and sometimes can access capital grants from statutory bodies and private donors. More companies, particularly in the UK, are beginning to appreciate the advantages of the foundation model and are creating charitable foundations to assist their strategic corporate responsibility programmes.[5] The development of the 'community interest company' (CIC) in the UK has added an interesting twist to intersectoral activity in that jurisdiction, allowing for-profit activities to be pursued by a legal vehicle designed to deliver 'community benefit' albeit non-charitable purposes. Since its inception in 2005, just over 3000 CICs have been established.[6]

Some charities have taken strategic decisions to engage in for-profit activity, at times totally unrelated to their charitable purposes, in an effort to create greater revenues to support their charitable activities than passive investment provides. Over the past decade, there has been a marked increase in the level of trading income earned by UK charities as a percentage of their total revenues, now accounting for almost 50 per cent of income for some charities.[7]

Developing a legal framework to manage the interactions between the worlds of commerce and charity presents challenges. Should there be situations in which charities can engage in trade in competition with for-profit firms? Should there be limits to the extent of any such involvement? Should the 'relatedness' of the business activity to charitable mission act as a mitigating factor? Or, should the ultimate 'destination' of the resulting income be the deciding factor in sanctioning charitable trading, regardless of the relatedness of the activity to the charitable mission? Should charity law or tax law control the extent to which the market–charity boundary accommodates incursions by either business or charity in the other sphere? Even to the degree to which such intersectoral activity is tolerated, what should be the financial and structural consequences for entities that engage regularly and substantively in such 'cross-border' activities?

TRADING AND CHARITY LAW

At common law, organisations wishing to benefit from charitable status must be established with exclusively charitable objects. This focus on charitable purpose is intended to ensure that charities devote their energies and resources to the attainment of their charitable objectives and do not become distracted by competing objects, particularly those concerned with the maximisation of profit. This common law determinant finds expression in many charity statutes. Thus, section 2 of the Irish Charities Act 2009 defines a charitable organisation as one that, inter alia, promotes a charitable purpose only and that, under its constitution, is required to apply all of its property (both real and personal) in furtherance of that purpose, except for moneys expended in the operation and maintenance of the body (such as moneys paid in remuneration and superannuation of its staff members).[8]

The question arises to what extent the carrying on of trade by a charity can be consistent with these charitable principles. What constitutes 'trade' is a matter of fact and law. The concept of 'trading' is not well defined in statute; Ireland and the UK share a rather unhelpfully circular definition of 'trade' as including 'every trade, manufacture, venture or concern in the nature of trade'.[9] Elaborating upon this vague concept, the UK Revenue and Customs service (HMRC) states that trading involves 'the provision of goods or services to customers on a commercial basis'.[10] It is irrelevant to this determination whether the profits are intended to be used for charitable purposes or not.[11] Although trading normally refers to commercial or business activity provided on an ongoing basis, a one-off venture or an occasional venture may still be treated as trading.[12] On the other hand, where a company owns an asset and the mere ownership of that asset produces an income, the company's income from this asset will not be classified as trading income – thus passive investment income may be tax-exempt.[13]

Case law provides further guidance as to what constitutes 'trading', as does a set of rules (known as 'the badges of trade') drawn up in 1955 by the UK Royal Commission on the Taxation of Profits and Income[14] which, although not legally binding, have been applied by courts in both jurisdictions.[15] Relevant factors to consider include: the subject matter of the transaction, the length of period of ownership, the frequency of the transaction, the degree to which supplementary work is incurred prior to the transaction in question, the circumstances surrounding the realisation, and the profit motive of the trader.[16] For comparative purposes, this chapter equates 'trade' with the concept of 'commercial activities' or 'business activities' as used in the American nonprofit literature.[17]

Charity law distinguishes between what is known in Ireland and England as 'primary purpose trading' (more commonly referred to as 'related business activity' in the US) on the one hand and 'non-primary purpose trading' (or 'unrelated business activity' in the US) on the other.[18] When a charity undertakes business activities in the course of carrying out its charitable activities, these activities are described as primary purpose trading activities. Typical examples of 'primary purpose trading' would include a charitable school or university charging students for tuition or a charitable hospital charging patients for medical or surgical procedures. In these cases, the trading activity is inextricably linked to the achievement of the charitable purpose. Profits made in the course of such activity, provided that they are used to achieve the charity's purposes and no private gains are made, do not cause charity law concerns.[19]

'Non-primary purpose trading' refers to business activities undertaken by a charity that are not directly related to the achievement of the body's charitable purpose. A typical example of non-primary purpose trading (that is, 'unrelated business income') is when a charity engages in business activity to raise funds for the charity. Such unrelated activity may cover a wide spectrum of activities from selling promotional goods in a charity gift shop[20] to running sideline businesses like funeral services or investment services. The compatibility of such activity with charitable status under charity law will depend on the extent of the activities rather than the ultimate destination of the income.

As a starting point, the Charity Commission for England and Wales (CCEW) will not register a charity when its purpose is, or includes, the carrying out of trade.[21] Even when registration is possible for a body with purely charitable purposes, charity law will prohibit that charity from engaging in 'non-primary purpose trading' or unrelated business activity to raise funds when that trading would involve significant risk to the assets of the charity.[22] The basis for this prohibition is the fear that if the costs of the trading endeavour exceed its turnover, the charity will be forced to finance the shortfall out of charitable assets. Depletion of those assets might prevent or, at the very least, undermine the charity's ability to benefit the public as efficiently as it might otherwise have done.

The exposure of charity assets to the risks of unrelated business activity may also have a detrimental effect on future donations by discouraging donors who believed that their contributions would be used directly for the charity's purposes or at least prudently invested, rather than risked in a commercial venture the purpose of which was solely to raise more money.[23] From a purely charity law perspective, therefore, although a charity can engage in business activity unrelated to its primary charitable purpose on a limited scale given the potential risks involved, it is more advisable for a charity to set up a separate trading subsidiary if it plans to trade in this manner on a regular basis.

Between these two categories of trading in furtherance of the charity's primary purpose (so-called 'related business activity') and non-primary purpose trading activities ('unrelated business activity') lies an assortment of activities that can be difficult to classify clearly. These 'grey area' activities, in truth, are either primary purpose or non-primary purpose activities. They would include the running of an interval bar for audience members by a theatre or the provision by a university of student accommodation on a rental basis. Most times, regulators will either prevaricate by stating that each case must be considered on its own merits in these situations or offer limited exemptions.[24] These types of activities are sometimes referred to as 'ancillary trading' activities, a vague expression meaning 'ancillary to the primary purpose of the charity'. Whether they will affect the charitable status of the charity will depend frequently on the scale of the activities in issue.

The CCEW has published guidelines on the statutory requirement that charities must have charitable purposes only and its effect on charities' ability to engage in trading activities.[25] The guidance distinguishes between primary purpose, ancillary and non-primary purpose trading. Under charity law, charities may engage in all three types of activity but engagement in non-primary purpose trading is permitted only insofar as there is no significant risk to the charity's assets.[26]

No similar written charity law guidance is available in Ireland. Prior to 2009 there was no body equivalent to the CCEW responsible for the regulation of charities in Ireland. The Revenue Commissioners determined whether a body was eligible for charitable tax-exempt status but their role was statutorily defined as one of fiscal rather than charitable oversight.[27] The Charities Act 2009 provides for the establishment of a new oversight body for charities, the Charities Regulatory Authority (CRA). The Act also decouples responsibility for the determination of charitable status (the role of the CRA) from that of deciding tax-exempt status (which remains the task of Revenue).[28] Irish charities that wish to engage in trade must now wait to see how the CRA will interpret the 2009 Act's provisions that not only require a charity to have exclusively charitable purposes but also preclude a charity from applying its property in furtherance of any other purpose (with the express exception of moneys expended in the operation and maintenance of the body).[29] It is possible that the CRA may adopt a similar approach under Irish charity law to the CCEW and permit a body with exclusively charitable purposes to engage in unrelated trading so long as such trading does not cause significant risk to charitable assets. Until the CRA is established, however, it remains the case that there is no clear *charity law* policy on this matter in Ireland.

CHARITY TRADING AND TAX LAW

Aside from charity law concerns regarding the types and degree of trading in which a charity may engage, there is an associated tax law question to be considered. A charity that carries on a trade is liable for tax on any resulting profits made in the course of that trade unless it is specifically exempted under revenue law. Irish and English tax laws on charitable trading are similar in many respects, though there is greater availability of published guidance from the English revenue authorities (HMRC) and of judicial authority than in Ireland.

The Irish Revenue Commissioners are quite circumspect when it comes to published guidelines for charities and trading. In October 1996, Revenue issued a technical note, CHY 7, *Trading by Charities: Exemption from Tax*, which laid down Revenue's conventions in dealing with both primary purpose trading and non-primary purpose trading. Revenue subsequently withdrew this guidance to revise and update it in relation to charity shops. The note has never been reissued.[30] It is, however, still referred to in the leading Irish treatise on income tax as an authoritative statement of Revenue practice and is available online from a third-party website.[31] The only current published Revenue guidance relating to charity trading and tax law is found in its Freedom of Information Manuals. In a short section entitled 'Trading Profits Relief', Revenue sets out the wording of the relevant tax provision governing tax exemption for trading profits but offers no elaboration on its terms or examples as to the scope or limits of its operation.[32] A lack of clarity thus exists in Irish tax law. In discussing the intersection of charity trading and tax law, therefore, the English position will be outlined, with reference to appropriate Irish guidelines or authorities, where possible.

There are a number of specific exemptions that apply to the conduct of charitable trading. To be liable for tax in the first instance, the activity in question must constitute 'trading', which bears the meaning discussed in the previous section. If liable for tax, a charity may seek an exemption in respect of its trading profits under a number of circumscribed headings. In all cases, it is a condition precedent for relief that the profits in question will be applied solely towards the primary charitable purpose. The exemptions considered below relate to:

(a) Primary purpose trading
    (i) Work in connection with trade mainly carried out by beneficiaries
(b) Ancillary purpose trading
(c) Non-primary purpose trading
    (i) Extraordinary concession for fundraising activities
    (ii) Small-scale trade exemption

Primary Purpose Trading Exemption

When a charity makes a profit from trade that is exercised in the course
of the actual carrying out of the charity's primary charitable purpose, that
profit is exempt from tax in both Ireland and the UK provided that the
income is applied solely to the purposes of the charity.[33] Since a charity
may have more than one primary purpose, it is possible to have multiple
forms of primary purpose trade. Thus, tuition fees charged by charitable
schools or universities, charges for medical procedures conducted by
charitable hospitals, and sales of reproductions of art works held by an
art gallery with charitable status are all exempt from tax.[34] HMRC has
taken a broad interpretation of what constitutes the primary purpose of a
charity in this regard to include within this tax exemption activities ancillary to the carrying out of the primary purpose.[35] In this regard, it gives
the example of the provision by a college of rented accommodation to its
students as falling within this exemption.[36]

**The work in connection with the trade is mainly carried on by beneficiaries
of the charity**
Many charities are engaged in activities where work is carried out by the
charity's beneficiaries. The work undertaken usually has an educational
or remedial purpose and will often qualify as a primary purpose activity.
However, even if the work is not a primary purpose activity (that is, it is
unrelated to the charitable purpose) it will still qualify for exemption from
tax as a trade where the work is carried out 'mainly' by the beneficiaries.
In all cases, the profits must be used for the purposes of the charity for the
exemption to apply.

The use of the word 'mainly' allows for other employees besides the
beneficiaries to be involved in the work without threatening the tax exemption. This situation would arise typically where the beneficiaries are disa-
bled or suffer from a learning difficulty and would be incapable, as a result
of their incapacity or lack of experience, of managing the business in question. Under its retracted CHY 7 guidance, Revenue states that, in order
to obtain exemption from tax, it is necessary to prove that the greater
part of a trade carried on by a charity is undertaken by the beneficiaries –
particularly where there are others involved, for example, employees
or volunteer workers who are not beneficiaries. It is unclear, however,
whether this measurement of involvement should be on a quantitative or
qualitative basis.[37]

A similar exemption exists under UK tax law.[38] According to the
HMRC guidance, where the work carried out by the beneficiaries has a
therapeutic, remedial or educational value, the profits from the trade may

qualify for exemption. Examples of such trades include the sale of goods manufactured by the beneficiaries of a disability charity or the running of a farm by agricultural college students.

Ancillary Purpose Trading

Trades which are not primary purpose activities in their own right may also qualify for trading exemption if they are ancillary to the carrying out of a charity's primary purpose.[39] In its guidance on ancillary trading, the CCEW further states that while the level of turnover is a factor in determining whether trade qualifies as ancillary or not, there is no specific level of annual turnover that decides this question. This principled, as opposed to mathematical, approach to the issue of ancillary trading strikes a common chord with the professed approach of the Inland Revenue Service in the US.[40] More importantly, trading the purpose of which is to raise funds for a charity does not qualify as ancillary purpose trading, such that these activities will be liable to tax unless otherwise specifically exempted.

HMRC takes a slightly more restrictive view of 'ancillary trading' in its guidance to charities. It describes 'ancillary trading' as trade which while not overtly primary purpose trading is nevertheless exercised in the course of carrying out the primary purpose and does not form a separate category of trade in its own right, which explains HMRC's rationale for bringing this type of activity within the tax exemption for primary purpose trading. Therefore, there should be a nexus between the primary purpose of the charity and the nature of the ancillary trading that is carried out. This would seem to make acceptable ancillary trading a form of 'related business activity' under the US model.

In Ireland, beyond providing some examples of what constitutes ancillary trading in its retracted CHY 7 guidelines, Revenue provides no published guidance for determining whether or to what extent an activity will be considered ancillary to an existing primary charitable purpose so as to qualify for tax exemption.

The Treatment of Non-primary Purpose Trading

Trading that is neither primary purpose trading nor ancillary in nature is classed as non-primary purpose trading (NPPT). NPPT is equivalent to the American concept of 'unrelated business activity'. A typical example would be trading that is intended to raise funds for a charity as distinct from trading which in itself furthers the charity's objects. When a charity engages in such NPPT, any profits resulting from this activity will, subject to the exemptions discussed below, be liable to tax regardless of the

ultimate destination of the income and may, depending upon the extent of
this activity, also threaten the charitable status of the organisation.

The difficulty caused by NPPT is exacerbated in Ireland by the existence
of a Revenue rule that does not allow for apportionment of income between
related and unrelated business activities carried out by charities. Thus, if
an Irish charity carries out both related business activities (which would be
exempt) and unrelated business activities (which do not enjoy exemption),
Revenue will consider which activity predominates. If Revenue determines
that the unrelated business activity predominates and the activity does not
fall within the scope of the exemptions outlined below, then *all* of the profits
arising from the event (including that part which is primary purpose trading)
will be liable to tax.[41] In other words, there is no equivalent to the US's unrelated business income tax (UBIT) in Ireland that can save unrelated trading
activity beyond the specific *de minimis* thresholds outlined below. In such
a situation, the charity will be forced to argue that the unrelated business
activity is a separate trade (and so severable from the exempt related business activity) or that it does not constitute 'trading' at all.

Prior to 2006, the UK revenue treatment of a charity engaged in both
related and unrelated business activities mirrored the Irish approach
outlined above. Thus, if a UK charity engaged in both primary and
non-primary purpose trading, the predominant form of trade coloured
the categorisation for tax purposes, resulting in the income being either
entirely exempt from tax or entirely liable for tax. The UK Finance Act
2006 amended the Income and Corporations Taxes Act 1988 so that, for
chargeable periods on or after 21 March 2006, UK law deems the primary
purpose and the non-primary purpose parts of the trade to be separate
trades.[42] The trade deemed primary purpose trade will be exempt from tax
as long as its profits are used for charitable purposes. The non-primary
purpose deemed trade is taxable, although the exemption for small trading
can apply to this trade (see below). Receipts and expenses relating to the
overall trade are apportioned to the separate trades on a reasonable basis.
The effect of these apportionment rules for charities now means that it is
possible for a charity *under UK tax law* to carry on more than small-scale
non-primary purpose trading activity in conjunction with its primary
purpose activity subject to the payment of tax on the unrelated business
activity. One must question whether this change in tax law amounts to a
surreptitious introduction of an American UBIT equivalent into UK law.

Extraordinary concession for fundraising activities

Ireland Revenue grants a concession from tax liability in respect of
profits from *small-scale* activities which have been run to raise funds

for charitable purposes only. No tax liability is incurred if the following conditions are satisfied:

(a)   the trading activities are not carried on regularly;
(b)   the trading activities are not in competition with other commercial traders;
(c)   the public supports the trading activities because they believe that the profits are intended for application to charitable purposes only;
(d)   the profits are applied for charitable purposes only.

It is implicit that if there is regularity to the fundraising activity it will not benefit from the concession so trading within the context of ongoing commercial activity, even if for the purpose of raising funds for charity, falls outside the scope of this exemption. The prohibition on commercial trade is emphasised further by condition (b) preventing charities from competing with commercial traders. This condition greatly limits the scope of this concession by confining charities to one-off events in the nature of dinners, bazaars, quizzes or shows. As to what is meant by 'small-scale activities', several factors are outlined in the retracted Revenue Guidance leaflet CHY 7, relating to:

● the level of both turnover and profit;
● the degree of commercial organisation involved;
● the level of input by outside bodies including professional fundraisers and well known personalities including individuals giving their services voluntarily;
● the number of people attending.

Revenue states that normally relief extends to all the profits of an activity including: (a) admission charges; (b) sale of refreshments; (c) sale of programmes; and (d) sale of advertisements, for example, in a programme. This concession is therefore quite narrow in its scope. There is no guidance as to what level of turnover or profit will cause a charity to lose the benefit and thus become liable to tax.

And yet occasionally Revenue has departed from these guidelines. In its 2001 Charities Manual, having reiterated the basic principle that an organisation set up solely to raise funds would not be considered charitable, Revenue qualified this statement to the effect that if 'the organisation specifies in its main object, the purpose for which it wishes to fundraise, *i.e.*, to further cancer research, to provide a cardiac unit in a named hospital etc., then such organisation would be regarded as established for charitable purposes'.[43]

In support of this finding, Revenue cites one example of an organisation the main object of which was to raise funds for charitable purposes and whose application for charitable tax-exempt status the Revenue Commissioners initially refused. Upon the subsequent advice of the Assistant Revenue Solicitor, Revenue reviewed this decision and granted exemption on condition that the funds raised were to be allocated to bodies which themselves had been granted charitable tax exemption under section 207 of the Taxes Consolidation Act 1997.[44] Since the outcome resulted in tax exemption, the case is a rare one in which one can identify the organisation involved (interestingly, The United Way of Ireland Ltd).[45]

Because no further details are given regarding the exemption,[46] this example does not aid our understanding of when a charity may have a main object of fundraising and still enjoy charitable status but also enjoy tax-exempt status in Ireland. It is unclear, for instance, what the intended nature of the fundraising activity was to be and whether if trading was intended such activity fell within the concessions either for small-scale fundraising or small-scale trading. Given that fundraising was listed as its main object, one might safely assume that neither concession applied. The decision in *United Way* thus sheds no light on the charitable tax treatment of fundraising or trading activity in Ireland. It may be that this case is an Irish subterranean version of the Australian High Court decision in *Commissioner of Taxation v Word Investments*[47] – that is, that once the destination of income is proven to be for charitable purposes, then the manner in which the income is raised does not detract from the otherwise charitable objects in question. And yet, in the absence of context and when placed beside Revenue's more generally available pronouncements on the treatment of fundraising and trading activities, this case study illustration merely serves to confuse rather than to clarify matters.

The United Kingdom   In contrast to the Irish guidance, the UK tax authorities are clearer with regard to the scope of the fundraising tax concession. HMRC operates a concessional tax relief in respect of certain fundraising activities under which certain events arranged by charities for the purposes of raising funds will fall outside the tax net if the event is of a kind that falls within the exemption from VAT under Group 12 of Schedule 9 to the VAT Act 1994 and the profits are transferred to charities or otherwise applied for charitable purposes.[48] To be a 'qualifying event' the event must have a charitable purpose and be organised by a charity or a trading subsidiary for the charity's own benefit. A limit is imposed on the number of times an event may be held in a given year so that if more than 15 events of the same kind are held at the same location during any financial year, none of the events will qualify for exemption. There is also a general exclusion of series of events (for example a weekly dinner dance) so that such regularity in trading would be liable to tax.

There are no particular restrictions as to the nature of the event held nor is there a turnover limit. So, in contrast to the Irish fundraising concession, the fundraising event is not required to be small-scale in order to avoid tax liability. A non-exhaustive list of events is provided covering dinners, fairs, shows, exhibitions, auctions, bazaars, contests. Given the lack of a turnover limit, this concession would allow charities potential tax relief for profits from substantial trading activities. However, in carrying out such business activities, a charity would need to be mindful of the charity law principle that unrelated business activities must not involve significant risk if carried out by charities directly.

The interface of charity law and tax law is particularly visible here since if a charity, concerned about violating the significant risk principle, chooses to set up a trading subsidiary to run the fundraiser, the profits from the fundraising event while being exempt from VAT[49] will nonetheless be subject to income or corporation tax. Yet, had the charity run the event itself instead of outsourcing it, no corporation tax liability would have arisen.[50]

Small trading income exemption – an exception to the NPPT rule?

Ireland Revenue makes available a small trading income exemption for non-primary purpose trading. Bearing in mind the 'all or nothing' classification rule for taxable activities in Ireland, the existence of a *de minimis* provision is a practical necessity for charities that carry out some unrelated business activity in addition to their charitable purpose activities. According to the retracted CHY 7 guidance, when a charity engages in both related and unrelated business activity the profits of the entire trading activity will be exempt if:

(a) that part of the trade which is NPPT activity is small, relative to the overall trading activity; and

(b) the turnover of that part of the trade which is NPPT activity is not greater than 10 per cent of the entire trading turnover.[51]

The United Kingdom The UK exemption for small-scale trading is more detailed and more generous to charities than its Irish equivalent. In the UK, the relevant statutory provisions are found in the Income Tax Act 2007 and the Corporation Tax Act 2009.[52] According to HMRC, the profits of 'small trading' carried on by a charity that are not otherwise already exempt may benefit from a small-scale exemption if:

- the total turnover from all of the charity's activities does not exceed the annual turnover limit (set at £5000 or if turnover is greater than £5000, 25 per cent of the charity's total incoming resources[53] subject to an overall upper limit of £50000), or
- if the total turnover exceeds the annual turnover limit, the charity had a reasonable expectation that it would not do so, and
- the profits are used solely for the purposes of the charity.

This exemption applies only to income and corporation tax and not to VAT. If the turnover of the unrelated trading exceeds the maximum threshold of £50000, the small-scale exemption will not apply unless the charity can prove that it had a 'reasonable expectation' at the start of the year that its trade income would not exceed this level. HMRC adopts an evidence-based approach to this test. To be entitled to the exemption, charities must produce evidence of previous trading figures (illustrating lower turnover) or evidence that expected grants had not materialised during the financial year to satisfy the revenue authorities as to the reasonableness of their belief.[54]

To illustrate this principle, assume Charity A has an unrelated business income of £40000 for the year and its total incoming resources, including this turnover, are £160000. In this scenario, the profits from the NPPT activity will be exempt because the turnover does not exceed either the 25 per cent threshold (£160000 × 25% = £40000) or the overall upper limit of £50000.

Compare this situation to that of Charity B, which has an unrelated business turnover of £60000 for a year in which its incoming resources amount only to £150000. In this case the turnover exceeds the overall upper limit of £50000 and the profits on the turnover may only be exempt if the charity can establish that it had a reasonable expectation at the start of the year that its turnover would not exceed this limit.

Under the new apportionment rules in the UK, HMRC would thus view Charity B as having both deemed primary purpose activity and deemed non-primary purpose activity in which case tax would be due only upon the profits from £60000 and not on the entire incoming resources of £150000. The UK law is thus more favourable to charities than Irish law, which does not operate an apportionment rule and under which the entire incoming resources would be liable to tax. It is difficult to distinguish the outcome in the UK in this instance from what the outcome would be in the US under UBIT. The qualifying charity law factor (as opposed to taxation factor) would relate to whether the scale of the unrelated business activities caused a significant risk to the charity's assets, in which case it would be advisable for the charity to set up a separate non-charitable trading subsidiary. One might imagine that once a charity exceeds the 25 per cent rule or the upper limit of £50 000 the onus of proving that the volume of trading does not pose a significant risk to charitable assets rests even more heavily with the charity in question.

In summary, therefore, a charitable organisation with purely charitable purposes may engage in primary purpose trading, the income of which, once applied for charitable purposes, will be tax-exempt in both Ireland and England. When trading occurs – whether primary purpose or non-primary purpose – once the work in relation to such activity is mainly carried out by the beneficiaries to the charity and the profits again applied for the charity's purposes, this too shall be exempt from tax. Unrelated business activity that is carried on by a charity in a manner that can be viewed as ancillary to its charitable purpose will also be exempt under a Revenue concession. The scale of such activity is a factor that will be taken into account.

When the trading activities of the charity are not related to the primary purpose of the charity at all but simply serve to raise income, unless these activities can be brought within the small-scale trade or extraordinary concession for fundraising activities, then any resulting profit from these activities will be liable to tax. Whereas in England since 2006 the conduct of both primary purpose trading and substantial NPPT will result in an apportionment of revenues between the two with tax payable only on the latter, tax law in Ireland is not so accommodating. Rather, the engagement in substantial unrelated business activity by a charity in conjunction with primary purpose business activity could result in the entire profits being subject to tax.

Aside from the taxation issues, trading that may cause significant risk to the charitable assets of the charity in question jeopardises the charitable status of the entity under UK charity law and presumably will have a similar effect under Irish charity law, in which case the setting up of a separate trading entity is advisable.

THE ORGANISATIONAL CHALLENGES OF CROSS-SECTORAL ACTIVITIES

To counter the legal and taxation challenges that affect charities wishing to engage directly in commercial activities in Ireland and the UK the use of a separate trading subsidiary is a commonly cited panacea. Setting up a separate trading company has a number of advantages for a charity. First, by distinguishing between a charity's main mission and its trading operations, a subsidiary can create both financial and organisational clarity for a charity. Second, an independent non-charitable subsidiary will not be constrained in its trading activities or the levels of profits that it makes from its business activities. Third, as discussed below, the use of separate structures may be tax efficient since the trading company can potentially eliminate its tax liabilities on trading profits donated back to the charity.[55] For this reason, even when use of a subsidiary is not required by charity law (for example, when the trading activities do not pose a significant risk to charitable assets), it may still be advantageous for a charity to set up a subsidiary structure.

However, there are downsides to this arrangement. Subsidiaries can be costly to set up and maintain for charities. They require separate administrative structures and when charity trustees sit on their boards, conflict of interest issues may arise. Moreover, these subsidiaries do not themselves enjoy charitable tax-exempt status. In setting up such entities, charity trustees are required to ensure that any charity money advanced by way of loan or otherwise to capitalise the subsidiary is invested in accordance with the charity's investment powers and properly secured so as not to risk the capital. The charity trustees are also subject to the broader charity legal obligations relating to prudent investment and diversification of investment assets.

Although the trading subsidiary would be liable for corporation tax on any profits made, it is possible for such companies to transfer back profits to the charity during the financial year in a tax-efficient manner. By using the Gift Aid Scheme in the UK or the Donations Scheme to Eligible Charities in Ireland, a trading subsidiary can transfer profits to its parent charity net of corporate tax.[56] Thus, if a subsidiary were to transfer its entire taxable profits to the charity, it would effectively eliminate its corporate tax liability.[57] As separate non-charitable legal entities, these subsidiaries are not restricted in the commercial activities in which they engage. However, trustees of charities that have trading subsidiaries must remember that in all decisions relating to the subsidiary the interests of the charity are paramount. It follows that the interests of the subsidiary, its directors or its creditors are all secondary to the interests of the charity.

Community Interest Companies – a Twist on the Trading Subsidiary?

Since 2004, charities in the UK wishing to establish a trading subsidiary have an additional organisational option beyond the private limited company in the form of the 'community interest company' (CIC), a limited liability company with the specific aim of providing benefit to a community. The CIC was introduced by the Companies (Audit, Investigations and Community Enterprise) Act 2004.[58] The CIC structure is not available to a charity as its main structure, but it can form part of a group that includes a charity – for example, the trading wing. This legal form can also be adopted by a range of social enterprises and nonprofit projects serving communities throughout the UK which combine the pursuit of a social purpose with commercial activities.

CICs can take one of three forms – a public limited company,[59] a private company limited by guarantee, or a private company limited by shares. If a CIC limited by shares aims to make a profit, that profit can (under certain checks and balances) be distributed to its members (who may or may not form part of the requisite community), thus allowing the potential for external equity investors.[60] In terms of structure, a CIC in the form of a company limited by shares or guarantee must have at least one member; there is no maximum number of members. The members of a company are the subscribers to the company's memorandum (who are deemed to have agreed to become members) and all other persons who have agreed to become members of the company. In a company limited by shares, members purchase shares, with their liability being limited to any amount owing to the company in respect of their shares. By contrast, in a company limited by guarantee, members agree to be liable to contribute a specified amount in the event of the company being wound up.

The CIC has a number of key features that distinguish it from other private limited companies. To be eligible as a CIC, an enterprise must pass the 'Community Interest Test'. This means that the CIC Regulator must be satisfied that a reasonable person might consider that the activities of that enterprise will be carried on for the benefit of the community. This test is intended to be a 'light touch' regulatory feature and does not equate to the public benefit requirements of charity.[61]

Another feature intended to reinforce this community benefit is the presence of a statutory 'asset lock'. The asset lock prevents the CIC giving away its assets for less than the true market value. The only exception is when the assets are transferred to another asset-locked body (such as a charity or CIC) or used to benefit the community that the CIC was set up to serve. The purpose of the asset lock is to provide legal protection against demutualisation and 'windfall profits' being paid out to its members and directors, without all the necessary checks and balances of mutuality or charitable status. In addition to their annual returns, CICs are required to submit an annual Community Interest report to the CIC Regulator. The purpose of the report is to show how the CIC is satisfying the Community Interest Test and that it is engaging appropriately with its stakeholders in carrying out activities which benefit the community.[62]

Thus, a CIC might be considered to be a halfway house between a fully commercial enterprise and a charity. On the one hand, it does not suffer from the constraints imposed upon charities relating to commercial activity and it can pay its directors reasonable remuneration. The downside is that it does not enjoy charitable tax exemption. On the other hand, the CIC is intended to be able to take advantage of the risk-taking features of a company, for example, by accessing the debt market for loans and bonds. If limited by shares, it may be able to expand through the selling of shares. Moreover, there is no limit to the level of profit a CIC is allowed to make, as this profit will be used to benefit the community it was set up to serve. Yet, the presence of the statutory asset lock (which applies as much to directors' remuneration as to company profits), the requirement of stated community benefit as both an aim in the objects and an outcome in the annual report and the statutory cap on the level of dividends that can be paid out to private individuals or corporations[63] all serve to differentiate the CIC from a regular for-profit enterprise.

Since its introduction in 2005, just over 3000 of these hybrid organisations have been established. Despite predictions of great take-up of this legal form,[64] the number of CICs established is relatively low when compared with the estimated number of social enterprises in Great Britain.[65] The difficulties lie with the limits imposed on this organisational form. First, a general problem relates to the arbitrary dividend cap imposed on CICs, which has made it difficult for CICs to attract adequate equity investment and forced some to rely on loans instead.[66] Until relatively recently, mainstream financial institutions were also slow to lend to charities. A major disincentive for the banks was the cost associated with assessing applications from voluntary organisations that did not fit the traditional debtor template.[67] Although matters have improved somewhat in the past five years with greater access to social financing opening up[68] and a growing expertise amongst commercial lenders, particularly in Britain, in evaluating and lending to charitable and social enterprises,[69] the inability to diversify beyond loan debt to equity leaves CICs vulnerable in times of recession.[70]

There are other perceived shortcomings in the CIC model. In a recent address at Harvard, Geoff Mulgan, Director of the London-based Young Foundation for Social Innovation (a charity with a 50-year track record of success in creating new organisations – public, private and nonprofit – as well as influencing ideas and policies) admitted that the Young Foundation has never once used the CIC format in creating its social innovation entities.[71] The CIC's statutory constraints have resulted in a preference for the use of the company limited by guarantee structure. Mulgan's admitted reluctance to avail of the CIC for spin-off enterprises is enlightening given that, in his former role as director of the government's Strategy Unit and Head of Policy in then Prime Minister Tony Blair's office, Mulgan helped create the original CIC model. Recognition of such shortcomings has forced the CIC Regulator to undertake a consultation process on the appropriateness of the current caps on the share dividends, aggregated dividends, and performance-related interest.[72]

THE POLITICAL AND ECONOMIC FORCES SHIFTING THE LINE

The changing nature of public service delivery, the replacement of grants with service contracts, the emergence of compacts and accords between the state and the voluntary sector and the growing demands on charities to provide greater services to beneficiaries, thereby increasing their need for greater resources, have had a visible impact upon the revenue streams of charities over the past ten years. Even those charities that continue to enjoy foundational grant support commonly find that they are being required to provide matching support when seeking grants, thereby increasing the pressure to find lucrative income outside the donations framework. Funders regularly urge charities to become more financially self-sufficient, which ultimately translates as a need to increase their earned income.

In the UK alone, recent figures published by the National Council for Voluntary Organisations (NCVO) reveal that over a five-year period in the UK the level of contract income earned by charities rose from £3.8 billion (in 2001) to £7.8 billion (in 2006). At the same time, charities experienced a reduction in statutory grants from £4.6 billion in 2001 to £4.2 billion in 2006–07.[73] NCVO's analysis of the income and expenditure trends of charities for the period 2006–07 reveals that, although voluntary income has continued to grow in absolute terms, its relative worth by 2006–07 had fallen to less than 41 per cent of total revenue. Conversely, earned income from contracts and sales of goods and services rose over the same period from 39 per cent of total revenue to 51 per cent.[74]

Corresponding figures are harder to come by in Ireland since there is neither a complete register of charities at present nor a database detailing government payments to nonprofit bodies. There appears to be a stronger reliance in Ireland on state funding (estimated to be in the region of 60 per cent), with most of this funding occurring in the areas of health and social services, education and social housing.[75] The limited evidence available, however, indicates that charities make a crucial contribution to public service delivery. A 2005 Joint Oireachtas Report estimated that the cost to the Exchequer of replacing the 475 000 volunteers who work with charities to provide beneficiary services would be in the region of €205 million to €485 million in wage costs per year.[76] Certain sectors, such as healthcare,

are particularly dependent on nonprofit organisations for public service delivery. In the area of disability services alone, the state paid out more than €877 million in service payments to nonprofit organisations in Ireland in the year 2003–04.[77] A 2006 Report, mapping the nonprofit sector in Ireland, estimated that state funding accounted for 59.8 per cent of the nonprofit respondents' income, with other earned 'fee' income accounting for 14.6 per cent.[78] These figures do not, however, indicate what percentage of the government funding took the form of grant funding and what proportion equated to contract payment.

Comparatively speaking, the level of charitable trading or contract payments for nonprofits in both Ireland and England falls short of the reported figures for Australian nonprofits, which show a 58 per cent reliance on earned income.[79] The Australian data do not indicate the degree to which this figure is influenced by the earned income of educational and healthcare institutions, which rely extensively on fee-for-service income in their budgeting models, and this, unless controlled for, would affect any figure attempting to estimate the entire sector's reliance on earned income. Nevertheless, the rate of commercial engagement, whether through primary purpose service delivery funded by contract or through for-profit engagement for funding purposes, appears to be growing in all three jurisdictions.

The larger policy question raised by these underlying trends towards commercialisation is whether such movement into for-profit ventures undermines the charitable mission of the organisation in question. Foster and Bradach have argued that many nonprofits lack the business perspective necessary to venture successfully beyond their primary charitable purposes, with the result that many for-profit enterprises detract from the charities' focus on their charitable mission and, more distressingly, frequently lose money.[80] In a similar vein, Weisbrod provides a litany of examples of charity–business alliances ranging from marketing relationships to joint ventures and other unrelated business activities that damaged the reputation of the charity in question or posed a serious conflict of interest with its charitable purposes.[81]

In one of the first empirical studies undertaken of how commercial income affects human services agencies, Guo has challenged a number of the assumptions generally associated with increased commercialisation in nonprofit entities.[82] Her findings suggest that commercial revenues do not necessarily help organisations to carry out their missions or deliver their services, a factor that has led Guo to argue that earned income does not guarantee improved services because what organisations gain in the way of additional income is offset by the demands of managing the business. The positive impact of earned income, according to Guo, manifested itself in organisations experiencing greater self-sufficiency and thus being positioned better to recruit and retain staff, thereby creating a positive circle for such organisations in which 'organisations with a better reputation can take advantage of this in their market practice, which further generates more economic return for nonprofits'.[83] Given the limited nature of the sample used and its non-representation of the broader sector of income generating nonprofits,[84] the study's findings should not be regarded as determinative but they do represent an interesting and rare empirical insight into this area, worthy of further inquiry.[85]

How does one begin to reconcile these conceptual and empirical difficulties of increased nonprofit commercialisation with the UK Cabinet Office's proposal to allow charitable organisations to carry out commercial activities directly without the need for a subsidiary trading organisation[86] or with the recent decision of the Australian High Court in *Commissioner of Taxation v Word Investments*,[87] allowing for unrestricted unrelated business activity by charities? The answer lies in distinguishing the policy questions underlying these proposals and outcomes. If one's only concerns with allowing charitable trading are taxation concerns and the preservation of competitive neutrality in the market place, then a 'play and pay' policy may seem to be the answer. Thus, we see greater freedom for nonprofits engaged in business activity in the US balanced against the requirement to pay unrelated business income tax.[88] The recent tax law changes in the UK, empowering HMRC to differentiate between a charity's non-taxable primary purpose trade, on the one hand, and its taxable non-primary purpose trade, on the other, would seem to mirror this approach. The existence of such a taxing power would seem to fit neatly with the Cabinet Office's 2002 proposal to lift restrictions on direct charitable trading.

And yet, the US experience to date implies that not even UBIT can fully protect the interests of the treasury (and, *a fortiori*, of for-profit competitors) from increased charity commercialisation. Recent US studies indicate that most UBIT returns report net losses.[89] One study estimated that by charging joint costs (that is, those not attributable directly to either program activities or for-profit activities) against taxable income, nonprofits annually report between US$500 million and US$2.3 billion more in total expenses to the IRS than they actually incur in their commercial activities.[90] In light of these findings, a government would have to consider seriously the potential loss to the treasury before introducing such a regime. If the loss to the treasury was balanced by better provision of public goods to the community at large, a state with a healthy surplus might make a policy decision to allow such activity to continue. If the alleged benefits were harder to prove or non-existent, a state might want to consider closer scrutiny of such trading adventures.

LIKELY FUTURE CHALLENGES FOR CONSIDERATION IN THE UK AND IRELAND

The pressures of increased intersectoral activity between charities and the market will continue to put pressure on the dividing line between the two sectors. It would be wrong to think, however, that this pressure flows only in one direction. There is evidence of increasing movement from the business side of the line to the borders of charity, which in turn will raise equally difficult questions relating to both charity and tax law. On the one hand, there has been a growth in the UK in recent years in the number of corporate foundations, that is, charitable foundations established, funded and staffed by commercial corporations, often with a view to assisting or furthering their corporate social responsibility agendas.[91] This generally positive development has raised issues regarding the independence of these foundations from their parent corporations. Governance questions arise over the level of corporation control over foundation boards and the subsequent influence such control has on the charity's programme activities. One recent study for the UK Cabinet Office and Charities Aid Foundation (CAF) found that 10 out of 29 foundations surveyed admitted that they were either completely or nearly completely controlled by their establishing corporate parents, despite the legal requirement for corporate foundations to be independent.[92]

More recently, hybrid organisations in the form of 'for-profit philanthropy' organisations have begun to emerge, further blurring the borderline between for-profit and nonprofit activity.[93] If, through a blurring of the borderline, we lose the ability to categorise an entity as either purely for-profit or purely nonprofit, what do we lose? In the first instance, we lose that clarity of legal purpose sought so keenly by lawyers and necessary for the application of charity law and regulation. Second, it seems inevitable that in a blurring of categorisation we injure organisations on both sides of the line, be they for-profit or nonprofit. As Payton pithily put it, 'Philanthropy owes its credibility to its altruistic imperative. It is not that self-interest does not yield altruistic benefits; what matters is that acts guided primarily by self-interest are called something else'.[94]

It is from their differing motivating purposes – self-interest versus public interest – that the differing legal and fiduciary obligations of for-profit officials and charity trustees flow. As Sugin and Brakman Reiser have argued, for-profit directors owe their fiduciary duties to shareholders when dealing with a company's assets; in contrast, charity trustees must steadfastly devote charity assets to their charitable mission in pursuit of public benefit.[95] Any mixing of the two forms in an orphaned hybrid entity raises immediate conflict of interest issues for directors apart from headaches for tax officials and charity regulators. Devoid of either pure charity or for-profit pedigree, the legitimacy of the resulting mongrel mix may depend on executive or judicial discretion. In practice, we have seen the former giving rise to a CIC-type model whereas the latter led to the decision in the Australian High Court in the *Word Investments* case;[96] neither result providing a particularly suitable basis on which to develop the law.

The regulatory challenges posed by charity–business hybrids force us to re-examine the policy choices that underlie the recognition rules for charitable entities and those characteristics that we deem fundamental in distinguishing 'charitable' from other nonprofit or for-profit activity. At its core, what constitutes a charitable purpose should be a political expression of the values that we, as a society, wish to foster on behalf of the community as a whole in the interests of pluralism as much as altruism. The tax reliefs that flow from such recognition should be a by-product of this understanding and not the raison d'être for its grant or its rejection. In practice, the implementation of such a perspective can be difficult given the predominant, if understandable, tendency of government to view the concept of charitable purpose through the lens of short-term political goals and current fiscal constraints.

NOTES

1. This chapter originated during the author's tenure as a Visiting Research Fellow at the Hauser Center for Nonprofit Organizations, Harvard University. The author wishes to thank Evelyn Brody, Anne Corrigan, Marion Fremont-Smith, and Debra Morris for their formative comments in the development of this chapter. Any remaining errors are, of course, my own.
2. On this point see Weisbrod, B. (2004), 'The Pitfalls of Profits', *Stanford Social Innovation Review*, 2(3), 40–47; Foster, W. and J. Bradach (2005), 'Should Nonprofits Seek Profits?', *Harvard Business Review*, 83(2), 92–100; cf. Jones, M.B. (2007), 'The Multiple Sources of Mission Drift', *Nonprofit and Voluntary Sector Quarterly*, 36(2), 299–307.
3. See Handy, C. (2000), 'The Privatisation of Social Housing: Capture and Commercialisation of the Voluntary Sector', in Dunn, A. (ed.), *The Voluntary Sector, the State and the Law*, Oxford: Hart Publishing, 107–19.
4. See the Charity Commission's approval in the UK of Wigan Leisure & Culture Trust and Trafford Community Leisure Trust, established by local councils to provide services formerly provided by them. In Ireland, the Health Service Executive, the body established by government to run the National Health Service, enjoys charitable tax-exempt status.
5. See Rigby, E. (2007), 'Foundations and Corporates Can Work More Closely Together', *Third Sector Online*, 20 July.
6. List of Community Interest Companies available at http://www.cicregulator.gov.uk/coSearch/companyList.shtml (accessed 17 December 2009).
7. In 2002, income from contracts and trading made up one-third of the total income of general charities in the UK: Cabinet Office, Strategy Unit (2002), *Private Action, Public Benefit: A Review of Charities and the Wider Not-for-Profit Sector*, para 4.42. Charities

   still obtained 50% of their total income from 'voluntary sources' split almost half and
   half between individuals and grants and corporate donations. In its 2009 edition of
   The UK Civil Society Almanac (formerly *The UK Voluntary Sector Almanac*), NCVO
   demonstrates that although voluntary income has continued to grow in absolute terms,
   by 2006–07 its relative worth had fallen to less than 41% of total revenue. Conversely,
   earned income from contracts and sales of goods and services rose over the same period
   from 39% of total revenue to 51%.

8. See also English Charities Act 2006, s. 1(1): '(1) For the purposes of the law of England
    and Wales, 'charity' means an institution which – (a) is established for charitable pur-
    poses only . . . '

9. UK Income and Corporation Taxes Act 1988 (c. 1), s. 832(1), as amended by Sched. 1,
    para 272 Corporation Tax Act 2009; Irish Taxes Consolidation Act 1997, s. 3(1).

10. HM Revenue and Customs (undated), *Charities – Trading and Business Activities*,
    Guidance Notes annex 4, London: HMRC, available at http://www.hmrc.gov.uk/chari-
    ties/guidance-notes/annex4/sectiona.htm (accessed 17 December 2009).

11. See below under 'Charity trading and tax law'.

12. See above n 10.

13. This would appear also to be the law in the United States. See Brody, E. (2009),
    'Business Activities of Nonprofit Organisations: Legal Boundary Problems', in Cordes,
    J.J. and C.E. Steuerle (eds), *Nonprofits and Business*, Washington: Urban Institute
    Press.

14. Royal Commission on the Taxation of Profits and Income (1955), *Royal Commission on
    the Taxation of Profits and Income Final Report*, Cmd 9497, London: HMSO.

15. In the UK, see *Lowe v Ashmore (JW)* [1971] Ch 545 (Ch); *Marson (Inspector of Taxes)
    v Morton* [1986] 1 WLR 1343 (Ch); *Chappell v Revenue and Customs Commissioners*
    [2009] STC (SCD) 11. In Ireland, see: *Airspace Investments Ltd v M Moore, Inspector
    of Taxes* [1994] 2 ILRM 151 (HC); earlier Irish case law dealing with the definition of
    trade includes *Davis v Superioress of Mater Misercordiae Hospital* [1933] IR 480 (SC);
    Pharmaceutical Society of Ireland v Special Commissioners of Income Tax [1938] IR 202
    (HC).

16. See Office of the Revenue Commissioners (2003), *Guidance on Revenue Opinions on
    Classification of Activities as Trading*, Dublin: Office of the Revenue Commissioners,
    available at http://www.revenue.ie/en/practitioner/tech-guide/trade.pdf (accessed 17
    December 2009).

17. See *Living Faith Inc v Commissioner*, 950 F 2d 365 (7th Cir 1991) on the 'commercial
    hue' test; cf. *Presbyterian Reformed Publishing v Commissioner*, 70 TC, 1070, rev'd, 743
    F 2d 148 (3rd Cir 1982).

18. For discussion of the law relating to related and unrelated business income in the US see
    Fremont-Smith, M. (2004), *Governing Nonprofit Organizations: Federal and State Law
    and Regulation*, Cambridge, MA: Harvard University Press, 289–99.

19. *Rowntree Memorial Trust Housing Association Ltd v Attorney General* [1983] Ch 159;
    Bryant Trust Board v Hamilton City Council [1997] 3 NZLR 343; *Barrington's Hospital
    v Commissioner of Valuation* [1957] IR 299 (SC).

20. The extent to which such sales would constitute non-primary purpose trading will
    depend on the context. The selling of art reproductions by a museum shop may consti-
    tute primary purpose trading whereas similar sales by a hospital shop may constitute
    non-primary purpose trade.

21. See Luxton, P. (2001), *The Law of Charities*, Oxford: Oxford University Press, at 20.2
    (citing refusal of Charity Commission of England and Wales to register entities with
    such objects as charities); Warburton, J. (2003), *Tudor on Charities*, 9th edn, London:
    Sweet & Maxwell, at 7.039.

22. Charity Commission for England and Wales (2007), *CC35 – Trustees, Trading and Tax:
    How Charities May Lawfully Trade*, London: Charity Commission, para C8.

23. Ibid.

24. In the US context in this regard, see IRC §513 (1954) setting out the 'convenience

doctrine', which exempts from unrelated business income tax (UBIT) any business activities operated by a tax-exempt organisation or college or university for the convenience of its members, patients, students, officers or employees. See also IRC §512 setting out 'modifications' to UBIT, which largely exclude certain types of income from the scope of UBIT.

25. Charity Commission, above n 22.
26. Charity Commission, above n 22 at para C8.
27. Office of the Revenue Commissioners (2005), *Applying for Relief from Tax on the Income and Property of Charities*, CHY 1, November, noting, 'The Revenue Commissioners are responsible for the administration of the relevant tax exemptions and for this purpose determine whether a body of persons or a trust claiming the benefit of any exemption is established for charitable purposes only'; Office of the Revenue Commissioners, Customs and Residence Division (2001), *Charities Manual 2001*, at 7 (stating, 'There can be misunderstandings in relation to the role of the Office of the Revenue Commissioners viz. a viz. [sic] charities . . . In a nutshell, the Office of the Revenue Commissioners does not fulfil the following functions, viz.: (a) In granting exemption from tax we do not grant charitable status per se . . . (b) We do not regulate the activities of charities'.)
28. Irish Charities Act 2009, s. 7.
29. Irish Charities Act, 2009, s. 2.
30. In correspondence with the Irish Revenue Commissioners in March 2009 the author was informed that Revenue does not now plan to reissue this guidance note but instead to deal with trading issues on a case-by-case basis as they arise.
31. See Judge, N.E. (2008), *Irish Income Tax 2008*, Haywards Heath: Tottel, para 18.204.
32. See Office of the Revenue Commissioners (undated), 'Charity Exemption – Tax Exemption for Charities under Sections 207 and 208 TCA 1997', in *Tax & Duty Manuals*, Section 16, Part 7, 7.1.6, para 5, available at http://www.revenue.ie/en/about/foi/s16/income-tax-capital-gains-tax-and-corporation-tax/part-07 (accessed 17 December 2009).
33. Irish Taxes Consolidation Act 1997, s. 208; UK Income Tax Act 2007, s. 525; and UK Income and Corporation Taxes Act 1988 (c. 1), s. 505(1)(e).
34. There is one exception to this rule in Ireland if the trade in question carried out by the charity is farming. In this case, exemption is granted under s. 208 of the 1997 Act if the profits are applied solely to the charity's purposes. In other words, it is not required that the charity's farming trade be carried out either mainly by the charity's beneficiaries or that it be exercised in the actual carrying out of the charity's primary purpose (s. 208(3)).
35. HM Revenue and Customs, above n 10 at 4.4.
36. Dawson, I. (2000), 'Taxation of Trades in the Charities Sector', in Dunn, A. (ed.), *The Voluntary Sector, The State and the Law*, Oxford: Hart Publishing, 177, at 186, is critical of this approach, arguing that 'as a matter of language, if one activity is ancillary to another, in performing the former one cannot be performing the latter' as is strictly required by statute.
37. See Dawson, above n 36.
38. UK Income and Corporations Taxes Act 1988, s. 505(1)(e)(ii) and UK Income Tax Act 2007, s. 525(1)(b).
39. See Charity Commission, above n 21 at C7; Office of the Revenue Commissioners (1996), *Trading by Charities: Exemption from Tax*, CHY 7, Dublin: Revenue Commissioners.
40. See General Counsel Memorandum 32689 (1963) and General Counsel Memorandum 32689 (1964) stating, '[The test is] essentially a test of proof. As such, it becomes a test of whether there is a real, bona fide, or genuine charitable purpose, as manifested by the charitable accomplishments of the organisation, and not a mathematical measuring of business purpose as opposed to charitable purpose'. See, further, Siegel, J. (2008), 'Commensurate in Scope: Myth, Mystery, or Ghost? – Part One', *Taxation of Exempts*, 20(3), 26–36.

41. Judge, above n 31 at 18.204.
42. Income and Corporations Taxes Act 1988, s. 505(1B), introduced by Finance Act 2006, s. 56 and Income Tax Act 2007, ss 525(2) and (3).
43. Charities Manual, above n 27 at 66. The Charities Manual was originally issued under the Irish Freedom of Information Acts 1997–2003.
44. Ibid.
45. CHY No. 10195.
46. Upon contacting United Way International's European Liaison Officer, the author was informed that the Irish branch was established in the 1980s and dissolved about 15 years later (prior to the compilation of the Revenue's 2001 Charities Manual). The founding board comprised agency executives rather than business and community leaders, which led to competition for funding. The domination of vested interests over community-wide interests inhibited the building of strong business connections and the ultimate failure to establish strong workplace giving practices. However, the Liaison Officer was unable to supply any background information on the tax concessions granted, which were awarded prior to her appointment.
47. *Commissioner of Taxation of the Commonwealth of Australia v Word Investments Ltd* [2008] HCA 55.
48. HM Revenue and Customs, Extra Statutory Concession, C4: Trading activities for charitable purposes.
49. In the UK, the supply of goods or services at or in connection with a wide range of fund-raising events is exempt from VAT. For VAT purposes, there is no distinction between primary purpose, beneficiary and non-primary purpose trading. Each can qualify as 'business activities' for VAT purposes, where 'business activity' is defined as anything that is carried on for a consideration. See, further, Group 12, Section 9 of the VAT Act 1994.
50. See, further, Charity Commission for England and Wales (2008), *CC20 – Charities and Fundraising*, London: Charity Commission; HM Revenue and Customs, above n 10 at para 36 ff.
51. See Office of the Revenue Commissioners, above n 39; HM Revenue and Customs, above n 10 at para 15.
52. UK Income Tax Act 2007, s. 526 and Sched. 1, Part 2, para 392 (amending Finance Act 2000, s. 46, to the effect that exemption applies to all small-scale trading carried out regardless of location); UK Corporation Tax Act 2009, Sched. I, Part 2, para 463 (amending Finance Act 2000, s. 46 but limiting exemption for charitable companies for small-scale trading to trading carried on wholly or partly within the UK).
53. Total incoming resources is defined by HMRC as the total receipts of the charity for the year from all sources (grants, donations, investment income, all trading receipts, etc.) calculated in accordance with normal charity accounting rules (whether the income would otherwise be taxable or not).
54. See HM Revenue and Customs, above n 10 at para 22. In this regard, HMRC will consider minutes of board meetings at which trading activities were discussed, copies of cash flow forecasts, and charity business plans along with previous years' accounts.
55. The position in Ireland and the UK differs in this regard from the position in the US, where a percentage limitation is imposed on the amount that a corporation can deduct from its tax liability through charitable contributions; cf. IRC §170(b)(2) restricting charitable donations by corporations to 10 per cent of the corporation's taxable income in any given tax year. Prior to 6 April 2001 a similar limitation on corporate donations to charity existed in Ireland under the Irish Finance Act 1998, s. 61 (which provided that qualifying donations to any one eligible charity could not exceed £10000 within a given accounting period; with an overall limit on relief for all qualifying donations of the lesser of £50,000 or 10% of the company's trading profits). The Finance Act 2001, s.45 replaced this provision; see below n 56.
56. On the UK Gift Aid scheme, see Income Tax Act 2007, s. 414, and Income and Corporation Tax Act 1988, s. 339. See also Charity Commission, above n 21 at D4.

On the Irish Eligible Donations scheme, see s. 848A, Sched. 26A, Taxes Consolidation Act 1997 as amended by Finance Act 2001, s. 45. See also Office of the Revenue Commissioners (2007), *Scheme of Tax Relief for Donations of Money or Designated Securities to 'Eligible Charities' and other 'Approved Bodies' under Section 848a Taxes Consolidation Act 1997*, CHY 2, Dublin: Revenue Commissioners. Note that it is a condition precedent under the UK regime that the recipient applies these transferred profits for charitable purposes only. No similar condition exists under the Irish scheme.

57. As the CCEW points out, when the level of taxable profits exceeds the level of profits for accounting purposes, the subsidiary may need to finance the profit transfer out of share capital since otherwise the trading subsidiary is likely to be insolvent. See Charity Commission, above n 22 at D5.

58. Companies (Audit, Investigations and Community Enterprise) Act 2004 (2004 Act), s. 26.

59. A 'plc' is a type of limited company in the UK and Ireland that is permitted to offer shares to the public through the stock exchange. A limited company grants limited liability to its owners. The public nature of the company allows it to sell shares to investors, which is useful for raising necessary capital.

60. Regulator of Community Interest Companies (2009), *Consultation on the Dividend and Interest Caps*, Cardiff: CIC Regulator, available at http://www.cicregulator.gov.uk/consultationintro.shtml (accessed 17 December 2009) – according to the consultation document, 1,836 CICs (73%) are companies limited by guarantee and 671 CICs (27%) are limited by shares.

61. See Regulator of Community Interest Companies (2006), 'Chapter 4 – Creating a CIC', *Guidance Notes*, Cardiff: CIC Regulator, available at http://www.cicregulator.gov.uk/guidanceindex.shtml (accessed 17 December 2009).

62. See Regulator of Community Interest Companies (2006), 'Chapter 8 – Statutory Obligations', *Guidance Notes*, Cardiff: CIC Regulator, available at http://www.cicregulator.gov.uk/guidanceindex.shtml (accessed 17 December 2009).

63. 2004 Act, s. 30 and the Community Interest Company Regulations 2005 (2005 No. 1788). Paras 17 to 22 of the 2005 regulations provide that a CIC limited by shares which adopts the appropriate clauses in its articles, and subject to company law requirements, may pay a dividend on shares if agreed by a resolution of its members. Dividends payable to certain types of shareholders (non-asset-locked bodies e.g. not a charity or CIC) are subject to a dividend cap. At present, the cap is a maximum dividend per share of 5% above the Bank of England base lending rate and a maximum aggregated dividend of 35% of the distributable profits. Unused dividend capacity can be carried forward for 5 years. There is also a cap on performance-related interest of 4% above the Bank of England base lending rate.

64. *Third Sector* reported the registration of the 1000th CIC in June 2007 ('CIC Register Swells to 1000', *Third Sector*, 15 June) with various predictions that this number would double within 6 months. In fact, the doubling took almost another 2 years, which means that on average only 500 CICs are being set up a year.

65. *A Survey of Social Enterprises Across the UK*: Research Report prepared for the Small Business Service (SBS) by IFF Research Ltd, The Small Business Service (July 2005), estimated that there were around 15,000 social enterprises in the UK at that time with a turnover of £18 billion. Given that the Office of the Third Sector now estimates the turnover of social enterprises to be in the region of £27 billion (http://www.cabinetoffice.gov.uk/third_sector/research_and_statistics.aspx, accessed 17 December 2009) the number of social enterprises has most likely increased in line with this figure, making the use of the CIC as an organisational form quite insignificant.

66. Warrell, H. (2008), 'News Analysis: What's the Price of Social Enterprise?', *Third Sector*, 2 July.

67. Bolton, M. and J. Kingston (2006), *Approaches to Financing Charitable Work: Tracking Developments*, Charities Aid Foundation, at 6.

68. For example the creation of the Social Finance Foundation in Ireland to enable

charities to access social finance capital at wholesale rates and similar social finance schemes in the UK with the creation of Charity Bank (www.charitybank.org) and Venturesome (http://www.cafonline.org/default.aspx?page=6903), both incubated within the UK Charities Aid Foundation.

69. See Bolton and Kingston, above n 67.
70. E.g., Ealing Community Transport, the UK's most successful social enterprise, which, due to cash-flow difficulties during the credit crisis, was forced to sell its profitable diversified businesses to a private company when the CIC structure hampered its efforts to raise further working capital. The deal has caused concern in the voluntary sector with some viewing the fate of ECT as illustrative of the structural shortcomings of the CIC organisational form in practice. See Cater, N. (2008), 'Company Buys Social Enterprise to Win Business', *Third Sector*, 11 June; Macalister, T. (2008), 'Going to Waste: The Rise and Fall of Flagship Refuse Firm ECT', *The Guardian*, 16 July 3.
71. Mulgan, G. (2009), *Social Innovation: Perspectives from England*, Hauser Center for Nonprofit Organizations, Harvard University, 12 March, in response to a question from the author.
72. See above n 60. Following the CIC Regulator's publication of *Summary of the Responses to the Consultation on the Dividend and Interest Caps* (October 2009), the Regulator is now consulting other stakeholders on whether to change the dividend caps. If any changes are to be made, it is intended that they would come into force in April 2010.
73. National Council for Voluntary Organisations (2009), *The UK Civil Society Almanac*, London: NCVO.
74. Ibid. See also Brindle, D. (2009), 'The Worst is Yet to Come', *The Guardian,* 18 February, 3.
75. Donoghue, F. and G. Prizeman (2006), *The Hidden Landscape: First Forays into Mapping Nonprofit Organisations in Ireland*, Dublin: Centre for Nonprofit Management, at 45.
76. Kelly, O. (2005), 'Voluntary Workers Save State €485m in Wages', *The Irish Times*, 26 January, 6.
77. Office of the Comptroller and Auditor General (2005), *Report on Value for Money Examination: Health Service Executive – Provision of Disability Services by Nonprofit Organisations*, Dublin: Comptroller and Auditor General, para 1.2.
78. Donoghue and Prizeman, above n 75 at para 4.3.
79. According to the National Roundtable of Nonprofit Organisations (undated), *The Nonprofit Sector in Australia: A Fact Sheet*, in 1999/2000, 58% of the nonprofit sector's income came from sale of goods or services as compared with only 30% from government grants and contracts.
80. Foster and Bradach, above n 2 at 97 (commenting with examples that 'Despite the hype, earned income accounts for only a small share of funding in most nonprofit domains, and few of the ventures actually make money').
81. Weisbrod, above n 2.
82. Guo, B. (2006), 'Charity for Profit? Exploring Factors Associated with the Commercialization of Human Service Nonprofits', *Nonprofit and Voluntary Sector Quarterly*, 35(1), 123–38 at 135.
83. Ibid, commenting, 'The nonrecursive model indicates that higher levels of commercial income can lead to higher assessments of the organization's reputation, and higher assessments of organization reputation, in turn, lead to higher levels of commercial income'.
84. Guo's data came from a survey of nonprofit ventures conducted by the Yale School of Management and the Goldman Sachs Foundation. Of the 519 respondent organisations, Guo limited her data to the survey's 67 human service agencies.
85. See Snibbe, A.C. (2006), 'What Profits Do for Nonprofits', *Stanford Social Innovation Review*, 4(2), 19–20, 20.
86. Cabinet Office, Strategy Unit (2002), *Private Action, Public Benefit: A Review of Charities and the Wider Not-for-Profit Sector*, London: HMSO, para 4.46.

87. *Commissioner of Taxation of the Commonwealth of Australia v Word Investments Ltd* [2008] HCA 55.

88. And yet, even in the US some see merit in the Anglo-Irish treatment of charitable trading. Cf. Yetman, R. (2005), 'Causes and Consequences of the Unrelated Business Income Tax', presented at National Tax Association Meeting, Miami, proposing the repeal of UBIT in return for a segregation by charities of their commercial activities into separate for-profit subsidiaries, cited in Brody, above n 13 at 113.

89. See Brody, above n 13 at 97, citing Riley, M. (2007), 'Unrelated Business Income Tax Returns, 2003: Financial Highlights and a Special Analysis of Nonprofit Charitable Organizations' Revenue and Taxable Income', *Statistics of Income Bulletin*, 26(3), 88–115 to the effect that 'only 4 percent of 263,353 charitable organizations filing Forms 990 or 990EZ also filed Form 990-T for 2003 and that the reported taxable unrelated business income from those 10,064 organizations came to only 1 percent of total revenue'.

90. Sinitsyn, M. and B. Weisbrod (2004), *Nonprofit Organization Behavior in For-Profit Markets*, Institute for Policy Research Working Paper WP–02–36, Evanston IL: Department of Economics, Northwestern University, cited in Weisbrod, above n 2 at 44. See also Sinitsyn, M. and B. Weisbrod (2008), 'Behavior of Nonprofit Organizations in For-Profit Markets: The Curious Case of Unprofitable Revenue-Raising Activities', *Journal of Institutional and Theoretical Economics*, 164, 727–50.

91. Smart Co (2007), *The Changing Nature of Corporate Responsibility: What Role for Corporate Foundations?*, Charities Aid Foundation.

92. Smart Co (2006), *Revealing the Foundations – A Guide to Corporate Foundations in England and Wales*, London: Cabinet Office and CAF.

93. Brakman Reiser, D. (2009), 'For Profit Philanthropy', *Fordham Law Review*, 77(5), 2437–74, 2472, arguing that 'the for-profit philanthropy model does not just push or question the boundaries the law has placed on philanthropy. It ignores the map altogether . . . [and in] doing so, for-profit philanthropy raises serious questions about whether the boundaries the law has placed on traditional charitable forms represent the right policy choices' Cf. Malani, A. and E.A. Posner (2007), 'The Case for For-Profit Charities', *Virginia Law Review*, 93(8), 2017–67 (discounting the need for a nonprofit form as a precondition for tax benefits for philanthropic activity) and Sugin, L. (2007), 'The Increasing Resemblance of Nonprofit and Business Organizations Law: Resisting the Corporatization of Nonprofit Governance: Transforming Obedience into Fidelity', *Fordham Law Review*, 76(2), 893–927 (arguing that 'The crucial difference between for-profit social entrepreneurship and nonprofit philanthropy is that only those in control of charitable organizations have the privilege and responsibility of subordinating all interests to the charitable mission of the organization . . . With the rise of for-profit philanthropy, increasing the resemblance of nonprofit governance to for-profit governance is a mistake because it fosters a type of accountability that is more suited to serving the private goal of profit than the public goal of mission').

94. Payton, R. (1989), 'Philanthropic Values', in Magat, R. (ed.), *Philanthropic Giving*, Oxford: Oxford University Press, at 40.

95. See above n 93.

96. See above n 47 and accompanying text.

7. Government–charity boundaries

Kerry O'Halloran

INTRODUCTION

The Preamble[1] was the initial legislative statement of matters construed by government to constitute charitable purposes in a common law context. It provided an outline of what was to become the core agenda for government's relationship with charity. The resulting implied partnership, as viewed by government, endured for four centuries and in many different cultural contexts across the common law world. During that period, judicial mediation on the balance to be struck between government interest in acquiring value for granting tax exempt privileges and the right of individuals to freely dispose of property in accordance with their particular altruistic wishes steadily broadened the range of purposes deemed to be charitable, the vagaries of donor choice often prevailing over government interest in acquiring value for tax exemption.[2]

The recent spate of charity law reform processes, completed or ongoing in many common law jurisdictions,[3] can be seen as a return to the Preamble drawing board: as government initiatives, often in the context of formal partnerships with charity, to revise and reformulate the terms on which it proposed to continue granting tax exemption and other privileges to charity. The legislative outcome of these processes reveals the new agenda for a 21st-century relationship between government and charity. Again, this is represented primarily in the nature and extent of the now statutorily stated charitable purposes. Four centuries after the Preamble, however, that relationship has grown more complex and diffused. Consequently, while core business continues to be embodied in the charitable purposes and ancillary conceptual definitions, we must also look to other matters accommodated within the new charity statutes, to tax law and to aspects of social and political context, in order to trace the new boundaries that now mark the territory owned by, and shared or disputed between, government and charity.

This chapter takes an overview of the re-drawing of the Preamble boundaries as manifested in those countries that have undergone charity law reform. It makes a start by examining the baseline for government–charity relations as first set out in 1601. Then, rather than dwelling on the various reform processes (addressed elsewhere in this book), it looks back on reform outcomes to consider the strategic significance of the changes effected, the degree of international consensus achieved and the implications arising for the future development of that relationship. This leads into a consideration of other aspects of the relationship, falling outside the confines of charity law, which have also contributed to shaping a new government–charity boundary for the 21st century.

THE PREAMBLE AND THE INITIAL GOVERNMENT–CHARITY BOUNDARY

Entitled 'An Acte to redresse the Misemployment of Landes Goodes and Stockes of Money heretofore given to Charitable Uses', the Statute of Charitable Uses 1601 was a reforming statute driven by a strategy comprising three distinct strands. Firstly, in order to fill the social care gap left by the dissolution of the monasteries and solicit the funds necessary to repair the damage caused by the ravages of war, it sought to channel private gifts towards priority areas of public need. Secondly, it aimed to reform the abuse of property donated to charities by listing the types of purposes thereafter to be recognised as charitable, and by establishing a body of Commissioners with the powers to supervise and inspect charitable trusts.[4] Thirdly, by enlisting the goodwill and assets of donors to assist government in addressing contemporary social need, it sought to build a new platform of collective civic responsibility in place of the institutional role vacated by the Church.[5] This strategy set out the terms of engagement that were to endure, substantially unaltered, for four centuries across the common law world. The government–charity boundary, reflecting the government's agenda for its relationship with charity at the dawn of the 17th century in England, was clearly evident in the following charitable purposes, stated in the Preamble to that Act:

> Releife of aged impotent and poore people, some for Maintenance of sicke and maymed Souldiers and Marriners, Schooles of Learninge, Free Schooles and Schollers in Universities, some for Repaire of Bridges Portes Havens Causwaies Churches Seabankes and Highwaies, some for Educacion and preferment of Orphans, some for or towardes Reliefe Stocke or Maintenance of Howses of Correccion, some for Mariages of poore Maides, some for Supportacion Ayde and Helpe of younge tradesmen Handicraftesmen and persons decayed, and others for reliefe or redemption of Prisoners or Captives, and for aide or ease

of any poore Inhabitantes concerninge paymente of Fifteenes, setting out of
Souldiers and other Taxes.

However imperfect the transference of modern social constructs, 'government' then as now can be seen declaring that charities will bear some
responsibility for public benefit provision: a partnership sealed with the
formal granting of tax exemption two centuries later.[6] The Preamble purposes were grouped into two broad categories: for the relief of the poor
and for public works. Because the purposes were treated from the outset
as being illustrative rather than definitive, although judicial uncertainty
initially prevailed as to whether they could be construed disjunctively or
conjunctively,[7] the list has been amenable to diversification and grew to
accommodate a wide range of analogous entities. Nonetheless, it is plainly
evident that government emphasis in the Preamble on the contribution
of charitable purposes to the following matters of public benefit has since
been sustained in all common law jurisdictions:

- health and social care provision
- training for employment
- public utility provision
- the physical maintenance of social infrastructure
- the protection of citizens.

In addition to several of the 'service' type public utilities then found
to be deserving of charitable status, there were also some of a 'social
control' nature. The maintenance of houses of correction, assisting
poor maids into marriage and the rehabilitation of prisoners are purposes indicating a legislative intent to promote a congruity between
the agendas of charities and government on the assumption that they
share a common interest in activities which conform with and tend to
preserve the values and institutions of contemporary society. There was
a presumption that charities would be supportive of government efforts
to maintain social order and ensure the continuation of the status quo in
society. By and large, this proved to be the case and the track record of
the government–charity relationship thereafter showed a willingness to
provide a level of mutual support that amounted to an implied partnership. During the ensuing centuries, pooled judicial precedents and not
dissimilar legal systems allowed this basic initial boundary to be maintained throughout the common law jurisdictions. Although differences in
tax regimes and welfare state commitments caused some national variation, 'the concepts of fiscal immunity and charitable status continue[d] to
march hand in hand'.[8]

PRELUDE TO CHANGE

The main driving force prompting modern governments to review their relationship with charity was essentially the same as that which had led to the Preamble: contemporary social need had outgrown affordable government provision (certainly in terms of social infrastructure); a new statute was needed to allow and attract private resources to fund a range of appropriate public benefit services. In particular, the inexorable logic of current demographic trends, together with the collapse of domestic manufacturing as production was outsourced to Asia, ensured that decreasing tax revenues would become progressively unable to sustain existing levels of government service provision for the growing numbers of elderly and infirm citizens: an inverse correlation between workers and dependants in such societies guaranteed the continued erosion of their traditional tax base; government would have to find new ways of sharing the cost of future public service provision.

Again, the absence of a charity specific regulatory regime, in any country other than England and Wales, was generally accepted as constituting a serious weakness; following a number of governance and financial abuse scandals in commercial companies (for example, Enron), the risk of similar or worse occurring in the virtually unregulated charity sector had become obvious. In addition, learning from experience in the private sector was important as this indicated the need to counter the trust legacy with more flexible legal structures to facilitate charitable activity. Consequently, a focus in a number of law reform processes was on the need for modern charity specific structures that married the benefits of incorporation with asset lock protection and allowed for direct regulatory control.

There was also a general recognition and concern among governments that, as expressed by Baroness Kennedy, 'the public's disengagement from organised politics has gathered pace as they have lost faith in the more traditional forms of political engagement'.[9] In the UK and some other common law jurisdictions (for example, the US) there was considerable debate as to how to narrow the gap between government and citizen, attract the participation of the latter in political matters and reawaken the democratic ethos. Moreover, the need to engage more volunteers in charitable activity seemed desirable not only on the grounds of reducing service costs but also because this would be likely to promote selfless altruism for community benefit and generate civic awareness that could translate into responsible participation in political matters.

While these were among the primary considerations that set the UK and like-minded jurisdictions on the road to charity law reform, other factors came into play later (not least that, in England, the National Council for

Voluntary Organisations (NCVO) was poised with a strategy and policy, eagerly grasped by the incoming Labour government, as the basis for sector–government partnership and a route to 'third way' politics) and influenced legislative outcome.

Once underway, the impetus and direction of reform was overtaken by two quite unforeseen global events: the perceived threat posed by international terrorism and the banking crisis that precipitated widespread economic recession. The first ensured that national regulatory reform would also have to make room for provisions that were compatible with international anti-terrorism measures. This concern to ensure that charities would not become the weak link in government's fight against terrorism was perhaps only to be expected but it was somewhat ironic that an initiative to liberalise charity law quickly reverted to the traditional approach of tightening regulatory scrutiny. The second raised questions regarding the role of charity in relation to capitalism – could the concepts of fiscal immunity and charitable status continue to march hand in hand if banks and other icons of the capitalist infrastructure were held to be fiscally immune and became appropriate recipients of tax revenue bailouts? In the light of global economic recession caused by systemic corporate greed, what was the relative importance of individual altruism and how could this now be encouraged by new charity legislation?

Boundary Adjustment

In the absence of legislative intervention[10] (with the notable exception of Barbados and, arguably, the US),[11] the government–charity boundary established by the Preamble has since been replicated, maintained and to a degree developed, with some consistency and uniformity, through the medium of judicial precedent, across the common law jurisdictions. In recent years a small minority of those jurisdictions chose to engage in charity law reform. The ripple effects of the changes then made, however, are likely to alter that boundary significantly across the common law world. The main outcomes achieved by the various charity law reform processes, as given effect in new legislation, were the statutory introduction of defined common law concepts and an extension of charitable purposes including the removal of the public benefit presumption; new charity specific regulatory mechanisms; and a further consolidation of the government–charity relationship.

Partnership

Four centuries and more of shared responsibility for public benefit provision (with a hiatus in the UK when government nationalised healthcare) would seem to have convinced government as to the merit of cultivating a partnership with charity and confirmed the main areas where they can work together best. In the UK,[12] as in Ireland,[13] formal partnership arrangements had been established prior to the launching of charity law reform. For such jurisdictions, the outcome of the charity law reform process was unavoidable – it had to be a legislative testament to the strength of the bond between government and charity, which confidently stated the terms of their intended partnership and set out their agreed common goals. The formative nature of the resulting charity legislation and the extent of the adjustments made to the regulatory framework would seem to bear out the strength of the partnership achieved in those jurisdictions.

The corollary – that without established, well worked through, formal partnerships in place, law reform outcomes would be of less substance – seemed to be demonstrated by the experience in Australia where the then government perhaps took the view that partnership with the sector was a political price too high to pay for the dubious reward of ultimately being able to share responsibility for future public service provision. The legislation to ultimately emerge from the Australian law reform process was only a salvaged remnant of promised provision. The process outcomes in New Zealand and Singapore were also less radical than in the UK and Ireland, reflecting the more compromised nature of the former's government–charity relations. Again, the lack of progress in the reform efforts of Canada and the US may also fairly reflect an inability to achieve the mature partnership context necessary to deal with government–charity boundary issues, though the complications resulting from the federated nature of those jurisdictions also undoubtedly played a part.

Where, as in the UK and Irish jurisdictions, mutual trust was established between government and the sector, this produced legislative provisions detailing the nature and extent of the new government–charity boundary; otherwise, taking into account complications arising from federated constitutions, the opposite proved to be true. However, sustaining and allowing for ongoing boundary review and adjustment required a further step: a system that would lock in the regulatory charity interface with overall government policy for the sector. This was provided in England and Wales in May 2006 by establishing the Office of the Third Sector, located in the Cabinet Office, to work in partnership with the sector and with a particular brief for charity law reform and the work of the Charity Commission: the Office liaises with Parliament on matters affecting the Commission. Set within the compact context, the Office is a well-placed strategic mechanism allowing government to closely monitor boundary issues.

It would seem wholly appropriate that the present adjustments to the

Preamble boundary are being led by the progenitor of charity law and it is highly probable, as illustrated by the new approach of the Australian government, that this partnership model will be accepted by other jurisdictions as a necessary precondition for similar boundary setting legislation. Equally necessarily, the corollary to achieving a successful legislative outcome is a stronger government–charity partnership.

The Statutory Encoding of Charitable Purposes and Other Definitional Matters

A sense of perspective is needed when considering the extent to which charity law reform has so far reset the Preamble boundary: of the 53 nations[14] that gained independence from the British Empire, very few engaged in the recent round of reforms; and while in England and Wales,[15] Scotland,[16] Northern Ireland[17] and Ireland[18] this concluded with legislative change to definitional matters, in New Zealand,[19] Australia,[20] Canada and Singapore[21] it concluded without any such change. Arguably however, the achievements of the few will in time accrue to others.

A legacy of imperial rule had left the same set of definitional matters to constitute the characteristic common law hallmarks of charity law, with some differences of emphasis, in those nations that once comprised the British Empire. The initial government–charity boundary, fixed by government in 1601, has been perpetuated by that set of definitions as interpreted and endorsed by judicial precedent. They require that to be a charity an entity must be confined exclusively to charitable purposes, be for the public benefit and be independent, non-profit-distributing and non-political (see, further, Chapter 2). Of those matters none is more important than the requirement that to acquire charitable status and consequent tax exemption privileges an entity must first satisfy the public benefit test. This principle, the gatekeeper to charitable status and tax exemption privileges, aided by the 'spirit and intendment' rule, also provided the only means whereby new interpretations of charitable purposes could be introduced to address emerging and local manifestations of contemporary social need. It has played a critical role in mediating between government and charity the responsibility for uncertain areas of public benefit service provision. The fact that the public benefit test was not uniformly applied in relation to the four heads of *Pemsel*,[22] nor with any consistency among the common law jurisdictions, had become an obstacle to planning the basis for future distribution of that responsibility.

As a consequence of charity law reform, the public benefit test and other essential definitional matters have now been placed on a legislative footing in Barbados,[23] England and Wales,[24] Scotland,[25] New Zealand,[26]

Northern Ireland[27] and Ireland.[28] Only in England and Wales,[29] Scotland[30] and Northern Ireland,[31] however, has the legal presumption of public benefit compliance been totally removed and the test declared to have an unequivocal mandatory application in respect of all charitable purposes,[32] thus allowing for a future closer alignment between charitable status and public benefit service provision. The statutory encoding of core definitional matters, even if largely restating their common law meanings, is a strategically important government step: it removes the interpretation and development of such matters from the ambit of judicial discretion, while also opening the door for further legislative amendment as and when this is deemed politically expedient. For charity in the UK and Irish jurisdictions, this may amount to government imposed change reminiscent of the Preamble. For charity in all other common law countries it raises the prospect of similar change being introduced either by government or the judiciary.

Pemsel Plus and the Terms of a New Government–Charity Contract

The UK jurisdictions, Ireland and to a very limited extent Australia,[33] alone among the common law nations, have chosen to statutorily extend the four heads of charity to include much the same set of '*Pemsel* plus' charitable purposes.[34] This development has introduced the first statutory definition of matters to be construed as 'charity' since the Preamble, with the exception of 'sport and recreation', which was so designated half a century ago. That such a significant and largely identical extension to the four *Pemsel* heads should now be made by these jurisdictions, fairly simultaneously and after several years of careful consideration and public consultation, indicates the level of importance attached by government to the *Pemsel* plus purposes. They can only be viewed as setting out the agenda of matters central to government's intended new partnership arrangement with charity.[35] Their importance is unlikely to remain restricted to the jurisdictions concerned, as others may well either replicate that statutory initiative or transfer its consequences by judicial proxy as the courts elsewhere in the common law world choose to follow new lines of precedents established in the courts of the UK and Ireland.

The new purposes list a number of activities that have gained judicial recognition over time including the advancement of animal welfare, the advancement of environmental protection or improvement and the advancement of the arts, culture, heritage or science (see, further, Chapter 2). However, they also, and with remarkable consistency, identify the following specific matters as having become of such central importance to government as to now warrant charitable status.

The prevention of poverty[36]
While this includes preventing those who are poor from becoming poorer and preventing persons who are not poor from becoming poor, it remains to be seen how or to what extent it will facilitate organisations dedicated to eradicating the causes of poverty. Whether it will permit a different approach to the established prohibition on charities tackling the causes of existing poverty, where this entails working to change existing laws or government policy, is open to question. Nonetheless, this provision represents a definite government commitment to focusing charity activity and resources on reducing poverty levels. The new focus should increase the numbers benefiting from localised schemes for dealing strategically with embedded poverty within the jurisdictions concerned and in underdeveloped countries.

The advancement of health or the saving of lives[37]
The specific recognition now given to this charitable purpose must again give a particular boost to those organisations involved in mass child inoculation programmes and in combating AIDS and other diseases in underdeveloped countries. It also indicates government willingness to facilitate a further transfer of health and social care service provision from the public sector.

The advancement of citizenship[38] **or community development**
This new charitable purpose reflects government awareness of the capacity of the charitable sector to generate social capital and of past difficulties experienced by local community organisations in attaining charitable status. It can be seen as an acknowledgement that opportunities for civic engagement and for forming localised participative democratic forums are of value to government because of their capacity to contribute to the building of a more cohesive and civil society. Encompassing as it does activities that promote urban and rural regeneration, community capacity building, civic responsibility and good citizenship, this provision should serve to encourage those organisations working with ethnic minorities and other deprived communities within the jurisdictions concerned.

The advancement of human rights, conflict resolution or reconciliation or the promotion of religious or racial harmony or equality and diversity[39]
On the face of it this new composite charitable purpose marks an important development in charity law: it reflects a government commitment to making that law compliant with the principles of human rights and equality. In particular, it plainly indicates that government wishes to encourage the involvement of charities with ethnic and other minority groups so as

to promote multiculturalism. The reference to promoting 'religious or racial harmony or equality and diversity' has a particular resonance in the present global context of a growing estrangement between Islam, or some of its followers, and the western democracies. It is a reference that also encourages mediatory activity on behalf of those who in a more domestic context feel discriminated against for reasons of race, disability, age, sexual orientation and so on. In addition, it would seem to accommodate activities intended to identify and address causes as well as effects of alienation or mutual estrangement. It has a strong preventative dimension.

However, clearly this new charitable purpose sits uneasily alongside the traditional and conspicuously unaltered common law constraints on political activity by charities (which may explain the absence of any reference to human rights in the Irish legislation) and until we see how the tension between the two is resolved it is difficult to estimate the potential for this purpose to transcend those constraints and effect real change. The political dimension to the government–charity boundary may well prevail.

The relief of those in need, by reason of youth, age, ill-health, disability, financial hardship or other disadvantage[40]

This charitable purpose maintains the very traditional focus of charity on those in need for reasons that have attracted compassion, protection and resources throughout the duration and extent of the common law. It accommodates relief in the form of specialist advice, equipment, care or accommodation and specialist housing, care centres, drop-in centres, and so on. While legislative specificity has its attractions it is difficult to see what, in this instance, it brings to the law when these groups have for some time been recognised as meriting charitable status. It is, however, a clear government statement that charity must direct its resources towards the needs of the most vulnerable in our society and opens wide the door for further government–charity contracts for provision of health and social care services.

The promotion of . . . the effectiveness or efficiency of charities[41]

The fact that the common law never had an interest in ascertaining whether the resources of the donor or charitable organisation are being prudently invested (beyond ruling that some causes are too absurd to merit charitable status[42]) resulted in numbers of charities providing overlapping services, or replicating existing services (for example cancer research) or applying resources greater than the need to be addressed. This charitable purpose (recognised as such for some years in England and Wales[43]) has now been statutorily introduced to address the misuse of resources. Although the UK and Irish jurisdictions have seen a shift from direct public service provision by government to regulating that provision by approved bodies, this purpose arguably marks a significant further step in that direction. The promotion of 'effectiveness' and 'efficiency' could license the introduction of quangos, or government-appointed agencies, to set and control standards in the charitable sector. Any such use of charity to control charity would constitute an interesting adjustment to the government–charity boundary.

Other purposes currently recognised as charitable or in the spirit of any purposes currently recognised as charitable[44]

Finally, this default provision continues the function provided by the fourth *Pemsel* head, at least for the UK jurisdictions, as there is no equivalent in the Irish statute. To gain charitable status such 'other purposes' will now be statutorily tied to the rule that a new purpose must be analogous to one already existing and so, by implication, the 'spirit and intendment' rule is discontinued. This purpose also carries over into the new legislative era the established capacity for partnership between government and charity by allowing for the continuation of charitable status in respect of those organisations that make a public service type contribution. So the provision of public works and services and the provision of public utilities (such as the repair of bridges, ports, havens, causeways and highways; the provision of water and lighting, a cemetery or crematorium; as well as the provision of public facilities such as libraries, reading rooms and public conveniences) are all thereby endorsed as charitable. Organisations and gifts for the relief of unemployment, for the social relief, resettlement and rehabilitation of persons under a disability or deprivation (including disaster funds) and for the benefit of a particular locality (such as trusts for the general benefit of the inhabitants of a particular place) will similarly continue to be entitled to charitable status.[45]

Collectively, these purposes signify the most fundamental government updating of its agenda with charity since the Preamble. Government has emerged from the process with a new statutory framework which clarifies the terms on which organisations may acquire charitable status and accompanying tax exempt privileges while directing and confining their public benefit activities and resources towards certain purposes. It is a framework now susceptible to ongoing statutory amendment. Such a clear and almost identical statement of additional matters, defined by several governments to be of contemporary public benefit and warrant charitable status, together with the established *Pemsel* charitable purposes and their derivatives, now constitute firm markers for the new government–charity boundary. These statutory purposes, newly born from recent reform processes, bear some resemblance to those that have long been codified in sub-sections 501(c)(3) and (4) of the US Internal Revenue Code. Arguably, such a convergence accurately reflects adjustments made in response to much the same social pressures and indicates an evolving boundary setting consensus among the developed common law nations.

Regulatory Control

The government–charity boundary has always been regarded with some suspicion by government as being vulnerable to abuse by persons and organisations seeking opportunities to exploit donors, charities or tax exemption entitlement. As was the case 400 years earlier, the recent law reform processes were also driven to some degree by a government concern to improve regulatory supervision of charities. This time, in addition to promoting the efficiency and effectiveness of charities as a charitable purpose, the legislation was focused on more specific aspects of regulatory control.

Decoupling responsibilities for determining charitable status and tax exemption

The traditional common law approach, which vested the tax collecting agency with the dual responsibility for determining both charitable status and tax exemption, had long been discontinued in England and Wales. There the Charity Commission has had exclusive responsibility for determining charitable status and for supervising and supporting those organisations that are on its register of charities. While the Inland Revenue continues in its traditional role it is required to defer to the Charity Commission on matters of status. In effect the Commission has in recent years come to displace the Revenue as gatekeeper to both charitable status and tax exemption privileges.

In that respect, as in others, the Charity Commission in England and Wales has stood apart from other national regulatory bodies. Four centuries after the Preamble, all other common law jurisdictions continued the traditional approach. As a consequence of law reform processes, this role demarcation has now been adopted by the other UK jurisdictions but not to the same extent elsewhere. In Ireland, as in Singapore and New Zealand, the responsibility for awarding charitable status has been surgically removed from the tax collecting agency and transplanted into the newly established and very similar Charities Regulatory Authority, Commissioner of Charities and Charity Commission respectively. These agencies have statutorily ascribed support functions in addition to the transferred policing component. However, as the new regulatory authority has no more discretion to interpret charitable purpose and definitional matters than the tax collecting agency had and is not vested with the necessary inherent powers of the High Court that would enable it to do so, and as its decisions remain subject to the right of the tax collecting agency to determine tax exemption privileges, it is unlikely that the statutory adjustment will cause the outcome for charities in these jurisdictions to differ greatly. Arguably, the efficient policing of the government–charity boundary requires the protection and development of charitable status to be treated separately from the administration of generic tax liability.

A charity specific regulator
Primarily, the Charity Commission in England and Wales stands apart from other national regulatory bodies in that it provides a charity specific regulatory function: the profile data of all charities, whatever their legal form, must be entered in the Commission's register and they must then subscribe to its regulatory regime as regards accountability, transparency, good governance and standards of practice; in particular, they must file annual reports with the Commission regarding their finances and activities. In return, the Commission provides charity specific advice and support while also mediating between government and the sector on charity issues. As mentioned above, a consequence of recent law reform processes has been the adoption of that regime wholly by the other UK jurisdictions and to a lesser extent in Ireland, Singapore and New Zealand, while Australia, Canada and the US continue with the traditional approach. The existence of a charity specific regulatory regime, if not a prerequisite for formal government–charity partnerships, at least reinforces the mutual confidence of both parties when it comes to negotiating boundary issues.

Anti-terrorism
An outcome of recent national law reform processes has been a government focus on bringing charities and other nonprofits within the reach of regulatory bodies so as to be able to locate them better, supervise their activities and monitor the flow of funds. The threat of international terrorism has prompted government to introduce tough legislative provisions designed to tighten its surveillance and control of the sector. This, coupled with the unchanged traditional constraints on charities engaging in political activities, will inevitably inhibit charities with the result that the mutual trust between charity and government, essential for partnership, is at risk of being eroded, which may be demonstrated in future boundary disputes.

National constraints have been compounded further by international initiatives, as governments acknowledge the global presence of many

charities – some of which have built up operational networks in pre-
cisely the same underdeveloped countries identified as associated with
international terrorism – and coordinate multi-national agreements to
intercept their activities. So, for example, the Financial Action Task Force
(FATF), an inter-governmental body established to combat money laun-
dering and the financing of terrorism, has led the way in negotiating such
agreements.[46]

The most significant definitional difference achieved by the new charity
legislation has been the reworking of the public benefit test. How this is
to be applied will depend very much on jurisdictional adjustments to the
regulatory framework and on whether the government strategy to build
the basis for a new partnership arrangement with the sector, underpinned
by reformed charity law, will now have to give way to the new international security imperative.

The Tax Regime

Control of a nation's purse strings has from feudal times provided its
government with the resources necessary to implement policy, while relaxing that control has always been central to its relationship with charity.
For the governments of most developed nations that relationship is now
managed through institutional regulatory arrangements, structuring the
tax regime and/or ongoing manipulation of the tax code. Manipulating
the tax regime through regulations or annual budgets, usually to introduce a 'stealth' tax, has become common government practice among the
developed nations as it offers a quick, informal, flexible and less accountable alternative to the legislative process. Once the primary legislation is
in place, as for example with VAT, then governments may adjust thresholds or extend categories and so on as needed in response to political pressures. The tax system offers government an important and discrete means
for managing boundary adjustments: tax code amendments provide a
revealing sub-text to declared government policy for its relations with
charity.

Regulatory institution

In countries such as the US, Canada and Australia, the government–
charity boundary relationship is dominated by a revenue driven approach,
perhaps unavoidable in federated jurisdictions, operationalised by the
designation of the Internal Revenue Service, the Canada Revenue Agency
and the Australian Taxation Office respectively as gatekeepers for charitable status with a brief to apply the tax regime in a uniform manner to all
persons and entities. The reverse is equally true, initially only in the case

of England and Wales but now also in the other UK jurisdictions, Ireland, Singapore and New Zealand, where the regulatory roles in respect of charitable status and tax liability have been institutionally separated. Relieving the tax collecting agency of responsibility for determining charitable status signifies an important policy change in government's approach to charity: the revenue driven approach is to be balanced by an at least equal weighting given to protecting and developing charitable purposes. Such a step demonstrates the willingness of government to adopt a new supportive role in relation to charity which is probably an essential basis for future partnership.

Structuring the tax regime
The approach adopted in the UK and Irish jurisdictions, whereby charitable status itself provides the sole passport to exemption across a range of taxes, has not been universally followed. In Australia and Singapore, for example, the tax regime is structured so as to draw a distinction between charities and Public Benevolent Institutions (PBIs) and between charities and Institutions of Public Character (IPCs) respectively: the former defines a PBI as a non-profit institution organised for the direct relief of such poverty, sickness, suffering, distress, misfortune, disability, destitution or helplessness as arouses compassion in the community. Something of the same structuring can be seen in the approach taken in the US, where sub-sections 501(c)(3) and (4) of the US Internal Revenue Code in effect set out a tax exemption continuum which benefits some entities more than others depending on the correlation between their activities and a hierarchical classification of social need. This approach has introduced a tiered approach to tax exemption on charitable grounds, enabling government to direct preferential tax credits to such areas of charitable activity it considers should be prioritised, and thereby allows a customisation of the government–charity boundary to fit the particular pattern of contemporary social need better.

Legal forms
A variation of the above approach is evident in the differentiation made in some jurisdictions between the legal form adopted to house charitable activity and consequent entitlement to tax exemption. While traditionally this has not been much in evidence in the UK and Ireland, other jurisdictions have favoured a gradation of legal forms. For example, in Canada a distinction is made between 'charitable organisation', 'private foundation' and 'public foundation', all of which can be a 'registered charity', while in the US a 'charitable organisation' may be a corporation, community chest, fund, foundation or sports association, with

endowed foundations being treated with most suspicion and community foundations being encouraged by the tax authorities. The recent and rapid rise of social enterprises in all modern common law jurisdictions also testifies to the importance of a supportive tax environment, as does the increasing pace of experimentation with hybrid legal structures (see, further, below).

Donor incentive schemes

Tax incentives to encourage donations from persons and companies, together with incentives for volunteering, help to shape a climate conducive to the growth of philanthropy. In the US, tax incentives for charitable giving have been part of the tax code since the 18th century.[47] In Australia, Canada, New Zealand, Ireland and the UK jurisdictions, donor incentive schemes have not been as popular as, to a large extent, they were displaced by government funding of charitable organisations. However, recently such schemes have been introduced in New Zealand and Singapore. In Australia, the formulation of Deductible Gift Recipient, which enables taxpayers to claim a deduction for certain gifts made to specified types of nonprofit organisations (deductible gift recipients), is a not dissimilar device. In the UK jurisdictions, Gift Aid and the 'Getting Britain Giving' campaign are donor incentive schemes, but it is the National Lottery that, as in Ireland, provides government with various opportunities for channelling tax revenues towards its favoured forms of public benefit activity.

Government Funding

The increasing dependency of charities on government funding, whether in the form of direct grants or contracts for service provision, is threatening to erode their traditional claim to be in the vanguard of non-governmental organisations. In the UK, for example, it has been noted that in the mid-1980s about 10 per cent of overall charitable revenue came from government sources;[48] by 1991, government funding accounted for 27 per cent of the sector's income;[49] and that has now grown to at least 38 per cent.[50] The State has become the largest single contributor to philanthropic causes.

The independence of charities is also being compromised by their need to engage in the 'contract culture', most evident in the growth of partnership arrangements with government bodies. This has been criticised by some as resulting in charities becoming compliant subjects of government as a 'muting of dissent' culture envelops those who need to prioritise their ongoing contractual arrangements.[51]

BOUNDARY SETTING TRENDS AND FUTURE GOVERNMENT–CHARITY RELATIONS

The Preamble footprint outlines the basis of current and future government–charity relations. The core components – fixed at a time of government insecurity, chronic lack of resources and awareness of fiscal abuse within the jurisdiction and enemies without – have recently and in not dissimilar circumstances been reviewed, confirmed and statutorily extended in the originating jurisdiction, then adopted by others.

The Politics of Partnership

The Preamble was underpinned by a basic premise–that government and charity should work in partnership for the public benefit to protect citizens, provide social infrastructure and utilities and deliver services to those in need. However, a premise that could be imposed in a feudal society required considerable political negotiation to gain broad acceptance four centuries later. The differing success rates among the various common law nations that have in recent years embarked upon charity law reform would seem to reflect the extent to which each had secured such a partnership. The UK jurisdictions, led by England and Wales, concluded with the most radical overhaul of charity law achieved by any country since the Preamble. This was no coincidence.

The problem of managing the retrenchment in health, housing, social care and education services was forced upon all developed nations in the late 20th century by the same inexorable demographic trends but it was in the UK, where the 'welfare state' had reached its apogee, that it was most acute. As a strategy for coping with the long retreat from its welfare state ideal, the UK government was forced earlier and under greater pressure than others to build a new national political consensus. Reworking the relationship between government, business, the not-for-profit sector and the citizen took decades and involved curbing the trade unions, carving out a new political constituency ('the third way') and finding room for participative forms of democracy to function alongside the traditional representative form. The terms of the new understanding needed to be formally set out in the negotiated framework of the various compacts. Only then could the Preamble premise be relied upon and consideration be given to how a new law could be shaped to govern the purposes and activities of charities.

Much the same process occurred in Ireland, was entered into in Canada, is now underway in Australia and may be about to commence in the US triggered by the proposed reform of the nation's health services. All modern democracies are now wrestling with the implications arising from privatising the delivery of essential services and working through the considerable challenges for sustaining civil society that flow from the consequent reshaping of relationships between governments, business, charity and the citizen. Arguably, the same social pressures are forcing the developed common law nations down much the same road, as demonstrated in a gradual convergence of boundary setting markers for future government–charity relations.

Civil Society Consolidation

For government, developing the capacity of the charitable sector is an investment in social stability. In the UK and Irish jurisdictions, the legislative extension of charitable purposes includes a definite emphasis on promoting the growth of civic responsibility and in all other developed nations governments are now also demonstrating an enthusiasm for encouraging the use of volunteers and involving faith based organisations in community work. Government can only gain from supporting a sector that generates a vibrant and diverse participative form of democracy, attracts the involvement of volunteers and bolsters a sense of social obligation and civic responsibility, thereby fostering the growth of social capital and consolidating civil society. Altruistic activity, a sufficient 'good' in itself, also acts as a model for others and can galvanise local communities into more responsible citizenship through bonding activities that accrue to the common good. In addition to engaging a growing proportion of the population in community care activity, closing the gap between citizen and government and being a catalyst for the development of a more civil and morally based society, the encouragement of altruistic conduct also has the happy consequence of reducing government expenditure (see, further, Chapter 9).

Because of their institutional nature, pastoral concerns and longevity, the larger charities are well positioned to reinforce and continue established social norms. Their longevity, coupled with financial and information resources, together with expertise and credibility established over generations of close engagement with vulnerable communities, places charities in a singularly strong position to provide the necessary continuity of concerned involvement to those communities with potential to threaten government stability. By absorbing the needs of minority groups, assuaging the dissatisfaction of the alienated, mediating on behalf of the socially excluded and involving armies of volunteers in community care activities, charities can make a unique contribution to maintaining social cohesion. With the continued constraints on their advocacy or political activity, their leadership role among non-government organisations and their reduced independence in the face of increased direct or indirect government funding, there is every reason to believe that charities will be of growing strategic importance to government as favoured partners in the task of building and maintaining social cohesion.

Public Benefit Service Provision

As at the time of the Preamble, the provision of health and social care services, training for employment, various aspects of public utility provision and the physical maintenance of social infrastructure are still very much the business of charities, as are education, housing and the general alleviation of those in impoverished circumstances. Although the line separating the public benefit service provision of government bodies and that of charities has always been uncertain, it has become more so in recent years.[52] Charities in these areas are now becoming more prominent as State services recede in all developed common law nations, while in some the *Pemsel* plus purposes specify a range of additional circumstances requiring charitable resources.

In the UK and Irish jurisdictions, future development of the already close relationship between charity and public authorities, fuelled by government grants and service contracts, will be firmly anchored on the public benefit test as now legislatively applied to all charitable purposes (excepting religious purposes in Ireland). The removal of the public benefit presumption in respect of the first three *Pemsel* heads is likely to promote further congruity between the purposes of charity and government and accelerate the former's public benefit service provision. As bodies such as public schools, independent hospitals, religious organisations and those established under the rules relating to 'poor relatives' and 'poor employees' are required in future to demonstrate that their services are also to some meaningful degree accessible to the poor or otherwise socially disadvantaged, this will nudge charity service provision into alignment with mainstream public services. The trend towards easing regulatory controls, so as to facilitate the delivery by charity of services previously assumed to be the responsibility of government, is now well established in a number of leading common law nations[53] and can only become firmer as *Pemsel* plus rulings channel the flow of charitable resources into social and health care areas of need.

Bridging the Public and Private Sectors

The withdrawal of government from health and social service provision has, in recent years, been matched by a similar retreat from its traditional responsibilities in respect of public utilities such as water supply, electricity and transport. For many in the UK, the privatisation of water supply in the late 1980s, followed by the disconnection of thousands of families from running water for failure to pay, provided stark evidence of a new public–private balance being struck in the distribution of responsibility for public benefit service provision.[54] Across the common law world, a similar move towards the privatisation of social utilities has enabled the State to leave the market to provide, at a price, services such as water, sanitation, transport, housing, prisons, electricity and gas. Wherever possible, government has engaged with private companies and non-profit organisations, including charities, to arrange for the transfer of such service provision while it retreats to controlling service provision, access and standards through regulatory legislation and inspectoral bodies.

This in turn has led to a proliferation of service delivery arrangements between government bodies, charities and commercial organisations entailing considerable experimentation with the new legal structures now required to balance public and private interests. The move away from trusts, never particularly popular in many countries such as the US and Australia, can only accelerate as social entrepreneurship gains more ground and new legal structures such as the community interest company and the charitable incorporated organisation prove more flexible. This trend is likely to be accompanied by appropriate adjustments to the regulatory framework. The regulatory failures in relation to banks, coupled with some evidence of the not-for-profit sector serving as a conduit for the flow of terrorist funds, have drawn government attention to the need to regulate for good governance in the charitable sector. Hybrid legal structures, tailored to accommodate a variable mix of public and private interests, regulated to ensure good governance, may well be features of the future government–charity boundary.

NOTES

1. Preamble to the Statute of Charitable Uses 1601 (43 Eliz. 1 cap. 4).
2. For example, the society for the protection of animals (1824) preceded the founding of the society for the protection of children (1884) and exceeds it in total wealth (in 2006, the RSPCA reported an income of £110.7 m, assets of £81.1 m and investments of £118 m while in the same year the NSPCC reported a total income of £116 m, assets of £54.9 m, and investment income of £2.8 m).
3. Concluded in England and Wales with the Charities Act 2006, in Scotland with the Charities and Trustee Investment (Scotland) Act 2005, in Northern Ireland with the Charities Act (Northern Ireland) 2008, in Barbados with the Charities Act 1989 and in New Zealand with the Charities Act 2005; in Australia, concluded with the withdrawal of the draft Charities Bill in May 2004 and the enactment of the Extension of Charitable

Purpose Act 2004; and in Singapore the process is currently at the stage of implementing the recommendations of the Inter-Ministry Committee on the Regulation of Charities and Institutions of Public Character established in October 2005.

4. The 1601 Act included a provision stating that 'the saide Commissioners . . . shall and may make Decrees and Orders for recompense to be made by any person or persons whoe, beinge put in Truste or havynge notice of the charitable Uses above mentioned, hathe or shall breake the same Truste, or defraude the same Uses'.

5. Parish-based relief systems for the poor were developed in many local English communities during the latter half of the 16th century in response to the collapse of the care facilities established and maintained by the Catholic Church until their removal by the Protestant Reformation. This system was extended by the Elizabethan legislation of 1597–1601 which secularised Church facilities. In 1598 the earliest form of State public service provision for the socially disadvantaged in Europe was introduced by the Elizabethan Poor Law Act, and it was amended by the Act for the Relief of the Poor 1601.

6. As noted in Picarda, H. (1999), *The Law and Practice Relating to Charities*, 3rd edn, London: Butterworths, at 733, 'the Income Tax Act 1799 exempted from the tax the income of any "corporation, fraternity or society established for charitable purposes". The 1799 Act was reinforced by the decision a century later in *Commissioners for Special Purposes of Income Tax v Pemsel* [1891] AC 531.

7. See e.g. *Re Ward* [1941] Ch 308 at 310 per Mackimmon LJ.

8. *Dingle v Turner* [1972] AC 601 per Cross LJ.

9. See Advisory Group on Campaigning and the Voluntary Sector, Chair: Baroness Helena Kennedy (2007), *Report of the Advisory Group on Campaigning and the Voluntary Sector*, London: the Advisory Group, 2.

10. Other than the inclusion of sport and recreation: the Recreational Charities Act 1958 (Eng & Wales) was replicated in many Commonwealth nations.

11. See the Charities Act, *The Laws of Barbados,* Vol. VIII, Title XVIII, Chap. 243, LRO 1989 and s. 501(c)(3) of the Internal Revenue Code respectively.

12. In May 1997, four separate compacts (for England, Scotland, Wales, and Northern Ireland) were developed; subsequently local compacts have been agreed and a new Compact Plus was introduced (2005).

13. See the national agreement: Department of the Taoiseach (2006), *Towards 2016: the Ten-year Framework Social Partnership Agreement 2006–2015*, Dublin: The Stationery Office; and Department of the Taoiseach (2008), *Towards 2016: Review and Transitional Agreement 2008–2009*, Dublin: The Stationery Office.

14. The Commonwealth consists of 53 independent sovereign nations all sharing a common law heritage from their experience as former colonies of the British Empire.

15. The Charities Act 2006.

16. The Charities and Trustee Investment (Scotland) Act 2005.

17. The Charities (Northern Ireland) Act 2008.

18. The Charities Act 2009.

19. The Charities Act 2005.

20. Concluded with the withdrawal of the draft Charities Bill in May 2004 and the enactment of the Extension of Charitable Purpose Act 2004.

21. Currently at the stage of implementing the recommendations of the Inter-Ministry Committee on the Regulation of Charities and Institutions of Public Character established in October 2005.

22. *Commissioners for Special Purposes of Income Tax v Pemsel* [1891] AC 531.

23. The Charities Act, *The Laws of Barbados,* Vol. VIII, Title XVIII, Chap. 243, LRO 1989, s. 4. This merely re-states the common law definition.

24. The Charities Act 2006, s. 3(1).

25. The Charities and Trustee Investment (Scotland) Act 2005, s. 7(1)(b).

26. The Charities Act 2005, s. 5(2)(a).

27. The Charities (Northern Ireland) Act 2008, s. 3(1).

28. The Charities Act 2009, s. 3.
29. The Charities Act 2006, s. 3(1).
30. The Charities and Trustee Investment (Scotland) Act 2005, s. 8(1).
31. The Charities (Northern Ireland) Act 2008, s. 3(2).
32. In New Zealand the removal of the presumption is implied in the Charities Act 2005, s. 5(2)(a). In Ireland, the test applies to all non-religious purposes, while in Australia and Canada the test continues to have no bearing on the first and third of the *Pemsel* heads, and some, but variable, bearing on trusts for the advancement of education, leaving only the fourth head to attract a stringent application of the public benefit test.
33. The Extension of Charitable Purpose Act 2004 simply added the provision of child care services on a nonprofit basis, self-help groups and closed contemplative religious orders as a charitable purpose (see further on this in Chapter 8).
34. In Barbados, a somewhat different statutory approach has been taken in which the 'benefit' requirement for 'public benefit' and the 'charitable purposes' requirements have been merged into one requirement which in turn provides a gateway to 26 separate heads of charity. Though note that in the US, s. 501(c)(3) of the Internal Revenue Code provides a codified list of tax exempt public benefit activity that extends beyond the four *Pemsel* heads.
35. Interestingly, the new statutory purposes bear some resemblance to those that have long been codified in ss 501(c)(3) and (4) of the US Internal Revenue Code.
36. See the Charities Act 2006, s. 2, as replicated in the Charities and Trustee Investment (Scotland) Act 2005, s. 7(2(a) and the Charities Act (Northern Ireland) 2008, s. 2(2)(a) and in the Charities Act 2009, s. 3(1)(a) where it is linked with the prevention of economic hardship.
37. The wording in the Charities Act 2006, s. 2(2)(d) 'the advancement of health or the saving of lives' is exactly replicated in the Charities and Trustee Investment (Scotland) Act 2005, s. 7(2)(d) and (e), and the Charities Act (Northern Ireland) 2008, s. 2(2)(d), but stated more fully in the Charities Act 2009, s. 3(11)(d) 'the advancement of health, including the prevention or relief of sickness, disease or human suffering'.
38. Again, the wording in the Charities Act 2006, s. 2(3)(c) 'includes – (i) rural or urban regeneration, and (ii) the promotion of civic responsibility, volunteering, the voluntary sector . . .' is exactly replicated in the Charities and Trustee Investment (Scotland) Act 2005, s. 7(3), and the Charities Act (Northern Ireland) 2008, s. 2(3)(c), and is expressed slightly differently in the Charities Act 2009, s. 3(11)(b) 'the advancement of community development, including rural or urban regeneration' and (c) 'the promotion of civic responsibility or voluntary work'.
39. The wording in the Charities Act 2006, s. 2(2)(h) is exactly replicated in the Charities and Trustee Investment (Scotland) Act 2005, s. 7(2)(j)(k) and (l), and in the Charities Act (Northern Ireland) 2008, s. 2(2)(h). Although the Charities Act 2009, s. 3(11)(e), includes 'the advancement of conflict resolution or reconciliation' it makes no mention of human rights but, in s. 3(11)(e), there is reference to 'the promotion of religious or racial harmony and harmonious community relations'.
40. The wording in the Charities Act 2006, s. 2(2)(j), 'the relief of those in need by reason of youth, age, ill-health, disability, financial hardship or other disadvantage', is exactly replicated in the Charities Act (Northern Ireland) 2008, s. 2(2)(j); is almost exactly replicated in the Charities and Trustee Investment (Scotland) Act 2005, s. 1(2)(n) 'the relief of those in need by reason of age, ill-health, disability, financial hardship or other disadvantage'; and is similarly expressed in the Charities Act 2009, s. 3(11)(d), 'the advancement of community welfare, including the relief of those in need by reason of youth, age, ill-health or disability'.
41. In the Charities Act 2006, s. 2(2)(l), the wording is 'the promotion of the efficiency of the armed forces of the Crown, or of the efficiency of the police, fire and rescue services or ambulance services', while the wording in the Charities and Trustee Investment (Scotland) Act 2005, s. 7(3)(b)(ii), 'the promotion of . . . the effectiveness or efficiency of charities' has been duplicated in the Charities Act (Northern Ireland) 2008, s. 2(3)(c)(ii),

and in the Charities Act 2009, s. 3(11)(i), it is 'the advancement of the efficient and effective use of the property of charitable organisations' that has now acquired charitable status.

42. See e.g. *Re Grove-Grady* [1929] 1 Ch 557 at 573–4 (a sanctuary or reserve for 'animals, birds or other creatures not human' was not charitable as they would only 'be free to molest and harry one another' per Lord Hanworth MR); *Thellusson v Woodford* (1799) 4 Ves 227 at 229 (a hospital for hedgehogs was too irrational and absurd); and *Re Pinion* [1965] Ch 85 at 107 ('I can conceive of no useful object to be served in foisting upon the public this mass of junk' per Harman LJ).

43. See e.g. the ruling of the Charity Commission in *Application for Registration of Guidestar UK,* 7 March 2003; and *Re White's Wills Trusts* [1951] 1 All ER 518.

44. The wording in the Charities Act 2006, s. 2(4)(b), 'any purposes that may reasonably be regarded as analogous to, or within the spirit of, any purposes falling within any of those . . .', is exactly replicated in the Charities Act (Northern Ireland) 2008, s. 2(4)(b) and virtually so in the Charities and Trustee Investment (Scotland) Act 2005, s. 7(2)(p): 'any other purpose that may reasonably be regarded as analogous to any of the preceding purposes'.

45. See also Charity Commission (2001), *RR1a – Recognising New Charitable Purposes,* London: Charity Commission.

46. Financial Action Task Force (undated), *Interpretative Note to Special Recommendation VIII: Non-Profit Organisations,* FATF–GAFI, available at http://www.fatf-gafi.org/dataoecd/43/5/38816530.pdf (accessed 20 December 2009).

47. See Howard, C. (1997), *The Hidden Welfare State: Tax Expenditures and Social Policy in the United States,* Princeton, NJ: Princeton University Press, as cited in Wright, K. (2002), 'Generosity vs. Altruism: Philanthropy and Charity in the United States and United Kingdom', *Voluntas,* 12(4), 399–416, 410.

48. Seddon, N. (2007), *Who Cares?,* London: Civitas, 28, citing *The Times,* 17 December 1984.

49. Ibid, citing Wilding, K. et al (2004), *The UK Voluntary Sector Almanac 2004,* 5th edn, London: NCVO.

50. Ibid.

51. See e.g. National Council for Voluntary Organisations, Commission on the Future of the Voluntary Sector (1996), *Meeting the Challenge of Change: Voluntary Action into the 21st Century,* London: NCVO, Volume 2 (the Deakin Report).

52. It has been recognised for some time that a charity providing a service that relieves local or general taxation is pursuing a legitimate charitable purpose, provided it is for the benefit of the public; see e.g. *AG v Bushby* (1857) 24 Beav 299.

53. See e.g. in England and Wales, the Charity Commission and Applications for Registration of (i) Trafford Community Leisure Trust and (ii) Wigan Leisure and Culture Trust (21 April 2004); in Australia, *Central Bayside Division of General Practice Ltd v Commissioner of State Revenue* [2006] HCA 43.

54. A policy since exported by the World Bank to the developing nations, international aid being conditional upon privatisation of national resources such as water and electricity, leading to greater hardship for those already below the poverty line and more emphatic social inequity in countries such as Ghana, Indonesia and Argentina.

8. Religion as a head of charity

Brian Lucas and Anne Robinson

This chapter proposes to deal with four questions: (1) why was the advancement of religion included as one of the heads of charity? (2) can religion be conceptualised as part of charity other than by tradition? (3) why should it continue to be included as one of the heads of charity? A subtext of these questions is: is it time to reform the religious head and strip back its privileges? So we might propose that the fourth question is: (4) should religious institutions be given special tax treatment?

ISSUES IN DEFINING RELIGION AS CHARITY

Definition of terms, not least legal terms, is an entirely purposive exercise. In other words, words are never defined for their own sake; they are attributed meaning for a specific reason and for specific contexts. In Australian common law, in much the same way as in the United Kingdom, the definition of the term 'charity' has come from three main applications.[1]

1. There are those cases where it was necessary for the court to determine the existence of a charitable trust because if they were not charitable they would be void, offending the rule against perpetuities; related to these were other cases where it was necessary to determine the charitable status of institutions to which gifts were given.
2. The term 'charity' and 'charitable' have been used in statutes (largely in the context of taxation and rate relief) without definition, so it has been necessary to resort to the judicial definitions.
3. The court's inherent jurisdiction to enforce, and sometimes vary, charitable trusts *cy près* has led to a number of judicial statements on when this jurisdiction arises and how it should be exercised.[2]

The terms 'charity' and 'charitable' are used in a number of contexts in statutes in Australia – most particularly federally in the Income Tax Assessment Act 1997 (ITAA), sections 50–1 and 50–5, and the Fringe Benefits Tax Assessment Act 1986 (FBTAA).

According to the Commissioner of Taxation (the Commissioner)'s public taxation ruling issued in 2005:

> A charitable institution is an institution established and maintained for purposes that are charitable in the technical legal sense . . . For a purpose to fall within the technical legal meaning of 'charitable' it must be:
> - beneficial to the community, or deemed to be for the public benefit by legislation applying for that purpose; and
> - within the spirit and intendment of the Statute of Elizabeth, or deemed to be charitable by legislation applying for that purpose.[3]

According to the Commissioner, charitable purposes are

> commonly grouped, following the terminology used in *The Commissioners for Special Purposes of the Income Tax v Pemsel* [1891] AC 531 . . . as the 'four heads of charity':
> - the relief of poverty;
> - the advancement of education;
> - the advancement of religion; and
> - other purposes beneficial to the community.[4]

It is noted that in the case of all heads of charity, regard is to be had to the purposes not the activities of the organisation, except to the extent that the actual activities may be evidence of the true purposes. The most significant difference between the regimes in England and Wales, Ireland and Australia is that in Australia the first three heads retain their common law presumptions of public benefit. Prior to considering the question of public benefit, it is useful to situate the discussion of why the advancement of religion is considered to be charitable at all within the historical context.

THE ORIGINS OF RELIGIOUS CHARITY IN AUSTRALIA

From the first century AD there has been a link between Christianity and charity because the word 'charity' itself is inextricably part of the Christian faith. This is not of course to say that Christianity is the only motivator of 'good works' or that Christians are the only charitable people. At the heart of Christian faith is the dual commandment of love of God and love of neighbour. We want to make some observations first about the Australian context of the development of social service delivery as an example – we could just as well look at education or overseas aid and development.[5]

The first thing to note is that the way in which social service is delivered in Australia is quite distinctive. Prior to the Second World War, social services were almost entirely delivered by charities and most of them were religious-based (Christian). For example, in New South Wales (NSW) the Benevolent Society was established in 1813 and was by some measures the first charity in Australia. While it is now no longer a specifically Christian organisation, its original name was the 'NSW Society for Promoting Christian Knowledge and Benevolence in these Territories and the Neighbouring Islands' and the men who founded it had mainly served as missionaries of the London Missionary Society. The founders were keen to spread the gospel as much as to relieve poverty and distress, but Governor Macquarie leant on them to focus on the latter object – and in NSW rather than the South Pacific.

In fairly quick succession district nursing services started (1820), asylums opened for the poor, blind, aged and infirm (1821), maternity hospitals (1866) and the first Women's Hospital in Australia commenced (1901). The Irish Sisters of Charity arrived in 1838, later opening St Vincent's Hospital in Sydney. In 1862, Sydney City Mission, 'an unsectarian Christian organisation', began to address poverty, and soon similar missions were in Brisbane (1859) and Adelaide (1867). The Society of St Vincent de Paul, founded by Frederick Ozanam in Paris in 1833, started its services in Sydney in 1881. Catholic religious orders such as the St John of God Sisters, Mercy Sisters and Little Company of Mary founded hospitals and hospices throughout Australia in the later part of the 19th century.

In the 20th century, HammondCare had its origins in Hammond's Social Services, and Hammond's Homes – the social services provided by the Anglican Church at St Barnabas Broadway where RBS Hammond was minister at the start of the 20th century. During the Depression years his Hammond's Social Services was one of the largest social service providers in Sydney, and pre-dated government-funded social welfare payments and support.

Around the country, prior to the Second World War, social services such as the distribution of food and clothing to the poor, housing relief, district nursing support and asylums for destitute children or the aged or the dying were overwhelmingly provided by Christian charities. It was not until after the Second World War and into the second half of the 20th century that the State throughout the western world took an increasing interest in the provision of social services. Jonathan Sacks, the Chief Rabbi of the United Kingdom, discusses this phenomenon as a 'nationalisation of compassion'. The increasing expectation was that it was up to the State, not the individual or the community group, to be responsible for social services. Charity, once needs-based, now became a universal entitlement. The result was that in western countries compassion was nationalised.[6]

This trend to increased State involvement in social service provision differed markedly in Australia from the United Kingdom as well as the United States. In Europe, public funding of these social services was viewed as 'public services' delivered by the bureaucracy or government-run departments or local authorities. In the United Kingdom there was huge growth in the provision of social services through the local government authority or through local health trusts. That did not happen in Australia.

In Australia, government largely took the view that there were already existing charities delivering these services and that it would be more effective and efficient if the increased government funding of these areas occurred through government subsidy of those existing services rather than by a replication of them through the creation or growth of government departments. This decision has had a profound impact on the character, nature and size of charities and nonprofit organisations in Australia compared with the United Kingdom or, indeed, the USA. Christian charities dominate in Australia in a way that they do not elsewhere. In the UK, only three of the largest 25 charities are Christian, and one other – Barnardo's – has had a Christian heritage. The UK data reveal that the largest 25 charities by income[7] represent arts, advocacy groups like cancer and heart organisations, and research organisations like the Wellcome Trust. About 40 per cent are providers of social service or are emergency relief organisations (for example Oxfam) or organisations which advocate for people with disabilities (for example Mencap). So Christian organisations are almost entirely absent at the top of what is called in the UK 'the third sector'. Even in the top 50 organisations by income the Christian presence is still less than 20 per cent.

In the United States a list of the top charities by income[8] shows that five of the top 25 charities are Christian, while another two (the YMCA and the YWCA) had Christian roots. Another faith-based nonprofit in the league table is the Jewish Federations of North America (until recently, known as the United Jewish Communities). So, at most one could suggest that 30 per cent of the top US charities were faith-based. Interestingly, the top US charities are also not focused on human social services.

The situation is markedly different among Australian charities. Twenty-three of the 25 largest Australian charities by income are Christian. If you exclude those charities that are focused on education, they are almost all focused upon social services, and the number that are Christian is still very high: 19 out of the top 25.[9] There are also more charities per capita in Australia than in England and Wales or Ireland.[10]

The historical evidence of creative and leading edge involvement in social inclusion, in Australia at least, belies the criticism that is sometimes directed towards Christian charitable institutions that they are not innovative or responsive to contemporary needs. More importantly, this evidence says a lot about the role of religious institutions and charities in Australia. The charitable activities are not undertaken in isolation: institutions may be separate entities for various legal reasons, but they are inherently part of, and come out of, communities of faith. It is misleading to split organisations into their 'religious' and 'charitable' (in the sense of social service) sectors. Each informs and supports the other.

RELIGION AND PUBLIC BENEFIT

Notwithstanding the extensive inquiry process from 2000[11] the federal government in Australia decided to adopt only three of the 27 recommendations of the Charities Definition Inquiry,[12] in particular declining to implement the recommendation to introduce a statutory definition of 'charity'. The Extension of Charitable Purpose Act 2004 (Cth) (Extension Act 2004) extended the definition for the purposes only of federal legislation to include child care, self-help groups and contemplative or closed religious orders. It could be said that 'Extension of Charitable Purpose Act' is a slight misnomer. The only true extensions relate to child care and the provision of rental accommodation under the National Rental Affordability Scheme; two other provisions are deeming provisions clarifying the issue of public benefit. One of these involved contemplative religious orders.

The first category of the Extension Act 2004 was the deeming provision in relation to contemplative orders and private prayer. Section 5 deems that an institution is taken to be for the public benefit to the extent it is 'a closed or contemplative religious order that regularly undertakes prayerful intervention at the request of members of the public'. The provision applies in the determination of whether an institution is charitable for the purposes of the ITAA 1997 and FBTAA and other Commonwealth legislation. The deeming provision was intended to overcome the doubts of some as to whether such closed religious orders are for the public benefit.[13] Arguably this deeming provision was unnecessary in Australia because of the well-established presumption of public benefit in the religion cases. Dal Pont explains it in the following way:

> The assumption is that private worship services are for the public benefit, in that such services equip adherents to apply religious principles in their role in society. This view is more consistent with the courts' modern approach, not only in presuming public benefit, but in the recognition that to deny charitable status to religious denominations or societies that hold private worship services, as opposed to those that hold public worship services, is to make the unjustified

assumption that the latter are directed to the public benefit whereas the former are not.[14]

The approach of Australian courts is illustrated importantly in the case of *Joyce v Ashfield Municipal Council*[15] where the NSW Court of Appeal upheld the grant of rating exemption to the Exclusive Brethren. The Commissioner comments that the Explanatory Memorandum of the Extension Act 2004 stated that 'in *Gilmour v Coats* [1949] AC 426 the House of Lords expressed the view that there is no proven or provable benefit to the community if the results of the contemplation are in no way communicated to the public'.[16] It is noted however that it is unlikely that *Gilmour v Coats* will be followed in Australian courts. The court in *Joyce* commenting on this case said: 'This doctrine that religious activities are subject to proof that they are for the public benefit could give rise to great problems in that it might lead to the scrutiny by the courts of the public benefit of all religious practices'.[17]

Dal Pont explains that in the Victorian case of *Crowther v Brophy*:[18]

> Gobbo J doubted whether *Gilmour v Coats* represents the law in Australia, where several decisions have recognized that the contemplative life may convey sufficient elements of public benefit to make assistance for its pursuit charitable. His Honour opined that the success of intercessory prayer is an inappropriate test for public benefit, and that the enhancement in the life, both religious and otherwise, of those who find comfort and peace of mind in their resort to inter-cessory prayer is a more appropriate consideration to adopt.[19]

Interestingly McGregor-Lowndes notes that prior to this 'extension' being enacted the Australian Taxation Office had already endorsed the vast majority of closed religious orders as charitable institutions.[20]

If the public benefit presumptions are removed there is a real risk that only those which are politically popular institutions or causes will be accepted as charitable. We do not want a return to discrimination similar to the sectarianism of the past or to create a situation where the marginal-ised peoples and causes are not considered to be charitable purposes – this would be in direct conflict with the appropriate application of the charities definition.

Much of the debate on the advancement of religion as a head of charity has been around whether religion has a public benefit, and whether the presumption should be retained. The presumption was removed in the UK under the Charities Act 2006. The expressed intention, according to the UK parliament, was that the time had come to have 'a level playing field'[21] – which paradoxically could have the opposite effect. Evidence must now be produced to demonstrate the public benefit. This is consistent with comments made by the Charities Commission in 2008: 'A religion must be capable of producing beneficial effects and evidence will need to be given to demonstrate that its beliefs, doctrine and practices have this capability'.[22]

Some comments on the current received wisdom about 'public benefit' are offered to stimulate further discussion. In the first place public benefit must be understood as being more than non-discriminatory 'good works'. If one accepts the premise that charity is about our relationship with 'the other', as will be outlined in more detail below, then it follows that there must be a 'public benefit' for all charity. In looking for public benefit, one must not limit 'benefit' to that which is only material. Nor does one determine benefit by evaluating the respective truth claims of diverse religions. Nor should one necessarily accept the trend of the case law to exclude benefits limited to the adherents of a religion. In this respect the inclusion of 'self-help' groups in an extended definition of charity[23] recognises that participation in the group is usually as much about what one does for the other as what one does for oneself.

It is said that 'fostering individual private piety is not charitable'.[24] Can one assume that personal piety, however demonstrated, does not have a public benefit? One's personal piety may well prove to be the very basis on which one develops and then demonstrates that love for others which is at the heart of charity. However, personal piety has a value in itself. By acknowledging and promoting the personal piety of the other, are we not encouraging the other to fulfil the spiritual dimension of human living and thus promoting human well-being?

One may speak of the edifying effect of public religious services in order to demonstrate public benefit but this is as incapable of proof as the benefit of private prayer. How is meditating by oneself different from meditating in a group? All that should be required is that the organisation promotes meditation (or prayer, or worship), assuming the other indicia of religion are present. Australian legislation sought to overcome the problem of finding 'public benefit' for contemplative religious orders by including in the extended charity definition a requirement that they 'regularly undertake prayerful intervention at the request of members of the public'.[25] One can only speculate how the tax authorities will define 'regularly' – each of the hours of the Divine Office perhaps? – and how they will distinguish prayers made at the request of the public from those that arise spontaneously from the members themselves.

This artificiality would not be necessary if one accepted that the promotion of the spiritual dimension of the human person is as 'charitable' as promoting the material needs of the poor, the physical needs of the sick, the educational needs of the ignorant, or the aesthetic needs of the culturally deprived. The public benefit presumption exists because of the unquestioned understanding that the Christian church with its faith commitment would deliver non-discriminatory 'good works' for the poor and needy. The presumption only began to be questioned in relation to other faiths or denominations or sects – first, politically, in relation to the Catholic closed orders, then in relation to the non-Christian sects, in particular the 'religion' of Scientology.[26] As Waters says, 'The approach of the law today is to stand back – to recognize freedom of belief, and to demonstrate the law's equality of treatment as between belief systems. That means that, if a purpose or organisation is to be held charitable, the remaining requirement of public benefit is of crucial importance'.[27]

Arguably it is dangerous to start doing what the Charities Commission in the UK (and ultimately the courts) must do and make judgments as to the public benefit of some religions over others. Is it their business? Will the determination of public benefit become a popularity contest? On what basis can the courts, or the Commission for that matter, make this determination – other than on the application of a disqualifying purposes test? In the end, would it not be better to keep the presumption of public benefit, which can be rebutted by evidence of social harm or unlawful activity – in effect a disqualifying purposes test?

There are those who are much more comfortable with the requirement in the UK of religious charities (together with all charities) to demonstrate their public benefit. However we would argue that in Australia, without at the very least a Charities Commission regulatory structure in place to moderate the process of assessing public benefit, the public benefit presumption in relation to charities for the relief (or prevention) of poverty and the advancement of education and religion should be retained – albeit with the onus on the regulator to rebut this presumption. We do not have in place in this country any appropriately holistic process for regulation of charities, so while the ATO is the gatekeeper for charity endorsement, the regulator does not in our experience have the capacity to make appropriate assessments of public benefit.

This is where a human rights model can be of assistance: the human right of religious freedom as defined in the International Covenant on Civil and Political Rights (ICCPR), article 18 of which states:

1. Everyone shall have the right to freedom of thought, conscience and religion. This right shall include freedom to have or to adopt a religion or belief of his choice, and freedom, either individually or in community with others and in public or private, to manifest his religion or belief in worship, observance, practice and teaching . . .
3. Freedom to manifest one's religion or beliefs may be subject only to such limitations as are prescribed by law and are necessary to protect public safety, order, health or morals or the fundamental rights and freedoms of others.

Australia ratified the ICCPR on 13 August 1980 and has adopted the United Nations Declaration on the Elimination of all forms of Intolerance and of Discrimination based on Religion or Belief 1981 (the Religion Declaration) as an international instrument relating to human rights and freedoms for the purposes of section 47 of the Australian Human Rights Commission Act 1986 (Cth). The right of religious freedom is importantly further expounded in this Religion Declaration, which states in article 6. In accordance with article 1 of the present Declaration, and subject to the provisions of article 1, paragraph 3, the right to freedom of thought, conscience, religion or belief shall include, inter alia, the following freedoms: . . . (b) to establish and maintain appropriate charitable or humanitarian institutions . . . (f) to solicit and receive voluntary financial and other contributions from individuals and institutions'. That is, these expressions of the right of religious freedom as elaborated in article 6 are subject to the limitation in article 1(3) that 'Freedom to manifest one's religion or belief may be subject only to such limitations as are prescribed by law and are necessary to protect public safety, order, health or morals or the fundamental rights and freedoms of others.' This means that states like Australia which have ratified ICCPR and adopted the Religious Declaration must ensure that limitations on the expressions of the right are prescribed by law, and necessary to protect public safety, order, health or morals or the fundamental rights and freedoms of others.

It is relevant to note here that religious freedom includes the right to express religious belief individually or in groups, including the right to establish and maintain philanthropic organisations and also to receive donation support. It is important to note also that there is a model in the international human rights instruments addressing the balancing of competing or conflicting expressions of rights. The limitation of such expression of religious freedom must be such as legislated. This model is not present in Australian law to any great extent, not least because there is no positive statement of human rights in most jurisdictions.

Pragmatically, we would also argue that it is best to leave the forces of human invention and creativity to solve social problems free of too much legislative intervention – history demonstrates well that charity has stepped in to fill the gaps of government service delivery. The presumption is accepted in relation to activities for the relief of poverty – that is, that they are worthwhile and will be treated as charitable without inquiry as to whether they are effective, represent best practice or are creditable. We know that if we start clambering all over such endeavours we will lose that precious spark of innovation, in particular the capacity of charities to 'plug the gaps'. History tells us that it has been the charities that provided support for the unemployed before society as a whole decided that governments should award the dole, provided for the homeless before public housing, and provided aged care services and pensions before government funding of these.

We could also ask the question another way: what is the public purpose or benefit in taxing the income of nonprofit, charitable institutions? What public purpose is being met? Do we want governments to provide equivalent institutions of social inclusion? Waters rightly asks whether the decline in Christian affiliation in some western countries, including Canada, has prompted the questioning of the place of religion as a head of charity.[28] It is demonstrably true that Canada, like parts of Europe, may be more 'post-Christian' than other countries. But Australians still hold a strong connectedness to religious institutions, even if they do not attend church as much as in previous generations. It is still very important to them that the Salvation Army is out there during bush fires; that they will be welcomed at Christmas or Easter services; and equally that the minority religious groups have a respected place in society, and that people have the opportunity to find and express the spiritual dimension of human living.

Waters asks whether public benefit is reasonably subject to judicial assessment.[29] He questions why, while the case law is 'still all over the place', the United Kingdom has opted to remove the presumption. Perhaps it is better to take the focus out, go up in the helicopter for a moment, and instead of concentrating on the question 'should advancement of religion continue to be accepted as a head of charity?' ask 'why would we want to tax nonprofit associations of citizens who come together for the pursuit of purposes – be they religious, cultural, sporting, community welfare, relief of poverty – particularly when, in the case of religious organisations, they do all or a number of these things?' The question of classification is relevant here – institutions usually exist for a number of purposes, perhaps only one of them being relevant for tax exemption reasons. These institutions are the way we join together to socialise, meet, and set the framework for friendship. For one person it might be Nippers on a Sunday morning, Scouts on Thursday evening, and the youth service on a Sunday evening or Friday night. For recently arrived Koreans it might be a Sunday afternoon service after a community lunch where the young people hang out and play games together.

In other words, the issue of the treatment of religious institutions as all charitable institutions is a much bigger issue today than the question of whether testamentary gifts will be valid in cases such as *Re Watson* or *Gilmour v Coats*.[30] Now that charitable institutions are more rarely established as trusts, and more commonly gifts are given for the purposes of identified institutions, it is important we do not keep engaging in the debates of the past but focus on the needs of society today.

Waters favours the public benefit presumption in the manner of Ireland's Charities Act 2009, which provides in section 3(4) that 'It shall be presumed, unless the contrary is proved, that a gift for the advancement of religion is of public benefit'. Dal Pont says that 'Religion's charitable status stems from the fact that, in English society, the concept of charity was essentially religious in origin'.[31] This is the reason why, in relation to charity for the advancement of religion, the public benefit is assumed unless the contrary is shown. The public benefit is absent if the beneficiaries are linked by 'blood, contract, family, association membership or employment'. This is potentially a problem for the smaller, ethnocentric or closed religious groups where it is hard to argue they are public institutions.[32]

HOW ARE WE TO DEFINE CHARITY?

The Judaeo-Christian rules for living require love of God and love of neighbour.[33] There were three Greek words for love: *eros, philia* and *agape*. *Agape* was used in the Greek translation of the Old Testament to translate the Hebrew *ahabà*. It became the preferred word for 'love' in the Greek New Testament. *Caritas* was the Latin translation of *agape* and forms the root of the English word 'charity'. They are complex words with manifold meanings. The context in which they appear in the Old Testament and New Testament is determinative of a subtlety of meaning that is lost with the simple translation into the English 'charity' or 'love'. There is a carnal and spiritual distinction. There are grades of love from what one might call a sense of the pleasant, through to the love of one's kinsfolk, through to the particular love of spouses, and culminating in the love of God.

At the heart of any appreciation of human love is awareness of the other and the well-being of the other, and, at its highest, a willing self-sacrifice for the sake of the other. This is expressed clearly in the Last Supper discourse of St John's Gospel: 'A man can have no greater love than to lay down his life for his friends'.[34] The origin of the word 'charity' suggests a broad meaning encompassing all that promotes human well-being. It includes, but is not limited to, practical assistance for those in need. The biblical response to the question of what love of neighbour means is the parable of the Good Samaritan[35] where the attention is given to the importance of caring for the outsider and the marginalised.

Concern and love of the other means love of the other in his or her totality and extends beyond meeting merely physical needs to identifying and responding to spiritual and emotional needs. From this starting point we can reflect on the different attributes of the human person and his or her needs – charity, love of the other, is a recognition and response to those needs. We might then construct an indicative list of human needs as the basis for discussion and identify organisations or activities that respond to them.

- Physical
  - health services
  - health promotion
  - disability services
  - aged care and child care
- Intellectual
  - education
  - training
  - science and research
- Spiritual
  - religion
- Aesthetic
  - arts and culture
  - heritage
- Material
  - relief of poverty and disadvantage
  - ecology.

Charity is about how we express our concern for the other in the broadest sense of what it means to advance human well-being. While it is not really possible to speak of 'Society' in an abstract sense, it is fair to say that those individuals who comprise human society collectively have an interest in promoting human well-being for themselves and for others. To be at peace spiritually, or find purpose and meaning in life through religious faith, is a worthwhile human aspiration. The spiritual dimension of the human person can rightly claim our concern. On that basis, the advancement of the spiritual dimension of human living is charitable in itself. Hence we propose an affirmative answer to the question: can religion be conceptualised as part of charity other than by tradition?

SHOULD THE LAW CONTINUE TO RECOGNISE RELIGION AS CHARITABLE?

The law does not, nor ought it to, recognise as charitable every organisation that might claim to be a religion. The High Court of Australia determined the meaning of the advancement of religion in Australia in *Church of the New Faith v Commissioner of Pay-Roll Tax (Vic)* (the *Scientology* case).[36] According to the decision of Mason CJ and Brennan J, 'the criteria of religion are twofold: first, belief in a supernatural Being, Thing or Principle, and second, the acceptance of canons of conduct in order to give effect to that belief, though canons of conduct which offend against ordinary laws are outside the area of any immunity, privilege or right conferred on the grounds of religion'.[37] To these two criteria Wilson and Deane JJ added three others: that a religion's ideas relate to man's nature and place in the universe and his or her relation to things supernatural; that its adherents are in identifiable groupings; and that its adherents see their ideas and practices as constituting a religion.[38]

The foundations of modern charity law were laid at a time when religion meant one religion only – Christianity. Migration and multiculturalism in many countries, including Australia, have led to a greater presence of other religious groups. Since the *Scientology* case decision, it has been necessary to consider whether other religions than Christianity should be given the same recognition and hence the same beneficial tax treatment. This has led to two challenging questions: (a) how far does the word 'religion' go and when is a group no longer a religion for these purposes?; and (b) if part of the justification for special tax benefits is their delivery of non-discriminatory provision of social welfare services, then what is to be done about religious groups that deliver their social welfare services on a discriminatory basis to people of their own religion? In other words, do we need to redefine the 'public benefit' of religious charities?

In Australia the charity sector still shows strongly the Christian foundations of its first institution. Arguably there is still a deeply held view in the Australian community that religious organisations or churches have their special tax exemption treatment because of the public benefits that they deliver: they are open to all; they deliver major social welfare services to the needy; they make their facilities open to community use; and they provide for the fulfilment of the spiritual aspiration of their adherents. The challenge of multiculturalism, and the modern face of diverse religious practice, is that this link is not always there, at least in the public perception. It is necessary to rely on another justification for supporting religion.

Having religious organisations is good for society as a whole – social inclusion is inclusion into a group of people, not a concept. We would argue that the Australian community accepts that there is an inherent value for society as a whole in having religious organisations which facilitate connectedness of people into religious groups. This is the case notwithstanding that they may not be open to those outside the group, and may not provide social welfare services to the broader community. Provided the religious groups do not engage in anti-social or illegal behaviour, most Australians would consider them to have a broader social good nonetheless. The elephant in the room is perhaps the role that the Christian religion has played in the wider work of charities based on the fundamental principles of love for God and love for neighbour – where, according to Jesus, neighbour is anyone in need, not just the Christian brother or sister. There is value to society as a whole in the provision of social welfare and other benefits to the group, even if these are not available on a non-discriminatory basis to the whole of society. We would suggest these two reasons present adequate justification for retaining the public benefit presumption in relation to religious organisations. The arguments in favour of the abolition of religion as a head of charity are not compelling. Prominent examples of these arguments are that we should not expect secular courts to judge whether there is or is not public benefit demonstrated from religious practice, and that the emergence of the modern welfare state has removed the need for reliance on religious bodies to perform charitable work.[39]

WHAT ORGANISATIONS OUGHT TO BE EXCLUDED?

Religious organisations that promote violence or disorder ought to be denied recognition. Likewise cults and sects that are manifestly harmful to adherents can be excluded. In some places there is a legitimate anxiety about links between religious groups and terrorist organisations. However, by way of caution, one might like to ponder the circumstances that led to the Penal Laws. Are there lessons there for today? One can use other 'anti-avoidance' provisions to deny recognition to groups that purport to be religious but operate only to enrich their promoters. There have been a number of scandals involving fake religions or some 'tele-evangelists' whose prime concern seems to be building a personal empire. Questions have been asked in the Australian Parliament about the Church of Scientology and claims made about financial exploitation. While such claims need to be investigated and assessed on their merits, the present law does have the capacity to resolve the issue. Another useful test is to ask whether the organisation that purports to be a religion would exist at all if the tax laws were different.

Two additional questions are relevant. Does the activity of religious groups contribute to 'bonding' rather than 'bridging' social capital? And where do human rights fit in here? – for example, is there a justification under the head of freedom of religion? We also consider there is no benefit in retaining the 'advancement of' limitation, which was more relevant to a categorisation of charitable gifts than to the purpose of a charitable institution. If 'charity' is to be defined statutorily, it would be preferable to separately express the terms for institutions and gifts – it makes more sense for an institution to exist for religious purposes, that is, as a religious institution, and for gifts to be given for the advancement of religion. In the same way, an institution can exist for education purposes, while gifts can be given for the advancement of education.

AN ENTITLEMENT TO SPECIAL TAXATION TREATMENT?

What would be the justification for trimming back privileges? The submission of the Atheist Foundation to the review of Australia's tax system has a useful statement of the argument that would deny taxation exemption to religious organisations:

> Equity requires that no individual or organisation, business enterprise or social club is given an unfair advantage. At the moment, religious practitioners, religions and religious enterprises are not required to pay income or land tax. This fails any reasonable test of equity and fairness, and by favouring, and therefore encouraging religion, makes a mockery of the notion that Australia is a secular state.
>
> As Mr. Justice Murphy of the High Court of Australia noted more than 20 years ago in the case of *Church of the New Faith versus Commissioner of Payroll Tax (Vict.)* 1983 154 CLR 120: '*... The crushing burden of taxation is heavier because of exemptions in favour of religious institutions, many of which have enormous and increasing wealth.*'[40]

There are a number of assumptions in this paragraph that require comment. Firstly it is more helpful to social analysis to regard Australia as a pluralist society rather than a secular one, if by 'secular' one means a society where there is no place for religion. Religious practitioners who earn an income do pay income tax. In some States, land taxes, including local government rates, are payable on land held by religious organisations, depending on its use. We mention these examples as illustrative of the confusion that exists at the popular level in relation to which bodies pay what taxes in various circumstances.

Concern on the part of some people about the wealth of religious bodies is perennial. The dissolution of the monasteries was one rather extreme response.[41] It is important to remember that assets held today by churches or other religious bodies are held in trust for charitable purposes – not the personal benefit of individual adherents. Sometimes it is hard to see this as some adherents can exercise such control over religious trust assets that they may as well be theirs beneficially. In order to eliminate abuses of such trusts, it would be most helpful in Australia either to have a charity regulator as a proactive watchdog on misuse of trust property (like the Charities Commission for England and Wales) or at least to have legislative amendment of the charitable trust legislation in each state. This could give state Attorneys General an active duty to protect charitable trusts, instead of the present role – that is, a passive, at best benign, bystander who will join actions in the Supreme Court, but only once a plaintiff can convince the Attorney that it has standing and the necessary funds to pursue the action.

Before one speaks of 'stripping back privileges' it is necessary to consider what we mean by privilege. One can easily identify any number of receipts of money by individuals or groups that are not liable to income tax. In Australia we do not impose income tax on the profits from the sale of a principal place of residence, the proceeds of an inheritance, gifts, lottery wins, or children's pocket money.[42] We do not always identify them as 'privileges' or 'tax exemptions'. Does a failure to impose income tax in these circumstances involve adding to 'the crushing burden of taxation'? Religious bodies and other charities do pay taxes of various kinds. Depending on which sub-category they fall into, they may pay fringe benefits tax, payroll tax, land tax, rates and various local government charges, stamp duty, car parking levies, and even toll road charges. Social policy dealing with taxation needs to consider:

- the type of tax
- its purpose
- those who should bear its burden, and why
- those who should not bear its burden, and why.

The decision of the High Court of Australia in the *Word Investments* case[43] has put the emphasis back onto 'purpose' as the determining element in characterising organisations as 'charitable'. In the context of 'religion' that purpose will be the advancement of the spiritual dimension of human living. This may then involve a myriad of other practical initiatives in the areas of health, social welfare, education, and the arts. These may be carried out through separate bodies leading to different taxation consequences. For example, religious organisations do not pay payroll tax, but their subsidiary bodies might. This was the outcome in the cases of the *Dominican Sisters*[44] (relating to a teachers' college) and *The Glebe Administration Board*[45] (relating to commercial and investment activities). Enterprises should be characterised taking into account their connection to the religious purpose which gives rise to them.

CONCLUSION

A more appropriate approach to understanding religion as charity is to begin with the acknowledgement of the spiritual dimension of human well-being. From that starting point one can then identify organisations that promote the development of spirituality. This may be done through public activity or the public promotion of private religious devotion. Those organisations are charitable institutions. Then, by way of exception one can exclude those that are manifestly harmful to adherents or members of the public, or are merely a sham, or a device for the enrichment of a few. From there we move to an entirely separate question: which charities pay which tax.

NOTES

1. The authors are indebted for material in this chapter to the key scholarly work of Gino Dal Pont in Dal Pont, G (2000), *Charity Law in Australia and New Zealand*, Melbourne: Oxford University Press.
2. Ibid, 6–7.
3. Australian Taxation Office (2005), 'Income Tax and Fringe Benefits Tax: Charities', *Taxation Ruling TR2005/21*, Melbourne: ATO, paras 7–8.
4. Ibid, para 13.
5. The material in this section draws from Judd, S. and A. Robinson (2006), 'Christianity and the Social Services in Australia: A Conversation', in Piggin, S. (ed.), *Shaping the Good Society in Australia: Australia's Christian Heritage: its Importance in our Past and its Relevance to our Future: Papers Read at the First Australia's Christian Heritage National Forum, Parliament House, Canberra, 6th–7th August 2006*, Sydney: Macquarie Centre. Dr Judd is the Chief Executive Officer of HammondCare.
6. Sacks, J. (2000), *The Politics of Hope*, London: Vintage.
7. CaritasData, *Top Charities Financials: the Guide to UK Charities*, http://www.topuk-charities.com/ (accessed 21 December 2009).
8. Based on data in Hudson, M. (2005), *Managing at the Leading Edge: New Challenges in Managing Nonprofit Organizations*, San Francisco: Jossey-Bass.
9. Based on figures in *Business Review Weekly*, 29 June–5 July 2006, pp. 56 ff.
10. See Productivity Commission (2009), *Contribution of the Not for Profit Sector: Issues Paper*, Canberra: Productivity Commission, which says there are probably at least 500 000 nonprofits for a population of some 22 million. According to 2008 data from the Australian Bureau of Statistics, in June 2007 there were approximately 41 000 non-profit organisations listed with an ABN. In England and Wales there are about 167 000 registered charities for a population of some 54 million, and in Ireland 7351 income tax exempt bodies for a population of some 4 million.
11. See, further, Chapter 1.
12. Australia, Inquiry into the Definition of Charities and Related Organisations (2001), *Report of the Inquiry into the Definition of Charities and Related Organisations*, Canberra: Treasury.
13. Explanatory Memorandum to the Extension of Charitable Purpose Bill 2004, referred to in Australian Taxation Office, above n 3 at paras 62 ff.
14. Dal Pont, above n 1 at 169.
15. [1975] 1 NSWLR 744.

16. Australian Taxation Office, above n 3 at para 63, which cited para 1.20 of the Explanatory Memorandum to the Extension of Charitable Purpose Bill 2004; and in comparison, the Australian cases *Association of Franciscan Order of Friars Minor v City of Kew* [1967] VR 732 and *Perpetual Trustee Co Ltd v Wittscheibe* (1940) 40 SR NSW 501.
17. Per Reynolds JA [1975] 1 NSWLR 744 at 750.
18. [1992] 2 VR 97 at 100.
19. Dal Pont, above n 1 at 171.
20. See, further, Chapter 1.
21. See discussion in Waters, D. (2009), 'The Advancement of Religion in a Pluralist Society', paper to the 2009 National Charity Law Symposium, presented by the Canadian Bar Association and Ontario Bar Association, Charity and Not-for-Profit Law Sections, 7 May, at 20.
22. Charity Commission (2008), *Analysis of the Law Underpinning the Advancement of Religion for the Public Benefit*, London: Charity Commission, para 1.6, available at http://www.charity-commission.gov.uk/Library/publicbenefit/pdfs/lawrel1208.pdf (accessed 21 December 2009).
23. Extension of Charitable Purpose Act 2004, ss 5(1)(a) and 5(2).
24. Charity Commission, above n 22 at para 2.6.
25. Extension of Charitable Purpose Act 2004, s. 5(1)(b); cf. *Cocks v Manners* LR 12 Eq 585, *Gilmour v Coats* [1949] AC 426; Charity Commission, above n 22 at para 2.6
26. Waters, above n 21 at 20.
27. Waters, above n 21 at 23.
28. Waters, above n 21 at 26.
29. Waters, above n 21 at 27.
30. *In Re Watson (deceased); Hobbs v Smith and others* [1973] 3 All ER 678; *Gilmour v Coats* [1949] AC 426.
31. Dal Pont, above n 1 at 147.
32. E.g. *Joyce v Ashfield Municipal Council* (1977) 51 ALJR 117 (the *Exclusive Brethren* case).
33. See Deut 6:5; Lev 19:18, 19:34; Luke 10:25–37; Matt 22:34–40; Mk 12:28–31.
34. John 15:13.
35. Luke 10:29 ff.
36. (1983) 154 CLR 120.
37. (1983) 154 CLR 120 at 136.
38. (1983) 154 CLR 120 at 174.
39. E.g. see Lockhart, A.W. (1984–87), 'Case Comment: Charitable Trusts: Centrepoint Community Growth Trust v Commissioner of Inland Revenue', *Auckland University Law Review* 5(2), 244–8, referred to in Waters, above n 21 at 24; see also Rationalist Society of Australia (2008), submission to *Australia's Future Tax System Review*, chaired by Dr Ken Henry, Secretary to the Treasury (the Henry Tax Review), available at http://www.taxreview.treasury.gov.au/content/submission.aspx?round=1 (accessed 23 December 2009).
40. Atheist Foundation of Australia (2008), submission to *Australia's Future Tax System Review*, para 3, available at http://www.taxreview.treasury.gov.au/content/submission.aspx?round=1 (accessed 23 December 2009) (emphasis in original).
41. For a discussion of this theme, see Lucas, B. (1992), 'The Wealthy Church – Some Myths', *Australasian Catholic Record*, 69(2), 139–46.
42. To use a frequently quoted example of Professor Myles McGregor-Lowndes.
43. *Commissioner of Taxation of the Commonwealth of Australia v Word Investments Ltd* (2008) 236 CLR 204.
44. *Commissioner for ACT Revenue Collections v Council of the Dominican Sisters of Australia* (1991) 101 ALR 417.
45. *Glebe Administration Board v Commissioner of Payroll Tax* (1987) 10 NSWLR 352.

PART III

The future of civil society organisations

9. The future of civil society organisations: towards a theory of regulation for organised civil society

Jonathan Garton[1]

INTRODUCTION

This chapter is a consideration of some rudimentary justifications for the state regulation of organised civil society as a cohesive economic sector. Despite flourishing bodies of literature on both civil society and regulation, such justifications have hitherto been largely overlooked, as there is little interaction between these disciplines, and it is particularly telling that the recent attempts to reform charity regulation which have taken place across much of the common law world have all been made on the assumption that regulation of organised civil society – specifically, regulation of the charitable sector – is justified. None of the bodies charged with drafting reform proposals in Australia, Canada, England, Ireland, New Zealand, Northern Ireland or Scotland, in their published findings at least, stepped back to consider whether this is indeed the case: the need for regulation was assumed, and all that was considered was the form that regulation should take. Yet this is an issue of the utmost importance given the scale of the sector and the nature of civil society activity. In Australia, for example, there are an estimated 700 000 nonprofit organisations, employing 604 000 people,[2] and nonprofits with paid workforces have a combined income in the region of $33.5 billion, a figure rivalling both the communications and agriculture industries.[3] Given the significant economic contributions made by civil society organisations (CSOs), and the social value of the activities they undertake, the questions of whether and when to regulate these organisations demand serious consideration.

With this in mind, this chapter takes a step back to consider five traditional justifications for state regulation, based on the private sector model, and considers their application to organised civil society. These are: monopoly power and anti-competitive behaviour; public goods; externalities; information deficits; and irregularity of production. We will see that, although instructive, key structural and functional differences between CSOs and private firms mean that it is inappropriate to assume that these justifications apply indiscriminately to the sector: some, such as the need to control monopolies, are of limited concern; others, such as the resolution of information deficits, have a particular relevance to civil society activity.

MONOPOLY POWER AND ANTI-COMPETITIVE BEHAVIOUR

Traditional regulation theory is based on the microeconomic model of a perfectly competitive private market, in which no one firm or consumer can influence the market price and the levels of supply and demand are the same. This state of affairs, referred to as market equilibrium, is desirable because it is both productively and allocatively efficient. It is productively efficient because it is not possible for a firm to increase output whilst maintaining costs, or reduce costs whilst maintaining output, and it is allocatively efficient because all parties are better off as a result of transactions: firms value revenue more than their products and consumers value products more than the money spent on their purchase. However, market equilibrium will only occur where there is a sufficiently large number of firms and consumers to prevent any one player from influencing the market price of a product. If one firm has a monopoly, lack of competition means that equilibrium is unlikely to be achieved naturally, as that firm has an obvious incentive to 'curtail . . . production in order to raise prices (from fewer sales) by gaining revenue through increased price on the units that are still sold'.[4] There is also a risk that the firm will be 'lazy' with regard to the costs of production,[5] as the lack of competition removes the incentive to keep such costs to a minimum, and it may fail to meet an appropriate level of customer service.[6]

A monopoly will typically arise if three conditions occur: (a) where the market is constituted by a single firm;[7] (b) where the good or service supplied is unique;[8] and (c) where 'substantial barriers' prevent potential rival firms from entering the market.[9] Similar problems will also arise in those markets where, although more than one firm is present, there is 'collusion' between firms who form cartels and engage in anti-competitive activities such as price-fixing.[10] Because the market is unable to correct these problems naturally, the existence or threat of a monopoly is viewed traditionally as justifying state intervention in the form of competition or antitrust law.[11]

So far as organised civil society is concerned, it is clear that there are two distinct spheres in which CSOs regularly operate on a monopolistic basis. First, a number of organisations that regulate entry into particular professions are constituted in such a way that they might properly be classed as falling within the sector. Nonprofit professional bodies (for example, in England, the General Medical Council (GMC) and the General Council of the Bar) exercise a gatekeeping function such that anyone wishing to practise (for example, as a doctor or barrister) must meet the training requirements and standards of conduct demanded of the respective body – accordingly, they have a monopoly on entry to their professions. Similarly, trade unions that operate on a closed shop basis effectively have a monopoly on entry into a particular trade. Secondly, some ideological organisations may operate on a monopoly basis if there are no other organisations with comparable belief systems – in other words, if the services provided are unique. For example, if a member of church x is told that if he breaches the church rules he will be excommunicated, then it will be of little consolation to him that he would be welcomed into churches y and z if those churches are not compatible with his religious beliefs.

However, aside from professional and ideological organisations, it is not clear that there are any other areas of civil society activity that are particularly likely to tend towards monopoly. Not only is there multiple CSO presence but the fact that no activity is the exclusive province of civil society means that there will typically be a public or private sector presence as well: consider, for example, the provision of healthcare and education. Although it is perfectly possible that within a specific field a CSO may develop a unique product which may warrant a specific regulatory response,[12] it would clearly be inappropriate to justify any broader, sector-based regulation by reference to the control of monopoly power. Similarly, if a CSO creates a new market, by identifying and responding to an area of social need not yet formally acknowledged,[13] it may gain a first-mover advantage and establish a dominant position analogous to a monopoly,[14] but regulation would be targeted better at the field in question rather than the sector at large.

Regulation may be appropriate, however, if CSOs engage in anti-competitive practices. Although some argue that competition is anathema to the concept of civil society,[15] resources are of course limited and it is inevitable that some CSOs, particularly those without an endowment fund large enough to cover all their activities, will find themselves competing with others for public or private funding. This can only be exacerbated (a) by the contract culture,[16] where organisations are forced to tender for government funding and demonstrate that they provide the most attractive package for service provision; and (b) where CSOs operate in the same sphere as private sector firms, such as healthcare and education. Those

CSOs feeling the pressure of competition have an incentive to engage in anti-competitive practices such as forming cartels with funding bodies in order to divert resources away from rival organisations.[17]

PUBLIC GOODS

Public goods are those goods and services which are non-rivalous and non-excludable. By non-rivalous, we mean that no matter how many consumers use the product it remains available to others, and it costs the producer the same amount to provide the product for many consumers as it does to provide it for a few.[18] By non-excludable, we mean that whilst the product is being provided it is impossible to prevent people from taking the benefit even if they do not pay.[19] Clean air is therefore a public good: it remains available for all to breathe, regardless of population size, and those who refuse to contribute to the cost of tackling pollution cannot be prevented from enjoying it. For-profit firms are typically unable to generate significant levels of public goods, because the rational citizen has an incentive to free-ride and enjoy the benefits without contributing to the cost, thereby limiting the achievable profit. Further, the difficulties in adequately evaluating the quality of public goods, given that they benefit society at large and often (as with much environmental activity) in a manner that will not be apparent for many years, mean that firms that do provide them have an incentive to compromise service quality in order to maximise profit. Accordingly, the second traditional microeconomic justification for regulating the private market is to secure the production of public goods,[20] as the market will be able to provide these with state intervention to raise sufficient finances to 'secure the supply' and determine the 'quality and quantity' of the goods in question.[21]

However, it is well established that, unlike the private market, CSOs are well suited to the provision of public goods.[22] Because they are not constrained by the need to maximise profit for their owners, as they are typically non-profit-distributing, CSOs are able to pursue an activity for its own sake. This means they can safely commit themselves to the production of a public good, as they are sheltered from the profit-related difficulties which result from non-rivalous consumption and non-excludability.[23] Further, as Henry Hansmann has argued,[24] they are particularly suited to providing goods and services in situations where there is information asymmetry between producer and consumer. Such information asymmetry arises when it is either impossible or highly impractical for the consumer to evaluate the quality of the goods in question. In the private goods context, the issue will usually be whether evaluation is possible before purchase;

post-purchase, most information deficits will be resolved, as the consumer will now have product experience.[25] In the public goods context, however, the problem is much bigger: as well as the difficulty of pre-purchase evaluation, there is the fact that consumers will typically not be able to judge the quality of the goods even after they have been supplied, for two reasons. First, because the beneficiaries extend far beyond those who are financing the good, it will be very difficult to obtain an accurate picture of the quality of the good overall.[26] This is compounded by the fact that the beneficiaries will not all have the same public goods preferences, so that even if it were possible for a representative sample to provide feedback it would be hard to eliminate the resulting bias. Secondly, the nature of many public goods means that some or all of their benefits will be either (a) incompatible with evaluation, because we lack the appropriate technology or tools of assessment, or (b) not apparent until some point in the future. When faced with a choice of potential service providers, consumers are therefore inclined to select the organisation which they consider most trustworthy, in order to minimise the risk that their public goods will be compromised in some way. Because CSOs are not susceptible to the perceived corrupting influence of profit, they are generally seen as more reliable and responsible than their private sector counterparts.[27]

Given that organised civil society has a strong public goods presence, which is in part explained by reference to private market failure, it is thus prima facie inapt to justify regulation of organised civil society by reference to the need to secure the provision of public goods. Furthermore, CSOs are by their nature often better placed than the state to determine the quality and quantity of public goods provision, making state regulation even less desirable. In a democracy, the state will at best[28] be able to meet the public goods preferences of the majority of its citizens,[29] but in any heterogeneous society there will be innumerable minority groups who desire either (a) public goods which are not supplied by the government or (b) different levels of those public goods which are so supplied.[30] Additionally, public goods provision may be targeted at resolving a problem which is actually caused by government activities.[31]

Lester Salamon identifies three reasons why CSOs are generally better suited than the state to the provision of public goods. The first is their comparative institutional efficiency, which results largely from their size.[32] CSOs are typically much smaller than government institutions, which means that their transaction costs are lower. Salamon notes that in order for government to start supplying a public good, 'substantial segments of the public must be aroused, public officials must be informed, laws must be written, majorities must be assembled, and programs must be put into operation'.[33]

This is exacerbated by the phenomenon of 'institutional stickiness', whereby large bureaucracies are unwilling to abandon established policies and activities, tending naturally towards inertia rather than change.[34] By comparison, CSOs can commence provision simply with 'a handful of individuals acting on their own' and will thus be more cost-effective.[35] There is support for this in microeconomic theory, which suggests that it will be less costly for smaller organisations to undertake new activities than for large organisations.[36] The small scale of CSOs enables them to 'form and disband' with ease,[37] minimising the response time to the 'unpredictable and often changing' public goods requirements of society.[38]

Whilst there is strength in this argument, it is dependent on CSOs being small organisations. In reality, the idea that CSOs are 'small' and government agencies 'large' is overly simplistic. Many successful CSOs are large organisations, whilst many government agencies are comparatively small, so it will not always be true to say that trustees will not be distanced from the grass roots by organisational structure,[39] or that it will be comparatively easy for a CSO to commence production of a novel public good. Furthermore, it is not clear that a small organisation will always be more efficient than a large organisation. Empirical research by Jeremy Kendall in the context of the provision of residential care, for example, suggests that CSOs have an edge over their private sector counterparts partly because they are 'relatively large'[40] and accordingly are able to take advantage of 'technical economies of scale and scope, cross-subsidy from other current activities . . . and historically accumulated reserves'.[41] Even in a sphere where CSOs are typically small, it does not follow that their efficiency turns on size alone – other factors, such as the ability to utilise volunteer labour,[42] or raise finances,[43] will also play a part.

However, CSOs are likely to be more efficient than either the state or the market in respect of 'relational goods', being those goods which depend on interpersonal relationships for their utility and which 'can be enjoyed only by participating in a social process'.[44] Avner Ben-Ner and Benedetto Gui argue that these relationships will be more 'satisfactory' when consumers are able to participate as stakeholders in the organisation,[45] as they will have a greater opportunity to 'express their intentions, opinions and desires' than if they engaged with a private firm or the state.[46] It seems likely that this will also, in part, turn on the size of any given CSO, as the greater the number of members or stakeholders, the quieter their individual voices will be.[47] The value of relational goods has been recognised by the courts in Australia, where maintaining the 'traditional ties' of an Aboriginal community is a charitable purpose.[48]

Salamon also suggests that the small size of CSOs compared with state institutions, and their diverse nature, will encourage expertise in service provision.[49] A minority preference group unhappy with the state's provision of a public good can either create a new CSO to supply the desired public goods or utilise an existing CSO with similar, if not identical, preferences to the group. The former strategy will obviously reflect their preferences, as the group will be able to set the CSO's service parameters. In the latter scenario, whilst the group's preferences might not exactly match those of an existing CSO, there is a greater likelihood, compared with government provision, that the group's particular preferences will be taken into account, as the relatively small size of the CSO means that their individual contributions (or potential contributions) will be proportionately more important and there is therefore an incentive for CSOs to 'tailor services to client needs'.[50] Moreover, there is a greater chance that these preferences will be accurately represented to high-level decision-makers within a CSO, as a smaller organisational structure means fewer opportunities for information to become distorted as it filters up through the various stages of administration from the coalface to the trustees.[51] In addition to the benefits for minority groups, the state itself may wish to utilise the expertise of CSOs for the same reasons. Public goods provision on a small scale also encourages diversity, providing greater 'consumer choice' of goods provision.[52]

Again, however, Salamon's argument is less applicable to larger CSOs, where trustees are likely to be distanced from the grass roots by organisational structure,[53] and we must note that, as with efficiency, there are factors other than organisational size which contribute to the expertise of CSOs. In particular, we should note the importance of the civil society 'ethos': the exchange theory of expertise holds that 'the more valuable to a person is the result of his action, the more likely he is to perform the action',[54] and so if some philanthropic or charitable satisfaction is derived by CSO workers and volunteers they will be encouraged to repeat their activities and, over time, develop specialised skills and knowledge.

Finally, Salamon notes that CSOs are relatively insulated from political considerations when compared with the state.[55] Because CSOs do not have to worry about being removed at the next election, unlike the government, they are less affected by the consideration of time,[56] which enables them to adopt a long-term strategy for their public goods provision; for the same reason, they are also freer to pursue innovative methods of production. The use of CSOs draws attention away from the government when the goods in question are 'culturally sensitive'.[57] On the other side of the coin, there may be a 'social stigma' attached to government intervention in a particular situation which organised civil society may also be able to avoid.[58] CSOs are also useful in garnering resources without alienating the electorate by increasing taxation.

However, it would be naïve to think that CSOs are unaffected by political considerations altogether – just as governments must appease voters and interest groups, so too must CSOs appease their own 'multiple constituents' and engage in micro-level politics.[59] As well as taking into account the preferences of their existing members and donation base, CSOs will need to consider their own image in order to increase levels of public support. In addition, CSOs which enter into funding arrangements with government bodies will also have to take their interests into account, as the terms of an individual contract or grant[60] will inevitably reflect the political concerns of the funding body. Furthermore, those CSOs which rely on government funding have an incentive to ensure they remain politically fashionable in order to secure future income. CSOs are also not immune from the macro-level politics more normally associated with government – those which engage in campaigning and lobbying of government, or, more formally, in consultation processes, necessarily occupy a space in the political arena,[61] and may need to consider whether shifting the focus of their activities to new public goods will see them cast as fickle service providers by the media.

For all these reasons, it is therefore inappropriate to justify the regulation of organised civil society by reference to public goods provision. This is not to say that CSO provision of such goods is without its problems: issues such as the ability of the sector to raise sufficient funds, or challenges to the sector's trustworthiness, may arise such as to warrant regulation. However, these problems are not specific to public goods and are discussed below.

EXTERNALITIES

The third traditional economic justification for regulation is as a response to externalities or spillovers[62] – the 'social costs' of a product that are not taken into account in pricing by firms or consumers.[63] For example, let us imagine that the manufacture of product x results in pollution affecting all the inhabitants of town y. If all of the inhabitants are able to co-ordinate themselves and bring an action in private law (for example, in the torts of negligence or nuisance), the cost of the pollution will be borne by the producer; this will then be reflected in the price of x. However, if the inhabitants are large in number, then concerted action by the affected individuals may well be hard to co-ordinate and may be affected by the free-rider problem. Furthermore, the nature of the pollution may be such that detrimental effects are not manifested until many years later, or such that the manufacture of x is only one of several contributory factors. In these situations it is unlikely that the producer will be forced to bear the cost – either because no action is brought (because the inhabitants do not co-ordinate their efforts or are unaware of the pollution) or because it is impossible to assess accurately the proportion of damage attributable to the production of x.

As far as CSOs are concerned, there is nothing inherent in civil society generally that suggests externalities are likely to result. Of course, individual activities carried out in pursuit of these functions may result in externalities: for example, a university's chemistry department may, in the pursuit of research, carry on experiments that contribute towards pollution in one of the ways described above. Where such externalities occur it may be that activity-based regulation is desirable. However, it is inappropriate to justify sector-wide regulation on this basis. Further, activity-based regulation would tend towards a coherent approach to the externality – in the example above, organisations outside civil society may pollute the environment as well, so we would not wish to restrict appropriate regulatory provisions to CSOs.

However, one area of CSO activity which is likely to lead to the production of externalities across the sector is political campaigning. Campaigning may result in externalities in that excessive lobbying can be a 'divisive and fragmenting influence'[64] which may overload any given decision-making process and lead to 'political paralysis'.[65] Accordingly, Eric Barendt notes that, in respect of freedom of expression in general, 'some regulation . . . must surely be conceded, if any expression is to be communicated effectively'.[66] Even if campaigning is undertaken on a more general basis, as opposed to being specifically targeted at official decision-makers, there is a risk that inaccurate or polemical campaigns will manipulate public opinion without due cause.[67] This problem may be exacerbated by the fact that, whereas campaigning by the state is called to account by opposition parties and CSOs, and private sector campaigning is called to account by rival firms, civil society campaigning has no natural control,[68] except insofar as rival CSOs may be competing for the same funding and thus have an incentive to disprove each other's inaccurate campaigning.

In addition to the risk of producing externalities, some regulation of campaigning can be justified on the ground that participation in the political arena risks compromising the independence of the sector, as individual CSOs may be tempted to form alliances with political parties or state officials in an attempt to secure the passing of a particular law or the implementation of a particular policy. Such arrangements may encourage those CSOs to take the interests of their political allies into account when making decisions and lose their 'non-partisan' reputation.[69] Loss of independence would not be insignificant: it would undermine the ability of the

sector to contribute towards the accountability of political players, especially were an individual CSO to be called upon to comment on the actions
of its ally; it may result in the application of a CSO's resources to activities
approved by its ally rather than its members or benefactors;[70] and, on a
more general level, may reduce trust and confidence in the sector, which
is likely, in turn, to exacerbate concerns relating to information deficits,
which we consider below. Further, we have already noted that one of the
reasons why organised civil society is an appropriate provider of public
goods is the fact that the sector is relatively insulated from 'populist pressures';[71] political campaigning is likely to raise the profile of a CSO and
remove a layer of political insulation.

INFORMATION DEFICITS

Regulation is traditionally justified where a particular market does not
tend towards the free flow of information that consumers need in order to
make rational purchasing decisions.[72] We have already noted that where it
is impossible or highly impractical to evaluate a particular good or service
prior to its purchase, and sometimes even after its purchase, consumers
will be ill-equipped to decide which products or combination of products
will be of the greatest utility. In this situation, although a producer could
rectify matters by making relevant information about its products freely
available, there will be a temptation to mislead consumers into selecting
its products over those of its rivals by supplying 'false information or by
omitting key facts'.[73] Accordingly, state intervention may be justified to
compel firms to provide sufficient (and accurate) information so as to
ensure that consumers are able to make rational choices.

It may seem prima facie that regulating organised civil society on the
ground of information asymmetry would be somewhat misguided. As we
noted above, Henry Hansmann's theory of contract failure uses the information deficits inherent in public goods to explain civil society's presence
in this area – the idea being that, because they generally do not operate on
a for-profit basis, CSOs lack the fiscal temptation to deceive consumers
in the way that a private firm might choose to do. This can also be used
to explain other CSO activities, such as the provision of complex private
services like education and healthcare, which involve similar information deficits between consumers and service providers.[74] If organised civil
society is itself a response to the private market's information asymmetry,[75] one might assume that there would be no need to regulate CSOs for
this reason. However, there are several reasons why the sector might suffer
from problems relating to information deficits.

First, organised civil society will only be a viable alternative to the market where consumers are confident that CSOs do, in fact, operate on a nonprofit basis. Without some form of regulation, organisations may decide to operate on a for-profit basis, in order to make money for the benefit of private concerns, but conceal this from donors and other stakeholders. Although one would hope that the civil society ethos would counter the incentive to operate a CSO for private benefit, Andreas Ortmann and Mark Schlesinger suggest that the more trustworthy organised civil society is perceived to be the more resources it will attract,[76] thereby increasing the incentive for abuse: paradoxically, those CSOs that are the most trusted initially are the ones most likely to have this trust 'eroded by subsequent violations'.[77] This problem has been acknowledged by the High Court of Australia in the context of religious charities, Mason ACJ and Brennan J noting that 'charlatanism is a necessary price of religious freedom'.[78] Accordingly, regulation to ensure the accountability of CSO directors and trustees has been described as a 'charm . . . expected to both prevent and cure the evils of sleaze and corruption'.[79]

It is also clear that certain CSOs operate legitimately on a for-profit basis. Hybrid organisations such as social enterprises, for example, distribute a limited amount of profit amongst investors.[80] Non-profit-distributing CSOs may decide to carry on profit-making activities that are ancillary to their main endeavours,[81] in order to replace or supplement income from donations or state grants[82] and thus fund other, loss-making activities.[83] Howard Tuckman notes that relevant considerations here will include: (a) whether a CSO has a need for additional resources; (b) whether it has a potentially sellable product which (c) doesn't 'substantially interfere' with the organisation's primary activities; and (d) whether it will be able to locate 'willing' consumers.[84] Without some form of control, these legitimate profit-making CSOs may succumb to the same problems as their illegitimate cousins. Furthermore, Burton Weisbrod notes that the pursuit of profit through ancillary activities may compromise a CSO's main objectives by 'distract[ing] management' or, more seriously, causing 'mission displacement' in order to satisfy potential customers.[85]

In any case, the pursuit of profit is not the only corrupting influence on an organisation – without some form of control, CSOs may be tempted to inflate administration costs unnecessarily in order to line the pockets of trustees or employees, for example by paying higher than average wages, remunerating needless expenses or providing extravagant facilities;[86] in fact, through 'everything from power, prestige, and other perks, to cross-subsidisation, influence costs, advocacy expenditures, and organisational slack'.[87] Trustees may also use their position to engage in political campaigning to secure their own interests rather than those of their members.[88]

Michael King notes that even the actions of those trustees whose 'motives are pure' may warrant regulation,[89] if, for example, in the case of charitable CSOs, they fail to understand the limits of the expenses for which they can legitimately be reimbursed.[90] By ensuring certain financial information is made available, regulation will also have the additional benefit of revealing to donors, who usually have 'no meaningful opportunity to learn about fund-raising costs',[91] that some administration costs are both legitimate and necessary.

The threats to the quality and quantity of a CSO's activities that stem from information deficits are exacerbated by three factors. First, whenever a CSO is funded by donations, its beneficiaries or consumers will typically be separated from its patrons, which will further hinder the latter's ability to evaluate the quality and quantity of the goods or services they have financed.[92]

Secondly, there is a long tradition of testamentary gifts to CSOs. Unlike *inter vivos* gifts, evaluation by a testator is, of course, not merely impractical but impossible. Similarly, those who set up CSOs rather than merely donate to them, whether *inter vivos* or by will, may be discouraged from their endeavours if they believe that, after their death, the organisation's aims may be corrupted.[93] This is particularly significant in the context of charitable CSOs as a charity's funds may be applied to a new purpose under the doctrine of *cy près*, if it is no longer appropriate for its purpose to be carried out. In theory, this purpose should be one that is 'as near as possible' to the original,[94] or a reasonable approximation,[95] but it is clear from the case law that this is not always the case.[96]

Thirdly, the structure of a CSO will often exacerbate accountability issues. Although the directors of those CSOs constituted as companies limited by guarantee must, in theory, account to their members, and whilst staff of CSOs must account to their trustees, Colin Rochester notes that the effectiveness of these mechanisms may be limited, for example: (a) where a board of lay trustees is intimidated by the expertise of employed staff;[97] (b) where a CSO is based around a small group of entrepreneurs who act both as trustees and as workers;[98] or (c) in the case of CSOs based on mutuality, where 'regular and close contact between the staff and members' may lead to problems of capture.[99]

CO-ORDINATION AND IRREGULARITY OF PRODUCTION

The final traditional economic justification for regulation is as a means of ensuring that the market is not disrupted by irregularity of production.

Irregularity may be geographical, in that firms may be discouraged from supplying goods in remote areas if the supply costs are higher than in non-remote regions – a practice known as 'cream-skimming'[100] – or it may be temporal, in that there may be a scarcity of resources from time to time[101] or demand may be 'cyclical'.[102] Certain consumers may find that they are unable to purchase goods by virtue of their location or the timing of their need and, as a consequence, regulation to co-ordinate production may be necessary in order to ensure an appropriate level of availability. Furthermore, where demand is cyclical, firms may find that they have to close down periodically and re-open according to whether demand is in a trough or at a peak, which will 'engender waste' from increased adminis-trative costs.[103] Regulation may prevent this as well.

Irregularity of production is particularly significant to CSOs in the context of public goods provision. Lester Salamon's theory of voluntary failure argues that CSOs will be limited in their ability to provide public goods where there is philanthropic insufficiency and philanthropic par-ticularism.[104] The former arises when the sector is unable to generate sufficient, stable resources to satisfy demands for public goods. Although we have already noted how CSOs can be used to circumvent free-riding, the phenomenon nevertheless affects organised civil society as well as the market, for there will always be consumers who consider free-riding to be an effective means of maximising their own utility.[105] Even where organised civil society as a whole is well resourced, there may be localised problems, such as difficulty in attracting funding for particular goods or a lack of CSO presence in a particular geographic area.[106] Lack of available funding for particular goods can in turn lead to particularism, whereby CSOs are naturally drawn to providing those public goods that attract the most resources.[107] This will mean that less 'lucrative' goods will be neglected, and low CSO activity may, in turn, mean that those who *are* willing to fund the goods have no vehicle to supply them. Conversely, high CSO activity in relation to more popular goods may result in 'wasteful duplication of services'.[108]

CONCLUSION

The regulation of private markets is traditionally justified by refer-ence to five economic conditions: monopoly power and anti-competitive behaviour, the supply of public goods, the production of externalities, information deficits, and irregularity of supply. Contemporary theories of organised civil society suggest that the first and third of these have little relevance to the regulation of organised civil society. There is nothing inherent in civil society activity which tends towards the domination of a particular market by a single CSO, such as the supply of unique goods or services or barriers preventing others from entering the market, and nothing to suggest that any individual CSOs are in a strong position to drive others from the market permanently through excessively competitive practices, whilst the level of organisational efficiency, expertise and political insulation of CSOs compared with state institutions means that they will often, although not always, be better placed than the state to provide public goods.

However, the remaining traditional microeconomic justifications for regulation are certainly relevant to organised civil society. First, advocacy and political campaigning may, if unchecked, result in externalities if decision-makers and the public are provided with inaccurate or misleading information, or if the marketplace of ideas is flooded with too much information to be of practical use. Secondly, although CSOs are perceived as being more trustworthy than for-profit firms because they are not motivated by the pursuit of profit, they are not immune from problems of information deficits, and they are only a viable alternative to the market when consumers are confident that they genuinely do operate on a nonprofit or limited profit basis. Furthermore, whenever CSOs rely on donations for funding, donors will rarely be able to appraise the quality and quantity of the services they fund, even where those services are of a kind that could otherwise be adequately evaluated. Thirdly, it is clear that the sector suffers from irregularities of production in the form of philanthropic insufficiency, where certain sections of the sector are unable to attract sufficient resources either temporally or geographically, and philanthropic particularism, where activities that readily attract funding are preferred by CSOs over others that do not.

Of course, the traditional microeconomic analysis of regulation is just the starting point in the development of any coherent policy for regulating organised civil society. The justifications identified above as relevant to the sector will not always be happy bedfellows, and an effective regulatory strategy will inevitably need to effect a compromise between competing goals – regulation to ensure the accountability of CSOs, in order to minimise information asymmetry, for example, may have implications for the sector's volunteer nature and its role as an innovator of service provision, whilst any regulation to co-ordinate resources may have ramifications for the sector's independence. There is also much to be learned about the sector's structure and operation from disciplines outside regulation theory, which have proved rather less reluctant to shift their attention away from the private market towards other social and economic sectors.[109] These, though, are matters for another study.

NOTES

1. Reader in Law, Charity Law Unit, University of Liverpool. This chapter is based on material taken from Garton, J (2009), *The Regulation of Organised Civil Society*, Oxford: Hart Publishing.
2. National Roundtable of Nonprofit Organisations (undated), *Australian Nonprofit Sector Factsheet*, Philanthropy Australia, available at, http://www.philanthropy.org.au/research/factsheets/nfpfactsheet.pdf (accessed 18 November 2009).
3. Ibid.
4. Breyer, S. (1982), *Regulation and its Reform*, Cambridge, MA: Harvard University Press, 15–16. See also Baldwin, R. and M. Cave (1999), *Understanding Regulation: Theory, Strategy, and Practice*, Oxford: Oxford University Press, 10.
5. Breyer, above n 4 at 16. The problem of organisational slack has also been noted in the civil society context: see Ortmann, A. (1996), 'Modern Economic Theory and the Study of Nonprofit Organizations: Why the Twain Shall Meet', *Nonprofit and Voluntary Sector Quarterly*, 25(4), 470–84, 472. This may be a particular problem for CSOs – Susan Rose-Ackerman notes that the lack of 'market discipline' (not specific to monopoly power but inherent in nonprofit distribution) may mean that an organisation continues to operate long after it has served its purpose or ceased to be effectual: Rose-Ackerman, S. (1997), 'Altruism, Ideological Entrepreneurs and the Non-Profit Firm', *Voluntas*, 8(2), 120–34, 125.
6. Breyer, above n 4 at 20.
7. Baldwin and Cave, above n 4 at 10; Gellhorn, E. and R. Pierce (1987), *Regulated Industries*, St Paul, MN: West Publishing, 33.
8. Baldwin and Cave, above n 4 at 10; Gellhorn and Pierce, above n 7 at 33.
9. Ibid.
10. See Cooter, R. and T. Ulen (2000), *Law and Economics*, Reading: Addison Wesley Longman, 40; Ogus, A. (1994), *Regulation: Legal Form and Economic Theory*, Oxford: Clarendon Press, 30.
11. See generally Breyer, S. (1990), 'Regulation and Deregulation in the United States', in G. Majone (ed.), *Deregulation or Re-Regulation? Regulatory Reform in Europe and the United States*, London: Pinter, 10; Cooter and Ulen, above n 10 at 40; Gellhorn and Pierce, above n 7 at 33–5, 44–9; Ogus, above n 10 at 30; Kay, J. and J. Vickers (1990), 'Regulatory Reform: An Appraisal', in Majone, ibid, 227–8; Sunstein, C. (1990), *After the Rights Revolution: Reconstituting the Regulatory State*, Cambridge, MS: Harvard University Press, 48–9.
12. CSOs that operate on a strictly nonprofit basis may limit some of the problems normally associated with monopolies: where an organisation does not operate so as to maximise profit it does not follow that in monopoly conditions it will reduce output and raise prices. However, other problems may still justify some form of regulation – for example excessive social and political power, or the risk of organisational slack: Steinberg, R. (1987), 'Nonprofit Organizations and the Market', in Powell, W. (ed.), *The Nonprofit Sector: A Research Handbook*, New Haven and London: Yale University Press, especially at 127–30.
13. Consider that, in England, organised civil society established the first universities, public libraries and hospitals: see Lawson, J. and H. Silver (1973), *A Social History of Education in England*, London: Methuen, 105; Douglas, J. (1983), *Why Charity? The Case for a Third Sector*, Beverly Hills and London. Sage, 13; Chesterman, M. (1979), *Charities, Trusts and Social Welfare*, London: Weidenfeld and Nicolson, 17.
14. See e.g. Conrad, C. (1983), 'The Advantage of Being First and Competition Between Firms', *International Journal of Industrial Organization*, 1(4), 353–64; Mueller, D. (1997),'First-Mover Advantages and Path Dependence', *International Journal of Industrial Organization*, 15(6), 827–50; Tuckman, H. (1998), 'Competition, Commercialization, and the Evolution of Nonprofit Organizational Structures', in

Weisbrod, B. (ed.), *To Profit or Not to Profit: the Commercial Transformation of the Nonprofit Sector*, Cambridge: Cambridge University Press.

15. See Gardner, J. (2000), 'The Virtue of Charity and its Foils', in Mitchell, C. and S. Moody (eds), *Foundations of Charity*, Oxford: Hart Publishing, who argues that the moral virtue of charity is incompatible with competition, though of course in practice neither the charitable sector nor organised civil society is synonymous with moral charity.

16. On which see generally: 6, P. and J. Kendall (eds) (1997), *The Contract Culture in Public Services*, Aldershot: Arena; Charity Commission (2007), *CC37 – Charities and Public Service Delivery – An Introduction and Overview*, London: Charity Commission; Warburton, J. and D. Morris (1991), 'Charities and the Contract Culture', *Conveyancer and Property Lawyer*, 21, 419–31.

17. See Downer, S. (2003),'Third Sector "Cartel" Blasted for Controlling NDC Funds', *New Start*, Bourne End, UK, 10 December, who notes unpublished research by Northumbria University's Sustainable Cities Research Institute detailing evidence of an attempt by three CSOs in Sunderland to 'control developments in the area in order to ensure that they dominate delivery'.

18. Hansmann, H. (1987), 'Economic Theories of Nonprofit Organization', in Powell, W. (ed.), *The Nonprofit Sector: A Research Handbook*, New Haven and London: Yale University Press, 29.

19. Cooter and Ulen, above n 10 at 42; Olson, M. (1971), *The Logic of Collective Action: Public Goods and the Theory of Groups*, Cambridge, MA and London: Harvard University Press, 14; Hansmann, above n 18 at 29.

20. See generally Baldwin and Cave, above n 4 at 13–14; Breyer, above n 11 at 22; Gellhorn and Pierce, above n 7 at 55–8; Ogus, above n 10 at 33; Sunstein, above n 11 at 49–52.

21. Ogus, above n 10 at 33.

22. Empirical work conducted by Estelle James and Susan Rose-Ackerman in the 1980s confirmed that the bulk of civil society presence is 'generally consistent with theories that stress . . . public goods' provision: James, E. and S. Rose-Ackerman (1986), *The Nonprofit Enterprise in Market Economies*, Chur, Switz. and New York: Harwood Academic Publishers, 60; this is acknowledged in a number of official publications: see e.g. Ontario Law Reform Commission (1996), *Report on the Law of Charities*, Toronto: Ontario Law Reform Commission, ch. 9, 10–11; Prime Minister's Strategy Unit (2002), *Private Action, Public Benefit: A Review of Charities and the Wider Not-For-Profit Sector*, London: HMSO, para 3.1.

23. See generally Weisbrod, B. (1986), 'Toward a Theory of the Voluntary Sector in a Three-Sector Economy', in Rose-Ackerman, S. (ed.), *The Economics of Nonprofit Institutions: Studies in Structure and Policy*, New York: Oxford University Press; Hansmann, H. (1986), 'The Role of Nonprofit Enterprise', in Rose-Ackerman, ibid.

24. Hansmann, H. (1987), 'Economic Theories of Nonprofit Organization', in Powell, W. (ed.), *The Nonprofit Sector: A Research Handbook*, New Haven and London: Yale University Press; Hansmann, above n 23.

25. Of course, this will not always be the case: some product qualities – for example, durability – must be assessed over a prolonged period of time.

26. It may be *technically* possible for all the beneficiaries to come together and evaluate the good, but the cost of doing so renders this impractical: see Krashinsky, M. (1986), 'Transaction Costs and a Theory of the Nonprofit Organization', in Rose-Ackerman, S. (ed.), *The Economics of Nonprofit Institutions: Studies in Structure and Policy*, New York: Oxford University Press, 117.

27. Hansmann, above n 23 at 29.

28. In practice, of course governments have an incentive to meet the public goods preferences of certain groups other than the majority, e.g. floating voters in marginal constituencies or those lobby groups with the loudest voices.

29. Levitt, T. (1973), *The Third Sector: New Tactics for a Responsive Society*, New York: AMACOM, 49–52.

30. Those public goods which are only considered desirable by a minority of citizens are deemed 'merit' goods by Robert Scott Gassler, whilst if a minority desire a lower level of a public good than the state is supplying, their attempts to achieve this are 'demerit' goods: Gassler, R.S. (1986), *The Economics of Nonprofit Enterprise: A Study in Applied Economics*, Lanham, MD: University Press of America, 29; Gassler, R.S. (1990), 'Nonprofit and Voluntary Sector Economics: A Critical Survey', *Nonprofit and Voluntary Sector Quarterly*, 19(2), 137–49, 142.
31. Levitt, above n 29 at 52.
32. Salamon, L. (1987), 'Of Market Failure, Voluntary Failure, and Third-Party Government: Toward a Theory of Government–Nonprofit Relations in the Modern Welfare State', in Ostrander, S. and S. Langton (eds), *Shifting the Debate: Public/Private Sector Relations in the Modern Welfare State*, New Brunswick: Transaction, 39; Morris, S. (2000), 'Defining the Nonprofit Sector: Some Lessons from History', *Voluntas*, 11(1), 25–43, 27.
33. Salamon, above n 32 at 39.
34. See generally Genschel, P. (1997), 'The Dynamics of Inertia: Institutional Persistence and Change in Telecommunications and Health Care', *Governance*, 10(1), 43–66.
35. Salamon, above n 32 at 39. See also Douglas, J. (1987), 'Political Theories of Nonprofit Organizations', in Powell, W. (ed.), *The Nonprofit Sector: A Research Handbook*, New Haven and London: Yale University Press, 49–50; James, E. (1990), 'Economic Theories of the Nonprofit Sector: A Comparative Perspective', in Anheier, H. and W. Seibel (eds), *The Third Sector: Comparative Studies of Nonprofit Organisations*, Berlin and New York: Walter de Gruyter, 24; Simon, J. (1990), 'Modern Welfare State Policy Toward the Nonprofit Sector: Some Efficiency–Equity Dilemmas', in Anheier and Seibel, ibid, 32; Knapp, M., E. Robertson and C. Thomason (1990), 'Public Money, Voluntary Action: Whose Welfare?', in Anheier and Seibel, ibid, 204–5.
36. Olson, above n 19 at 5–55. See also: Coase, R. (1988), *The Firm, the Market, and the Law*, Chicago and London: University of Chicago Press, 42–7; Anheier, H. (2001), 'Foundations in Europe: a Comparative Perspective', in Schlüter, A., V. Then and P. Walkenhorst (eds), *Foundations in Europe: Society Management and Law*, London: Directory of Social Change, 69.
37. Salamon, above n 32 at 44. See also: Home Office (1989), *Charities: A Framework for the Future*, Cmnd 694, London: HMSO, para 1.4; Knapp et al, above n 35 at 205–6.
38. Morris, D. (2000), 'Paying the Piper: The "Contract Culture" as Dependency Culture for Charities', in Dunn, A. (ed.), *The Voluntary Sector, the State and the Law*, Oxford: Hart Publishing, 128.
39. See Bennett, J. and T. DiLorenzo (1989), *Unfair Competition: The Profits of Nonprofits*, Lanham, MD: Hamilton Press, 48–9.
40. Kendall, J. (2003), *The Voluntary Sector*, London: Routledge, 169.
41. Ibid.
42. See e.g. Kendall, above n 40 at 169, in the context of day care provision.
43. See e.g. Kendall, above n 40 at 192, in the context of environmental organisations and the dissemination of information.
44. Ben-Ner, A. and B. Gui (2003), 'The Theory of Nonprofit Organisations Revisited', in Anheier, H. and A. Ben-Ner (eds), *The Study of the Nonprofit Enterprise: Theories and Approaches*, New York: Kluwer/Plenum, 4. See also Gui, B. (1994), 'Interpersonal Relations: a Disregarded Theme in the Debate on Ethics and Economics', in Lewis, A. and K. Wärneryd (eds), *Ethics and Economic Affairs*, London: Routledge.
45. On the stakeholder theory of CSOs generally, see Ben-Ner, A. and T. van Hoomissen (1991), 'Nonprofit Organizations in the Mixed Economy: A Demand and Supply Analysis', *Annals of Public and Cooperative Economics*, 62(4), 519–50.
46. Ben-Ner and Gui, above n 44 at 16.
47. This suggests that it is in fact inappropriate to classify relational goods as public goods, as some commentators do: see Ben-Ner and Gui, above n 44 at 14. If a network's effectiveness depends upon its small size, then, beyond a certain point, the

greater the number of members, the less utility each will have. Therefore, it cannot be said that the goods are non-rivalrous. Nor are they non-excludable in any meaningful sense, as it will always be a simple matter to restrict membership.

48. *Shire of Derby/West Kimberley v Yungngora Association Inc* (2007) 157 LGERA 238 at para 54 (Newnes AJA).
49. Salamon, above n 32 at 44; Morris, above n 32 at 27.
50. Salamon, above n 32 at 44. See also Home Office, above n 37 at para 1.4.
51. Referred to as the sector's 'modelling function': Langton, S. (1981), 'The New Voluntarism', *Nonprofit and Voluntary Sector Quarterly*, 10(1), 7–20, 11. See also: Salamon, above n 32 at 44; Clark, J. (1997), 'The State, Popular Participation and the Voluntary Sector', in Hulme, D. and M. Edwards (eds), *NGOs, States and Donors: Too Close for Comfort*, Basingstoke and London: Macmillan, 46.
52. Knapp et al, above n 35 at 202. See also: Salamon, above n 32 at 44; Rose-Ackerman, above n 5 at 124; Voluntary Sector Roundtable Panel on Accountability and Governance in the Voluntary Sector (1999), *Building on Strength: Improving Governance and Accountability in Canada's Voluntary Sector: Final Report*, Voluntary Sector Roundtable, 12; Douglas, above n 35 at 46–8.
53. See Bennett and DiLorenzo, above n 39 at 48–9.
54. Gaines, B. (1994), 'The Collective Stance in Modelling Expertise in Individuals and Organizations', *International Journal of Expert Systems*, 7, 21 at 33.
55. See Saidel, J. (1989), 'Dimensions of Interdependence: The State and Voluntary-Sector Relationship', *Nonprofit and Voluntary Sector Quarterly*, 18(4), 335–47, 343; also Douglas, above n 35 at 50.
56. Gassler (1990), above n 30 at 143; Anheier, above n 36 at 69.
57. Boris, E. (1999), 'Nonprofit Organizations in a Democracy: Varied Roles and Responsibilities', in Boris, E. and E. Steuerle (eds), *Nonprofits and Government Collaboration and Conflict*, Washington, DC: Urban Institute Press, 21.
58. Douglas, above n 35 at 50.
59. O'Regan, K. and S. Oster (2000), 'Nonprofit and For-Profit Partnerships: Rationale and Challenges of Cross-Sector Contracting', *Nonprofit and Voluntary Sector Quarterly*, 29(Suppl), 120–40, 123. Consider, e.g., the disputes between the National Trust and the Devon and Somerset Staghounds and Quantock Staghounds in relation to the use of land owned by the Trust: *R v National Trust for Places of Historic Interest or Natural Beauty, ex parte Scott* [1998] 1 WLR 226 and *Scott v National Trust* [1998] 2 All ER 705; and between the RSPCA and various pro-hunting lobby groups in relation to excluding pro-hunting activists from its membership: *Royal Society for the Prevention of Cruelty to Animals v Attorney General* [2002] 1 WLR 448.
60. Government grants will frequently be as prescriptive as contracts: Garton, J. (2000), 'Charities and the State', *Trust Law International*, 14, 93 at 95–6.
61. E.g. the social housing sector and, to a lesser extent, the provision of care for the elderly: see Kendall, above n 40 at 144–5, 176–8.
62. Breyer, above n 4 at 23; Breyer, above n 11 at 10.
63. Ogus, above n 10 at 35. See generally Baldwin and Cave, above n 4 at 11–12; Gellhorn and Pierce, above n 7 at 55–8; Kay and Vickers, above n 11 at 226–7; Sunstein, above n 11 at 36, 54–5.
64. Boris, E. (1999), 'Nonprofit Organizations in a Democracy: Varied Roles and Responsibilities', in Boris, E. and E. Steuerle (eds), *Nonprofits and Government: Collaboration and Conflict*, Washington, DC: Urban Institute Press, 23. See also James, above n 35 at 24.
65. Jenkins, J. (1987), 'Nonprofit Organizations and Policy Advocacy', in Powell, W. (ed.), *The Nonprofit Sector: A Research Handbook*, New Haven and London: Yale University Press, at 296. See also: 6, P. and A. Randon (1995), *Liberty, Charity and Politics: Non-Profit Law and Freedom of Speech*, Aldershot: Dartmouth, 139; Blair, H. (1997), 'Donors, Democratisation and Civil Society: Relating Theory to Practice', in

Hulme, D. and M. Edwards (eds), *NGOs, States and Donors: Too Close for Comfort*, Basingstoke and London: Macmillan, 30.

66. Barendt, E. (1985), *Freedom of Speech*, Oxford: Clarendon Press, 13.
67. Boris, above n 64 at 23. Debra Morris notes that this may be a particular problem in respect of those CSOs with charitable status, as their perceived elevated status may enhance their standing in the eyes of the public: Morris, D. (1995/96), 'The Media and the Message: An Evaluation of Advertising by Charities and an Examination of the Regulatory Frameworks', *Charity Law and Practice Review*, 3(3), 157, 172. Guidelines for Private Voluntary Organizations, published by InterAction, the American Council for Voluntary International Action, stress the importance of ensuring that campaigns draw a balance: 'An organization's communications . . . shall neither minimize nor overstate the human and material needs of those whom it assists': InterAction (2009), *PVO Standards*, InterAction, para 5.3.
68. See Bennett, J. and T. DiLorenzo (1994), *Unhealthy Charities: Hazardous to your Health and Wealth*, New York: BasicBooks, 31.
69. InterAction, above n 67 at para 8.3.
70. See generally Meier, R (1999), 'The Darker Side of Nonprofits: When Charities and Social Welfare Groups Become Political Slush Funds', *University of Pennsylvania Law Review*, 147(3), 971–1008.
71. Blair, above n 65 at 40.
72. See generally Breyer, above n 4 at 26–8; Kay and Vickers, above n 11 at 228–30; Ogus, above n 10 at 38–41; Sunstein, above n 11 at 52–3.
73. Breyer, above n 4 at 27. It should be noted that the problem of lack of information is not one that only blights consumers – firms may also suffer at the hands of information asymmetry. Kay and Vickers note that in the insurance industry it is the consumers who hold the upper hand and have an incentive to conceal personal information that would otherwise cause their premiums to increase: Kay and Vickers, above n 11 at 230.
74. The similarities are sufficiently strong that these are often erroneously described as public goods in the civil society literature, despite being inherently neither non-rivalous nor non-excludable.
75. Albeit a very different one from regulation. The latter is an attempt to shape the operation of the market artificially, whereas the former is an organic attempt to provide an alternative to the market.
76. Ortmann, A. and M. Schlesinger (1997), 'Trust, Repute and the Role of Non-Profit Enterprise', *Voluntas*, 8(1), 97–119.
77. Ibid, 103.
78. *Church of the New Faith v Commissioner of Pay-Roll Tax (Victoria)* (1983) 154 CLR 120 at 141.
79. Belcher, A. (2000), 'Board Responsibilities in the Voluntary Sector: The Case of Housing', in Dunn, A. (ed.), *The Voluntary Sector, the State and the Law*, Oxford: Hart Publishing, 62. Just as Breyer notes, above n 4 at 28, that there can be 'little quarrel' with regulation that remedies information deficits in the private sector context, there is general agreement among both civil society theorists and official publications that regulation of the sector is justifiable on these grounds. See e.g. Home Office (1998), *Home Office Annual Report 1998–99*, London: HMSO, para 24.1; InterAction, above n 67 at para 5; Leat, D. (1996), 'Are Voluntary Organisations Accountable?', in Billis, D. and M. Harris (eds), *Voluntary Agencies: Challenges of Organisation and Management*, Basingstoke and London: Macmillan, 66; Parliamentary Select Committee on Public Accounts (1998), *Charity Commission: Regulation and Support of Charities*, HC 408, London: House of Commons, para 6; Rochester, C. (1995), 'Voluntary Agencies and Accountability', in Davis Smith, J., C. Rochester and R. Hedley (eds), *An Introduction to the Voluntary Sector*, London and New York: Routledge, 193; Salamon, above n 32 at 45; Scottish Charity Law Review Commission (2001), *Charity Scotland: The Report of the Scottish Charity Law Review Commission* (the McFadden Report), Edinburgh:

Stationery Office, recommendation 39; Voluntary Sector Roundtable Panel on Accountability and Governance in the Voluntary Sector, above n 52 at 14.

80. See e.g., the UK community interest company established by the Companies (Audit, Investigations and Community Enterprise) Act 2004, Pt 2.

81. Note the distinction between 'ancillary' trading, which is only undertaken in order to increase revenue for other activities, and trading which is 'mission-related': Weisbrod, B. (1998), 'The Nonprofit Mission and its Financing: Growing Links Between Nonprofits and the Rest of the Economy', in Weisbrod, B. (ed.), *To Profit or Not to Profit: the Commercial Transformation of the Nonprofit Sector*, Cambridge: Cambridge University Press, 18. We are concerned here with the pursuit of profit as an influence on an organisation's behaviour; however, Weisbrod acknowledges the fact that not every CSO commercial activity will be motivated by the pursuit of profit – trading may reflect 'social-service missions to reach particular target populations' or 'distributional mission[s]': at 11. See also: Weisbrod, B. (1998), 'Modeling the Nonprofit Organization as a Multiproduct Firm: A Framework for Choice', in Weisbrod, ibid, 52–5, 61; Steinberg, R. and B. Weisbrod, 'Pricing and Rationing by Nonprofit Organizations with Distributional Objectives', in Weisbrod, ibid.

82. On the relationship between commercial income and other revenue streams, see generally Steinberg and Weisbrod, above n 81 at 56–61; James, E. (1998), 'Commercialism among Nonprofits: Objectives, Opportunities, and Constraints', in Weisbrod, B. (ed.), *To Profit or Not to Profit: the Commercial Transformation of the Nonprofit Sector*, Cambridge: Cambridge University Press, 272; Segal, L. and B. Weisbrod (1998), 'Interdependence of Commercial and Donative Revenues', in Weisbrod, ibid.

83. See James, E. (1986), 'How Nonprofits Grow: a Model', in Rose-Ackerman, S. (ed.), *The Economics of Nonprofit Institutions: Studies in Structure and Policy*, New York: Oxford University Press, 185–95. Indeed, many of the reports of the English Charity Commission's inquiries into the administration of charities made under s. 8 of the Charities Act 1993 highlight these issues, e.g. the Bournemouth Aviation Charitable Foundation inquiry (11 January 2005); Frankgiving Ltd inquiry (11 January 2005); Clownes Foundation inquiry (2 September 2003).

84. Tuckman, above n 14 at 36.

85. Weisbrod, above n 81 at 54.

86. See Ortmann and Schlesinger, above n 76 at 102–105; Bennett and DiLorenzo, above n 68 at 46–7; Hansmann, above n 23 at 77.

87. Ortmann, above n 5 at 472.

88. Blair, above n 65 at 30.

89. King, M. (2000), 'Trustee Benefit', *Charity Law and Practice Review*, 6(3), 185, at 187.

90. Ibid, 186–7. See *Re Barber* [1887] LR 34 Ch D 77 at 81 (Chitty J).

91. Espinoza, L. (1991), 'Straining the Quality of Mercy: Abandoning the Quest for Informed Charitable Giving', *Southern California Law Review*, 64(3), 605–84, 605.

92. See generally Krashinsky, M. (1986) 'Transaction Costs and a Theory of the Nonprofit Organization', in Rose-Ackerman, S. (ed.), *The Economics of Nonprofit Institutions: Studies in Structure and Policy*, New York: Oxford University Press; Possett, J. and T. Sandler (1988), 'Transfers, Transaction Costs and Charitable Intermediaries', *International Review of Law and Economics*, 8(2), 145–60; Bennett and DiLorenzo, above n 68 at 47, 50; R. Steinberg, 'Competition in Contracted Markets', in 6, P. and J. Kendall (eds) (1997), *The Contract Culture in Public Services*, Aldershot: Arena, 166.

93. The European Foundation Centre notes 'the importance of operating in accordance with the wishes of founders who provide initial capital': European Foundation Centre (2002), *Principles of Good Practice*, Brussels: European Foundation Centre, 'Preamble', notably missing from the 2007 edition of the same document; the Ontario Law Reform Commission emphasises the need for 'loyalty to purpose': Ontario Law Reform Commission (1996), *Report on the Law of Charities*, Toronto: Ontario Law

Reform Commission, 9. However, whilst the need to protect the interests of founders may prima facie strengthen the argument for regulation, it is important that the 'dead hand' of the settlor does not needlessly hinder the operation of a CSO in later years, particularly where the settlor's concerns do not relate to mismanagement or abuse but simply to a change in direction or organisational ethos: Simon, J. (1990), 'Modern Welfare State Policy Toward the Nonprofit Sector: Some Efficiency–Equity Dilemmas', in Anheier, H. and W. Seibel (eds), *The Third Sector: Comparative Studies of Nonprofit Organisations*, Berlin and New York: Walter de Gruyter, 41.

94. See e.g. *Cook v Duckenfield* (1743) 2 Atk 562; *Re Avenon's Charity* [1913] 2 Ch 261.
95. See e.g., in the US, Restatement (Third) of Trusts, s. 67 (2003).
96. See e.g. *Attorney General v Ironmongers' Company* (1834) 2 My & K 576, where funds originally devoted to the redemption of slaves were applied *cy près* to educational establishments; noted in Luxton, P. (2001), *The Law of Charities*, Oxford: Oxford University Press, 551. Note also the new English position, whereby regard is had, not just to the spirit of the original gift and the closeness of the new purpose to the original, but also to the prevailing social and economic circumstances: Charities Act 1993, ss 14B(2), 14B(3).
97. Rochester, above n 79 at 196.
98. Rochester, above n 79 at 194–5.
99. Rochester, above n 79 at 194.
100. Ogus, above n 10 at 32.
101. See Breyer, above n 11 at 11; Gellhorn and Pierce, above n 7 at 51–2; Ogus, above n 10 at 42; Sunstein, above n 11 at 45.
102. Ogus, above n 10 at 43.
103. Ogus, above n 10 at 43.
104. See Salamon, above n 32 at 44; Salamon, L. (1987), 'Partners in Public Service: The Scope and Theory of Government-Nonprofit Relations', in Powell, W. (ed.), *The Nonprofit Sector: A Research Handbook*, New Haven and London: Yale University Press, 111–12.
105. Salamon, above n 32 at 39. On the issue of securing stable resources, see generally Mitchell, C. (2002), 'Saving for a Rainy Day: Charity Reserves', *Charity Law and Practice Review*, 8, 35; Morris, above n 32.
106. Salamon, above n 32 at 40; Salamon, above n 104 at 111. See also Kendall, above n 40 at 118–19.
107. Salamon, above n 32 at 41; Salamon, above n 104 at 111–12. See also Kendall, above n 40 at 119–20; Kuti, E. (1990), 'The Possible Role of the Non-Profit Sector in Hungary', *Voluntas*, 1, 26, 27. For empirical data confirming philanthropic particularism, see Salamon, L. (1984), 'Nonprofits: the Results are Coming', *Foundation News*, 25, 16.
108. Salamon, above n 32 at 41.
109. See further Garton, above n 1 chs 2–3.

10. Modernising charity law: steps to an alternative architecture for common law charity jurisprudence

Matthew Turnour

INTRODUCTION

This chapter addresses the question, how can the common law concept of charity law be modernised? There are difficulties with the present jurisprudential conception. The focus of the chapter is not on those difficulties, however, but rather on the development of an alternative architecture for common law jurisprudence. The conclusion to which the chapter comes is that charity law can be modernised by a series of steps to include all civil society organisations. It is possible if the 'technical' definition of charitable purpose is abandoned in favour of a contemporary, not technical concept of charitable purpose.[1] This conclusion is reached by proposing a framework, developed from the common law concept of charities, that reconciles into a cohesive jurisprudential architecture all of the laws applying to civil society organisations, not just charities.

In this section, first the argument is contextualised in an idea of society and located in a gap in legal theory. An analogy is then offered to introduce the problems in the legal theory applying, not just to charities, but more broadly to civil society organisations. The substantive challenge of mapping an alternative jurisprudence is then taken in steps. The final substantive section conceptualises the changes inherent in a move beyond charities to a jurisprudence centred on civil society organisations and how this would bring legal theory into line with sectoral analysis in other disciplines.

Social Context

Dissatisfaction and frustration with the doctrine of charitable purpose as it is presently applied is of such a magnitude that common law countries have had almost thirty inquiries into the law and regulation of charities over the last 60 years. Australia,[2] Barbados,[3] England and Wales,[4] Northern Ireland[5] and Scotland[6] have passed legislation defining and/or extending the *technical* common law definition of charitable purpose. None of the 22 African, Caribbean Island, and Pacific Island states that are members of the Cotonou Agreement have a statutory definition of 'charity' but there, too, statutory extensions to the common law 'definition' are common.[7] The technical common law definition of charitable purpose therefore continues to underpin legal developments.

Even in countries where it seems that there is a complete statutory definition, such as Barbados, where what appears to be an exhaustive list has been passed into statute, the technical common law definition continues to inform legal development.[8] A similar approach has been taken in the United States of America. There the Supreme Court relied upon the common law understanding of charitable purpose to deny access to deductibility on at least one occasion to a civil society organisation, even though there is not express reference to charitable purpose in the omnibus list of civil society organisations entitled to favours under section 501(c)(3) the Internal Revenue Code.[9]

From these reports, statutes and the surrounding literature, what is known can be stated quite simply: there are multitudinous difficulties due in part to the way the common law, technical definition of charitable purpose has been applied to the development of the law of charities. Reform proposals have accepted that the problems are rooted in the Preamble to the Statute of Charitable Uses[10] and the way the cases have developed following *Pemsel's case*, which categorised the technical definition of charitable purpose into four principal divisions.[11] Proceeding by way of a list and analogy from already accepted charitable purposes, as *Pemsel's case* requires, remains, though, the accepted method – even after legislative intervention purporting to remedy defects in the common law.[12] It follows that legislative patches to the common law are a fix that is being used more frequently to overcome the problems but this does not address the underlying lack of a genus. Jurists required to differentiate these listed and analogous charitable purposes from other purposes remain without explicit rationale for differentiation. Ostensibly recognising these problems, New Zealand,[13] Scotland,[14] England and Wales[15] have empowered regulators of charities to assist in scoping the definition. A similar approach has been followed in Northern Ireland.[16] The Canada Revenue Agency discharges this role in Canada and the Australian Taxation Office fulfils a similar role in Australia. In South Africa, the South African Revenue Service discharges this role, but defines charitable purposes, narrowly, 'to mean direct poverty relief'.[17]

The underlying problems confronting jurists across the common law

world are, then, fundamentally the same: how to modernise the law applying to entities defined by reference to a concept of charitable purpose. The
challenge is to expand the definition to include an ever increasing class of
organisations. The concept of charitable purpose at law takes a technical
definition which is unsatisfactory. The puzzle for all common law countries is how to define this extended class of organisations satisfactorily:
organisations that belong to a class frequently now known as civil society
organisations. This puzzle is compounded by a supplementary problem.
As pursuing charitable purposes is a gateway to accessing favour,[18] the
supplementary problem is: what favours should particular organisations
enjoy, if any? The answer presently dominating legal discourse is that the
organisations are to be defined by reference to the four principal divisions
in *Pemsel's case*, extended by statute where needed. Entitlement to favours
is also to be determined with respect to that definition. This response of
adding extensions can only go so far. The more extensions are added, and
the more diverse those extensions are, the more apparent it is that this
approach is unsatisfactory. Dissatisfaction and frustration with the inad-
equacies of the common law doctrine[19] are compounded, not addressed,
by these extensions and their diversity.

What is needed is a fresh approach. Justice Kirby of the High Court of
Australia has invited an alternative jurisprudence and his fellow judges
have observed that without an alternative being argued before the court, the
court is obliged to remain within the current orthodoxy.[20] This chapter proposes an alternative. It proposes that the technical definition be abandoned
in favour of a definition of charitable purpose that resonates with popular
conceptions and current non-legal academic theory. A precise but dynamic
definition of charitable purpose is developed that extends to include all civil
society organisations. A definition of charitable goods is also developed
within this architecture justifying entitlement to access favours.

Charitable Purpose in the Context of Civil Society

This fresh approach begins by contextualising charitable purposes and
more broadly the law for civil society organisations within a conception of
society. Society is complex and so, for analytical purposes, the literature
often divides society into four sectors:[21]

1. business (the first sector)
2. government (the second sector)
3. not-for-profit, non-government, voluntary, intermediary (the third
   sector)
4. family (the fourth sector).

In this broader literature, organisations with charitable purposes are discussed as a part of the third sector, which is here caught up in the concept of civil society.[22] Legal theorists may focus on particular forms of organisation (those with charitable purposes), but the broader literature does not.[23] The broader literature is significantly informed by the sectoral analysis of society with a focus on civil society organisations as a part of the third sector – not just charities. This broader literature informs my focus on civil society organisations rather than charities and my object of sketching outlines of an architecture for a jurisprudence for civil society. This broader approach is necessary because there is a gap in legal theory relative to the organisations that make up civil society.

The scope of this alternative jurisprudence is determined, then, by the scope of the definition of civil society. Defining civil society is difficult:[24] it is a contested concept[25] used to label a significant space.[26] Helmut Anheier's definition of civil society is taken as the working definition for the purposes of this chapter. It is as follows: 'Civil society is the sphere of institutions, organisations and individuals located between family, the state and the market in which people associate voluntarily to advance common interests'.[27]

As charities and other expressions of civil society that are the subject of legal rights and obligations are best conceptualised as organisations (as distinct from individuals or institutions), it is organisations that are the focus of this chapter.[28] There are two reasons for this. First, it is the *purposes* pursued through organisations that are critical to the identification of charitable purposes and non-charitable purposes and thus it is at this level that the legal theory discussion is framed. Second, and at a more general level, it is the gathering of people to pursue common purposes through organisations that is the dominant expression of civil society. With this brief introduction of civil society and its organisations and foreshadowing further exploration, I turn now to introduce the way in which law has come to be analysed.

Jurisprudential Context

Law is complex and so, for analytical purposes, it too is often divided according to sectors. A common initial division of law, now well established in the literature of jurisprudence, is between public law and private law.[29] The division between public law, which relates to government (second sector), and private law, which relates to business and family (first and fourth sectors), can be traced back into Roman law.[30] It significantly informs European law.[31] It is still widely adopted in common law jurisdictions[32] including the United States, where the division is still 'not

uncommon',[33] although it is not as popular.[34] Public law is principally concerned with delimiting and regulating the use of coercive powers by government.[35] Private law is concerned with legal relations between citizens
as citizens.[36] A major subset of private law with its own jurisprudential
framework is commercial law, which is founded in contract law and its
focus is the facilitation and regulation of an informed market to ensure
that profits are acquired justly.[37] Laws enabling association for non-
commercial purposes are often analysed as a part of commercial law.[38] The
further division of private law does not follow neat categorisation, but for
present purposes it is sufficient to note that within private law there is a
further separation of commercial law from that which regulates families
as families. Families have family law and estate law[39] to ensure persons
within families are treated equitably.[40] Equity is a subsection of private law
that applies to both business and families.[41] As Lord Macnaghten pointed
out, 'Charitable uses or trusts form a distinct head of equity'.[42] The division between public and private is foundational to the law of charities.[43]

Returning to the sector analysis of society mentioned earlier, it is important to highlight that the third sector is absent in this sub-segmentation of
law, but that analysis of law has loosely followed the sectoral divisions for
the other sectors into which analysis of society has been divided.[44] In legal
analysis it is possible to identify segmentation into:

- public law for government
- private law for citizens as citizens, with further sub-division into:
  - commercial law for business
  - estate and family law for families.

But a jurisprudence for the third sector[45] and, more broadly, civil society
has not developed.[46]

The law of charities (which sometimes arises for consideration in the
context of estate law) remains a subset of equity and consequently is a
subset of private law.[47] There is 'no single structure in English law specifically designed for charities' and 'charities have had to make do with a
legal structure fashioned largely (in the case of trusts) for family property
holding, or (in the case of the company) for commercial endeavour'.[48]
So, whilst it may be said that jurisprudential divisions follow divisions
of the first, second and fourth sectors and distinct heads of law for those
sectors are readily identifiable, the same cannot be said for the laws applying to civil society. At the beginning of the third millennium, there is no
clearly identifiable jurisprudence for the third sector. Analysis of its law
seems to have lagged in development in a way similar to the way analysis
of the third sector has lagged.[49] The division of society into four sectors

(business, government, civil society and family) which is common in a range of social science discourses, including economics, sociology and politics, has not flowed into jurisprudence.[50] It is suggested in this chapter that the time has come for this division to inform legal theory development in relation to civil society organisations. An analogy may help to introduce the argument.

An Analogy

The present description and legal analysis of civil society organisations within the common law framework of the law of charities (plus some heads added by statute in some jurisdictions), with assistance from commercial, association and corporation law, is like explaining the solar system in pre-Copernican terms. It is possible, but is becoming progressively more difficult. A simpler theory that explains this 'legal universe' more completely is required.[51] So, just as Copernicus urged upon his readers the acceptance of 'that which is easiest to grasp'[52] and pointed out that his ideas were not that radical for they could be found in a pedigree leading back to the early Greeks,[53] so in this chapter I argue that a simpler theoretical framework is discernible in the common law. I suggest that this simpler framework is identifiable in the ancient roots of the law of charities but has been lost in the present convolution. I begin by asking questions such as: if the presently recognised charitable purposes are planets, to what particular universe do they belong? What else belongs in that universe? What distinguishes these planets from planets that belong to other universes? What is the gravitational force that holds these planets together? The great puzzle for lawmakers has been the difficulty in recognising what purposes truly belong to this legal universe.[54]

Under the common law, only advancement of religion, relief of poverty and advancement of education have had a secure place.[55] Beginning with Barbados in 1979,[56] where a complete statutory definition of charitable purpose was provided, it has become progressively more fashionable for common law countries to add by legislative fiat to the common law heads of charities.[57] The legislation for England and Wales recognises as charitable a broad range of purposes that edify society and promote the basic freedoms essential to the foundational enjoyment of citizenship.[58] In Australia, certain childcare organisations, self-help groups and closed and contemplative religious orders also enjoy that status by legislative fiat.[59] The Barbados list included such things as the provision of *facilities* for family planning and the relief of distress caused by natural disaster and catastrophe.[60] These statutory extensions amount to securing a place in this legal universe for those purposes so added. What, though, is the underlying rationale for these inclusions? What has led these governments to add these particular yet different purposes and not others to the law of charities? It is not enough, theoretically, to add to or take away from a list. The additions must all share some common characteristics. Whether purposes belong to this particular area of law or not should be determined by reference to characteristics – real definable essence and distinguishing features.

I theorise that the characteristics may be labelled 'charitable purpose', but not 'charitable purpose' as the term is presently understood as a technical, legal conception. Rather, as one overruled superior court summarised, I suggest:

> 'Charitable' must . . . be understood in its 'popular' sense. That does not admit of any rigid or undeviating connotation. It is flexible to an immeasurable degree, as can be seen by reference to the judgments of such eminent masters of law and language as the Judges who sat in *Pemsel's Case*.[61]

I suggest that charitable purpose, like gravity, is evident at different strengths, in different contexts.[62] At the weakest level is the minimum fellowship and friendliness necessary to sustain involvement in a voluntary association.[63] Those purposes that are sufficiently charitable are considered to be included within this legal universe. I suggest that legal theory divide the legal cosmos into four universes and that the third be a universe recognised as being held together by the gravitational force called, in common parlance, 'charitable purpose'.

Complication arises with declaring that all civil society organisations evidence charitable purposes because acceptance into that legal universe brings with it access to certain favourable treatment. Under the common law doctrine of charitable purpose as it is presently understood, there is not a differentiator between those organisations that evidence weak charitable purpose and those that evidence charitable purpose strongly. Because of the favourable treatment implications of being recognised as belonging to the universe of 'charitable purpose', I argue that it is necessary to distinguish, within the class, between civil society organisations that show only weak evidence of charitable purpose and those where charitable purpose is incontrovertibly and overwhelmingly evident.

I theorise that 'charitable purpose' understood in the way discussed in this chapter is the gravitational force that holds all of the laws of this legal universe together. Closer to the centre of the universe, 'charitable purpose' (as here defined) is more evident.[64] In this context, the purposes recognised as 'charitable purposes' at law are but the characteristics of planets in this legal universe. It does not follow, under this approach, that all planets must enjoy preferential treatment. Belonging to the universe is one thing. Deciding which planets enjoy favours is another.

An Alternative Architecture

How, then, can charity law, as it is presently conceived, be modernised into a fully fledged jurisprudence for civil society? The process is undertaken in a series of steps. First the doctrine of charitable purpose, which is a one-dimensional concept, must be developed into a two-dimensional *space* that encompasses all the laws that *enable* participation in civil society through civil society organisations. The doctrine of charitable purpose also performs the function of acting as a gateway to favour and this is a third dimension. So the two-dimensional space is then developed into three dimensions to accommodate *favour*. A discussion of how ordinal, and possibly cardinal, units of measure might be applied within the now completely constructed framework follows.

ONE DIMENSION – REDISCOVERING THE HEART OF CHARITABLE PURPOSE

As the common law presently stands, charitable purpose has lost its heart. It is technically defined and it is one-dimensional – a civil society organisation either has a technically defined charitable purpose or it does not. The analysis is confined to nominal measurement: to which class does an organisation belong, charitable or not charitable? This concept of charitable purpose does not provide any way of distinguishing the regulating function of law from the favouring. Further, in the context of favouring based on charitable purpose there is not a basis for distinguishing between more and less favourable treatment. This is significant because there is more and less favourable treatment afforded civil society organisations that pursue charitable purposes in common law countries.

In this new alternative jurisprudence, a common meaning of charitable purpose takes centre stage, and not a technical definition. The heart of charitable purpose is rediscovered. This is not achieved by abandoning the theory from which the technical meaning emerged, but rather by returning to it and fulfilling it more completely. Second, within the class of charitable purposes there are presently the four 'heads': relief of poverty, advancement of religion, advancement of education, and other purposes beneficial to the community; but these classes (as presently limited) do not advance inquiry beyond 'nominal' measurement. They simply assist in answering the broader question: charitable purpose or not? As presently applied, they are not useful classes for differentiating between purposes. These heads do point, however, to reasons why the common law grants favour to civil society organisations. The challenge taken up from this one-dimensional approach is to develop, from within this jurisprudential space, differentiated classes that are helpful in distinguishing between civil society organisations and their others, and also for differentiating within the class of civil society organisations.

In summary then, the one-dimensional mapping of the common law into charities and non-charities, following the current orthodox approach of the law of charities, is not a particularly useful categorisation for analytic purposes. However, it provides a way of identifying essence; it points to indicia of differentiation; and it suggests characteristics of classes for more sophisticated sub-categorisation. A better form of 'measurement' of the organisations regulated or favoured as civil society organisations would be preferable. Toward that outcome, the next two sections build from these core concepts.

TWO DIMENSIONS – REDISCOVERING DIFFERENTIA

Introducing the Components of the Theory

In the orthodox understanding of the doctrine of charitable purpose, the regulating function is not distinguished from the role of favouring. The scope of the regulating dimension of the jurisprudence is all of the laws that enable and regulate voluntary association for common purposes, whether or not those purposes are recognised as charitable at common law as the law stands at present. It is the subject of this section. At the centre of the regulating dimension of the jurisprudence is the formation, conduct, regulation and dissolution of civil society organisations including (but not limited to) charities. It is necessary to define the characteristics of civil society organisations so that it is clear which organisations are within the class of organisations to be enabled or regulated, as the case may be, and which are not. Clearly it is necessary to go beyond the Preamble and the categorisations from *Pemsel's case* for the definition, as the scope is broader than charities.

In this alternative architecture it is theorised that civil society organisations have, as their essence, charitable purpose (not technically defined) and, as their 'other' business, government and family. It follows for the reasons developed in this chapter that, as charitable purpose is not technically defined, civil society organisations are those organisations that manifest:

1. Altruism
2. Benefit for the public
3. Coercion being sufficiently absent for the association to be voluntary.

For the purposes of this jurisprudential analysis, altruism, benefit of others and absence of coercion are identified by a combination of two of three factors. The three factors are:

1. the otherwise remoteness of the people associating (*xenos*[65] – for convenience labelled 'X')
2. the reason for associating being voluntarily to benefit others ('why' – for convenience labelled 'Y')
3. the number of persons associating (for convenience labelled 'Z').

Altruism

George Lewes introduced the word 'altruism' into the English language in 1853 with his translation of Comte's *Philosophy of the Sciences*.[66] When using the term, Comte intended 'to establish the opposite reference point to the self-gratifying, utility-maximizing "economic man" of economic theory'.[67] In theoretical analysis, it is part of a broader class called 'prosocial behaviour'.[68] *The Oxford English Dictionary* defines altruism as: 'Devotion to the welfare of others, regard for others, as a principle of action; opposed to egoism or selfishness'.[69]

One of the great challenges facing reform of the doctrine of charitable purpose is how to move beyond the 'spirit and intendment' of the Preamble. I argue that it is possible by replacing the 'spirit and intendment' with altruism and the absence of coercion, in a manner consistent with the dissenting judgment of Justice Gonthier in *Vancouver Society of Immigrant and Visible Minority Women*.[70] I argue that altruism stands alongside public benefit as the second essential characteristic of charitable purpose.[71] This is not a novel proposition. The Charities Definition Inquiry in Australia reported that the Preamble 'has now outlived its usefulness'[72] and recommended that 'to be regarded as charitable, an entity must have a dominant purpose which is altruistic and for the public benefit'.[73]

There is a long line of cases from diverse jurisdictions setting out the principle that altruism is central to charitable purpose.[74] I argue that it is a 'mark or test of what is truly charitable' as opined by Justice MacDermott in the *Baptist Union of Ireland* case.[75] The difficulty is not with the idea. The puzzle is how to theorise it. Altruism has not been theorised as an alternative to the Preamble in a way that is suitable for jurisprudential development of the common law. I argue that when strangers associate to pursue purposes which transcend private benefit, altruism is present. I theorise, then, that there are two factors that inform altruism: remoteness and motive. Altruism can be assessed by a combination of 'X' and 'Y'. The more disparate the origins of the persons (remoteness) and the more the reasons are to benefit others (why) then the greater the altruism. A civil society organisation is altruistic. When goods are transferred in or through a civil society organisation, some altruism is evident.

Furthermore, these variables might be measurable beyond nominal measurement. The United Nations *Handbook on Non-Profit Institutions in the Systems of National Accounts* provides a method for valuing volunteer labour input, having regard to the two presently dominant methods of opportunity cost and market or replacement cost.[76] As gifts of time and money are indicia of altruism and are capable of quantitative measurement, they could be utilised in law as indicia of charitable purpose. There is a vast array of organisational forms that all manifest altruistic purposes to differing extents. The altruism manifest in the purposes of these organisations is not the same. Some purposes are more altruistic than others. It follows that organisations might be ranked or valued according to the extent to which they manifest altruistic purposes. A manifestation of altruistic purposes could be, for example, the source or application of resources being gifts of time or money. The ranking or value could be set out diagrammatically as in Figure 10.1

Different courts, legislators or regulators may draw upon different factors to inform them of how much, or how little, altruism is evident in a particular purpose. As Lord Macnaghten observed: 'Many people, I think, would consider a gift for the support of a lifeboat a charitable gift', and 'even a layman might take the same favourable view of a gratuitous supply of pure water for the benefit of a crowded neighbourhood'[77] but how are judges, legislators and regulators to decide? The problem is how to measure, and possibly compare, altruism as an indicium of charitable purpose in lifesaving organisations and aquaduct service providers. There is no universally agreed means of measurement of altruism. However, factors that inform altruism and indicia of altruism capable of quantitative measurement do exist.[78] Therefore it may be possible not only to rank but to quantitatively compare organisations according to the extent that

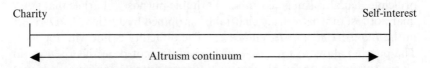

Figure 10.1   Altruism continuum

they manifest altruistic purposes. Reducing the measurement to a percentage or scale of zero to 100, a continuum emerges.[79]

Benefit

It is clear from the cases on charitable purpose that manifestations of public benefit are necessary for charitable purpose to be established and that the level of publicness in those manifestations varies within the four heads of charitable purpose set out in *Pemsel's case*.[80] If the purposes of an organisation are for public benefit, those purposes satisfy one or two criteria of charitable purpose at common law. I theorise that benefit can be assessed by a combination of 'X' and 'Z'. If a large number of people who would otherwise be strangers voluntarily associate, then the association is public. If a small number of people associate for private purposes (such as a family gathering to celebrate Christmas), the association is private. A civil society organisation is public benefiting.

The level of publicness required for advancement of religion or relief of poverty is significantly lower than that required to establish a charitable purpose based on advancement of education or the fourth head, other purposes beneficial to the community.[81] Scholarship over the last 30 years has theorised public benefit, refining it significantly beyond the general proposition set out in the cases on charitable purposes.[82] As with altruism, there is evidence in the literature of methods of grading or ranking publicness, and objective criteria by which publicness can be assessed.[83] That ranking turns upon the extent to which the purpose is to benefit the public as distinct from being for private benefit.[84] Between the completely public purposes which lie at the heart of charitable trusts, and the purposes of civil society organisations that exist entirely for the private benefit of families, there is a continuum of publicness. At one extreme is the most public of trusts. At the other there are small private clubs.[85] This continuum is conveniently labelled the 'benefit continuum' and can be represented diagrammatically as in Figure 10.2.

Whilst different courts, legislators or regulators may draw upon different factors to inform them of how much, or how little, public benefit must be evident to belong to civil society, and different factors may be

Figure 10.2   Benefit continuum

taken into account, or differently weighed, in deciding the extent to which public benefit is evident, some quite sophisticated criteria for categorising publicness have emerged.[86] These criteria could significantly inform the more general principles for legal theory development. All charitable trusts were originally considered public trusts[87] and if charitable trusts are taken as the foundation typology of the voluntary public organisational form for the supply of goods (which they were), then charitable purpose resides at one extreme of the 'benefit continuum' and at the other there are organisational forms which are purely for private purposes. So ranking or categorising of public benefit provides a basis for legal theory to go beyond the general idea of 'public' to a continuum of publicness whereby organisations may be ranked on a benefit continuum or categorised for the purposes of favouring particular categories in particular ways.

Coercion

Charitable trusts, and more generally charitable organisations, are recognised by the voluntariness of involvement and the voluntariness of supply of goods and services.[88] In that voluntariness, these organisations are distinguishable from government.[89] Similarly, where the government pursues purposes such as repairing a seabank or contributing to poverty relief, a citizen does not have freedom to choose whether or not to contribute, as contributions are compellable by law and the transfer of assets to government for those purposes is coerced through taxation.

As with the recognition of altruism and public benefit in civil society organisations, it was noted that coercion is not one-dimensional. There is a continuum of coercion in the context of a discussion of civil society organisations. At one extreme, again, is the religious charitable trust where the common law protects the right to voluntary involvement in the pursuit of objects that advance religion.[90] At the other extreme are civil society organisations over which government exercises substantial control, for example through statutory setting of purposes, control over who is appointed to or removed from the board and control over funding. Examples of this extreme include some professional bodies with responsibility for regulation of whole sectors of society such as those overseeing the registration and conduct of various professions.[91] It follows that absence of coercion can be theorised by a combination of 'Y' and 'Z'. If the association is a large group of persons but the reason for association is coerced, then the fundamental character of voluntariness is missing. It is an arm of government. A civil society organisation is a voluntary association. As there is a continuum of coercion the continuum between these extremes can be illustrated by Figure 10.3.

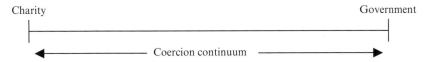

Figure 10.3 Coercion continuum

The philosophical contests over the extent to which citizens should be permitted to associate free of the coercive influences of government are such that different courts, legislators and regulators may draw upon different factors to inform them of how much, or how little, communities should be allowed to self-organise and self-regulate through civil society organisations. There may be debates over whether too much external regulation might be a threat to the trust and charity which are the very essence of the sector itself.[92] Different factors may be taken into account, or differently weighed, in deciding the extent to which such freely chosen organisation must be for common good for it to be allowed to occur. There is no dispute, though, that there is a coercion continuum between the religious freedom enjoyed at common law and the complete control by government. At some point the level of coercion is so great that the organisation is an arm of government.

CIVIL SOCIETY SPACE

All of the continua have charitable purpose as a starting point and charity is differentiated from three others. Those three others are: business (the first sector); government (the second sector); and family (the fourth sector). Charities and related organisations are included in the third sector. At some point on these lines, drawn between organisations with charitable purposes and each of these others, a boundary is crossed from civil society (as it is emerging) to one of these others.

When drawn as shown by Figure 10.4, the overlapping conceptions between charity and civil society are even more apparent. Civil society is differentiated from business by altruism, from family by benefits being public not private, and from government by its voluntariness, that is, absence of coercion. At a certain point there is insufficient altruism, public benefit or voluntariness to call the organisation a civil society organisation. When the concept of a charitable purpose is expanded in the way proposed here, it reaches to the borders of civil society. By joining the lines, then, a theoretical space is created which is the bounds of this new jurisprudence for civil society, with charitable purpose – as expanded – at its centre. That space looks, in a theoretical sense, like Figure 10.5.

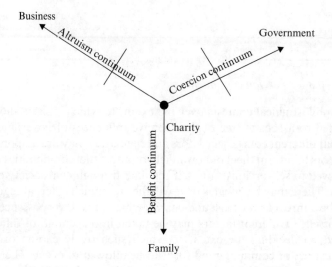

Figure 10.4   Charity continua

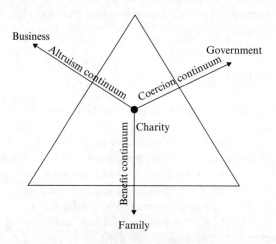

Figure 10.5   Charity continua and civil society space

The theoretical space will change shape according to the society. For example, in the context of a small government state where voluntary philanthropic organisations are constrained compared with business and family but carry a larger share of responsibility for meeting society's needs, the space would be diagrammatically expressed as in Figure 10.6. In a society where the government, business and family dominate, the space would be contracted on all sides and might be expressed as in Figure 10.7.

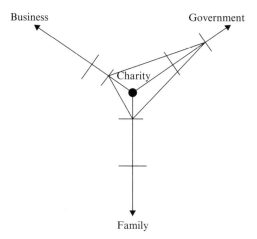

Figure 10.6   Defining boundaries and expanded civil society

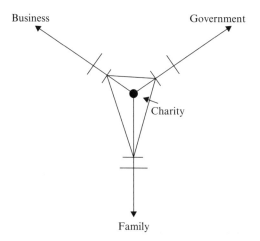

Figure 10.7   Defining boundaries and constrained civil society

INTRODUCING DYNAMIC BOUNDARIES

Once a definition of the whole of civil society is set out in this way, it is apparent that there will be contests over where each of these theoretical boundaries is to be drawn. In the Scottish context, the common law concept of the public trust[93] might be rediscovered as a progenitor of the common law civil society organisation in addition to, or separate from, the creatures of statute in that country. In the United States there are hundreds of thousands of organisations, including literary clubs, sporting organisations, unions, trade associations, political organisations, churches, hospitals, condominium and neighbourhood associations, which are exempt from income tax and yet their exempt status is not linked explicitly to pursuing a common law, charitable purpose. There the link is to a list in a statute – the scope is set by section 501(c)(3) of the Internal Revenue Code. The Australian,[94] New Zealand[95] and United Kingdom[96] governments assess differently what is, and what is not, to be favoured with donor favoured status,[97] with a more direct focus on charitable purpose. There are, though, many organisations that enjoy the same favours as charities but which are not charities.[98] A notion of dynamic boundaries is needed to accommodate these differences, for some common law countries may wish to include some organisations thought to be at the margins which others wish to exclude. Examples include charitable trading that might be considered business,[99] small religious organisations that might be considered family,[100] and some government-controlled professional associations.[101]

However, so far as is relevant to the development of this jurisprudence the contests over where these boundaries lie are reducible to three. They are over:

1. the extent to which the purpose is *altruistic*, which is manifest in the contest over where the boundary between the space for civil society should end and the space for business begin;
2. whether the association is private or *public*, which is manifest in the contested boundary between civil society on the one hand and small private groups such as family on the other;
3. *freedom*, which is manifest in the contest over the boundary between the space for civil society on the one hand and the extent of government intrusion into that space on the other.

Diagrammatically, the space for civil society, and consequently its organisations, is then described better in the more complex way seen in Figure 10.8, with charitable purposes as the essence. On each of the three continua of altruism, benefit and coercion, there is a contested point where the space for civil society ceases and its other begins. That is the point of differentiation.

For convenience this body of law, the subject of which is association in civil society, is called Association law. Diagrammatically, Association law is represented by the triangular space in Figure 10.8 with charity at the centre and bordered by business, government and family. Association

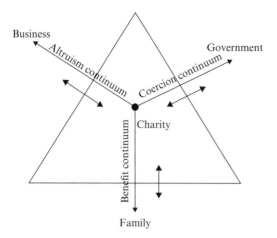

Figure 10.8   Dynamic boundaries for civil society space

law marks out more than just a space for association. It also involves a basis for entitlement to favour. It is now appropriate to introduce the next dimension into this alternative jurisprudence.

THREE DIMENSIONS – ADDING DEPTH BY FAVOUR

Introducing the Elements of Favour

This jurisprudence also provides an architecture for analysing entitlement to favour. This framework goes beyond, but is built from, the general proposition that the common law grants favour to civil society organisations that manifest charitable purposes. The common law favours are, though, relatively modest compared with the statutory, particularly taxation, favours. The common law classification is important more as a gateway to statutory favours than in its own right. I theorise that once there is evidence of voluntariness and altruism it is the public benefit that justifies favour. As the subject is benefit, for convenience this body of law, of which entitlement to favour is the object, is called Benefit law. How, though, to assess public benefit? I suggest there are two ways. Jurists can either look to the extent that the public benefits or they can look to the nature of the public benefit supplied.

The *extent* of benefit is the simpler case and can be stated quite briefly. If the extent of benefit is taken as the relevant criterion then benefit can be theorised as on a continuum between private and public. Once the requisite level of publicness is attained entitlement to favour follows. The greater the extent of public benefit the greater the justification for entitlement to favour.

If the *nature* of the public benefit is the criterion, then the analysis is a little more sophisticated. In this context I propose that the current classes of charitable purposes – relief of poverty, advancement of religion, advancement of education, and other purposes beneficial to the community – become the guides to broader categories justifying favour based on the nature of the benefit to the public. Within this alternative architecture, favours are enjoyed by civil society organisations when they pursue charitable purposes the nature of which is for public benefit. I foreshadowed at the outset a definition of charitable goods justifying favour. I now theorise that charitable goods arise, are recognisable and may be a gateway to favours when charitable purposes lead to the delivery of public benefit in one of three contexts:

1. private goods supplied to a *person* for the purposes of 'dealing with disadvantage' thereby advancing *equality*;
2. quasi-public or public goods supplied to *people* for the purposes of 'encouraging edification' thereby advancing *fraternity*;
3. ligaments binding together the *polis* (the community as a whole) which 'facilitate freedom' to advance *liberty*.[102]

Each of these three forms of charitable goods is now discussed in turn.

Dealing with Disadvantage

When dealing with disadvantage, even the supply of private goods to individual persons at a disadvantage is for public benefit. Relief of poverty is the head of the doctrine of charitable purpose from which this category is developed. The framework goes beyond relief of poverty, though, to the supply of the goods that enable those at a disadvantage to enjoy the basic rights and obligations of citizenship equally with other citizens. It advances equality. The charitable purpose cases relating to poor relations and poor employees suggest that as the law presently stands, when dealing with disadvantage, the goods supplied may be private goods and the transferee could be a relative or an employee.[103] It is to the public benefit for private goods to be supplied to a person at a disadvantage, for example bread to be supplied to a starving person, whether or not the person is a relative. When dealing with disadvantage to bring equality, a common good can be a private good supplied to an individual person.

Encouraging Edification

To be classified as a common good that encourages edification and thus advances fraternity, greater publicness in either the goods supplied, or the class of recipient for the good or service, is required.[104] Advancement of education and the more general category of other purposes beneficial to the community are the heads of the doctrine of charitable purpose from which this category is developed. The framework goes beyond advancement of education and other purposes beneficial to the public, though, to the supply of goods that are at least quasi-public and that encourage the edification of communities – or at least subsections of communities which are sufficiently large to be considered public. The provision of social goods, such as the arts and other cultural activities, is an example of this kind of common good, as is the provision of physical infrastructure like bridges, seabanks, public libraries and public museums. A greater level of public benefit is required when pursuing purposes classed as 'encouraging edification' than when pursuing purposes 'dealing with disadvantage'.[105]

As the law presently stands, to be entitled to favour for pursuing purposes that encourage edification, a civil society organisation is likely to be required to supply at least quasi-public goods and many *people* must enjoy the benefit. In the case of this class of encouraging edification, the quasi-public good may be enjoyed by rich as well as poor[106] (as the object is advancement of fraternity not equality). In economic terms, to be common goods that encourage edification, it is arguable that the goods or services supplied must be both non-rivalrous and non-excludable. When encouraging edification, a common good must be for people, not just a person.

Facilitating Freedom

Facilitating freedom is the basis for favour based on holding society together. It is founded upon, but goes beyond, the favour granted at common law to charitable trusts for the advancement of religion. The charitable purpose cases make it clear that religion is to be favoured. The public benefit in the advancement of religion was self-evident in the much more homogeneous social context in which the law of charities developed. Religion plays a role in binding people together in society through encouraging self-restraint and concern for others. Etymologically, religion is that which binds together. It has its root in Latin *ligare* from which the English word 'ligament' is derived.[107] This etymology suggests a way of conceptualising the role of religion as that which binds a body together, but that is not the way the common law has developed. If the law were to rediscover this etymological foundation then there would be a basis for favour that is founded upon the favour granted at common law to charitable trusts for the advancement of religion, but extends beyond that to all organisations which bind society together. This binding together voluntarily reduces the need for unity coerced by government and thus facilitates freedom. This advances liberty. As a stream of early United States cases pointed out, this basis for favour, built on a foundation of liberty, is 'the surest basis on which to rest the superstructure of social order'[108] and is 'necessary to the advancement of civilization and the promotion of the welfare of society'.[109]

It follows from this reasoning that advancement of religion need not be the only purpose entitled to favour. The recent extension of charitable purpose by statute in England and Wales to include advancement of citizenship or community development, the advancement of human rights and conflict resolution or reconciliation shows that these purposes can all be included within this aspect of this legal universe.[110] The scope of the definition of this class is a matter for each common law country to determine. At its narrowest, the class could be confined to advancement of religion as it has been at common law.[111] At its broadest, the class could be extended to include all civil society organisations that are vehicles by which social cohesion is strengthened. The class could be extended to include organisations pursuing political purposes and, more generally, lobbying and advocacy.[112] This means that goods that are both rivalrous and non-rivalrous, excludable and non-excludable could be within this class.

Summary of Third Dimension of Favour

In summary then, within the framework of this jurisprudence, favour is afforded to civil society organisations that voluntarily provide public goods that advance equality, fraternity or liberty. The good of the *polis* is the basis for favouring civil society organisations with purposes that 'facilitate freedom'. The benefiting of *people* is the basis for 'encouraging edification' in civil society organisations. When 'dealing with disadvantage' is the basis for favouring a civil society organisation, it is enough that the public benefit manifests in the supply of a good to a *person* who is at a disadvantage. This could be summarised as in Table 10.1.

In the same way that concepts of measurement were applied to altruism, benefit and coercion, measurement principles can be applied generally to public benefit or to the specific expressions of equality, fraternity and liberty. So within this jurisprudence, these concepts can be treated as dynamic. Entitlement to favour will move with the values of the particular

Table 10.1   Extent of benefit guide to essential characteristics

	Extent of benefit	Rivalry	Excludability
Dealing with disadvantage	Person	Rivalrous	Excludable
Encouraging edification	People	Non-rivalrous	Non-excludable
Facilitating freedom	*Polis* (community as a whole)	Both rivalrous and non-rivalrous	Both excludable and non-excludable

common law country along a continuum of favour, if all are aggregated as public benefit, or along continua of equality, fraternity and liberty if considered separately. Laying each of these concepts out on a continuum or continua, rather than confining the discourse within the rigid heads of *Pemsel's case*, sets out the architecture for a more expansive discussion.

It follows that because both 'public' and 'benefit' are contested concepts, different levels of publicness are required for 'dealing with disadvantage', 'encouraging edification' and 'facilitating freedom'. Further, different common law countries will place different weight, at different times, on different forms of benefit. Some jurisdictions might confine the concept of charitable purpose, and with that entitlement to favour, to the supply of charitable goods that deal with disadvantage, but others might extend it to include purposes that encourage edification and facilitate freedom. It is to be expected, then, that theorists will sometimes return to the foundational variables for identifying civil society organisations and apply those variables to valuing the supply of public goods. It will be recalled that the foundational variables are:

1. the otherwise remoteness of the people associating (*xenos*, for convenience labelled 'X');
2. the motive for associating being voluntarily to benefit others ('why', for convenience labelled 'Y');
3. the number of persons associating (for convenience labelled 'Z').

So I suggest that, as with charitable purpose generally, entitlement to favour due to the supply of charitable goods for public benefit will also be informed by reference to a combination of 'X', 'Y' and 'Z'.

As a matter of logic, entitlement to favour extended to civil society organisations cannot ever be greater than the space allowed for association through civil society organisations. So in the context of this jurisprudence,

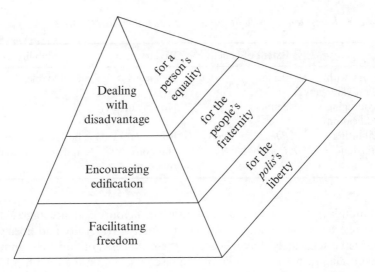

Figure 10.9   Civil society space and the favour dimension pyramid

Benefit law can be considered as a third dimension built upon Association law.[113] This entitlement to favour is also built upon and developed from the conceptions of charitable purpose, so it makes sense conceptually to set favour as a third dimension. It is appropriate to express it diagrammatically as a third dimension in the form set out in Figure 10.9.

MOVING BEYOND 'NOMINAL' MEASUREMENT OF CHARITABLE PURPOSE

Measurement is not a simple concept.[114] Its application to concepts like charitable purpose, altruism, public benefit and coercion is problematic.[115] One group debated the concept of measurement for six years[116] and at the conclusion of that debate it was said that 'the 19 members of the committee came out by the routes they entered'.[117] Following this debate, SS Stevens of Harvard University published a paper clarifying measurement into four classes.[118] These four categories, now labelled Representational Theory, stand alongside and differ from Operational Theory and Classical Theory approaches to measurement.[119] The language of Stevens's Representational Theory is deeply embedded in the discourses of occidental thought and the categories are adequate for the purposes of this discussion, so they are adopted even though they are not without difficulties.[120] The four classes or scales of measurement Stevens postulated were: nominal, ordinal, interval and ratio.[121]

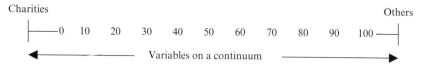

Figure 10.10   Variables on a continuum measured quantitatively

At the outset it was noted that the analysis of charitable purpose was limited to 'nominal' measurement (charitable purpose or not). Moving beyond nominal measurement, to at least ordinal ranking of altruism, public benefit and coercion, is clearly a possibility in light of developments in disciplines other than law. Authors such as Hansmann,[122] Atkinson[123] and James[124] have offered alternative classifications and rankings for division of the social *space* occupied by civil society organisations. Ordinal and even ratio measurement was proposed by Weisbrod for classification of these organisations, according to contributions to public benefit, through a collectiveness index.[125] Colombo and Hall pointed to the use of money received (which is ratio measured) by way of donation in the context of deciding taxation *favours* for charities.[126] These are important insights that could inform common law development of the theoretical analysis of the space occupied by civil society organisations, and entitlement to favours associated with the provision of charitable goods in civil society. Without an overarching framework that shows how these insights can be located in common law theory, however, they remain of no practical use to a jurist seeking to give voice to the underlying philosophical battles in a policy context. Adopting an alternative jurisprudence which centres not on charities but on civil society organisations, in the way proposed here, facilitates adoption of these insights into common law theory development. This is possible because, even at the highest level of ratio measurement, there is the possibility of objectively and numerically measuring the variables with ratio measures such as money, time or hours. If that is so, then each of the variables could be set out not just on a continuum but on a continuum which is quantitatively measured. Figure 10.10 shows an example.

Whilst it is beyond the scope of this chapter to descend into policy, it should be noted that over the thirty years since Weisbrod's collectiveness index[127] economists have developed quite sophisticated models of measurement.[128] These insights could inform jurists seeking to develop policy if they could be set free from the present orthodox understanding, an understanding which requires reasoning by analogy from a long list of purposes, some of which are irrelevant (payment of sixteens), and some of which are inappropriate (marriage of poor maids).

APPLYING A JURISPRUDENCE FOR CIVIL SOCIETY TO GO BEYOND CHARITIES

The Possibility of Bright Lines

At the threshold level this chapter argues that there is a boundary line between civil society organisations and their other. The other organisations are excluded because they are defined by insufficient evidence of charitable purpose. Businesses do not evidence sufficient altruism; in family organisations the benefit is private; and government organisations are evidenced by insufficient voluntariness. The dynamic nature of this definition of charitable purpose, informed by the variable continua of altruism, benefit and coercion, permits different jurisdictions to draw different but nevertheless quite bright lines between what is a civil society organisation and what is not. For example, one jurisdiction might determine that any control of an organisation by government, such as a veto right with respect to appointment of a board member, might take the organisation out of the class of civil society organisations into the class of government organisations. Another might consider an organisation to be a government organisation only if the majority of the board were appointed by government.[129] A third might look only to the capacity of government to control membership. In each case, the line between what is a civil society organisation and what is a government organisation is clear, but different. Where the boundary line is drawn will almost certainly be different from one common law country to another but what is critical for theory development is that the boundary can be drawn *and* in different places.

Location in Current Jurisprudential Theory

Just as the sectoral analysis of society led to recognition of what was initially called the third sector, and which is here labelled civil society, so there is a need for law to also acknowledge this third space in legal theory. Just as civil society is characterised by voluntary participation, so the law in this area takes two characteristics – one enabling voluntary association and the other favouring voluntary contribution. The alternative jurisprudence proposed in this chapter encompasses only two types of laws: laws that enable and laws that grant favour. Where people wish to contribute voluntarily for public benefit, the task of a lawmaker changes from that of proscribing to one of enabling, with minimum limitations, and possibly favouring. The laws by which society enables, and sometimes favours, those who participate and contribute to society voluntarily (other than through business, government or family) set the scope of this alternative framework.

The re-categorisation to include a jurisprudence for civil society is based on segmenting out the applicable law for civil society, which, it is argued, is capable of division into two sub-categories. *Association law* is the first sub-category. It is the umbrella under which are gathered all the laws that enable persons to associate freely for the voluntary pursuit of common, non-commercial interests. *Benefit law* is the second. It is the sub-category of law that grants favours to organisations that contribute to public benefit which a society wishes particularly to encourage by granting favours.

Civil society law stands between, but is differentiated from, the two great dividers of legal theory: private law and public law.[130] It warrants its own space in legal theory. It may be asked why Benefit law is not drawn as a complete subset of Association law. It is true that most of the time it will be a subset of Association law. There are cases, though, where civil society is strengthened by preferring businesses through such things as favourable income tax treatment and grants, and for that reason it seemed better to treat it as a separate division.

CONCLUSION

A theoretical framework, bringing together the laws applicable to the third sector, has now been outlined. Arguably the gap in legal theory which surrounded the third sector's law has been filled. The doctrine of charitable purpose has been defined, expanded and located in a wider jurisprudence, linked to the sectoral analysis discernible in the jurisprudential analysis of other categories of law. An outline has been sketched for a way in which the common law can be developed beyond the currently dominant doctrine of charitable purpose, to a jurisprudence for civil society. A jurisprudence for civil society has been offered that brings into a unifying whole the common law centred on the doctrine of charitable purpose that enables and favours voluntary contributions to common good. It offers a simpler and more cohesive explanation of this 'legal universe'. It is not referent to an ancient statute or dependent upon inadequate categories set down in a 19th-century case, but rather is drawn from and integrated into current conceptions of civil society. To repeat Copernicus, it is 'that which is easiest to grasp'.

In this jurisprudential universe it is 'charitable purpose' in its ordinary broad sense that is the central concept. This concept of charitable purpose identifies *charitable organisations* by their altruism, public benefit and absence of coercion. It is a concept of charitable purpose that identifies *charitable goods* by altruism, public benefit and absence of coercion in their contribution. It is this concept of charitable purpose that is the gravitational force that holds all of the laws of this legal universe together. Closer to the centre of this universe, charitable purpose is more evident because altruism, voluntarism and the benefit to the public are more evident. The more evident altruism, voluntarism and public benefit, the more favour is justified. Acknowledging that departure from reference to the Preamble and *Pemsel's case* is a paradigm shift, I nevertheless contend that it is a logical development and one well overdue. Within this framework civil society organisations fit perfectly as the expression of charitable purpose.

NOTES

1. The requirement that, at law, charitable purpose must take a 'technical definition' is traced to Lord Macnaghten's judgment in *Commissioners for Special Purposes of Income Tax v Pemsel* [1891] AC 531 (*Pemsel's case*).
2. Extension of Charitable Purpose Act 2004 (Aus).
3. Charities Act, The Laws of Barbados, Volume VIII, Title XVIII, Chapter 243, LRO 1989.
4. Charities Act 2006 (UK), c. 50.
5. Charities Act 2008 (NI), c. 12.
6. Charities and Trustees Investment (Scotland) Act 2005 (Asp. 10), s. 7.
7. Lakshman, C. (2002), 'The Cotonou Agreement, Civil Societies and Charities in Pacific Member States of the ACP', 8(1) *Third Sector Review*, 173–209, 184–6.
8. Corporate Affairs and Intellectual Property Office (2001), *The Charities Act, Cap. 243*, St Michael: CAIPO, available at http://www.caipo.gov.bb/corp/inner/charities.html (accessed 18 December 2009).
9. *Bob Jones University v United States*, 461 US 574 at 591 (1983) discussed in Atkinson, R. (1997), 'Nonprofit Symposium: Theories of the Federal Income Tax Exemption for Charities: Thesis, Antithesis, and Syntheses', *Stetson Law Review*, 27(2), 395–431, 426.
10. Statute of Charitable Uses 1601, 43 Eliz. c. 4.
11. Judgment of Macnaghten LJ, [1891] AC 531 at 583–4.
12. See Drache, A. (2002), 'Hostage to History: the Canadian Struggle to Modernize the Meaning of Charity', *Third Sector Review*, 8(1), 39–65; Bromley, B. (1993), 'Contemporary Philanthrophy – Is the Legal Concept of "Charity" Any Longer Adequate?', in Waters, D. (ed.), *Equity, Fiduciaries and Trusts*, Scarborough, Ont: Carswell, 59–98.
13. Charities Act 2005 No 39 (NZ), s. 8.
14. Charities and Trustees Investment (Scotland) Act 2005, s. 1(1).
15. Charities Act 2006 (UK) c. 50, s. 6.
16. Charities Act 2008 (NI) Part 2, particularly s. 6(1).
17. Nelson, K. (2004), 'Tax and the Non-profit Sector – The South African Experience', in Bater, P., F. Hondius and P.K. Lieber (eds), *The Tax Treatment of NGOs: Legal, Ethical and Fiscal Frameworks for Promoting NGOs and Their Activities*, New York: Kluwer Law International, 193–208, 193–4.
18. 'The Court of Chancery has always regarded with peculiar favour those trusts of a public nature which, according to the doctrine of the Court derived from the piety of early times, are considered to be charitable': *Pemsel's case* [1891] AC 531 at 583 (Lord Macnaghten).
19. For the status of charitable purpose as a doctrine see *Pemsel's case* [1891] AC 531 at

583 (Lord Macnaghten) and also *National Anti-Vivisection Society v Inland Revenue Commissioners* [1948] AC 31 at 52 (Lord Porter).

20. *Central Bayside General Practice Association Limited v Commissioner of State Revenue* (2006) 229 ALR 1 at 15–37 (Kirby J). The Australian High Court stands alone in this request. The Canadian Supreme Court has eschewed responsibility for this development, declaring that 'wholesale reform [as distinct from] incremental change . . . is best left to Parliament . . . [and] substantial change in the definition of charity must come from the legislature rather than the courts'. See *AYSA Amateur Youth Soccer Association v Canada (Revenue Agency)* 2007 SCC 42 at [44] (Rothstein J, delivering the judgment of McLachlin CJ, Bastarache, Binnie, LeBel, Deschamps, Fish, Charron and Rothstein JJ).

21. Analysis of society in terms of sectors, particularly when discussing civil society organisations, came to prominence through the Commission on Private Philanthropy and Public Needs (Filer Commission) in the United States, although it was initially suggested by Amitai Etzioni.

22. Civil society is a term sometimes used to describe the amalgam of the third and fourth sectors, but refers throughout this chapter only to the third sector. This division is important for legal analysis as part of resolving the definitional puzzle of which the 'poor relations cases' are an example. *Oppenheim v Tobacco Securities Trust Co* [1951] AC 297 at 317–18 (Lord MacDermott dissenting); *Internal Revenue Commissioners v Baddeley* [1955] AC 572 at 590; *Dingle v Turner* [1972] 1 All ER 878 at 888.

23. Garton, J.E. (2005), 'The Regulation of Charities and Civil Society', D Phil Thesis, University of London, 14, 30.

24. Anheier, H. (2004), *Civil Society Measurement, Evaluation, Policy*, London: Earthscan. See also O'Connell, B. (2000) 'Civil Society: Definitions and Descriptions', *Nonprofit and Voluntary Sector Quarterly*, 29(3) 471–8, 474, whose model I do not adopt, in part because it labours under (what I consider to be) the definitional difficulties that beset legal analysis, in that the author excludes some nonprofit and some charity from civil society.

25. Whilst the origins of the contest are traceable into the roots of occidental philosophy, the foundational work setting out the two dominant alternative contested views lies in the work of one of the founders of sociology. See Ehrenberg, J. (1999), *Civil Society – The Critical History of an Idea*, New York: New York University Press; Tönnies, F. (2001), *Community and Civil Society*, J. Harris trans, Cambridge: Cambridge University Press.

26. Van Til, J. (2000), *Growing Civil Society – From Nonprofit Sector to Third Space*, Bloomington: Indiana University Press.

27. Anheier, above n 24 at 22. This definition has been chosen as it underpins the structural–operational model that was used for much early research and it now underpins the civil society diamond concept which is used in more recent research. The structural–operational model has been utilised in a number of different systems of accounts including the Global Nonprofit Information System Project, the European System of National Accounts, and various national accounting methods including, for example, the Australian Nonprofit Data Project.

28. Anheier, above n 24 at 23–6; Luxton, P. (2001), *The Law of Charities*, Oxford: Oxford University Press, 5.

29. Farrar, J. (1977), *Introduction to Legal Method*, London: Sweet & Maxwell, 15; Harlow, C. (1980), '"Public" and "Private" Law: Definition Without Distinction', *The Modern Law Review*, 43(3), 241–65, 242.

30. Girard, P. (2000), *A Short History of Roman Law*, Toronto: Canada Law Book Co.

31. Samuel, G. (1988), 'Government Liability in Tort and the Public Private Division', *Legal Studies*, 8(3), 277–302.

32. Farrar, above n 29; Harlow, above n 29; Deegan, A. (2001), 'The Public/Private Dichotomy and its Relationship with the Policy/Operational Factors Distinction in Tort Law', *QUT Law & Justice Journal*, 1(2), 241–65.

33. Farnsworth, E.A. (1996), *An Introduction to the Legal System of the United States*, 3rd edn, Dobbs Ferry, NY: Oceana Publications, 96.
34. In the United States this jurisprudential division can be traced into the work of Henry Terry in the 1880s, whom Herget describes as 'the first American author of a significant text on jurisprudence': Herget, J.E. (1990), *American Jurisprudence, 1870–1970*, Houston: Rice University Press, 357. See also *Garner v Teamsters Union*, 346 US 485 at 494 (1953).
35. Arrowsmith, S. (1996), 'The Impact of Public Law on the Private Law of Contract', in Halson, R. (ed.), *Exploring the Boundaries of Contract*, Aldershot: Dartmouth, 3, at 3.
36. Ibid.
37. E.g. in Australia, the Trade Practices Act 1974, where the intent is expressed in s. 2 as 'to enhance the welfare of Australians through the promotion of competition and fair trading and provision for consumer protection'.
38. A reason for this is possibly that the association may be understood as a contract between members but in situations where the purpose of the association is not the pursuit of self-interest but provision of charitable goods the division is by no means tidy. As Ford notes, 'In so far as a body corporate is formed to advance some purpose or the interests of a class of persons the body corporate may be thought to be like a trustee': Ford, H.A.J. and W.A. Lee (1996), *Principles of the Law of Trusts*, Sydney: LBC, para [1560].
39. Succession law, whilst technically different from estate law, is, for present purposes, incorporated as within estate law.
40. E.g. in Australia, the Family Law Act 1974 (Cth) which regulates family disputes that cannot be resolved privately, and the Succession Act 1981 (Qld) which, in the state of Queensland, provides for the passing of property justly, following death.
41. For the purpose of this chapter, the distinction between law and equity is not important. The practice now adopted by legislators like the Queensland government of not distinguishing between equitable and legal forms chosen for pursuit of charitable purpose is adopted.
42. *Pemsel's case* [1891] AC 531 at 580 (Lord Macnaghten).
43. Charity Commission (2008), *Charities and Public Benefit: The Charity Commission's General Guidance on Public Benefit*, London: Charity Commission, 13; Warburton, J., D. Morris and N.F. Riddle (2003), *Tudor on Charities*, London: Sweet & Maxwell, 9–10.
44. For discussion of why the common law seems fixed around private law see Howard, C. (1984), 'Public and Common Law', in Galligan, D.J. (ed.), *Essays in Legal Theory*, Melbourne: Melbourne University Press, 1–28.
45. The concept of third sector is virtually absent from the Australian legal landscape.
46. The phrase 'civil society' has begun to appear more in Australian judicial decisions. Five recent (at 8 September 2008) High Court of Australia cases where the term is used illustrate its application to freedom of association, freedom of communication and (reward for) voluntary contribution.
47. Although Luxton avers that 'We are witnessing the encroachment of trusts law by stealth': Luxton, above n 28 at 17.
48. Ibid.
49. See Atkinson, R. (2000), 'Problems with Presbyterians: Prolegomena to a Theory of Voluntary Associations and the Liberal State', in Mitchell, C. and S. Moody (eds), *Foundations of Charity*, Oxford: Hart Publishing, 125–74.
50. James, E. (1989), *The Nonprofit Sector in International Perspective*, New York: Oxford University Press; Anheier, H. and L. Salamon (1992), 'In Search of the Non-profit Sector – I: The Question of Definitions', *Voluntas*, 3(2), 125–51; Anheier, H. and L. Salamon (1992), 'In Search of the Non-profit Sector II: The Problem of Classification', *Voluntas*, 3(3), 267–309.
51. A qualification about this metaphor is central to the chapter, and that is that theory in

the natural sciences involves the discovery of immutable patterns but the discovery of similar patterns in law, which is an artificial construct, is an incidental exercise in (re) organisation and definitions. Were that not so then this argument would not be possible, for it postulates not that the law is different but that by adopting an alternative way of viewing the object – law – a better understanding of it evolves.

52. Copernicus, N. (1542), *On the Revolutions of the Heavenly Spheres*, 2nd edn, 508.
53. Ibid.
54. Levin suggests that 'all [l]aw is a puzzle at least to the ordinary individual, uninitiated in the mysteries and ritual of the legal process': Levin, J. (1992), *How Judges Reason: The Logic of Adjudication*, New York: Lang, 13.
55. See *Pemsel's case* [1891] AC 531.
56. The Charities Act 1979 (Barbados) Cap. 243.
57. Charities Act 1979 (Barbados) Cap. 243, LRO 1989; Extension of Charitable Purpose Act 2004 (Cth); Charities and Trustees Investment (Scotland) Act 2005, s. 10; Charities Act 2006 (UK) c. 50; and Charities Act 2008 (NI). The Supreme Court of Canada considered and rejected the idea of adding a head on the grounds that it would 'do little to enhance the fairness or flexibility of the law': *Vancouver Society of Immigrant and Visible Minority Women v Minister of National Revenue* (1999) 169 DLR (4th) 34 at para 203 (Iacobucci J).
58. See Charities Act 2006 (UK), s. 2(2)
59. Extension of Charitable Purpose Act 2004 (Cth), ss 4, 5.
60. Carmichael, T.A. (2004), 'Charity Law Development in the Commonwealth Caribbean', in Bater, P., F. Hondius and P.K. Lieber (eds), *The Tax Treatment of NGOs: Legal, Ethical and Fiscal Frameworks for Promoting NGOs and their Activities*, New York: Kluwer Law International, 59–74, 61.
61. *Chesterman v Federal Commissioner of Taxation* (1923) 32 CLR 362 at 384 (Isaacs J). This was also the position taken in overruled decisions in lower courts in *Pemsel's case* as Lord Watson observed: 'The learned judges of the Court of Session refused to attach to "charitable purposes" the comprehensive meaning which the words admittedly bear in English law, being of opinion that they have no technical significance in the law language of Scotland': [1891] AC 531 at 556.
62. Charity is often viewed from two (allegedly) antithetical perspectives: one, that charity is voluntary gift; the other, that it is the fulfilment of a positive duty. Kymlicka, W. (2001), 'Altruism in Philosophical and Ethical Traditions: Two Views', in Phillips, J., B. Chapman and D. Stevens (eds), *Between State and Market: Essays on Charity Law and Policy in Canada*, Montreal: McGill-Queen's University Press, 87. It is not the function of this chapter to arbitrate between the two perspectives but rather to lay out a platform for a debate that may encompass both. This debate (about why people behave charitably) is of significance to this argument though, for altruism is a justification for favour and therefore is of importance later, when setting out an alternative basis for favour different from the Preamble. The view that the perspectives are necessarily opposed is also not well founded. There is a pedigree of ideas leading back to at least the 13th century which positions charitable acts on a continuum between self-interest and self-sacrifice. For the eight degrees of charity drawn from ancient Jewish roots see Maimonides, M. (1840), *The Laws of the Hebrews, Relating to the Poor and the Stranger*, London: Richardson.
63. At its very basest it is rudimentary pro-social behaviour. For a brief introduction to the scientific study of pro-social behaviour see Piliavin, J.A. and Charng, H.W. (1990), 'Altruism: A Review of Recent Theory and Research', *Annual Review of Sociology*, 16, 27–65.
64. The idea that charity may be analysed in this graduated way is both ancient and current. For the ancient roots see Maimonides, above n 62; see also Ting, J.-C. and Piliavin, J.A. (2001), 'Altruism in Comparative International Perspective', in Phillips, J., B. Chapman and D. Stevens (eds), *Between State and Market: Essays on Charity Law and Policy in Canada*, Montreal: McGill-Queen's University Press, 51.

65. The classical Greek word for stranger.
66. Lewes, G. (1890), *Comte's Philosophy of the Sciences*, G. Lewes trans, London: Bell & Sons. Comte evidently invented the word, possibly drawing upon the Italian *altrui*, or the French legal phrase *alteri huic*: Anheier, H. and R. List (2005), *A Dictionary of Civil Society, Philanthropy and the Non-Profit Sector*, London: Routledge, 6; Simpson, J.A. and E.S.C. Weiner (eds) (1989), definition of 'altruism', *The Oxford English Dictionary*, 2nd edn, Oxford: Clarendon.
67. Anheier and List, above n 66 at 6.
68. Vaughan, G. and M. Hogg (1998), *Introduction to Social Psychology*, Sydney: Prentice Hall, 324; Shaffer, D. (2000), *Social and Personality Development*, Belmont, CA: Wadsworth, 306.
69. Simpson and Weiner, above n 66.
70. *Vancouver Society of Immigrant and Visible Minority Women v Minister of National Revenue* (1999) 169 DLR (4th) 34 at paras 37, 50.
71. See *Toronto Volgograd Committee v Minister of National Revenue* [1988] 3 FC 251 at 258–9, where Marceau J held: 'There is one difficulty however with Lord Macnaghten's judgment, a difficulty which, in my opinion, is too often overlooked: it was a judgment strictly concerned with charitable trusts and was elaborated with a view to reaching all possible objects capable of giving validity to institutions set up in an altruistic spirit for the furtherance of some beneficial objective'.
72. Australia, Inquiry into the Definition of Charities and Related Organisations (2001), *Report of the Inquiry into the Definition of Charities and Related Organisations*, Canberra: Treasury, 6.
73. Ibid, 111.
74. Whilst altruism as a word was only introduced into the English language in 1853 the concept was established before Sir William Grant MR famously held in 1804 that the word charity 'in its widest sense denotes all the good affections, men ought to bear towards each other; in its most restricted and common sense, relief of the poor' but that in 'neither of these senses is it employed in this Court. Here its signification is derived chiefly from the statute 43 Eliz., c. 4 [relating to charitable gifts]': *Morice v Bishop of Durham* [1804] 9 Ves Jr 399; 1803–1813 All ER Reprints 451 at 454.
75. *Baptist Union of Ireland (Northern) Corporation Ltd v Commissioners of Inland Revenue* 26 Tax Cas 335 at 357 (MacDermott J).
76. United Nations, Department of Economic and Social Affairs, Statistics Division (2003), *Handbook on Non-Profit Institutions in the System of National Accounts*, Studies in Methods, Series F, No 91, Handbook of National Accounting, New York: UN, 69.
77. *Pemsel's case* [1891] AC 531 at 584 (Lord Macnaghten).
78. United Nations, Department of Economic and Social Affairs, Statistics Division, above n 76 at 69; Atkinson, R. (1990), 'Altruism in Nonprofit Organizations', *Boston College Law Review*, 31(3), 501–639; Benabou, R. and J. Tirole (2003), 'Intrinsic and Extrinsic Motivation', *Review of Economic Studies*, 70(2), 489–520; Piliavin and Charng, above n 63; Ting and Piliavin, above n 64.
79. Anheier, above n 24 at 32.
80. Atiyah, P.S. (1958), 'Public Benefit in Charities', *The Modern Law Review*, 21(2), 138–54.
81. *Oppenheim v Tobacco Securities Trust Co Ltd* [1951] AC 297 at 305.
82. E.g. Weisbrod, B.A. (1977), 'Not-for-Profit Organizations as Providers of Collective Goods', in Weisbrod, B.A. (ed.), *The Voluntary Nonprofit Sector*, Lexington, MA: DC Heath, 1, 1; Hansmann, H. (1981), 'Reforming Nonprofit Corporation Law', *University of Pennsylvania Law Review* 129(2), 497–623, 500, 504; James, E. (1987), 'The Nonprofit Sector in Comparative Perspective', in Powell, W. (ed.), *The Nonprofit Sector: A Research Handbook*, New Haven: Yale University Press, 397.
83. Weisbrod, B.A. (1977), 'Toward a Theory of the Voluntary Nonprofit Sector in a Three-Sector Economy', in Weisbrod, B.A. (ed.), *The Voluntary Nonprofit Sector*,

Lexington, MA: DC Heath, 51; Atkinson, above n 78; Colombo, J. and M. Hall (1995), *The Charitable Tax Exemption*, Boulder, CO: Westview Press.

84. Weisbrod, above n 83.
85. Ibid, 60; Weisbrod, B.A. (1991), *The Nonprofit Economy*, Cambridge MA: Harvard University Press, 59.
86. Atkinson, above n 78 at 565–6.
87. *Pemsel's case* [1891] AC 531 at 580 (Lord Macnaghten).
88. *Pemsel's case* [1891] AC 531 at 584 (Lord Macnaghten); but note comments against this, and authorities cited, by Lord Halsbury at 544.
89. *Central Bayside General Practice Association Limited v Commissioner of State Revenue* (2006) 228 CLR 168 at 181.
90. E.g., *Magna Carta* 1215 signed by King John; *Magna Carta* 1216, 1217, 1225 signed by King Henry III; *Magna Carta* 1297 signed by King Edward I; signed by each succeeding monarch until Henry V in 1416; United States Constitution, Preamble; Cannon, H.L. (1909), 'The Character and Antecedents of the Charter of Liberties of Henry I', *The American Historical Review*, 15(1), 37–46.
91. E.g. in Australia, the Legal Profession Act 2007 (Qld) and similar legislation in other Australian jurisdictions.
92. Power, M. (1999), *The Audit Society: Rituals of Verification*, Oxford. Oxford University Press, 97–8
93. In that jurisdiction it is clear that public trusts are a broader class and charities are a subclass of that class; and the effect of the passing of the Charities and Trustees Investment (Scotland) Act 2005 has been that the ranks of non-charitable public trusts may well be increased by trusts which either are unable to satisfy the new public benefit requirement or choose not to register as a charity under the legislation. See The Scottish Law Commission (2007), *Report on Variation and Termination of Trusts*, Report No 206, Edinburgh: the Law Commission, para 6.4. See also Barker, C.R. (2004), 'The Reform of Charity Law in Scotland', in Bater, P., F. Hondius and P.K. Lieber (eds), *The Tax Treatment of NGOs: Legal, Ethical and Fiscal Frameworks for Promoting NGOs and their Activities*, New York: Kluwer Law International, 33–58, 34.
94. Income Tax Assesment Act 1997 (Cth), Div. 30.
95. Income Tax Act 2004 (NZ), s. CW36.
96. Income Tax Act 2007 c. 3 (UK), ss 413–46.
97. The expression 'donor favoured' describes favours extended to donors such as deductibility for gifts and tax credits. It is used throughout this chapter as the form and type of favour varies from country to country. Examples of such favours are contained within the (Australian) Income Tax Assessment Act 1997 (Cth), Div 30; Internal Revenue Code (US), ss 501(c)(3) and 170; Income Tax Act 2004 (NZ), ss BD2, DV8 and DV9; Income Tax Act 2007 (UK) c. 3, ss 521–3; Income Tax Act (Can) (1985) c. 1 (5th Supp), ss 110.1(1)(a)(ii), 118.1(1)(b), 118.1(3), and 149(1)(l)).
98. For example, political parties in Australia enjoy limited donor favoured status: Income Tax Assessment Act 1997 (Cth), s. 30–242.
99. *Federal Commissioner of Taxation v Word Investments Ltd* (2006) 64 ATR 483; Hansmann, H. (1989), 'Unfair Competition and the Unrelated Business Income Tax', *Virginia Law Review* 75(3), 605–35; Atkinson, above n 78; McGregor-Lowndes, M. (1994), 'The Regulation of Charitable Organisations', PhD Thesis, Griffith University; Colombo and Hall, above n 83; Stone, E.G. (2005), 'Adhering to the Old Line: Uncovering the History and Political Function of the Unrelated Business Income Tax', *Emory Law Journal*, 54(4), 1475–1556.
100. *Cheung Man Yu v Lau Yuen Ching and Ors* (Hong Kong Court of Appeal, 20 July 2007).
101. *Central Bayside General Practice Association Limited v Commissioner of State Revenue* (2006) 228 CLR 168.
102. In this alternative jurisprudence, equality, fraternity and liberty are treated as values

and diversity is acknowedged. For example, in classical Greek theory, three kinds of equality are recognised: isonomia (equality before the law); isotimia (equal respect for all); and isegoria (equal freedom of speech and political action). In post-enlightenment theory, the three kinds tend to be covered by one of a trilogy of principles (liberty, fraternity, and equality): Nygh, P.E. and P. Butt (eds) (1998), *Butterworths Concise Australian Legal Dictionary*, 2nd edn, Sydney: Butterworths, 152. My limited purpose is to label three ideals. A particular jurisprudential worldview or common law country may give shape and expression to the value in a particular context.

103. *Dingle v Turner* [1972] 1 All ER 878 at 888.
104. *Gilmour v Coats* [1949] AC 426 at 449.
105. *Oppenheim v Tobacco Securities Trust Co Ltd* [1951] AC 297; *Lloyd v Federal Commissioner of Taxation* (1955) 93 CLR 645 at 662 (McTiernnan J), 667 (Fullagar J), 670 (Kitto J); *Pemsel's case* [1891] AC 531 at 559 (Lord Watson); *In Re Lopes Bence-Jones v Zoological Society of London* [1931] 2 Ch 130; *Re Pinion* [1965] Ch 85.
106. *Pemsel's case* [1891] AC 531.
107. Definition of 'ligament', *Oxford English Dictionary Online*, available at http://dictionary.oed.com (accessed 7 June 2008).
108. *Holland v Peck* (1842) 37 NC 255, 258.
109. *People ex rel Seminary of Our Lady of Angels v Barber* (1886) 3 NY St Rep 367, affirmed in (1887) 13 NE 936.
110. Charities Act 2006 (Eng & W) c. 50, s. 2(2).
111. Ellis-Jones, I. (2007), 'Beyond the Scientology Case: Towards a Better Definition of What Constitutes a Religion for Legal Purposes in Australia Having Regard to the Salient Judicial Authorities from the United States of America as well as Important Non-Judicial Authorities, PhD Thesis, University of Technology Sydney.
112. For an example of statutory amendments see the Charities Act 2006 (Eng & W) c. 50. For discussion of the relevant theory see: 6, P. and A. Randon (1995), *Liberty, Charity and Politics: Non-Profit Law and Freedom of Speech*, Aldershot: Dartmouth; Breen, O.B. (2008), 'EU Regulation of Charitable Organizations: The Politics of Legally Enabling Civil Society', *International Journal of Not-for-Profit Law*, 10(3), 50–78.
113. An important caveat which is beyond the scope of this chapter to explore is that businesses sometimes enjoy benefits similar to civil society organisations, e.g. in Australia, the Export Expansion Grants Act 1978 (Cth).
114. Sarle, W. (1997), *Measurement Theory: Frequently Asked Questions*, Cary, NC: SAS Institute Inc, available at ftp://ftp.sas.com/pub/neural/measurement.html (accessed 21 December 2009); Velleman, P. and L. Wilkinson (1993), *Nominal, Ordinal, Interval, and Ratio Typologies are Misleading*, available at http://www.helsinki.fi/~komulain/Tilastokirjat/Nominal_to_ratio_misleading.pdf (accessed 21 December 2009); Michell, J. (1986), 'Measurement Scales and Statistics: A Clash of Paradigms', *Psychological Bulletin*, 100(3) 398–407.
115. Stevens, S.S. (1946), 'On the Theory of Scales of Measurement', *Science*, 103(2683), 677–80; Michell, above n 114; Velleman and Wilkinson, above n 114.
116. Stevens, above n 115 at 677.
117. Ibid.
118. Ibid, 678.
119. Michell, above n 114 at 398.
120. Watanabe, H. (2005), 'Coarse-Grained Information in Formal Theory of Measurement', *Measurement*, 38(4), 295–302; Velleman and Wilkinson, above n 114; Michell, above n 114.
121. Stevens, above n 115.
122. Hansmann, above n 82 at 503.
123. Atkinson, above n 78 at 565–6.
124. James, E. (1989), 'The Nonprofit Sector in Developing Countries: The Case of Sri Lanka', in James, E. (ed.), *The Nonprofit Sector in International Perspective – Studies*

in *Comparative Culture and Policy*, New York: Oxford University Press, 289–318, 292.

125. Weisbrod, above n 83 at 73.
126. Colombo and Hall, above n 83 at 217.
127. Weisbrod, above n 83 at 73.
128. See e.g. Chillemi, O. and G. Benedetto (1991), 'Uninformed Customers and Nonprofit Organization: Modelling "Contract Failure" Theory', *Economics Letters*, 35(1), 5–8; Cullis, J., P. Jones and C. Thanassoulas (1984), 'Are Charities Efficient "Firms"? A Preliminary Test of the UK Charitable Sector', *Public Choice*, 44(2), 367–73, 369.
129. *Central Bayside General Practice Association Limited v Commissioner of State Revenue* (2006) 228 CLR 168 at 181.
130. Farrar, J. and A.M. Dugdale (1994), *Introduction to Legal Method*, 3rd edn, London: Sweet & Maxwell, 15.

Conclusion

Kerry O'Halloran

This volume began with an overview of developments in charity law since 2001, as apparent from the charity legislation recently introduced in the UK and Irish jurisdictions, and so also in Singapore, Canada, New Zealand and Australia. It explored the meaning of 'public benefit', as now newly defined in such legislation, giving particular attention to its distinctive attributes in Irish law and to its significance as the principle that ultimately distinguishes charity in a common law as opposed to a civil code context and as illustrated by the progress currently being made in China and Japan.

That led, inevitably, into the matter of central concern to the book and to the future of charity: a consideration of the fluctuating boundaries between charity, religion and the more sectoral interests of business and government; noting also the significance of jurisdictional boundaries, the impact of global anti-terrorism provisions and economic recession, and the particular difficulties faced by federated jurisdictions. Beginning with a focus on the charity–business boundary, it explained why charity is now a growing presence in the marketplace and assessed the significance of: marrying public and private interests; corporate philanthropy; partnerships between charity and business; and the challenge of social entrepreneurship. Turning then to focus on the charity–government boundary, it explored and explained the reasons why this boundary is now changing: the rolling back of the 'welfare state'; governments retreating from providing to regulating public benefit services and broadening the range of charitable purposes as a means of sharing the responsibility for such services with charity; and the need for government to generate more civic engagement and forge the alliances necessary to consolidate civil society. It then examined the charity–religion boundary and pursued four lines of enquiry: the inclusion of religion as one of the heads of charity; its conceptualisation as part of charity; the justification for its continuance as a separate head; and the entitlement of religious institutions to special tax treatment. It was suggested that the working subtext to these issues was: is it time to reform the religious head and strip back its privileges?

The book concluded with two critiques of the notion of charity and civil society organisations. One challenged the underpinnings of common law charity regulation and sought to reconceptualise it to make it a fit legal framework for the whole of civil society. The other challenged the assumption that the regulatory approach is conducive to the growth of civil society: the rationale for extending the same regulatory approach to civil society entities as is applied to justify regulating private interests was assessed, challenged and judged to be inappropriate. The incremental nature of policy reform in liberal democracies militates against such grand designs, but both contributions shed light on the essential structural issues at the foundations of the charity framework.

In the main, the recent developments in charity law comprised incremental statutory improvements to the regulatory framework and the encoding of common law concepts. However, modernisation was found to vary across a considerable spectrum. At one extreme lie the UK and Irish jurisdictions. There, new regulatory mechanisms have been put in place including, where they did not previously exist, the statutory introduction of: charity specific, lead regulatory bodies; charity registers, together with more stringent governance and accountability requirements; appeals tribunals to hear appeals against registration decisions; and provisions to promote charity efficiency and effectiveness. They have also extended the range of charitable purposes significantly and reversed the established public benefit presumption, making all new purposes subject to that test (excepting the advancement of religion in Ireland). The nature and extent of charity law modernisation in the UK and Ireland distinguishes that group of jurisdictions from all others, places them in a position to interface and to further develop wide-ranging case law, and strengthens their respective well-established government–charity partnerships. It may also have created a permanent rift in the fabric of charity law.

At the other extreme are those jurisdictions, most notably Australia and Canada, where charity law reform has so far completely failed to fulfil its promised potential. There, the traditional regulatory framework led by the tax collecting agency, together with the *Pemsel* definition of charitable purpose and the accompanying public benefit presumption, remains firmly in place. While modernisation in both is undoubtedly more difficult to achieve due to the constitutional complexities and associated constraints of their federated jurisdictions, in the case of Canada there also seems to be a lack of any drivers for reform capable of forming a united front around a clearly identified national reform agenda and sustaining the momentum necessary to accomplish desired reform outcomes.

In between these extremes lie the cautious legislative steps towards modernisation made in Singapore and New Zealand. In both, the primary achievement has been to improve the regulatory framework: mainly by decoupling institutional responsibility for determining charitable status and tax exemption; vesting the former in a new lead, charity specific, regulatory body loosely resembling the UK Charity Commission model; and establishing charity registers together with a regime for supervising and supporting those registered. Like Australia and Canada, neither Singapore nor New Zealand has taken any legislative steps to broaden the traditional *Pemsel* list of charitable purposes or to alter the public benefit presumption. However, and unlike Canada, both these jurisdictions have now placed the key common law concepts onto the statute books – thereby, in keeping with the UK and Irish jurisdictions, giving their legislatures the future capacity to amend and extend the *Pemsel* list and adjust the public benefit rules.

Reflecting on the varied jurisdictional progress towards modernisation recorded in this book, there is a clear correlation between reform outcomes and the strength of established government–sector links. Following the lead given in the UK by government success in building formal links with the sector (compacts, accords, protocols, Office of the Third Sector and so on), similar initiatives were taken in Ireland, Singapore and New Zealand and, more recently, in Australia. The results seem to indicate that where there is a thoroughly worked through and negotiated understanding between government and the sector then effective and far-reaching charity law reform can follow. Without that platform in place, notwithstanding the admittedly more complex dynamics present in federated jurisdictions, it is probable that mutual uncertainty, if not suspicion and defensiveness, between government and the sector will prevent radical change in an area of such strategic importance to both parties. This, of course, raises the question: what exactly is it in the political context that is conducive or otherwise to the promotion of formal linkages between government and the sector? Further questions then follow. How, if at all, does that linkage relate to business, traditional legal structures and religion? And what, if any, are the implications for the future of civil society? While it would be a mistake to venture too far down a path that risks over-reaching the remit of this book, it would also, perhaps, be equally remiss not to take some steps in the direction indicated by the contributors and consider what light possible answers to such questions might shed on the future modernisation of charity law.

POLITICAL CONTEXT

The relationship between government and the sector (charities being sector leaders) lies at the heart of democratic society. Arguably, there are at least two main strands to this relationship: one that concerns responsibility for public benefit provision; and the other to do with the mechanisms for government engagement with the community and with citizens.

In the UK, the broad legal parameters of that relationship were laid down in the Preamble and subsequently adjusted, largely through charity case law but also by legislation and more recently through the mediation of the Charity Commission. The significant upheaval that skewed this relationship in the post-war years, with the nationalisation of public utilities and healthcare services, has since been readjusted by government action to subdue the trade unions, followed by the winding back of nationalisation. This inevitably led to charity law reform as the means for changing the balance of responsibility for future provision from government to sector, which coincided with government's electoral strategy of pursuing a 'third way' approach to capture that growing middle ground of disenchanted constituents who felt equally alienated by the politics of 'left' and 'right'.

As noted in Chapter 1, both strands combined to persuade government that it needed to develop and vigorously pursue a policy that would enable it to close the distance between governing and the governed, win the trust of community and sector representatives and thereby motivate enough politically disillusioned citizens to risk supporting the present government in the next election. This policy came to be operationalised through tactics that promoted the growth of a 'participative' form of democratic politics alongside the more traditional 'representative' form.

In a possibly unprecedented and sustained campaign to break down or bypass the established institutional linkages between government and citizen, many new avenues of direct communication were opened up: constitutional devolution was accompanied by devolution of power to local communities; a layer of quangos sprang up to co-ordinate policy and resources in designated areas of social need (for example housing, child care, and poverty); formal and well-used networks linked government and the sector (for example the NCVO); many 'experts' were appointed as consultants to government bodies, to ministers and to the prime minister; and, in short, the government quickly established avenues of communication which were intended and used to allow its policies to be directly influenced by sector bodies without any electoral mandate. As a consequence, in the early years of the Labour administration, government and sector were perhaps more closely aligned in their mutual engagement across a broad range of domestic social care policy issues than had been the case for some decades. The rationale and process for launching charity law reform flowed logically from that engagement: it had become clearly evident that the terms of reference for future public benefit service provision needed to be negotiated; it was readily accepted that a review of the law that, for four centuries, had distributed between government and charity the responsibility for such provision was the appropriate framework for doing so; and the parties concerned had by then achieved well-established working relations and a sufficient level of mutual trust and sense of common purpose to embark on an intrusive examination of the basis of their relationship and its durability.

The main point to emerge from this is that successful charity law reform in the UK jurisdictions was demonstrated to be both cause and effect of a secure and stable government–sector alliance, a point illustrated by the relative lack of success in other jurisdictions where government–sector relations are weaker (see Chapter 7). The eagerness with which the current government in Australia is seeking to replicate the formal and informal links with the sector, as pioneered in the UK, would seem to indicate that the point was well taken in that jurisdiction. Of the other jurisdictions studied, only in Ireland was a similar partnership approach adopted. Since 1987, the Irish government had cultivated a model of social partnership with certain groups designated as 'pillars' of Irish society (employers, the trade unions and the farming organisations). The community and voluntary sector was seen as the fourth pillar in this partnership arrangement with government. In Ireland, the incentive for partnership was driven by EC requirements for infrastructure grants but it has proved to be a solid and sustainable working framework and one which has facilitated the only thorough modernisation of charity law achieved outside the UK.

CHARITY AND LEGAL STRUCTURES

The clearer line drawn by charity law reform between charitable and all other enterprises indicated government's intention to leave the market to determine the future provision of those utilities and services, currently designated 'public services', that could not be assigned to charity under the new *Pemsel* plus list of charitable purposes as policed by the public benefit principle. In many cases, however, there were operational restrictions (due to matters such as the knowledge base, deeds of ownership, public trusts or access to resources) that impeded a straightforward sale, lease or transfer of responsibility from government to the private sector. The existence of such complications acted as a catalyst for the creation of a new generation of legal structures that could marry public and private interests and operate with some flexibility in the new and uncertain frontier land that separated government, charity and commerce.

The recent and rapid spread of hybrid organisations and forms of social entrepreneurship has been one of the more interesting aspects of modernisation. It has been very apparent that innovation in legal structures commenced in the US, where the more 'open' market has acted as an inducement for experimentation with types of limited liability corporate structures that may provide suitable vehicles for a mix of both public and private interests, allowing philanthropy to bridge the for-profit–charity dichotomy and form partnerships or joint ventures between government, commercial and charitable entities. The L3C (low-profit limited liability company – L x 3), for example, is seen as offering an attractive investment opportunity for foundations, as well as individuals and government agencies, through the purchase of an equity position or other means, such as loans. These investments, by providing capital for socially beneficial activities such as keeping a small-town factory in business or building low cost housing, offer a mix of funding sources to deliver community regeneration projects beyond the reach of most charities. Such experimentation, together with community foundations and a broad range of social entrepreneurship, has since taken root in the UK, Irish, Canadian and Australian jurisdictions but appears to be less evident in Singapore and New Zealand.

Charity law reform in the UK jurisdictions, but nowhere else, specifically addressed the need for new legal structures. It introduced the community interest company (CIC), a limited liability company designed to use its profits and assets to achieve social missions. This tailor-made vehicle for social entrepreneurs has several distinguishing features: it must pass a 'community interest test' that ensures that it operates in the public interest; it must file an annual report detailing payments to directors, dividends paid on shares, interest paid on loans, and the ways it has fostered involvement of stakeholders in the company's activities; it also must operate under an 'asset lock', which prohibits it from distributing assets or profits to its members except in cases where shareholders have an equity stake in the company. In those cases, returns to shareholders must be modest and are capped so that most of the profits are distributed to the broader community. Charities cannot qualify as CICs, but they can invest in them or own them. The UK jurisdictions also introduced the charitable incorporated organisation (CIO), which is created specifically to meet the needs of charities and is available exclusively to charities. There is every reason to believe that similar steps will be taken to extend the range of legal structures in other jurisdictions as governments move to facilitate the spread of social entrepreneurship.

The corollary to such a sudden and prolific experimentation with new legal structures is, perhaps, at least two-fold: continued reliance on the traditional structures, particularly the trust, is likely to fade; and the simple demarcation between charities and other non-profits may prove untenable in the near future. It seems likely that the dynamics of the market will exert such pressure that form will be dragged into line with function and charity will have no option but to participate in the eclectic fusion of new legal structures that are now emerging, to compete in the public benefit space abandoned by government and compromised by the recent excesses of capitalism.

CHARITY, THE MARKET AND GOVERNMENT

The undoubted achievement of the UK Labour government in cultivating a multi-level engagement with the sector, assisted by the latter's eagerness to seize the strategic opportunity provided by 'third way' politics and hoist its banner alongside that of government, was paralleled by its success in continuing policies initiated by its Conservative predecessor in opening up new opportunities for business in the privatised utilities market. This was a policy thrust upon a new government that had no possibility of undoing the fire sale approach of its predecessor towards such hitherto core nationalised public utilities as water and electricity supply, the rail network and so on. In furthering the process of lessening the burden on government, there was considerable experimentation with public–private finance initiatives that allowed commercial entities to invest vast amounts of private money into public benefit infrastructure such as schools, hospitals, roads, and so on, subject to government regulation but often on a for-profit basis. It was a process that had been adopted much earlier in the US, where government had never assumed anything like the level of responsibility for public benefit service provision that had been achieved in the UK, and consequently the latter jurisdiction had to proceed more urgently and radically. As this progressed, questions inevitably arose as to the preferred mix of government–charity–business provision.

The reality, that many core public benefit utilities had already been privatised, challenged the government to formulate a rationale for determining why all remaining such utilities and services should not follow suit, or at least to clarify the basis for their future distribution between government, sector and business. This issue was one that again pointed towards charity law reform as the forum for negotiating responsibility for future public benefit service provision – the argument being that a reformed charity law, by outlining a modern schema of purposes to be addressed by charity, would thereby determine what remained as the responsibility of government, some of which it could then choose to sell, franchise out or share with business. In that context, the public benefit principle was crucial: charity being restricted to purposes that delivered on that principle, it defined those areas of provision that could not fall to be undertaken by charitable organisations. Removing the presumption that the principle could be satisfied by certain traditional purposes and requiring instead its application to all new ones, together with the retention of other common law rules such as those relating to exclusiveness and profit distribution, reflected a new government resolve to firm up on the role played by this gate-keeping rule; it would in future serve to confine charity.

However, and most unexpectedly, government was faced with a challenge from the opposite direction: it was required to precipitately redesignate icons of private enterprise as public benefit utilities. While modernisation of charity law had been preoccupied with clarifying the charity remit and extending it in some jurisdictions through the *Pemsel* plus approach to charitable purposes – thereby facilitating a transfer of responsibility for public utilities to charity – the partial collapse of the banking and financial system resulted in government having to facilitate a reverse transfer of responsibility for banks, car manufacturers and others from the private to the public sector. This reverse flow, ironically occurring at the same time that the outlet from public to private had largely been freed up, has placed government and to some extent charity in a considerable quandary. If public benefit is the distinguishing characteristic of charity then how is it that organisations such as Help the Aged, Chrysler, Save the Children, AIG, Fannie Mae and Freddie Mac can now shelter equally under that umbrella, sharing the space reserved for altruism? Is it possible that both the most profit driven and the most philanthropic organisations can equally satisfy the public benefit test and thereby qualify for assistance from the public purse? If car manufacture constitutes public benefit, where does this leave the 'civil society' paradigm? What does the speed, scale and ease with which unprecedented amounts of wealth were transferred from the public to the private sector say about the meagre tax concessions that filter the flow from the public to the charitable sector? If politics rather than law is the true arbiter of matters deemed to meet the test, where does this leave charity and what weighting does charity law actually have relative to the imperatives of commerce and politics? While at present there is no indication of any government willingness to square this particular circle, all government initiatives to adjust the social role of charity must now also be seen in the light of its response to the damage caused by the excesses of capitalism.

In a sense, the market simply prevails. In the long run, although the interests of both charity and commerce occasionally require government intervention (for example, to protect, police or subvent), market dynamics probably just absorbs such intrusions, makes the necessary adjustments and moves on. However, there are particular lessons arising for the role played by the public benefit principle. The demarcation between public and private interests, an integral component of charity law in a common law context (a legacy of the law of trusts and the duties of trustees), never neatly represented by government–charity and commerce respectively, now needs to be interpreted with considerable elasticity. Given that the sliding door of the public benefit principle can admit both commerce and charity to taxpayer subvention, there is an argument for accommodating all entities with capacity to satisfy the principle, whether wholly or partially, within a graduated scheme that confers a degree of charitable status and tax exemption commensurate with their level of satisfying the principle. Arguably, at one end of that spectrum would lie charities, being those entities found to be exclusively serving the public interest, and at the other those essentially commercial entities which also deliver some level of public benefit. In between would lie all other nonprofits including social enterprises, community foundations, L3Cs and the diverse range of newly emerging hybrid entities. The modernisation of charity law must allow for entities that variously blend public and private interests if it is to achieve coherence and ensure the relevance of charities in the contemporary marketplace.

CHARITY AND RELIGION

As uncertainty comes to characterise the new space between citizen, government and market, with fluctuating boundaries and a lack of clarity regarding the distribution of public and private interests, it was to be expected, perhaps, that religion would assume greater importance. This volume revealed considerable jurisdictional variation in the treatment of religion, appropriately reflecting respective cultural contexts (see Chapters 2, 3 and 8), which gives rise to questions regarding the future of the charity–religion boundary and its significance for civil society. It explored the issues in defining religion as charity, the difficulties associated with determining its public benefit and the temptation, in some jurisdictions, to secularise charity law and thereby neuter its traditional approach to the characteristics of religion as a charitable purpose (see Chapter 8).

In all common law nations, 'religion' in the context of charity law has for the most part been tied to a belief in God, usually interpreted (if only by default) to mean a Christian deity, while religion, religious organisations and their activities have usually had no difficulty meeting the legal definition of 'charity'. In some, such as Ireland, these organisations attract preferential treatment through statutory endorsement of the rule that gifts to and the activities of religious bodies are presumed to be for the public benefit and therefore charitable. In all other jurisdictions studied, this rule applies despite not being embodied in statutory form. Considerable jurisdictional variation was found to exist in relation to the range of activities held to merit charitable status, particularly in relation to closed contemplative religious orders.

Charity law reform did not significantly alter the jurisdictional approach to religion with the notable exception of the UK where, as in all aspects of reform, it has taken modernisation a step further. There, the presumption of public benefit has been statutorily repealed and religious organisations are now as subject to the public benefit test as any other organisation. Moreover, in England and Wales, charity law now no longer requires that 'religion' be restricted to belief in one god nor indeed to belief in any god as non-theistic religions are deemed to be charitable. Should other jurisdictions ultimately follow the tentative lead now being given by the Charity Commission in recognising value and belief systems as included within the definition of 'religion', together with the requirement that the public benefit test be applied as with any other organisation seeking charitable status, then the point will have been reached where it will be open to question just what it is about this head of charity that warrants its continuance as a separate and distinct charitable purpose.

The past contribution of religious organisations to total charitable activity, to the work of the wider voluntary sector, to statutory services provision and thereby to the creation of institutional and pastoral support for communities in all common law jurisdictions has been inestimable. Ireland, Australia, New Zealand, Singapore, the US and Canada are all indebted to religious organisations which laid much of the foundations for their present health and education systems and often provided the staff and resources for their functioning and maintenance. In the future, the role of charitable religious organisations is likely to be shaped by domestic opportunities resulting from the contraction of government services and on an international basis by the escalating scale and diversity of human suffering in developing nations. In both the domestic and international contexts, the essentially Christian ethos of religion and charity in those nations will have to adjust to meet the challenges presented by a sustained influx of migrants, the necessity to engage with and accommodate the needs of those from other cultures and the mounting pressure to address the grievances of a resurgent Islam. However, the contribution of religious organisations to the consolidation of civil society, past or present, has not been beyond reproach. From at least the time of the Crusades, religion has demonstrated a capacity to divide as well as unify societies.

In terms of the contemporary charity–religion boundary, both strands have attracted controversy, usually centred on their capacity, separately and jointly, to promote pluralism rather than simply defend sectional interests. The increased secularisation of social infrastructure in the jurisdictions studied has allowed, if not stimulated, mounting scepticism as to the benefits inherent in maintaining religion as a distinct head of charity. An ever-expanding raft of national and international legislation underpinning entitlements to human rights, equity, equality and non-discrimination has cast some doubt on the social role of charity. Both religion and charity bear with them into the 21st century considerable baggage associated with divisiveness, deference, condescension and acceptance which does not sit comfortably alongside a modern rights awareness. Both, however, are also bringing the values, particularly of compassion and good neighbourliness, which have done much to bind communities facing adversity in past generations and will doubtless similarly contribute to consolidating civil society in the future.

CHARITY AND CIVIL SOCIETY

Arguably, the constructs 'charity', 'religion' and 'civil society' share a natural mutual affinity: they are underpinned by much the same sense of structure, sets of beliefs and values, while their adherents tend to be mutually supportive and collectively motivated towards the introduction of legislation that positively discriminates in favour of entities dedicated to constructive purposes within and between societies. As yet, however, although there are sound working definitions of 'civil society' (such as those referenced in this book), there is no firm consensus as to where its boundaries with commerce and religion may lie and this poses a serious challenge. While the modernisation of charity law carries implications for all three constructs, its likely impact on the future of civil society is the most difficult to assess.

Chapters 9 and 10 considered civil society in structuralist terms and, perhaps, with what in the present circumstances may appear to be iconoclastic vision. There is much to be said in favour of government legislative initiatives to advance the systemic building of a civil society infrastructure, if only as a long-term policy commitment, but there is little evidence of any such government intent. The concerted international investment of government energy and resources into bolstering the systemic capacity of the banking and financial system is without any equivalent in relation to the institutions of civil society. The law reform processes have scrupulously left the traditional common law constraints on political activity by charities relatively intact, while the complexities of the aid–trade relationship between developed and developing nations continues its pernicious effects on the latter, by maintaining their poverty levels and hampering the growth of an indigenous and authentic civil society. As the international proliferation of anti-terrorism legislation is used to track the flow of charity funds and steadily imposes further constraints on civil liberties, so it becomes progressively less possible to be optimistic as regards the willingness of governments to legislate for the creation of a civil society institutional framework.

However, the outcomes of recent charity law reform processes clearly reveal the content of 'civil society' as the subject of direct and positive legislative intervention by government. The *Pemsel* plus charitable purposes will, for the foreseeable future, exercise most influence in promoting the currency of civil society by underpinning social institutions and reinforcing civic responsibility. The fact, nature and spread of new statutory charitable purposes designed to increase volunteering, reconciliation, religious and racial harmony and multi-culturalism constitute clear government recognition of the importance of civil society and the role that charity must play in furthering its development. In conjunction with purposes intended to prevent poverty, advance human rights and facilitate social inclusion, it is the *Pemsel* plus purposes that will, over time, introduce national and international benchmarks for growing civil society. This, together with the general effects of globalisation and the international tendency towards increasing government audit and regulation of nonprofits, may well eventually pave the way for more structural policies which, it is hoped, will allow the growth of a civil society infrastructure that best fits the needs of local communities.

Index